Microsoft® Office Word 2010

A SKILLS APPROACH, COMPLETE

Cheri Manning
Catherine Manning Swinson
Triad Interactive, Inc.

The McGraw-Hill Companies

MICROSOFT® OFFICE WORD 2010: A SKILLS APPROACH, COMPLETE
Published by McGraw-Hill, a business unit of The McGraw-Hill Companies, Inc., 1221 Avenue of the Americas, New York, NY, 10020.

This book is printed on acid-free paper.

1 2 3 4 5 6 7 8 9 0 RMN/RMN 1 0 9 8 7 6 5 4 3 2 1

ISBN 978-0-07-739499-8
MHID 0-07-739499-2

Vice president/Director of marketing: *Alice Harra*
Publisher: *Scott Davidson*
Sponsoring editor: *Paul Altier*
Director, digital products: *Crystal Szewczyk*
Development editor: *Alan Palmer*
Editorial coordinator: *Allison McCabe*
Marketing manager: *Tiffany Russell*
Digital development editor: *Kevin White*
Director, Editing/Design/Production: *Jess Ann Kosic*
Project manager: *Marlena Pechan*
Buyer II: *Laura M. Fuller*
Senior designer: *Srdjan Savanovic*
Senior photo research coordinator: *Keri Johnson*
Manager, digital production: *Janean A. Utley*
Media project manager: *Brent dela Cruz*
Media project manager: *Cathy L. Tepper*
Outside development house: *Barrett Lyon*
Typeface: *10.5/13 Garamond Premier Pro*
Compositor: *Laserwords Private Limited*
Printer: *R. R. Donnelley*
Cover credit: © Plainview, iStockphoto; back cover: © Okea, iStockphoto
Credits: The credits section for this book begins on page WDI-6 and is considered an extension of the copyright page.

Printed in the United States of America.

Library of Congress Cataloging-in-Publication Data

Manning, Cheryl.
Microsoft Office Word 2010 : a skills approach, complete / Cheri Manning, Catherine Manning Swinson.
p. cm.
Includes index.
ISBN-13: 978-0-07-739499-8 (alk. paper)
ISBN-10: 0-07-739499-2 (alk. paper)
1. Microsoft Word. 2. Word processing. I. Swinson, Catherine Manning. II. Title.
III. Title: Word 2010.
Z52.5.M52M354 2012
005.52—dc23

2011023727

www.mhhe.com

contents

office and word 2010

word 2010

preface

How well do you know Microsoft Office? Many students can follow specific step-by-step directions to re-create a document, spreadsheet, presentation, or database, but do they truly understand the skills it takes to create these on their own? Just as simply following a recipe does not make you a professional chef, re-creating a project step by step does not make you an Office expert.

The purpose of this book is to teach you the skills to master Microsoft Word 2010 in a straightforward and easy-to-follow manner. But *Microsoft® Office Word 2010: A Skills Approach, Complete* goes beyond the ***how*** and equips you with a deeper understanding of the ***what*** and the ***why.*** Too many times books have little value beyond the classroom. The *Skills Approach* series has been designed to be not only a complete textbook but also a reference tool for you to use as you move beyond academics and into the workplace.

ABOUT TRIAD INTERACTIVE

Triad Interactive is a small business and a District of Columbia Qualified High Technology Company specializing in online education and training products.

Triad's flagship program is SimNet®—a simulated Microsoft Office learning and assessment application developed for the McGraw-Hill Companies. SimNet development began in 1999 with SimNet 2000, a CD-ROM-based program used to measure students' understanding of the Microsoft Office 2000 applications. In 2000, for Office XP, Triad expanded the SimNet platform to include a learning component with lessons written by Cheri Manning and Catherine Manning Swinson. Over the past 10 years, the SimNet series has continued to evolve from a simple CD-ROM program into a robust online learning and assessment system. More than 500,000 students worldwide have used SimNet to learn the skills necessary to master Microsoft Office.

Triad is also actively involved in cancer education and in research projects to assess the usefulness of technology for helping high-risk populations make decisions about managing their cancer risk and treatment.

about the **authors**

CHERI MANNING

Cheri Manning is the president and co-owner of Triad Interactive. She is the author of the Microsoft Excel and Microsoft Access content for the SimNet series of online assessment and learning programs. She has been authoring instructional content for these applications for over 10 years. Cheri is also the co-author of McGraw-Hill's *What's New in Microsoft Office 2003* and *What's New in Microsoft Office 2007.*

Cheri began her career as an Aerospace Education Specialist with the Education Division of the National Aeronautics and Space Administration (NASA), where she produced materials for K–12 instructors and students. Prior to founding Triad Interactive, Cheri was a project manager with Compact Publishing, where she managed the development of McGraw-Hill's Multimedia MBA CD-ROM series.

CATHERINE MANNING SWINSON

Catherine Manning Swinson is the vice president and co-owner of Triad Interactive. She is the author of the Microsoft Word, Microsoft PowerPoint, and Microsoft Outlook content for the SimNet series of online assessment and learning programs. She has been authoring instructional content for these applications for over 10 years. Catherine is also the co-author of *What's New in Microsoft Office 2003* and *What's New in Microsoft Office 2007.*

Catherine began her career at Compact Publishing, one of the pioneers in educational CD-ROM-based software. She was the lead designer at Compact and designed every edition of the *TIME Magazine Compact Almanac* from 1992 through 1996. In addition, she designed a number of other products with Compact, including the *TIME Man of the Year* program and the *TIME 20th Century Almanac.*

The authors would like to extend a special thank-you to the Triad staff especially to Torger Wuellner for keeping the show running while we were writing the text and to Katie Lawson and Jodi Sandvick for staying late and coming in on the weekends to help with graphics. Thanks to Marlena Pechan, Barrett Lyon, and Alan Palmer for their patience working with two authors new to the print world. Thanks to Liz Haefele and Scott Davidson for the opportunity to expand our digital collaboration into print. And a final thanks to Paul Altier for his extraordinary vision of what this series could be and for all of his encouragement and support throughout the process. We deeply appreciate all of the hard work by the contributors, technical editors, reviewers, and everyone at McGraw-Hill to develop this new series.

contributors

word projects

Randy Nordell
American River College

Melissa Prinzing
Sierra College

Dennis Walpole
University of South Florida

from the perspective of

Marlene Roden
Asheville-Buncombe Technical Community College

Bonnie Smith
Fresno City College

technical editors

Mary Carole Hollinsgworth
Georgia Perimeter College

Carol Lloyd
Cuyamaca College

Sue McCrory
Missouri State University

Gary Sibbetts
St. Louis Community College

Pam Silvers
Asheville-Buncombe Technical College

Lynne Stuhr
Trident Technical College

reviewers

OUR THANKS GO TO ALL WHO PARTICIPATED IN THE DEVELOPMENT OF *MICROSOFT® OFFICE WORD 2010: A SKILLS APPROACH.*

Rosalyn Amaro
Florida State College at Jacksonville

Beverly Amer
Northern Arizona University

Wilma Andrews
Virginia Commonwealth University

Tom Ashby
Oklahoma City Community College

Robert Balicki
Cleary University

Diana Baran
Henry Ford Community College

Nathan Barker
Southern Utah University

Alfred Basta
Kaplan University

Judy Bennett
Sam Houston State University
Jan Bentley
Utah Valley University
Judy Brierley
Seminole State College
Eva Brown
San Jacinto College
Judy Brown
The University of Memphis
Katharine Brown
University of North Florida
Menka Brown
Piedmont Technical College
Sylvia Brown
Midland College
Peter Cardon
University of South Carolina
Patricia Casey
Trident Technical College
Gerianne Chapman
Johnson & Wales University
Dan Combellick
Scottsdale Community College
Paulette Comet
Community College of Baltimore County
Sissy Copeland
Piedmont Technical College
Jami Cotler
Siena College
Penny Cypert
Tarrant County College
Don Danner
San Francisco State University
Raphael De Arazoza
Miami Dade College
Darren Denenberg
University of Nevada–Las Vegas
Joy DePover
Minneapolis Community and Technical College
Charles DeSassure
Tarrant County College
Kim Ellis
Virginia Western Community College
Jean Finley
Asheville Buncombe Technical Community College
Dave Fitzgerald
Jackson Community College
Deborah Franklin
Bryant & Stratton College
Susan Fuschetto
Cerritos College
Amy Giddens
Central Alabama Community College

Fred Goldberg
Community College of Philadelphia
Barbara Gombetto
Bryant & Stratton College
Kemit Grafton
Oklahoma State University–Oklahoma City
Marilyn Griffin
Virginia Tech
Andrew Hardin
University of Nevada–Las Vegas
Michael Haugrud
Minnesota State University Moorhead
Terri Hayes
Broward College
Cheryl Heemstra
Anne Arundel Community College
Marilyn Hibbert
Salt Lake Community College
Mary Carole Hollingsworth
Georgia Perimeter College
Lister Horn
Pensacola State College
Jennifer Ivey
Central Carolina Community College
Linda Johnsonius
Murray State University
Barbara Jones
Golden West College
Sally Kaskocsak
Sinclair Community College
Hazel Kates
Miami Dade College Kendall Campus
Judith Keenan
Salve Regina University
Hal Kingsley
Trocaire College
Linda Kliston
Broward College
Kitty Koepping
Shepherd University
Charles Lake
Faulkner State
Jackie Lamoureux
Central New Mexico Community College
Nanette Lareau
University of Arkansas Community College at Morrilton
Kevin Lee
Guilford Technical Community College
Patricia Lee
Florida State College at Jacksonville
Kate LeGrand
Broward College
Mary Locke
Greenville Technical College

Donna Lohn
Lakeland Community College
Nicki Maines
Mesa Community College
Daniela Marghitu
Auburn University
Juan Marquez
Mesa Community College
Phil Marshall
University of South Carolina
Prosenjit Mazumdar
George Mason University
Robert McCloud
Sacred Heart University
Sue McCrory
Missouri State University
Daniel McKee
Mansfield University of PA
Patricia McMurray
Kaplan Career Institute ICM Campus
Dawn Medlin
Appalachian State University
Alanah Mitchell
Appalachian State University
Susan Mitchell
Davenport University
Kathleen Morris
University of Alabama
Carmen Morrison
North Central State College
Melissa Nemeth
Kelley School of Business Indianapolis
Brenda Nielsen
Mesa Community College
Philip Nielson
Salt Lake Community College
Maria Osterhoudt
St. Petersburg College
Judy Pento
Seacoast Career School
Rene Polanco
Austin Community College
Don Rhyne
San Joaquin Valley College
Steven Rosen
Keiser University
Kathy Ruggieri
Lansdale School of Business
Charles Salazar
Clackamas Community College
Diane Santurri
Johnson & Wales University
Paul Schwager
East Carolina University
Vicky Seehusen
Metro State College of Denver
Steven Singer
Kapiolani Community College
Cindi Smatt
Texas A&M University
Bonnie Smith
Fresno City College
Thomas Michael Smith
Austin Community College
Candice Spangler
Columbus State Community College
Diane Stark
Phoenix College
Allen Truell
Ball State University
Kari Walters
Louisianna State University
Eric Weinstein
Suffolk County Community College
Stu Westin
University of Rhode Island
Billie Jo Whary
McCann School of Business and Technology Sunbury Campus
Melinda White
Seminole State College
Katherine Winters
University of Tennessee at Chattanooga
Judy Wynekoop
Florida Gulf Coast University
Laurie Zouharis
Suffolk University
Matthew Zullo
Wake Technical Community College

Instructor Walkthrough

Microsoft Office Word 2010:
A Skills Approach, Complete

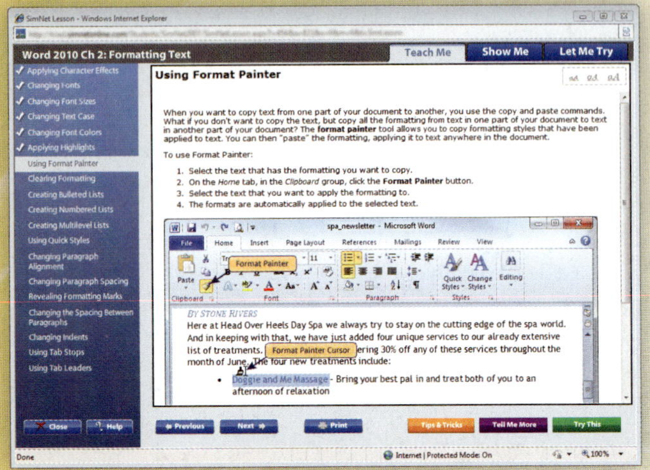

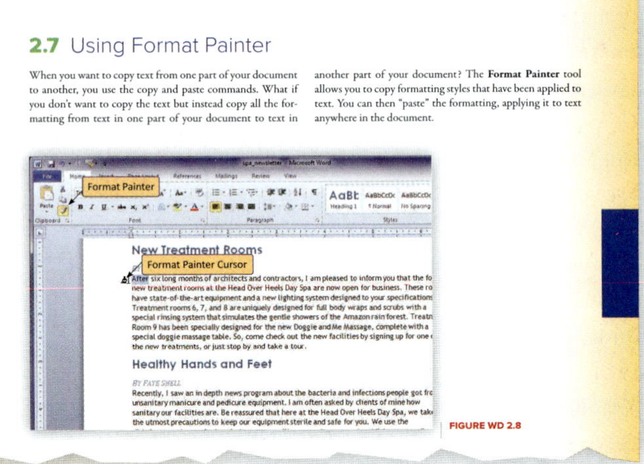

2.7 Using Format Painter

When you want to copy text from one part of your document to another, you use the copy and paste commands. What if you don't want to copy the text but instead copy all the formatting from text in one part of your document to text in another part of your document? The **Format Painter** tool allows you to copy formatting styles that have been applied to text. You can then "paste" the formatting, applying it to text anywhere in the document.

FIGURE WD 2.8

❯ **1-1 Content in SimNet for Office 2010**

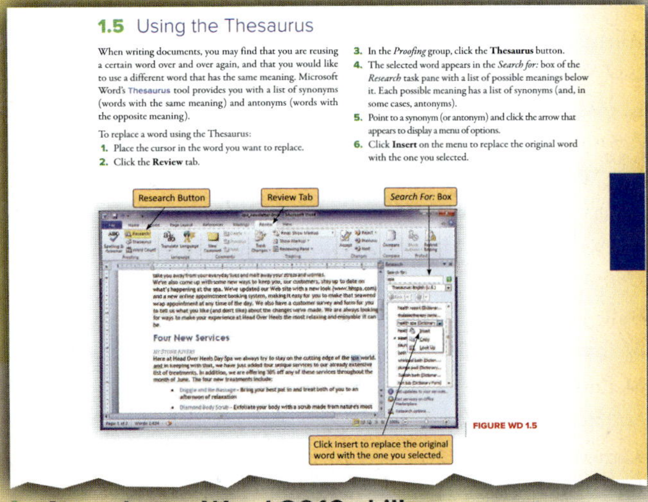

1.5 Using the Thesaurus

When writing documents, you may find that you are reusing a certain word over and over again, and that you would like to use a different word that has the same meaning. Microsoft Word's **Thesaurus** tool provides you with a list of synonyms (words with the same meaning) and antonyms (words with the opposite meaning).

To replace a word using the Thesaurus:

1. Place the cursor in the word you want to replace.
2. Click the **Review** tab.
3. In the *Proofing* group, click the **Thesaurus** button.
4. The selected word appears in the *Search for:* box of the *Research* task pane with a list of possible meanings below it. Each possible meaning has a list of synonyms (and, in some cases, antonyms).
5. Point to a synonym (or antonym) and click the arrow that appears to display a menu of options.
6. Click **Insert** on the menu to replace the original word with the one you selected.

Research Button | Review Tab | Search For: Box

Click Insert to replace the original word with the one you selected.

FIGURE WD 1.5

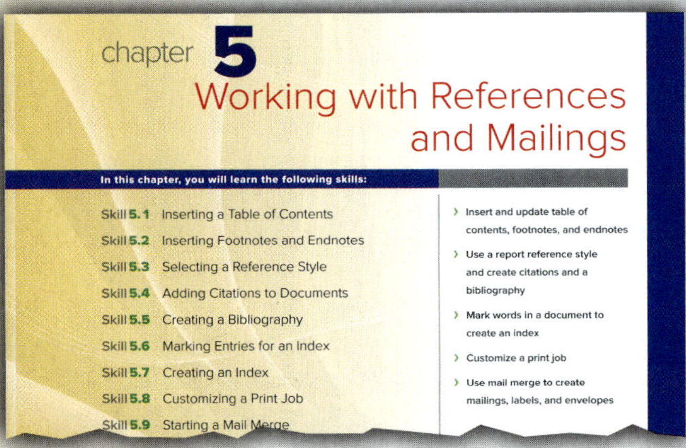

chapter **5**

Working with References and Mailings

In this chapter, you will learn the following skills:

- Skill 5.1 Inserting a Table of Contents
- Skill 5.2 Inserting Footnotes and Endnotes
- Skill 5.3 Selecting a Reference Style
- Skill 5.4 Adding Citations to Documents
- Skill 5.5 Creating a Bibliography
- Skill 5.6 Marking Entries for an Index
- Skill 5.7 Creating an Index
- Skill 5.8 Customizing a Print Job
- Skill 5.9 Starting a Mail Merge

- Insert and update table of contents, footnotes, and endnotes
- Use a report reference style and create citations and a bibliography
- Mark words in a document to create an index
- Customize a print job
- Use mail merge to create mailings, labels, and envelopes

❯ **Introduction—Learning Outcomes are clearly listed.**

❯ **At-a-glance Word 2010 skills**

Quick, easy-to-scan pages, for efficient learning

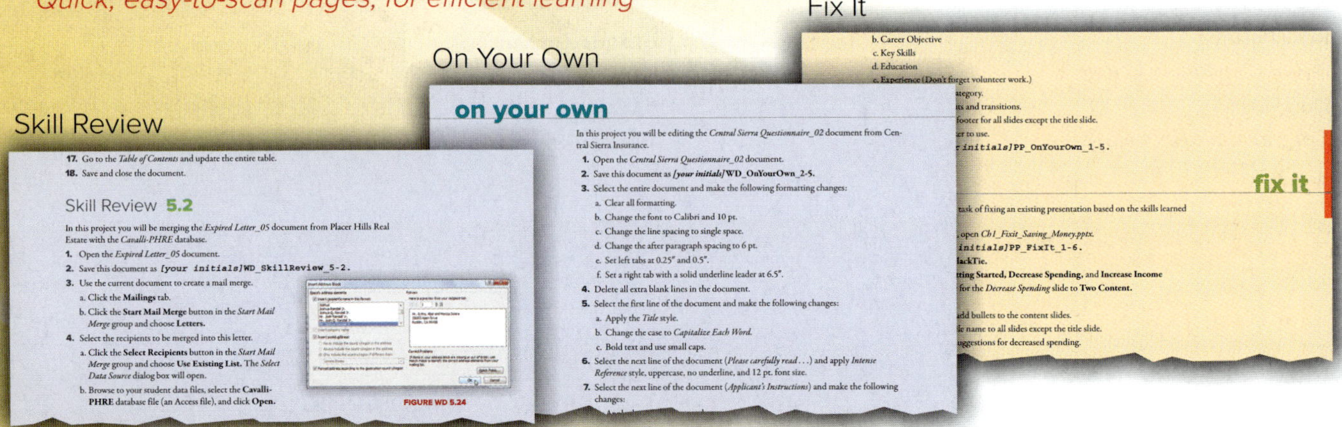

Skill Review

17. Go to the *Table of Contents* and update the entire table.
18. Save and close the document.

Skill Review **5.2**

In this project you will be merging the *Expired Letter_05* document from Placer Hills Real Estate with the *Cavalli-PHRE* database.

1. Open the *Expired Letter_05* document.
2. Save this document as *[your initials]WD_SkillReview_5-2*.
3. Use the current document to create a mail merge.
   a. Click the **Mailings** tab.
   b. Click the **Start Mail Merge** button in the *Start Mail Merge* group and choose **Letters**.
4. Select the recipients to be merged into this letter.
   a. Click the **Select Recipients** button in the *Start Mail Merge* group and choose **Use Existing List**. The *Select Data Source* dialog box will open.
   b. Browse to your student data files, select the **Cavalli-PHRE** database file (an Access file), and click **Open**.

FIGURE WD 5.24

On Your Own

on your own

In this project you will be editing the *Central Sierra Questionnaire_02* document from Central Sierra Insurance.

1. Open the *Central Sierra Questionnaire_02* document.
2. Save this document as *[your initials]WD_OnYourOwn_2-5*.
3. Select the entire document and make the following formatting changes:
   a. Clear all formatting.
   b. Change the font to Calibri and 10 pt.
   c. Change the line spacing to single space.
   d. Change the after paragraph spacing to 6 pt.
   e. Set left tabs at 0.25" and 0.5".
   f. Set a right tab with a solid underline leader at 6.5".
4. Delete all extra blank lines in the document.
5. Select the first line of the document and make the following changes:
   a. Apply the *Title* style.
   b. Change the case to *Capitalize Each Word*.
   c. Bold text and use small caps.
6. Select the next line of the document (*Please carefully read . . .*) and apply *Intense Reference* style, uppercase, no underline, and 12 pt. font size.
7. Select the next line of the document (*Applicant's Instructions*) and make the following changes:

Fix It

b. Career Objective
c. Key Skills
d. Education
e. Experience (Don't forget volunteer work.)

fix it

❯ **Diverse end-of-chapter projects**

Projects that relate to a broad range of careers and perspectives, from nursing, education, business, and everyday personal uses.

Features:

Tips and Tricks

From the Perspective of...

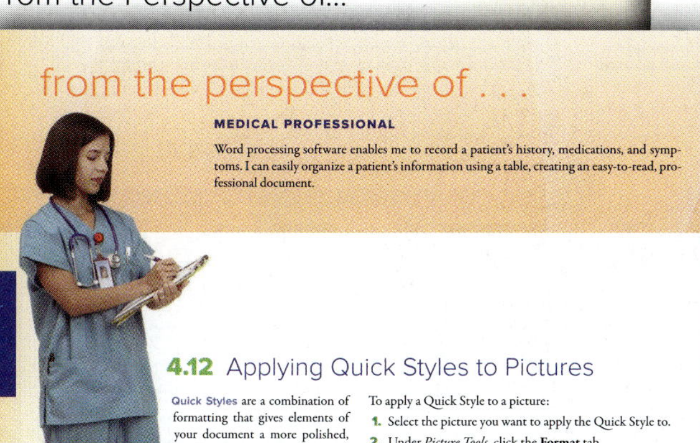

from the perspective of . . .

MEDICAL PROFESSIONAL

Word processing software enables me to record a patient's history, medications, and symptoms. I can easily organize a patient's information using a table, creating an easy-to-read, professional document.

4.12 Applying Quick Styles to Pictures

Quick Styles are a combination of formatting that gives elements of your document a more polished, professional look without a lot of work. Quick Styles for pictures

To apply a Quick Style to a picture:

1. Select the picture you want to apply the Quick Style to.
2. Under *Picture Tools*, click the **Format** tab.
3. In the *Picture Styles* group, click the **More** button

tips & tricks

- Click the **Next Footnote** button to navigate to the next footnote in the document. Click the arrow next to the **Next Footnote** button to display a menu allowing you to navigate to previous footnotes and between endnotes in the document.
- To delete a footnote, you must first select the reference mark in the document and press **Delete** on the keyboard. If you select and delete the text of the footnote, the reference mark will remain and the footnote will not be removed from the document.

Try This

Tell Me More

tell me **more**

If you want to modify letters individually, click **Edit individual letters . . .** Then, in the *Merge to New Document* dialog box, select the records you want to change and click **OK.** Word opens a new document based on the selected records. Make any changes you want, and then print or save the document just as you would any other file.

If you want to send the document via e-mail, click **Send E-mail Messages . . .** Enter the subject line and mail format. Select the recipients you want to send the document to and click **OK.**

try **this**

You can start a numbered list by:

- Typing a 1, a space, and your list item, then pressing the [←Enter] key.
- Clicking the **Numbering** button, typing your list item, then pressing the [←Enter] key.
- You can convert text to a numbered list by right-clicking the selected text, pointing to **Numbering,** and selecting an option.

Instructor materials available on the online learning center, www.mhhe.com/office2010skills

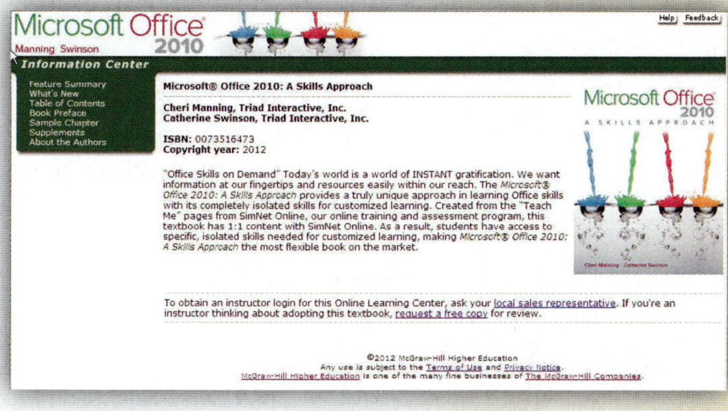

- Instructor Manual
- Instructor PowerPoints
- Test Bank
- Project Data and Solution Files

SimNet for Office **2010**

Online training and assessment

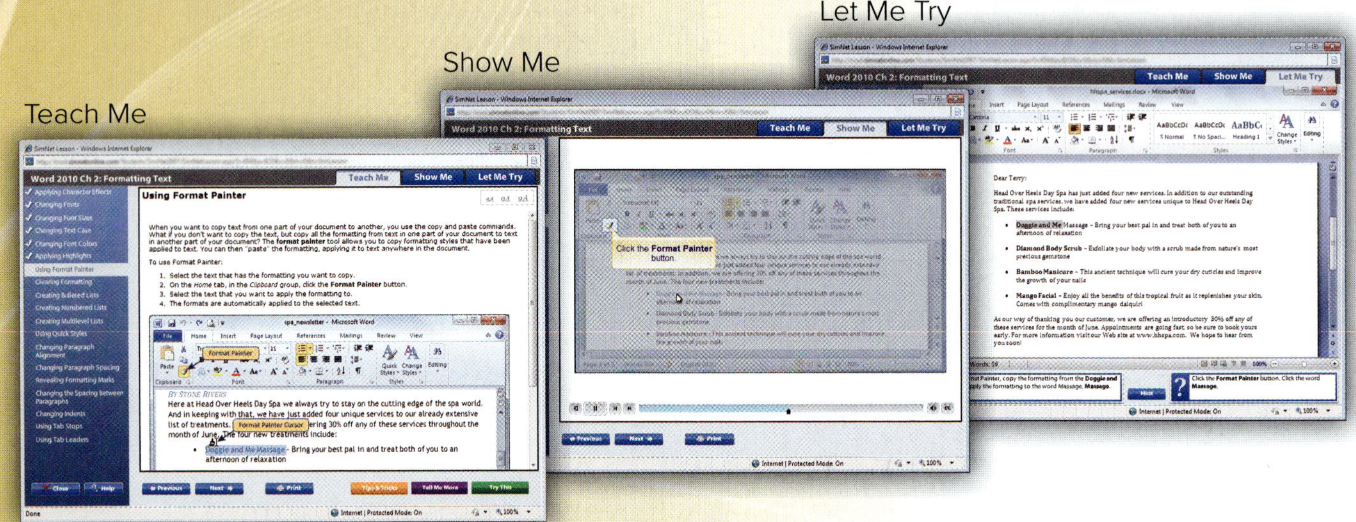

INCLUDES:

- Microsoft® Office Suite
- Microsoft® Outlook
- Windows XP
- Windows Vista
- Windows 7
- Internet Explorer 7
- Internet Explorer 8
- Computer Concepts

Since 1999, instructors have been using SimNet to measure student outcomes in a virtual Microsoft® Office environment. Now completely online, with nothing to install, students can practice and study their skills at home or in the school lab. Moreover, this resource is an ideal course solution, but even more valuable, as it can be used beyond the course for self-study! For more information, contact your McGraw-Hill sales representative or visit the SimNet Online Web site, **www.mhhe.com/simnet2010**

IT'S EASY!

SimNet is an EASY & INTUITIVE, true turnkey design. Instructors can quickly and efficiently assign content around the needs of your course, edit throughout the semester, and copy to multiple sections and instructors! SimNet is scannable so students can quickly scan the tasks in a lesson to identify the skills they know and the ones they don't…saving them time!

STUDENTS LEARN BEYOND THE BOOK!

SimNet offers a complete computer-based learning side that presents each skill or topic in several different modes:

- *Teach Me:* combines instructional text, graphics, and interactivity to present each skill.
- *Show Me:* uses animation with audio narration to show how the skill is implemented.
- *Let Me Try:* allows students to apply and practice what they have learned on their own to master the learning objective.

STUDENTS LEARN BEYOND THE COURSE!

SimNet allows students to perform their best in the course, and SimNet allows students to continue learning Office skills for future classes and beyond through its self-study material! Need to learn an advanced topic or a refresher on a certain skill? Use SimSearch to search or pull up specific content when you need it.

Essential Skills for Microsoft Office and Word 2010

Essential Skills for Microsoft Office and Word 2010

In this chapter, you will learn the following skills:

- Learn about Microsoft Office 2010 and its applications: Word, Excel, PowerPoint, and Access
- Recognize Microsoft Word 2010 common features and navigation elements
- Create new Word 2010 documents
- Demonstrate how to open, save, print, and close Word documents
- Use Microsoft Help
- Perform basic editing tasks and use the Office Clipboard

Skill **0.1** Introduction to Microsoft Office 2010
Skill **0.2** Exploring the Word 2010 User Interface
Skill **0.3** Customizing Word
Skill **0.4** Opening a Document
Skill **0.5** Understanding Security Warnings in Word
Skill **0.6** Creating a New Blank Document
Skill **0.7** Creating a New Document Using a Template
Skill **0.8** Using the Status Bar
Skill **0.9** Modifying Document Properties
Skill **0.10** Viewing Document Statistics
Skill **0.11** Using Help
Skill **0.12** Using Undo and Redo
Skill **0.13** Using Cut, Copy, and Paste
Skill **0.14** Using the Office Clipboard
Skill **0.15** Using Paste Special
Skill **0.16** Checking Spelling
Skill **0.17** Checking Grammar
Skill **0.18** Previewing and Printing a Document
Skill **0.19** Saving a Document
Skill **0.20** Closing a Document
Skill **0.21** Exiting Word

skills

introduction

This chapter introduces students to Microsoft Office and Microsoft Word 2010. Students will learn about the shared features across the applications of Microsoft Office 2010 and how to navigate common interface elements such as the Ribbon and status bar. Students will become familiar with basic editing skills including checking spelling and grammar; using cut, copy, and paste; and managing the Office Clipboard. Introductory features such as creating, opening, saving, and closing files; using Office Help; and previewing and printing are explained.

0.1 Introduction to Microsoft Office 2010

Microsoft® Office 2010 is a collection of business "productivity" applications (computer programs designed to make you more productive at work, school, and home). The most popular Office applications are:

Microsoft Word—a word processing program. Word processing software allows you to create text-based documents, similar to how you would type a document on a typewriter. However, word processing software offers more powerful formatting and design tools, allowing you to create complex documents including reports, résumés, brochures, and newsletters.

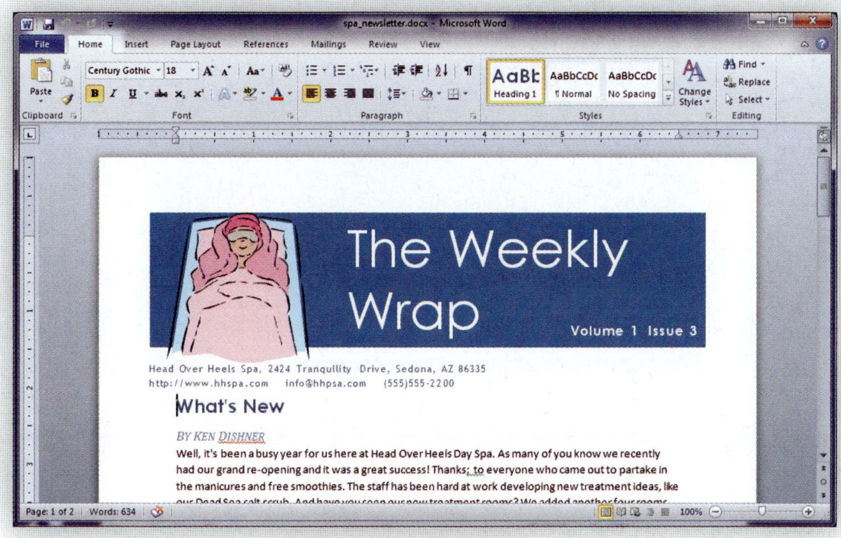

A Word Document

FIGURE WD 0.1

Microsoft Excel—a spreadsheet program. Originally, spreadsheet applications were viewed as electronic versions of an accountant's ledger. Today's spreadsheet applications can do much more than just calculate numbers—they include powerful charting and data analysis features. Spreadsheet programs can be used for everything from personal budgets to calculating loan payments.

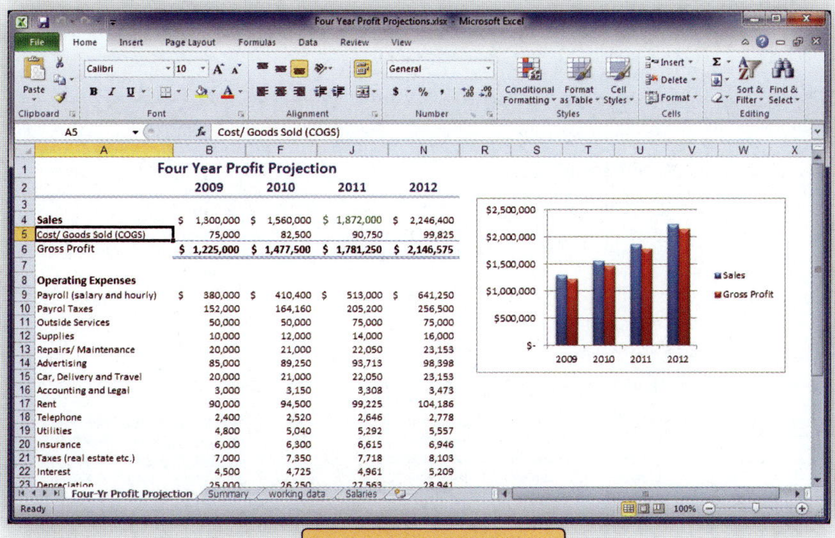

Four Year Profit Projection

	2009	2010	2011	2012
Sales	$ 1,300,000	$ 1,560,000	$ 1,872,000	$ 2,246,400
Cost/ Goods Sold (COGS)	75,000	82,500	90,750	99,825
Gross Profit	**$ 1,225,000**	**$ 1,477,500**	**$ 1,781,250**	**$ 2,146,575**
Operating Expenses				
Payroll (salary and hourly)	$ 380,000	$ 410,400	$ 513,000	$ 641,250
Payrol Taxes	152,000	164,160	205,200	256,500
Outside Services	50,000	50,000	75,000	75,000
Supplies	10,000	12,000	14,000	16,000
Repairs/ Maintenance	20,000	21,000	22,050	23,153
Advertising	85,000	89,250	93,713	98,398
Car, Delivery and Travel	20,000	21,000	22,050	23,153
Accounting and Legal	3,000	3,150	3,308	3,473
Rent	90,000	94,500	99,225	104,186
Telephone	2,400	2,520	2,646	2,778
Utilities	4,800	5,040	5,292	5,557
Insurance	6,000	6,300	6,615	6,946
Taxes (real estate etc.)	7,000	7,350	7,718	8,103
Interest	4,500	4,725	4,961	5,209
Depreciation	25,000	26,250	27,563	28,941

An Excel Spreadsheet

FIGURE WD 0.2

Microsoft PowerPoint—a presentation program. Presentation applications enable you to create robust, multimedia presentations. A presentation consists of a series of electronic slides. Each slide contains content, including text, images, charts, and other objects. You can add multimedia elements to slides, including animations, audio, and video.

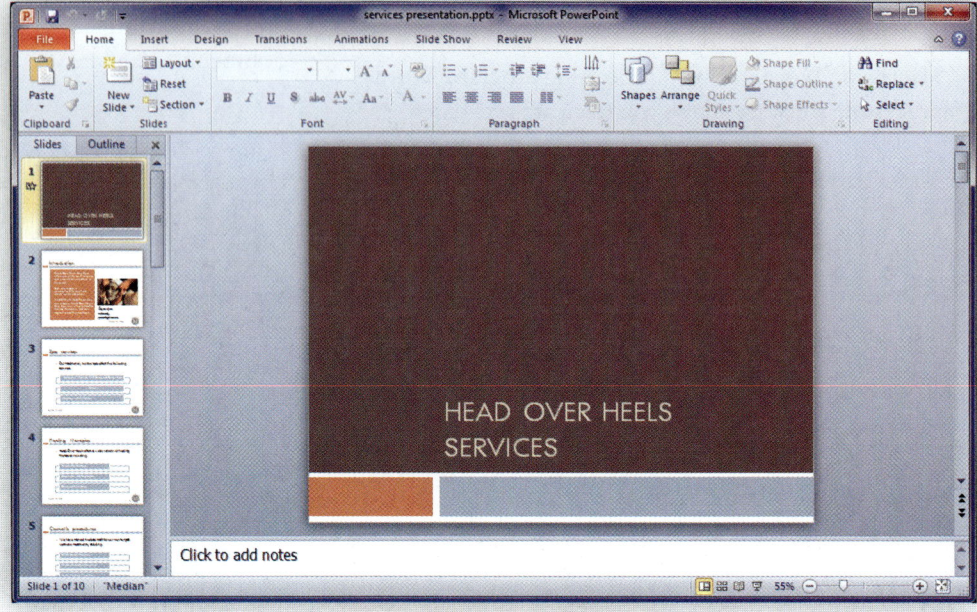

FIGURE WD 0.3 A PowerPoint Presentation

Microsoft Access—a database program. Database applications allow you to organize and manipulate large amounts of data. Databases that allow you to relate tables and databases to one another are referred to as *relational* databases. As a database user, you usually see only one aspect of the database—a *form.* Database forms use a graphical interface to allow a user to enter record data. For example, when you fill out an order form online, you are probably interacting with a database. The information you enter becomes a record in a database *table.* Your order is matched with information in an inventory table (keeping track of which items are in stock) through a *query.* When your order is filled, a database *report* can be generated for use as an invoice or a bill of lading.

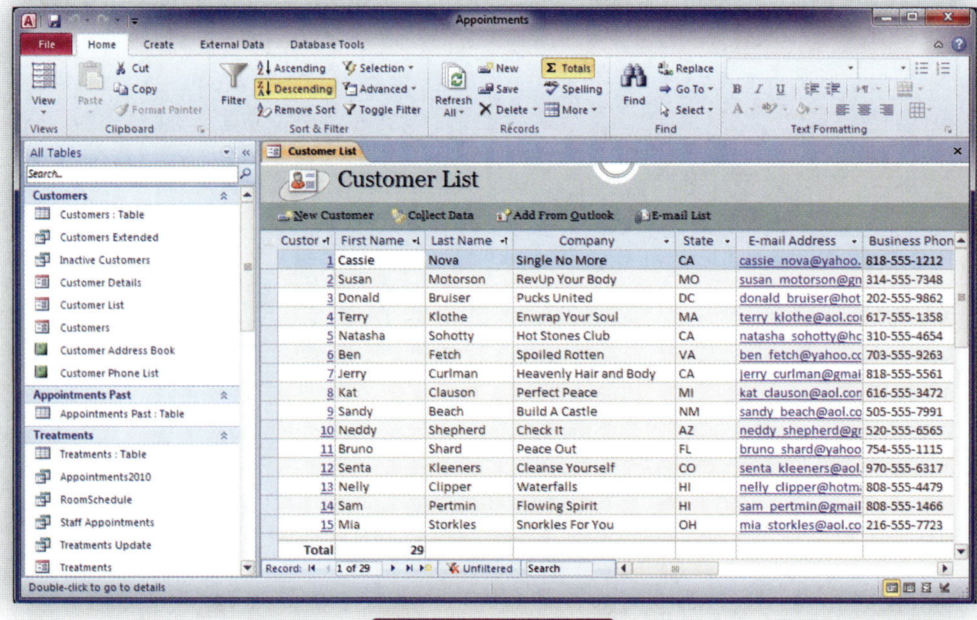

FIGURE WD 0.4 An Access Database

To open one of the Office applications:

1. Click the Windows **Start button** (located in the lower-left corner of your computer screen).
2. Click **All Programs.**
3. Click the **Microsoft Office** folder.
4. Click the application you want to open.

Word, Excel, and PowerPoint open a new blank file automatically; Access opens to Backstage view, where you are asked to give the database a file name first.

tips & tricks

You can download a free trial version of Microsoft Office from Microsoft's Web site (http://office.microsoft.com). The trial allows you to try the applications before buying them. When your trial period ends, if you haven't purchased the full software license yet, you will no longer be able to use the applications (although you will continue to be able to open and view any files you previously created with the trial version).

tell me more

There are three popular versions of Microsoft Office, each offering a different combination of programs.

Office Home and Student—includes *Word 2010, Excel 2010, PowerPoint 2010,* and *OneNote 2010* (a note-taking and organizational program). This version of Office is intended for home use only. Use by commercial or nonprofit businesses is prohibited.

Office Home and Business—includes the same applications as the Home and Student version, and adds *Outlook 2010* for e-mail, contacts, and calendar management.

Office Professional—includes the same applications as the Home and Business version, and adds *Access 2010* and *Publisher 2010* (a desktop publishing application).

try this

A shortcut for starting one of the Office applications is to type the application name in the *Instant Search* box at the bottom of the *Start* menu:

1. Click the **Start** button.
2. In the *Instant Search* box, type `Access`, `Excel`, `PowerPoint`, or `Word`, and then press ←Enter.
3. The application will open a new blank file.

0.2 Exploring the Word 2010 User Interface

THE RIBBON

If you have used a word processing program in the past, you may be surprised when you open Word 2010 for the first time. Beginning with Word 2007, Microsoft redesigned the user experience—replacing the familiar menu bar/toolbar interface with a new Ribbon interface that makes it easier to find application functions and commands.

The **Ribbon** is located across the top of the application window and organizes common features and commands into tabs. Each **tab** organizes commands further into related **groups**. When a specific type of object is selected (such as a picture, table, or chart), a contextual tab will appear. **Contextual tabs** contain commands specific to the type of object selected and are only visible when the commands might be useful.

The **Home tab** contains the most commonly used commands. In Word, the Home tab includes the following groups: *Clipboard, Font, Paragraph, Styles,* and *Editing.*

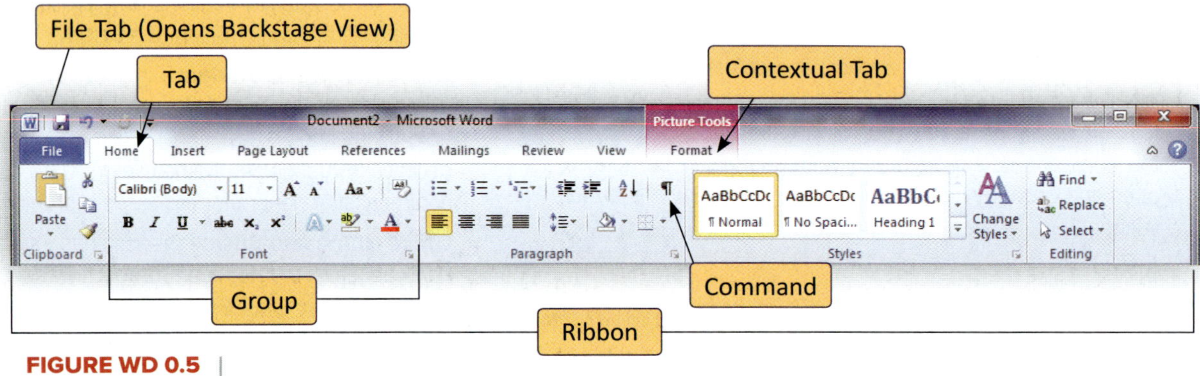

FIGURE WD 0.5

BACKSTAGE

The **File tab** appears at the far left side of the Ribbon. Clicking the *File* tab opens the **Microsoft Office Backstage™ view**, where you can access the commands for managing and protecting your documents including *Save, Open, Close, New,* and *Print*. Backstage replaces the *Office Button* menu from Word 2007 and the *File* menu from previous versions of Word.

tips & tricks

If you need more space for your document, you can minimize the Ribbon by clicking the **Minimize the Ribbon** button in the upper-right corner of the Ribbon (or press Ctrl + F1). When the Ribbon is minimized, the tab names appear along the top of the window (similar to a menu bar). When you click a tab name, the Ribbon appears. After you select a command or click away from the Ribbon, the Ribbon hides again. To redisplay the Ribbon permanently, click the **Expand the Ribbon** button in the upper-right corner of the window. Double-click the active tab to hide or display the Ribbon.

KEYBOARD SHORTCUTS

Many commands available through the Ribbon and Backstage are also accessible through keyboard shortcuts and shortcut menus.

Keyboard shortcuts are keys or combinations of keys that you press to execute a command. Some keyboard shortcuts refer to F keys or function keys. These are the keys that run across the top of the keyboard. Pressing these keys will execute specific commands. For example, pressing the F1 key will open Help in any of the Microsoft Office applications. Keyboard shortcuts typically use a combination of two keys, although some commands use a combination of three keys and others only one key. When a keyboard shortcut calls for a combination of key presses, such as Ctrl + V to paste an item from the Clipboard, you must first press the modifier key (Ctrl), holding it down while you press the V key on the keyboard.

FIGURE WD 0.6

try **this**

Many keyboard shortcuts are universal across applications—all applications, not just Microsoft Office applications. Some examples of universal shortcut keys include:

Ctrl + X = Cut

Ctrl + C = Copy

Ctrl + V = Paste

Ctrl + Z = Undo

Ctrl + O = Open

Ctrl + S = Save

SHORTCUT MENUS

Shortcut menus are menus of commands that display when you right-click an area of the application window. The area or object you right-click determines which menu appears. For example, if you right-click in a paragraph, you will see a shortcut menu of commands for working with text; however, if you right-click an image, you will see a shortcut menu of commands for working with images.

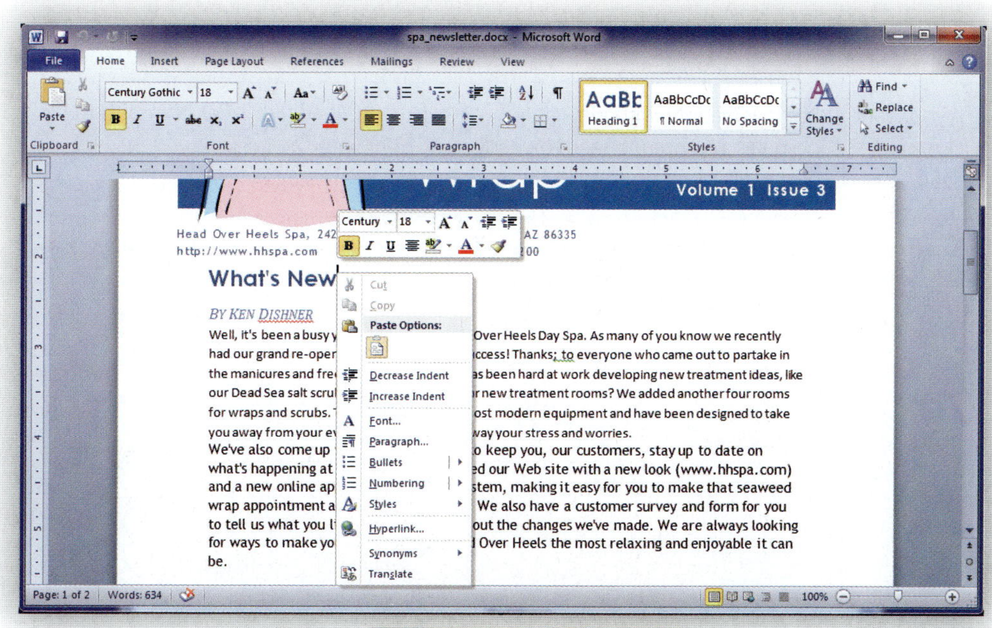

FIGURE WD 0.7

QUICK ACCESS TOOLBAR

The **Quick Access Toolbar** is located at the top of the application window above the *File* tab. The Quick Access Toolbar, as its name implies, gives you quick one-click access to common commands. You can add commands to and remove commands from the Quick Access Toolbar.

To modify the Quick Access Toolbar:

1. Click the **Customize Quick Access Toolbar** button located on the right side of the Quick Access Toolbar.
2. Options with check marks next to them are already displayed on the toolbar. Options with no check marks are not currently displayed.
3. Click an option to add it to or remove it from the Quick Access Toolbar.

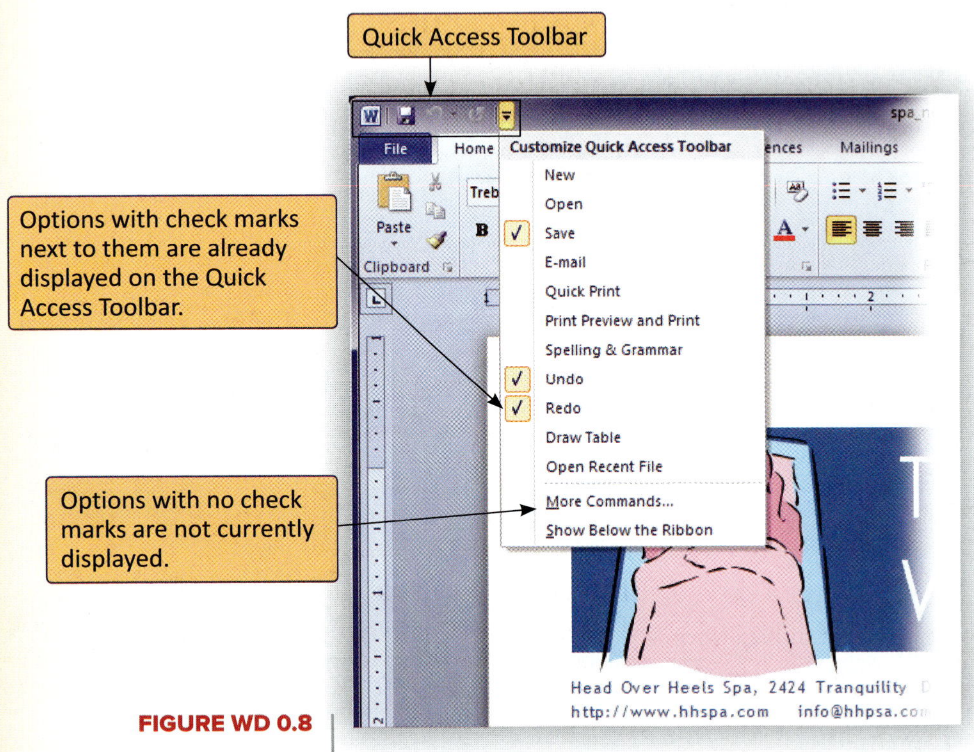

FIGURE WD 0.8

tips & tricks

If you want to be able to print with a single mouse click, add the *Quick Print* button to the Quick Access Toolbar. If you do not need to change any print settings, this is by far the easiest method to print a file because it doesn't require opening Backstage view first.

THE MINI TOOLBAR

The **Mini toolbar** gives you access to common tools for working with text. When you select text and then rest your mouse over the text, the Mini toolbar fades in. You can then click a button to change the selected text just as you would on the Ribbon.

To display the Mini toolbar, you can also right-click the text. The Mini toolbar appears above the shortcut menu.

try **this**

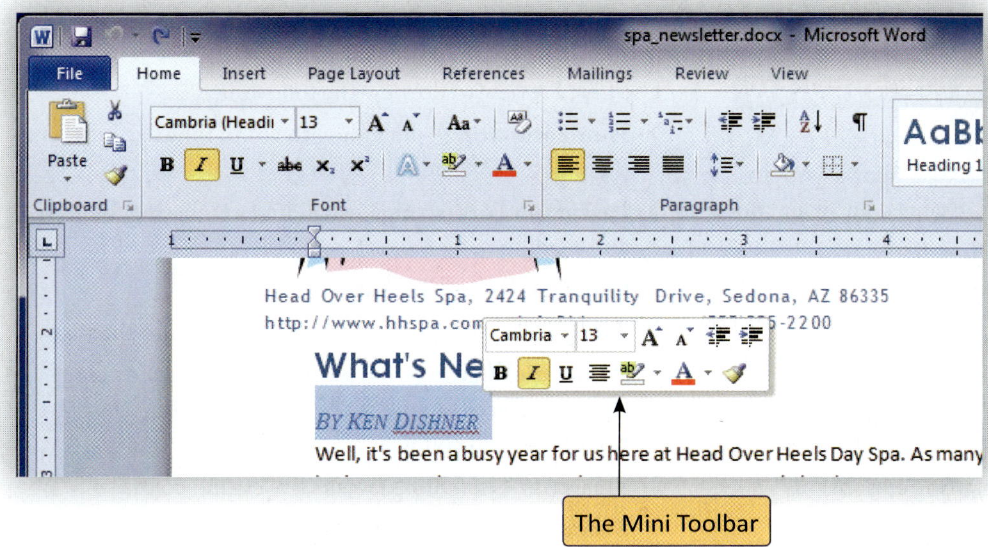

FIGURE WD 0.9

ENHANCED SCREENTIPS

A **ScreenTip** is a small information box that displays the name of the command when you rest your mouse over a button on the Ribbon. An **Enhanced ScreenTip** displays not only the name of the command but also the keyboard shortcut (if there is one) and a short description of what the button does and when it is used. Certain Enhanced ScreenTips also include an image along with a description of the command.

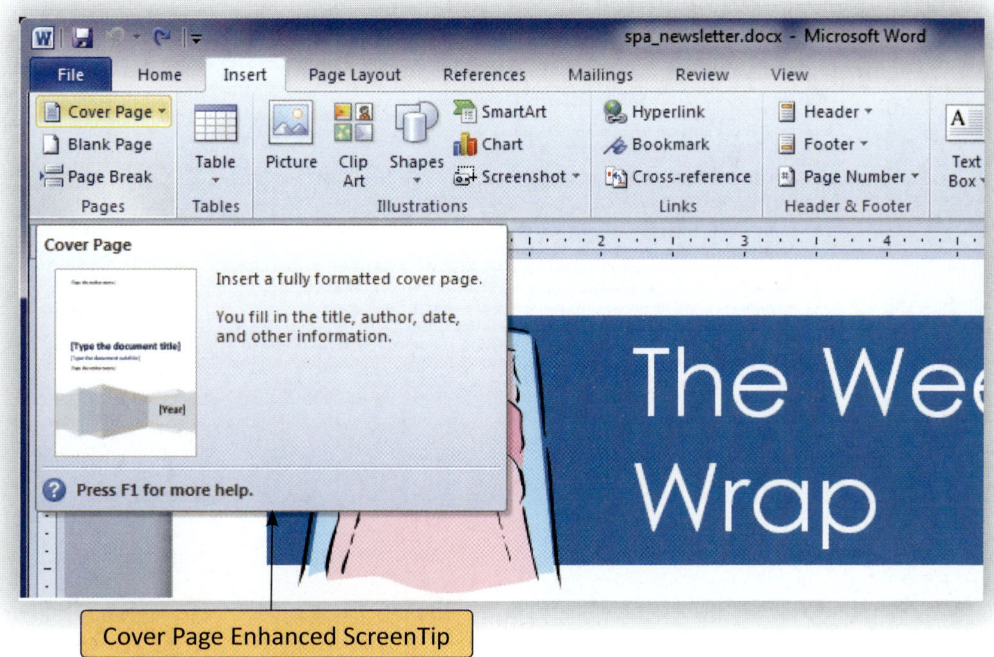

FIGURE WD 0.10

from the perspective of . . .

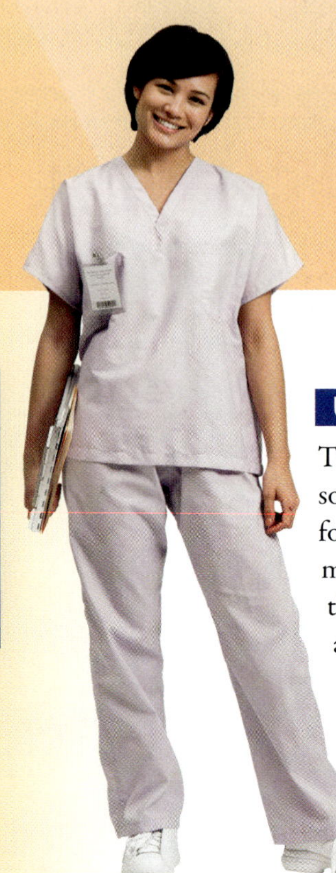

VETERINARY ASSISTANT

As a veterinary assistant, I never thought word processing would be part of my job! However, I constantly need to write reports and maintain research information. Cut, copy, and paste are my new best friends!

USING LIVE PREVIEW

The **Live Preview** feature in Microsoft Word 2010 allows you to see formatting changes in your document before actually committing to the change. When Live Preview is active, rolling over a command on the Ribbon will temporarily apply the formatting to the currently active text or object. To apply the formatting, click the formatting option.

Use Live Preview to preview the following:

- **Font Formatting**—including the font, font size, text highlight color, and font color
- **Paragraph Formatting**—including numbering, bullets, and shading
- **Quick Styles and Themes**
- **Table Formatting**—including table styles and shading
- **Picture Formatting**—including correction and color options, effects, picture styles, borders, positioning, brightness, and contrast
- **SmartArt**—including layouts, styles, and colors
- **Shape Styles**—including borders, shading, and effects

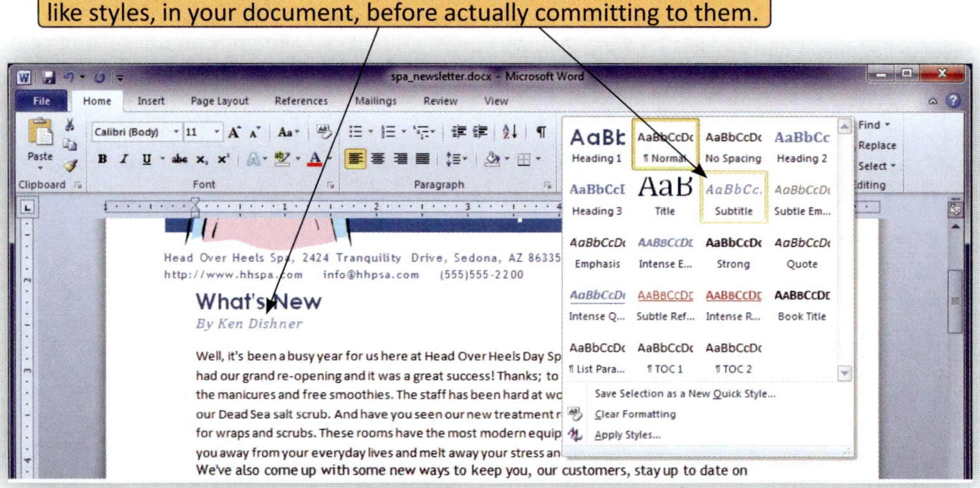

FIGURE WD 0.11

0.3 Customizing Word

When first installed, every version of Word has the same features enabled. However, you can enable and disable some of the user interface features through the *Word Options* dialog. You can even change the colors used in the Word interface.

1. Click the **File** tab to open Backstage view.
2. Click **Options.**
3. Make the changes you want, and then click **OK** to save your changes.
   - Check or uncheck *Show Mini toolbar on selection* to control whether or not the Mini toolbar appears when you hover over selected text. (This does not affect the appearance of the Mini toolbar when you right-click.)
   - Check or uncheck *Enable Live Preview* to turn the Live Preview feature on or off.
   - Change the color scheme used for the Word interface by expanding the *Color scheme* list and selecting *Silver, Blue,* or *Black.*
   - Make a selection from the *ScreenTip style* list:
     - *Show feature descriptions in ScreenTips* displays Enhanced ScreenTips when they are available.
     - *Don't show feature descriptions in ScreenTips* hides Enhanced ScreenTips. The ScreenTip will still include the keyboard shortcut if there is one available.
     - *Don't show ScreenTips* hides ScreenTips altogether, so if you hold your mouse over a button on the Ribbon, nothing will appear.

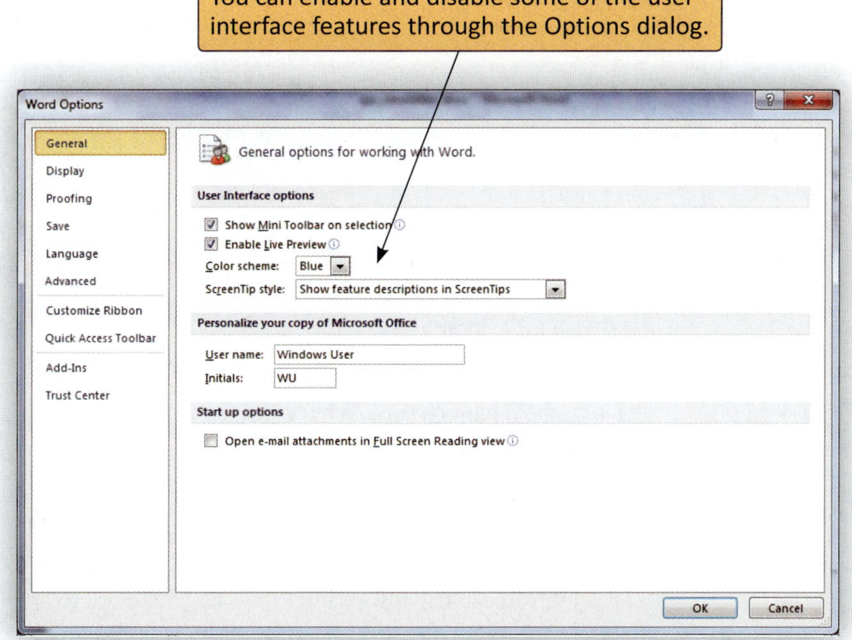

FIGURE WD 0.12

The *Word Options* dialog also allows you to control features such as AutoCorrect, displaying formatting marks, and autosaving the document while you work.

tell me **more**

0.4 Opening a Document

Opening a document retrieves it from storage and displays it on your computer screen.

To open an existing document:

1. Click the **File** tab to open Backstage view.
2. Click **Open.**
3. The *Open* dialog box appears. If necessary, navigate to find the folder location where the document you want is stored.
4. Select the document name in the large list box.
5. Click the **Open** button in the dialog box.

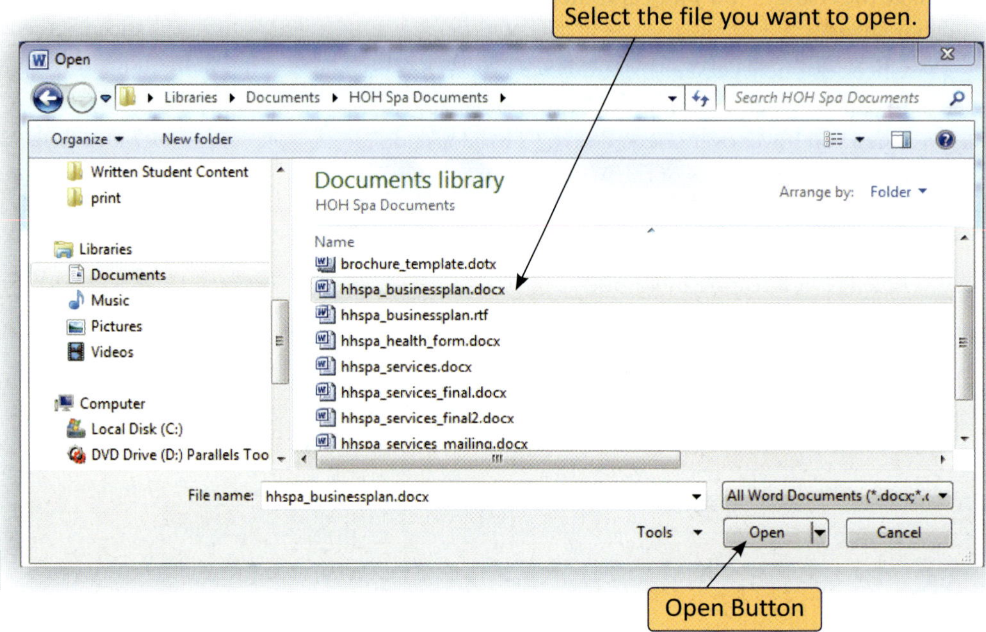

FIGURE WD 0.13

tips & tricks

The screen shot shown here is from Word 2010 running on the Microsoft Windows 7 operating system. Depending on the operating system you are using, the *Open* dialog box will appear somewhat different. However, the basic steps for opening a document are the same regardless of which operating system you are using.

tell me more

You can find documents that you have recently worked on.

1. Click the **File** tab to open Backstage view.
2. Click **Recent**.
3. The *Recent Files* list shows the most recent documents you have worked on. Click a document name to open it.

If you don't see the document you need in the *Recent Files* list, you can use the *Recent Places* list to browse to a specific folder. Click a folder in the *Recent Places* list to open the *Open* dialog showing files in that location.

try this

To open the *Open* dialog box, you can also press Ctrl + O on the keyboard.

To open the document from within the *Open* dialog box, you can:

- Press the ←Enter key once you have typed or selected a file name.
- Double-click the file name.
- Click the **Open** button arrow and select **Open**.

0.5 Understanding Security Warnings in Word

When you download a document from a location that Word considers potentially unsafe, it opens automatically in Protected View. **Protected View** provides a read-only format that protects your computer from becoming infected by a virus or other malware. Potentially unsafe locations include the Internet, e-mail messages, or a network location.

Files that are opened in Protected View display a yellow warning bar at the top of the window, below the Ribbon. To disable Protected View, click the **Enable Editing** button in the yellow warning bar.

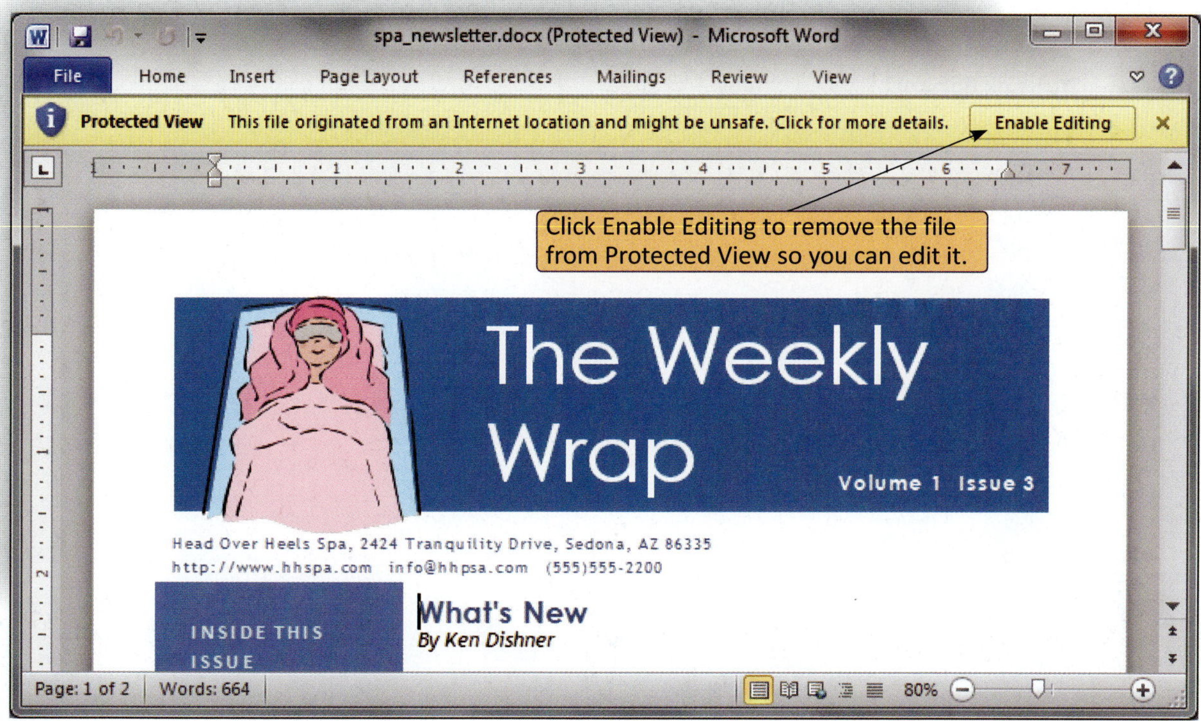

FIGURE WD 0.14

tell me **more**

You can modify the Protected View settings to add or delete specific locations or types of locations.

To review or modify the Protected View settings for Word:

1. Click the **File** tab.
2. If you are currently in Protected View, the *Info* tab will include a link to go to the Protected View settings. If you are not currently in Protected View, click the **Options** button to open the *Word Options* dialog.
3. Click **Trust Center**, and then click the **Trust Center Settings** button.
4. The *Trust Center* dialog opens. Click **Protected View** to enable or disable Protected View for different locations such as the Internet and Outlook attachments.
5. To exempt specific locations from Protected View, click **Trusted Locations,** and add the locations you trust (such as secure network locations).

0.6 Creating a New Blank Document

When you open Microsoft Word from the *Start* menu, a new blank document appears on your screen ready for you to begin work. But what if you want to create another new document? Will you need to exit the program and launch it again? The **New** command allows you to create new documents without exiting and reopening the program.

To create a new blank document:

1. Click the **File** tab to open Backstage view.
2. Click **New.**
3. Under the *Home* section, the *Blank* option is selected by default. To create a new blank document, simply click the **Create** button beneath the preview of the blank document.

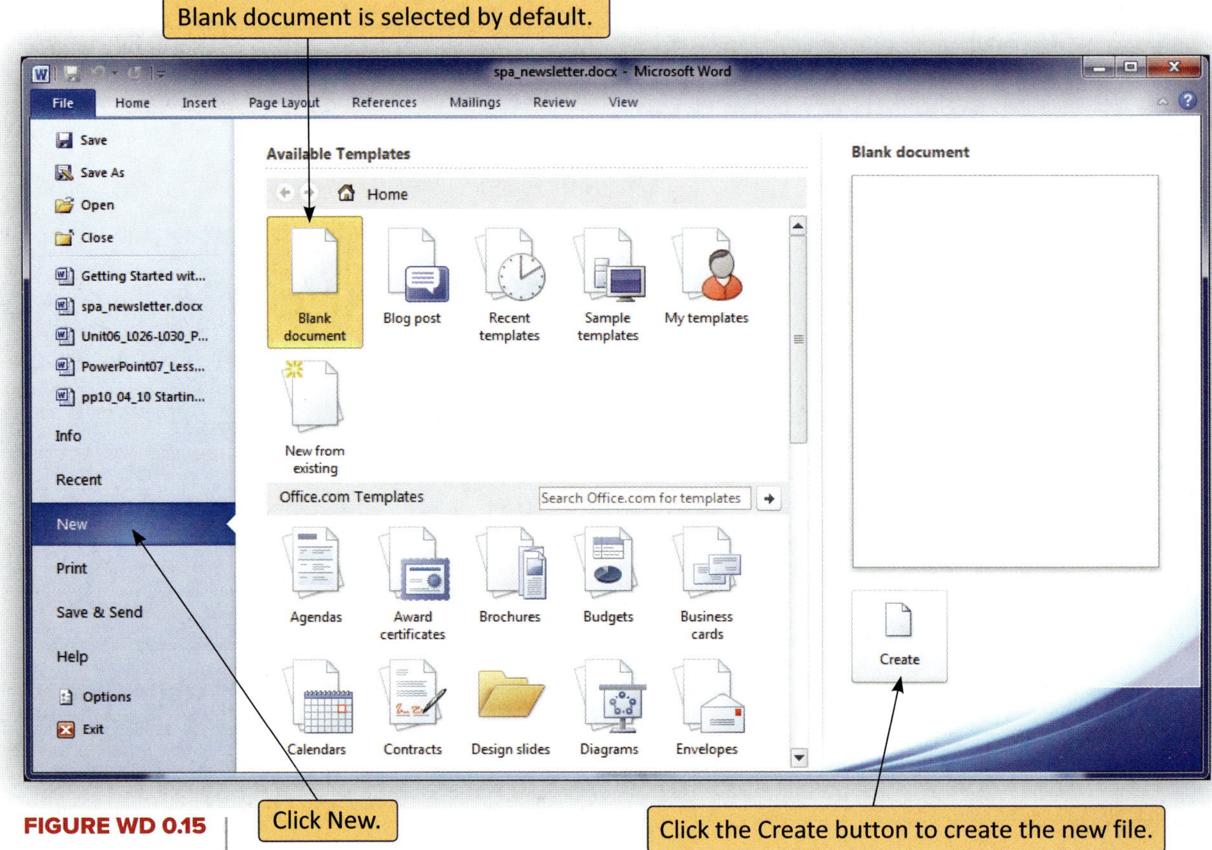

FIGURE WD 0.15

try this To bypass Backstage view and create a new blank document, press Ctrl + N on the keyboard.

0.7 Creating a New Document Using a Template

A **template** is a document with predefined settings that you can use as a pattern to create a new file of your own. Using a template makes creating a fully formatted and designed new file easy, saving you time and effort. There are templates available for letters, memos, résumés, newsletters, and almost any other type of document you can imagine.

To create a new document from a template:

1. Click the **File** tab to open Backstage view.
2. Click **New.**
3. Notice that the entire right pane is labeled *Available Templates.* Even the *Blank Document* option is considered a template. The *Home* section gives you access to all the templates located on your computer.

   The *Office.com* section gives you access to hundreds of templates available from Office.com, but you must have an active Internet connection to download a template from this section.
4. To find a template from Office.com, click one of the categories in the *Office.com* section.
5. Click each template image to see a preview of the file and a brief description of the template.
6. When you find the template you want to use, click the **Download** button.
7. A new document opens, prepopulated with all the template elements.

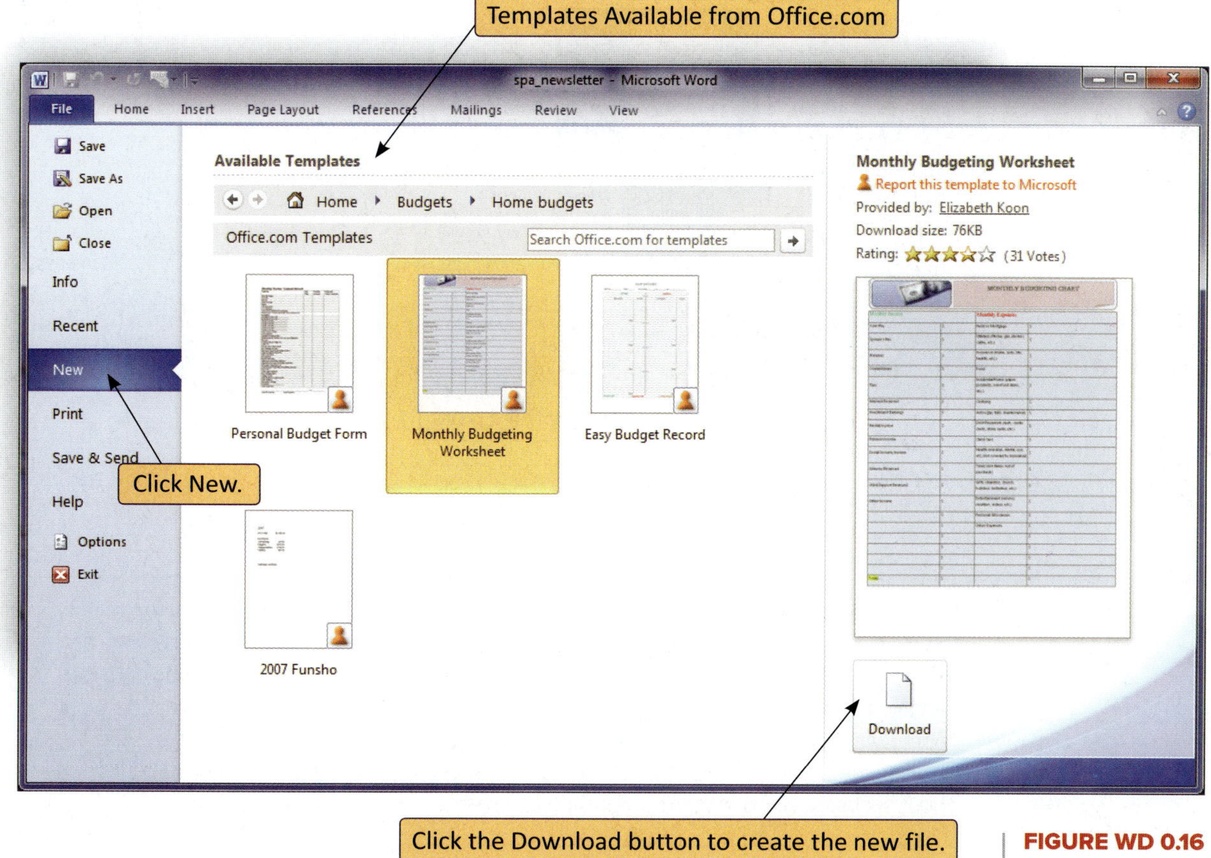

FIGURE WD 0.16

tell me more

Microsoft Word includes a set of templates that are copied to your computer when you install the application. These templates are always available from the *Home* section of the *Available Templates* page, in the *Sample templates* category.

0.8 Using the Status Bar

The **status bar** appears at the bottom of the Word window and displays information about the current document. By default, the status bar displays the page number, number of words in the document, and whether or not there are spelling and grammar errors. You can customize the status bar to show other information about the document, such as section, the current vertical position of the cursor in the document, and whether Caps Lock is on or off.

To change the information shown on the status bar:

1. Right-click anywhere on the status bar.
2. The *Customize Status Bar* menu appears. Options with check marks next to them are currently active. Options without a check mark are not currently active.
3. Click an item on the menu to add it to or remove it from the status bar display.

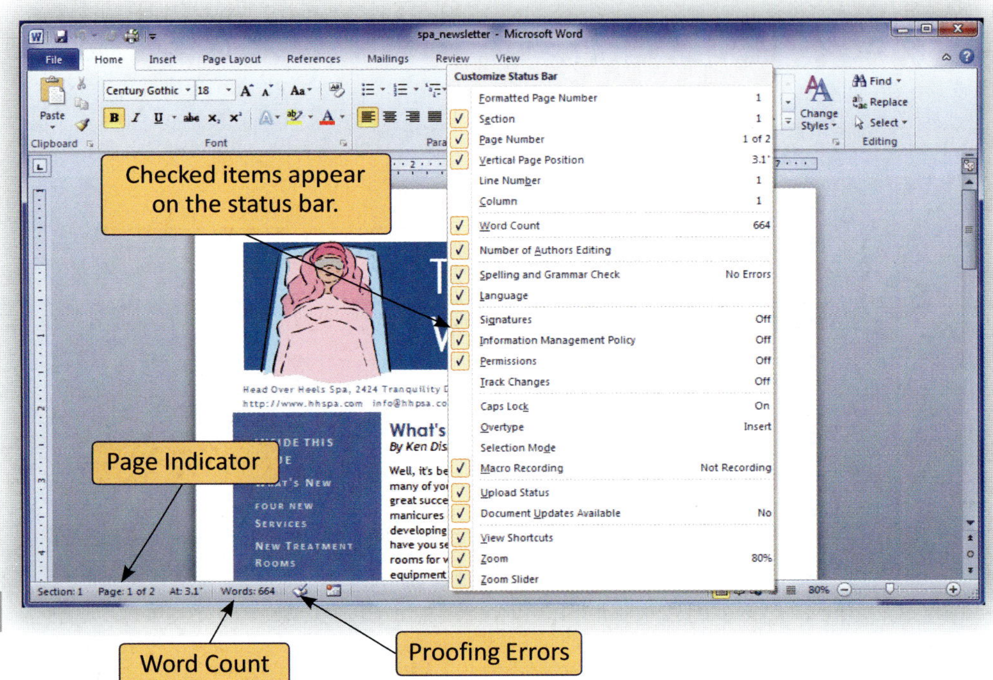

FIGURE WD 0.17

tips & tricks

Word includes a **zoom slider** at the right side of the status bar to allow you to control how the file appears on screen. Drag the slider to the right to increase the zoom percentage and make text and images appear larger; drag the slider to the left to decrease the zoom percentage to make text and images look smaller. For more information about using the Word zoom feature, refer to the skill *Zooming a Document* in Chapter 1.

The status bar also displays buttons for changing the file view. For more information about changing views in Word, refer to the skill *Using Views* in Chapter 1.

0.9 Modifying Document Properties

Document properties provide information about a document such as the location of the document, the number of pages and words, when the document was created and last modified, the title, and the author. Properties also include keywords, referred to as **tags**, that are useful for grouping common files together or for searching. All this information about a file is referred to as **metadata**.

To view a document's properties, click the **File** tab to open Backstage view. Properties are listed at the far right of the *Info* tab.

To add keywords to a document, click the text box next to *Tags* and type keywords that describe the document, separating each word with a comma.

The Author property is added automatically from the name entered when you installed and registered Word. You can change the author name or add more names by editing the Author property.

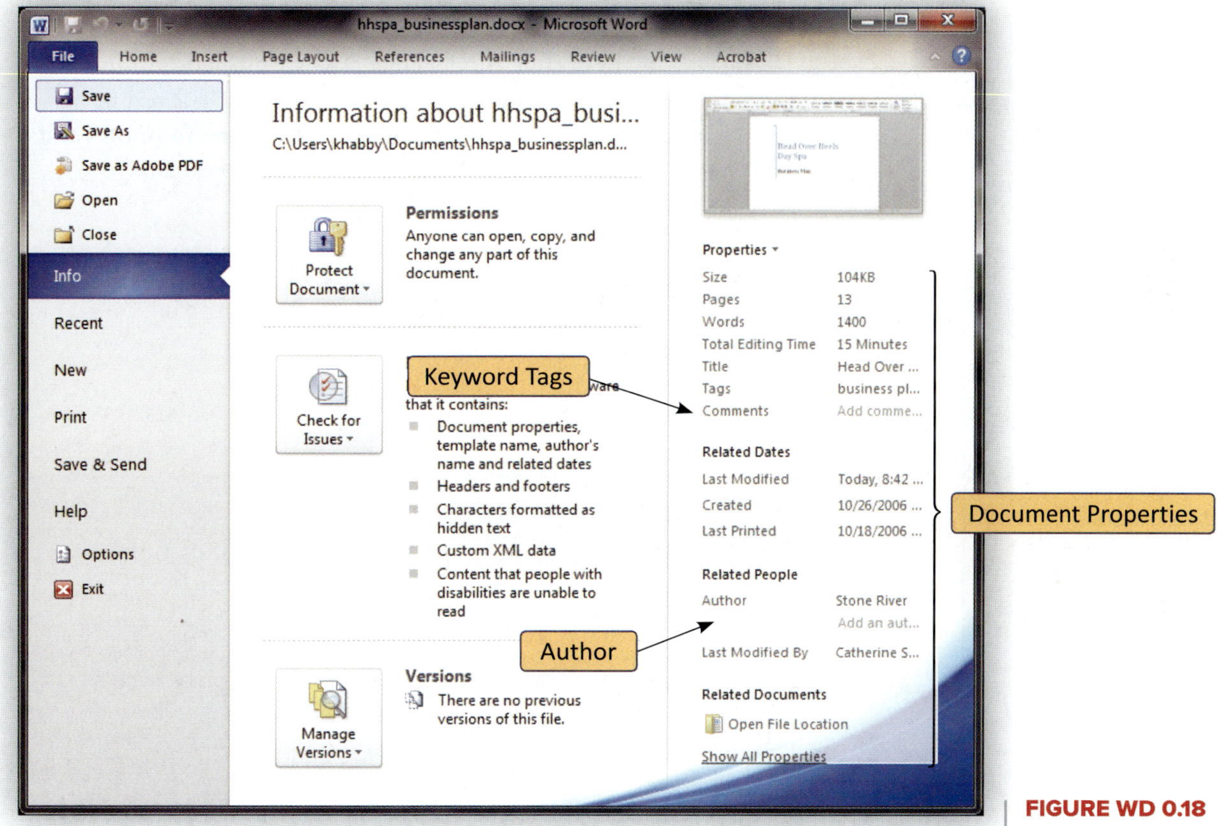

FIGURE WD 0.18

tips & tricks

Some document properties are generated automatically by Windows and cannot be edited by the user, such as the date the file was created and the size of the file.

tell me more

The Windows Vista and Windows 7 operating systems take advantage of the enhanced properties in Office 2010 documents by allowing you to search for files based on metadata, including author and keywords. When you select a file in the Explorer, its metadata are displayed in the *Details* pane.

0.10 Viewing Document Statistics

Have you ever had to write a 250-word essay or submit a 3,000-word article? You don't need to guess if your Word document is long enough (or too long). Word's **Word Count** feature provides the current statistics of the document you are working on.

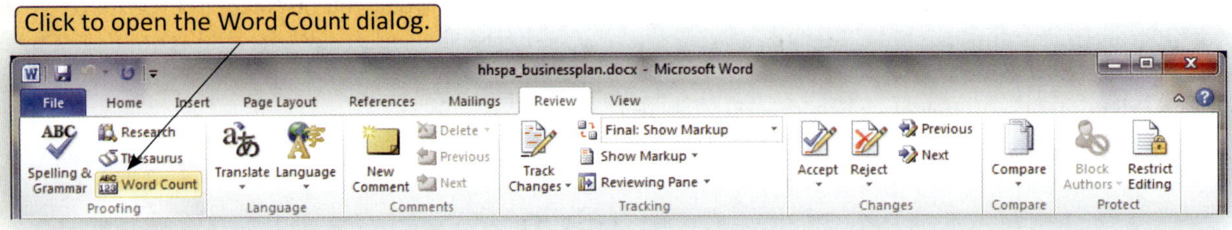

FIGURE WD 0.19

To view document statistics:

1. From the *Review* tab, in the *Proofing* group, click the **Word Count** button.
2. The *Word Count* dialog opens and displays the statistics for the document.
3. By default, the document statistics include text in text boxes, footnotes, and endnotes. To exclude text in these areas, click the **Include textboxes, footnotes and endnotes** check box to remove the checkmark.
4. Click **Close** to close the dialog.

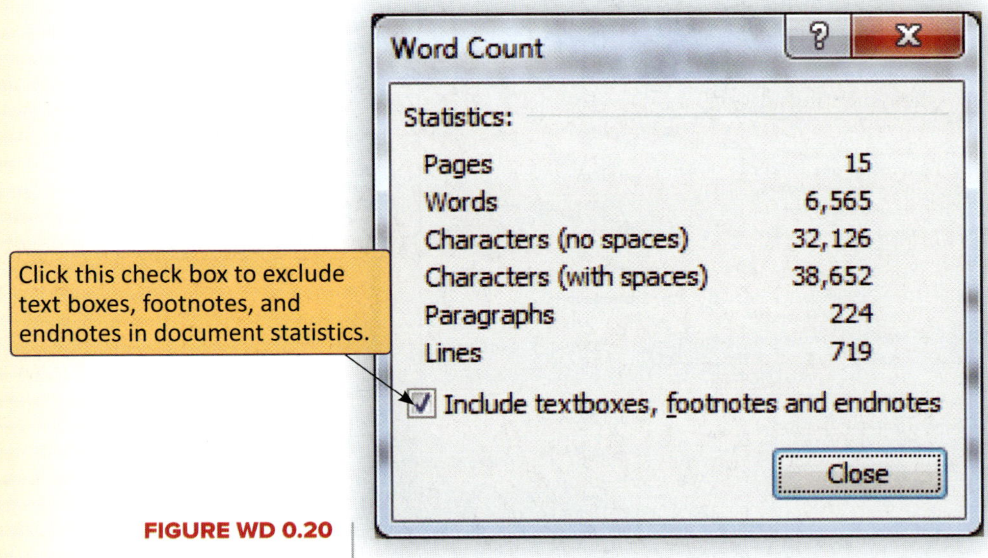

FIGURE WD 0.20

tips & tricks

The number of words and the number of pages in the document are also displayed as part of the document properties available from the *Info* tab in Backstage view.

0.11 Using Help

If you don't know how to perform a task, you can look it up in the Microsoft Word Help system. The Help system includes several ways of displaying help topics, including articles, online training, and videos. When Microsoft Word Help first opens, the Home page displays. From the Home page, you can click any of the links to learn more about that topic. If you are looking for specific information, use the search box at the top of the Help window.

To search for a topic using the Microsoft Word Help system:

1. Click the **Microsoft Word Help** button. It is located at the far right of the Ribbon.
2. In the *Type words to search for* box, type a word or phrase describing the topic you want help with.
3. Click the **Search** button.
4. A list of results appears.
5. Click a result to display the help topic.

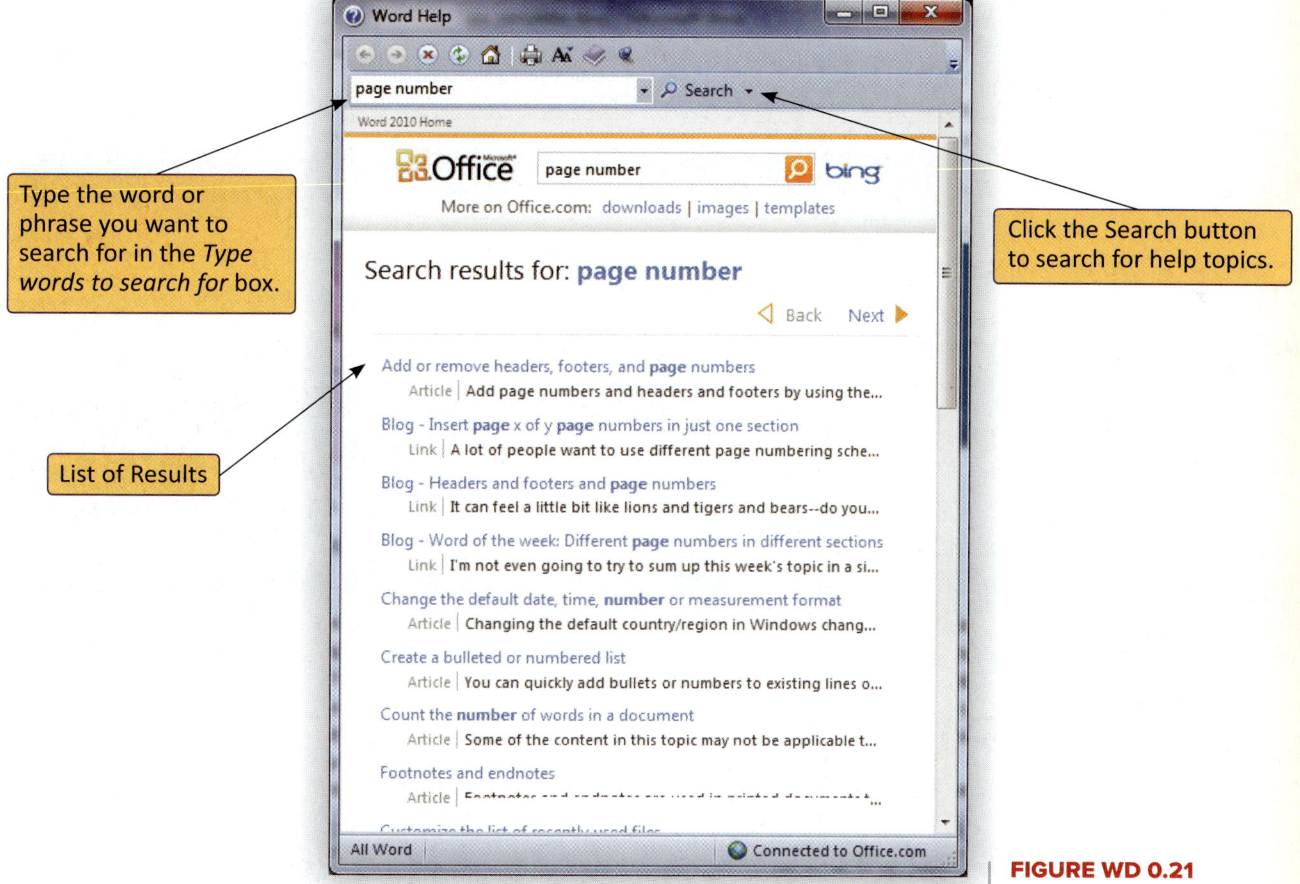

FIGURE WD 0.21

tips & tricks

At the bottom right of the Help window there is a button indicating whether you are connected to Office.com or whether you are working offline. If you are working offline (and not connected to Office.com), Help is still available, but it is limited to the topics that are installed as part of the Office applications. If you are connected to Office.com, the Help system adds material from the Office.com Web site including templates and links to other Web sites.

tell me more

The Help toolbar is located at the top of the Help window. This toolbar includes buttons for navigating between screens, reloading the current screen, and returning to the Help Home page. Click the printer icon on the toolbar to print the current topic. Click the pushpin icon to keep the Help window always on top of the Microsoft Word window.

try this

To open the Help window, you can also press F1 on the keyboard.

0.12 Using Undo and Redo

If you make a mistake when working, the **Undo** command allows you to reverse the last action you performed. The **Redo** command allows you to reverse the *Undo* command and restore the file to its previous state. The Quick Access Toolbar gives you immediate access to both commands.

To undo the last action taken, click the **Undo** button on the Quick Access Toolbar.

To redo the last action taken, click the **Redo** button on the Quick Access Toolbar.

To undo multiple actions at the same time:

1. Click the arrow next to the *Undo* button to expand the list of your most recent actions.
2. Click an action in the list.
3. The action you click will be undone, along with all the actions completed after that. In other words, your document will revert to the state it was in before that action.

FIGURE WD 0.22

try this

To undo an action, you can also press Ctrl + Z on the keyboard.
To redo an action, you can also press Ctrl + Y on the keyboard.

0.13 Using Cut, Copy, and Paste

The *Cut, Copy,* and *Paste* commands are used to move text and other objects within a document and from one document to another. Text or an object that is **cut** is removed from the document and placed on the Office Clipboard for later use. The **Copy** command places a duplicate of the selected text or object on the Clipboard without changing the document. The **Paste** command is used to insert text or an object from the Clipboard into a document.

To move text within a document:

1. Select the text to be cut or copied.
2. On the *Home* tab of the Ribbon, click the appropriate button:

   Cut

   or

   Copy

3. Place the cursor where you want to insert the text from the Clipboard.
4. Click the **Paste** button.

These same steps apply whether you are cutting, copying, and pasting text, pictures, shapes, video files, or any type of object in a Word document.

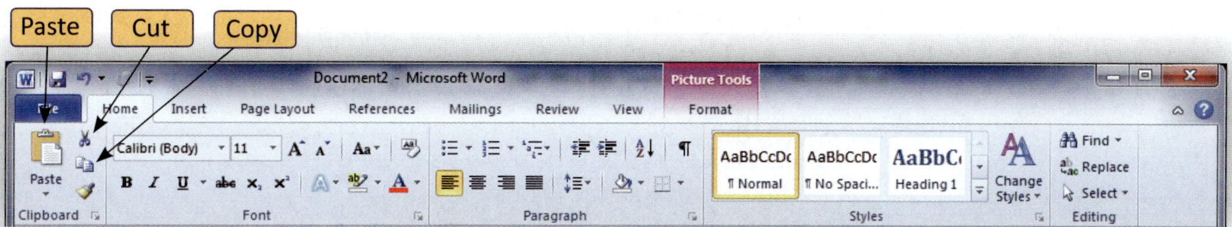

FIGURE WD 0.23

tell me more

The *Paste* button has two parts—the top part of the button pastes the topmost contents of the Clipboard into the current document. If you click the bottom part of the button (the *Paste* button arrow), you can control how the item is pasted. Each type of object has different paste options. For example, if you are pasting text, you may have options to keep the source formatting, merge the formatting of the source and the current document, or paste only the text without any formatting. Move your mouse over the icon for each paste option to see a preview of how the paste would look, and then click the icon for the paste option you want.

try this

To apply the *Cut, Copy,* or *Paste* command, you can use the following shortcuts:

- **Cut** = Press Ctrl + X on the keyboard, or right-click and select **Cut.**
- **Copy** = Press Ctrl + C on the keyboard, or right-click and select **Copy.**
- **Paste** = Press Ctrl + V on the keyboard, or right-click and select **Paste.**

0.14 Using the Office Clipboard

When you cut or copy items, they are placed on the Office Clipboard. The icons in the Clipboard identify the type of document from which each item originated (Word, Excel, Paint, etc.). A short description or thumbnail of the item appears next to the icon, so you know which item you are pasting into your document. The Office Clipboard can store up to 24 items for use in the current document or any other Office application.

To paste an item from the Office Clipboard into a document:

1. Place your cursor where you want to paste the item.
2. On the *Home* tab, in the *Clipboard* group, click the **Clipboard** dialog launcher.
3. The *Office Clipboard* task pane appears.
4. To paste an item from the Clipboard into your document, click the item you want to paste.
5. To remove an item from the Office Clipboard, point to the item, click the arrow that appears, and select **Delete.**
6. To add all the items in the Office Clipboard at once, click the **Paste All** button at the top of the task pane.
7. To remove all the items from the Office Clipboard at once, click the **Clear All** button at the top of the task pane.

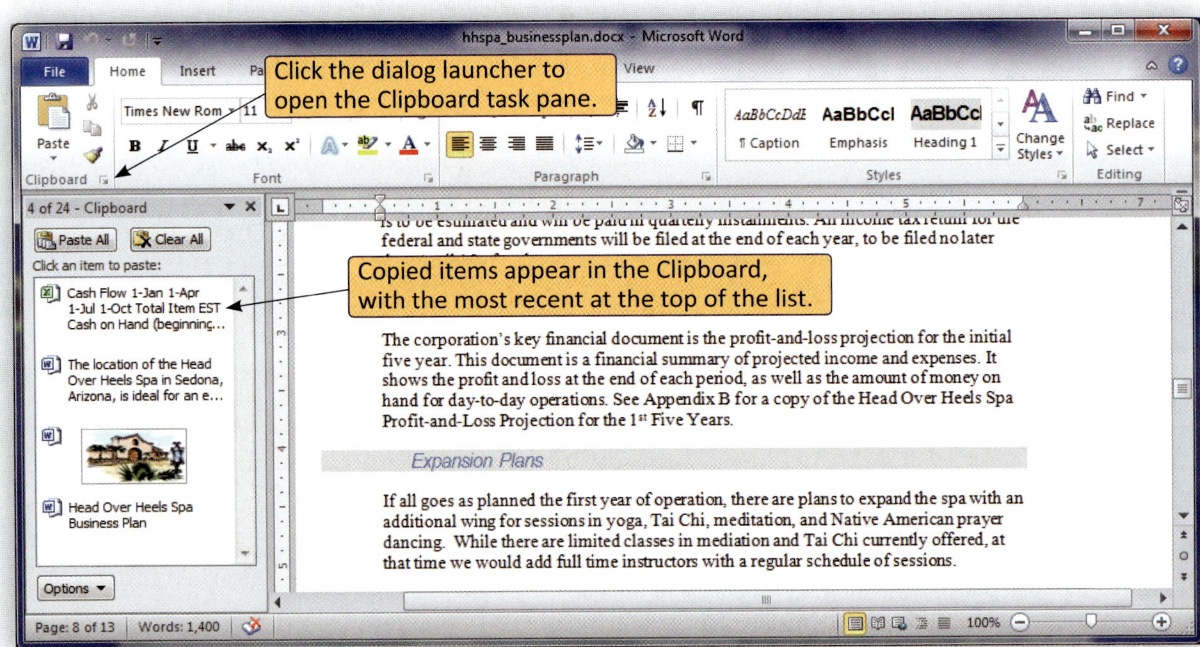

FIGURE WD 0.24

tips & tricks

The Office Clipboard is common across all Office applications—so you can cut text from a Word document and then paste that text into an Excel spreadsheet or copy a chart from Excel into a PowerPoint presentation.

try this

To paste an item, you can also point to the item in the *Clipboard* task pane, click the arrow that appears, and select **Paste.**

0.15 Using Paste Special

Using the **Paste Special** command, an object from another Office application (for example, an Excel spreadsheet) can be inserted into a Word document. When pasting source material from another program, you have two choices:

Linked objects. Linked data are stored in the source file. Information in a linked object is updated if the source file is edited. The destination file stores only the location of the source file and displays a representation of the linked data. Double-click the linked object to open the source file.

Embedded objects. Once pasted into your Word document, embedded objects are independent of the original source. Information in an embedded object does not change if you modify the source file. Double-click the embedded object to edit it within the Word document (using the source program, but not the source file).

To use the *Paste Special* command:

1. Copy the object you want to paste.
2. On the *Home* tab, in the *Clipboard* group, click the **Paste** button arrow and select **Paste Special.**
3. Select a format for pasting the object in the *As* box. Different formats are available depending on the source of the pasted material.
4. If you want to paste the material as a linked object, click the **Paste link** radio button.
5. Click **OK.**

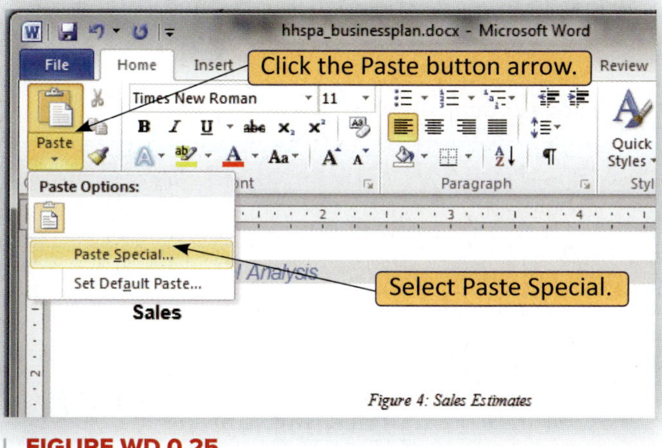

FIGURE WD 0.25

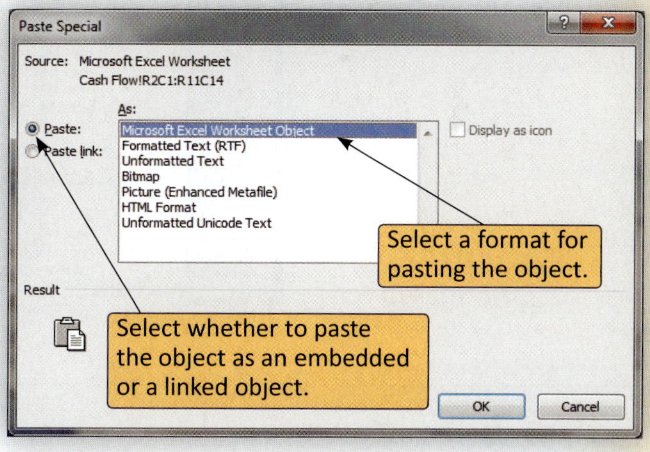

FIGURE WD 0.26

tips & tricks

The *Paste Special* options available vary depending on the type of source material. Some objects may only be available to paste as an embedded object, not a linked object.

tell me more

Information in a linked object is updated every time you open the document. To update an object manually, right-click the object and select **Update Link.**

0.16 Checking Spelling

Regardless of the amount of work you put into a document, a spelling error or typo can make the entire document appear sloppy and unprofessional. All the Office applications include a built-in spelling checker. In Word, the *Spelling and Grammar* command analyzes your entire document for spelling errors. It presents any errors it finds in a dialog box, enabling you to make decisions about how to handle each error or type of error in turn.

To check a document for spelling errors:

1. Click the **Review** tab. In the *Proofing* group, click the **Spelling & Grammar** button.
2. The first spelling error appears in the *Spelling and Grammar* dialog box.
3. Review the spelling suggestions and then select an action:
   - Click **Ignore Once** to make no changes to this instance of the word.
   - Click **Ignore All** to make no changes to all instances of the word.
   - Click **Add to Dictionary** to make no changes to this instance of the word and add it to the main dictionary, so future uses of this word will not show up as misspellings. When you add a word to the dictionary, it is available for all of the Office applications.
   - Click the correct spelling in the *Suggestions* list, and click **Change** to correct just this instance of the misspelling in your document.
   - Click the correct spelling in the *Suggestions* list, and click **Change All** to correct all instances of the misspelling in your document.
4. After you select an action, the spelling checker automatically advances to the next suspected spelling error.
5. When the spelling checker finds no more errors, it displays a message telling you the check is complete. Click **OK** to close the dialog and return to your document.

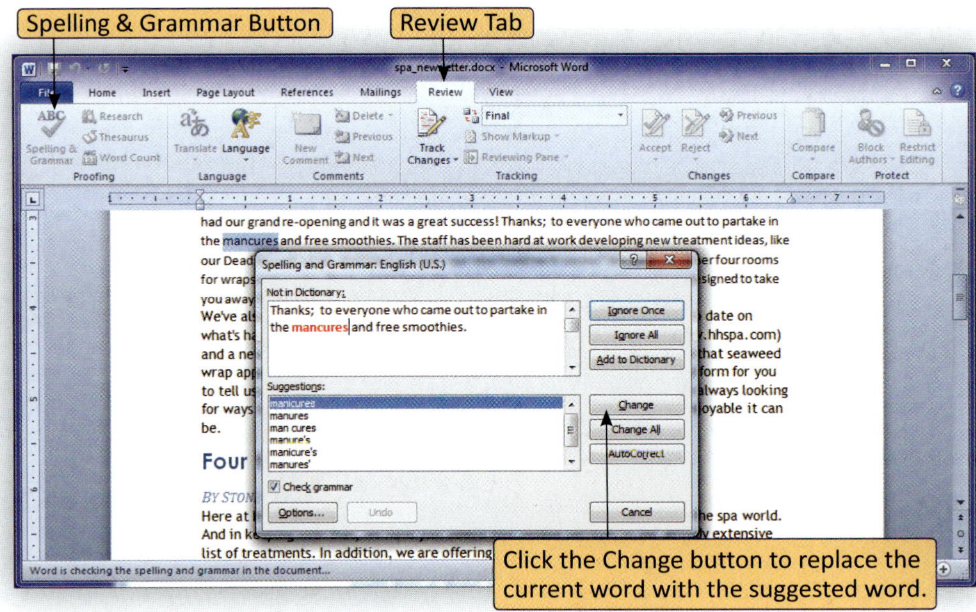

FIGURE WD 0.27

tips & tricks

Whether or not you use the Spelling tool, you should always proofread your files. Spelling checkers are not infallible, especially if you misuse a word yet spell it correctly—for instance, writing "bored" instead of "board."

If you misspell a word often, the next time the spelling checker catches the misspelling, use this trick: Click the correct spelling in the *Suggestions* list and then click the **AutoCorrect** button. Now, when you type the misspelled version of the word, it will be corrected automatically as you type.

tell me more

If you have typed the same word two times in a row, Word will flag the second instance of the word as a possible error. In the *Spelling and Grammar* dialog box, the *Change* button will switch to a *Delete* button. Click the **Delete** button to remove the duplicate word.

try this

To open the *Spelling and Grammar* dialog box, you can also press the F7 key.

0.17 Checking Grammar

In addition to checking spelling, the *Spelling and Grammar* command can analyze your document for grammar errors. It presents any grammar errors it finds in a dialog box, enabling you to make decisions about how to handle each error or type of error in turn.

To check a document for grammar errors:

1. Click the **Review** tab.
2. In the *Proofing* group, click the **Spelling & Grammar** button.
3. If necessary, click the **Check grammar** check box.
4. The first error appears in the *Spelling and Grammar* dialog box.
5. Review the grammar suggestions to determine which one is correct.
   - Click **Ignore Once** to skip just this instance of the grammar error.
   - Click **Ignore Rule** to skip all instances of the grammar error.
   - Click **Next Sentence** to skip this error and advance to the next.
   - The *Suggestions* box displays potential corrections. Click the correction you want to use, and then click the **Change** button.
   - For more information about why Word considers this a grammatical error, click the **Explain** button.
6. A message appears to tell you when the spelling and grammar check is complete. Click **OK** to close the *Spelling and Grammar* dialog.

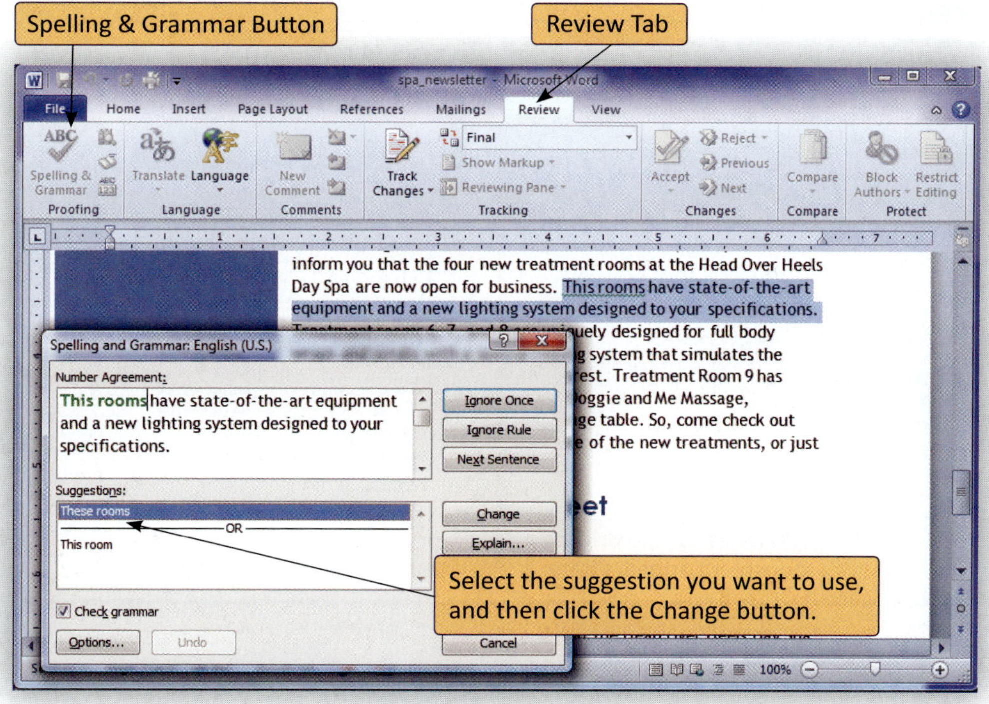

FIGURE WD 0.28

tell me **more**

You can control which grammar rules Word checks for.

1. From the *Spelling and Grammar* dialog, click the **Options** button at the lower-left corner, or from Backstage, click the **Options** button to open the *Word Options* dialog, and then click **Proofing.**
2. In the *When correcting spelling and grammar in Word* section, click the **Settings** button to specify the type of grammar rules to apply to your documents.
3. You can set the grammar checker to look for errors in writing style as well as grammar. Expand the *Writing Style* list and select the option you want: **Grammar & Style** or **Grammar Only.**

try **this**

To open the *Spelling and Grammar* dialog box, you can also press the F7 key.

0.18 Previewing and Printing a Document

Printing has changed significantly in Word 2010. Previous versions of Word relied on the *Print* dialog box for setting printing options. In Word 2010, all the print settings are combined in a single page along with a preview of how the printed document will look. From the *Print* tab in Backstage view, you can adjust your settings to print specific pages, including the current page or a range of pages. You can also control the number of copies to print from the *Print* tab in Backstage view.

To preview and print a document:

1. Click the **File** tab to open Backstage view.
2. Click the **Print** tab.
3. At the right side of the page is a preview of how the printed document will look. Beneath the preview there is a page count. If there are multiple pages, use the *Next* and *Previous* arrows to preview all the pages in the document. You can use the scroll bar to the right to scroll through the preview pages.
4. Verify that the correct printer name is displayed in the *Printer* section.
5. In the *Settings* section, click the first button to select which pages to print.
6. Type the number of copies you want to print in the *Copies* box.
7. Click the **Print** button to print.

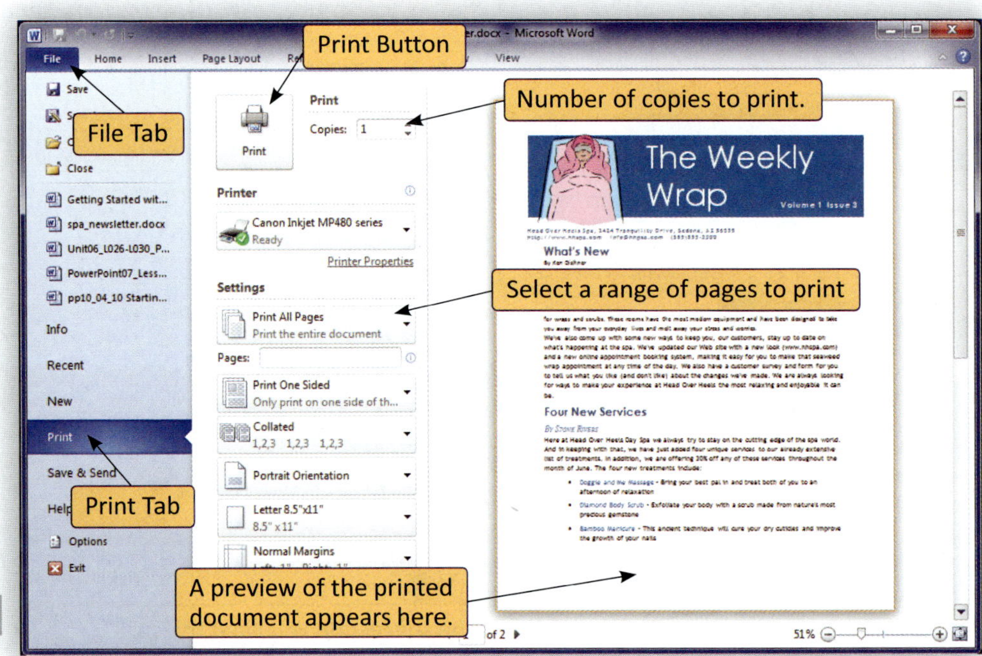

FIGURE WD 0.29

tips & tricks

Add the *Quick Print* command to the Quick Access Toolbar so you can print with a single mouse click. If you do not need to change the default print settings, you can click the *Quick Print* button instead of going through the *Print* tab in Backstage view.

tell me more

You can specify which pages to print by typing a print range in the *Pages:* box under *Settings.* To print a range of pages, separate the numbers by a hyphen. For example, typing 3-7 will print pages 3, 4, 5, 6, and 7. To print nonconsecutive pages, separate the numbers by a comma. For example, typing 3, 7 will print pages 3 and 7, but not pages 4, 5, and 6.

try this

- To open the *Print* tab in Backstage view, you can use the keyboard shortcut Ctrl + P.
- You can click the up and down arrows to change the number of copies to print.

0.19 Saving a Document

As you work on a new document, it is displayed on-screen and stored in your computer's memory. However, it is not permanently stored until you save it as a file to a specific location. The first time you save a document, the *Save As* dialog box will open. Here you can enter a file name, select the file type, and choose where to save the document.

To save a document for the first time:

1. Click the **Save** button on the Quick Access Toolbar.
2. The *Save As* dialog box appears.
3. If necessary, navigate to the location where you want to save the document.
4. If you want to create a new folder, click the **New Folder** button near the top of the file list. The new folder is created with the temporary name *New Folder*. Type the new name for the folder and press **Enter.**
5. Click in the *File name* box and type a file name.
6. Click the **Save** button.

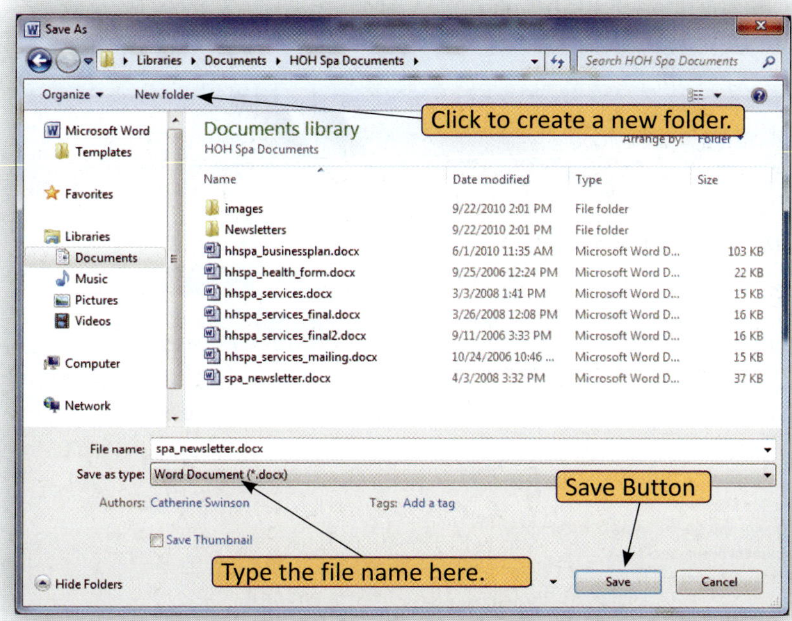

FIGURE WD 0.30

The next time you save this document, it will be saved with the same file name and to the same location automatically. The *Save As* dialog will not open again.

As you are working with documents, be sure to ***save often!*** Although Word 2010 includes a recovery function, it is not foolproof. If you lose power or your computer crashes, you may lose all the work done on the document since the last save.

tips & tricks

The screen shot shown here is from Word 2010 running on the Microsoft Windows 7 operating system. Depending on the operating system you are using, the *Save As* dialog box will appear somewhat different. However, the basic steps for saving a document are the same regardless of which operating system you are using.

try this

To save a document, you can also:

› Press Ctrl + S on the keyboard.

› Click the **File** tab, and then select **Save.**

To open the *Save As* dialog box, you can also click the **File** tab and then select **Save As.**

tell me more

Beginning with Word 2007, Microsoft changed the file format for Word documents. Documents created with Word 2007 and Word 2010 will not work with older versions of Word. If you want to share your documents with people who are using Word 2003 or older, you should save the documents in a different file format.

1. Click the **File** tab.
2. Click **Save As.**
3. The *Save As* dialog opens. Click the arrow at the end of the *Save as type* box to expand the list of available file types.
4. To ensure compatibility with older versions of Office, select *Word 97–2003 Document.*

0.20 Closing a Document

Closing a document removes it from your computer screen and stores the last-saved version for future use. If you have not saved your latest changes, Word will prevent you from losing work by asking if you want to save the changes you made before closing.

To close a document and save your latest changes:

1. Click the **File** tab to open Backstage view.
2. Click the **Close** button.
3. If you have made no changes since the last time you saved the document, it will close immediately. If changes have been made, Word displays a message box asking if you want to save the changes you made before closing.
   - Click **Save** to save the changes.
   - Click **Don't Save** to close the document without saving your latest changes.
   - Click **Cancel** to keep the document open.

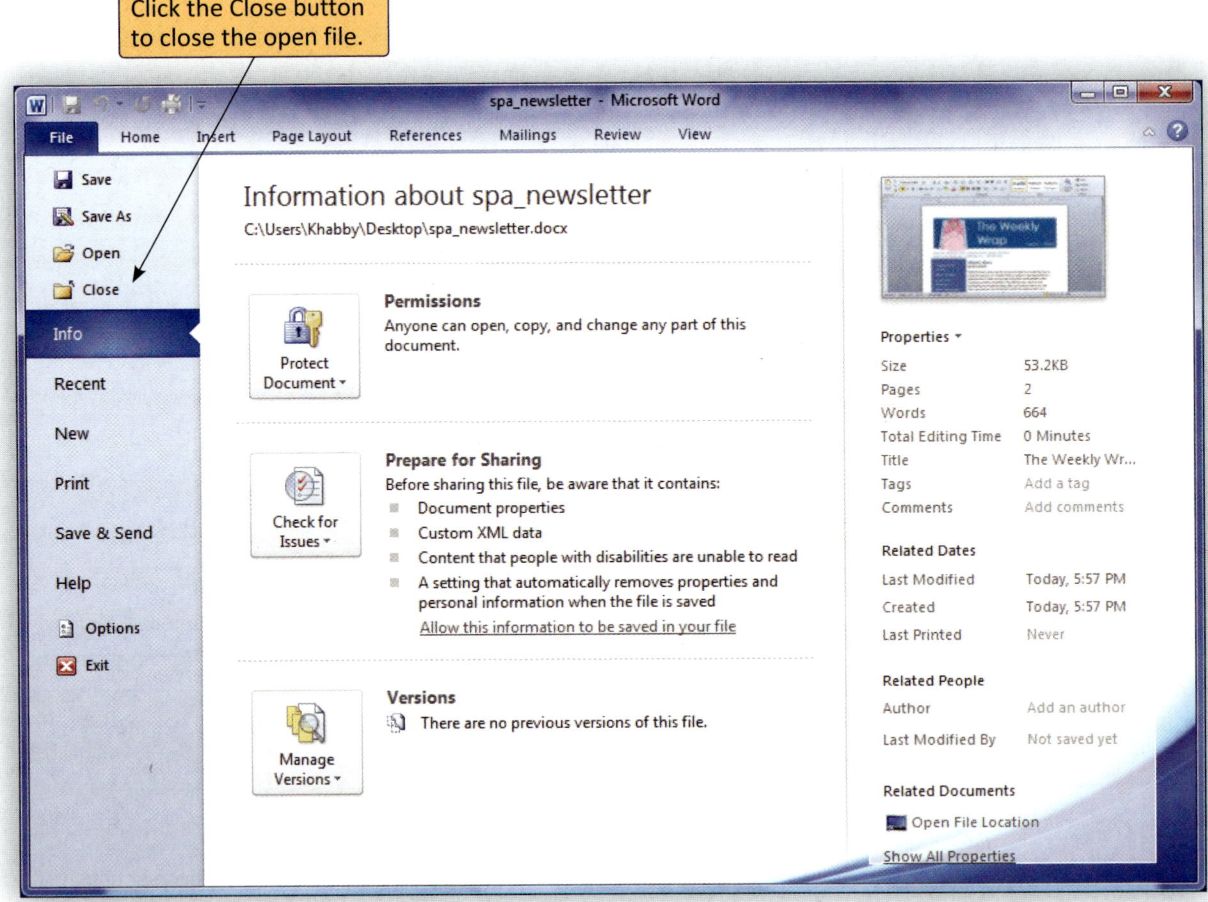

FIGURE WD 0.31

try this

To close a document, you can also press Ctrl + W on the keyboard.

0.21 Exiting Word

When you close a document, Microsoft Word stays open so you can open another document to edit or begin a new document. Often, when you are finished working on a document, you want to close the document *and* close Microsoft Word at the same time. In this case, you will want to *exit* Microsoft Word.

To exit Microsoft Word:

1. Click the **File** tab to open Backstage view.
2. Click the **Exit** button.
3. If you have made no changes since the last time you saved the document, Word will close immediately. If changes have been made, Word displays a message box asking if you want to save the changes you made before exiting.
   - Click **Save** to save the changes.
   - Click **Don't Save** to exit Word without saving your latest changes.

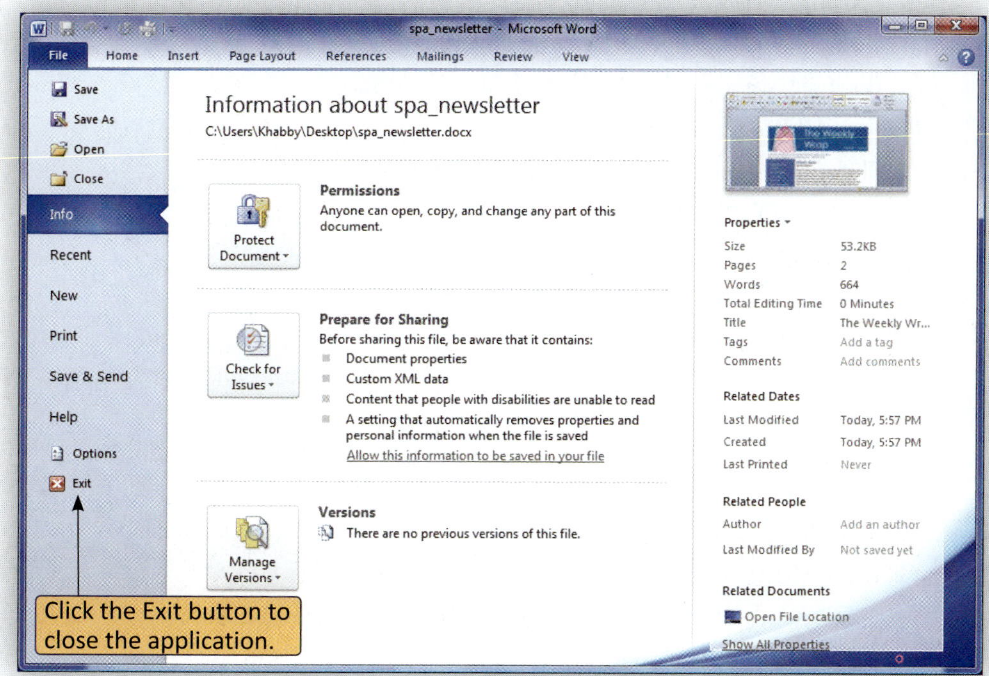

FIGURE WD 0.32

tips & tricks

Click **Cancel** in the message box to not exit the application. This action keeps Word and all documents open.

try this

To exit Word, you can:

- Click the [X] in the upper-right corner of the application window.
- Right-click the title bar of the application window and select **Close**.

projects

Data files for projects can be found on
www.mhhe.com/office2010skills

Skill Review 1

In this project you will create two icebreaker documents using Microsoft Word 2010. The first will be a simple poster to introduce yourself. The second will utilize a résumé template to create a document listing your own objectives for this course and your prior experience with computers. Also, you will be linking some text from the résumé document to the poster document. When changes are made to the first, the link will cause the same changes to be made to the other document.

1. Start Microsoft Word 2010 as follows:

   Click the **Start** button. If you see Microsoft Word 2010 on the *Start* menu, you can click it.

   If you don't see Microsoft Word 2010 on the *Start* menu:

   a. Point to **All Programs.**

   b. Scroll if needed, and then click **Microsoft Office.**

   c. Click **Microsoft Word 2010.**

   After Word 2010 launches, a new blank document is opened.
   This document starts with the default name *Document1.*

2. Use Word Help:

   a. Click the Microsoft Word **Help** button. It is a blue circle with a question mark, located at the far right of the Ribbon.

   b. Type `Backstage view` in the *Search* box at the top of the *Help* window and click the **Search** button.

   c. Click the **What and where is Backstage view** topic to display that article.

   d. Close the Help window.

3. Type: `Introduction` at the top of the document. Press the **Enter** key.

4. Save your document as follows:

   a. Click the **Save** button on the Quick Access Toolbar.

   b. The *Save As* dialog box appears.

   c. Navigate to the location where you will be saving your completed documents. Pay careful attention to where you save this file. You will be opening it later in this skills review project.

   d. Click in the *File name:* box, and type the new file name:
   ***[your initials]*WD_SkillReview_0-1_Me.**

   e. Click the **Save** button in the *Save As* dialog box. You will see that file name *Document1* has been replaced with the new file name in the title bar of the document.

5. Use the status bar and customize Word:

   a. Drag the slider at the right side of the status bar to adjust the zoom percentage to your preference.

   b. View document statistics on the status bar. You should see the number of words. If you do not, customize the status bar as follows:

      (1) Right-click anywhere on the status bar.

      (2) Click **Word Count** on the menu to add it to the status bar display.

c. Continue entering text in your document. Type the following text. Press Enter after each word:

Outgoing

Motivated

Energetec

Detail Oriented

Sensitive

Reliable

d. Notice the word count on the status bar has increased. Click the **Word Count** button on the status bar to view document statistics.

e. Click **Close.**

6. On the Quick Access Toolbar:

Click the **Save** button to save the *[your initials]WD_SkillReview_0-1_Me* file.

7. Check your *[your initials]WD_SkillReview_0-1_Me* document for spelling errors:

a. Click the *Review* tab on the Ribbon.

b. Click the **Spelling & Grammar** button in the *Proofing* group.

c. Change the misspelling *Energetec* to *Energetic.*

d. Click **OK** in the message box.

8. Use Ctrl + S keyboard shortcut:

Hold the Ctrl key and tap the S key to save the spelling corrections to *[your initials]WD_SkillReview_0-1_Me.*

9. Close the *[your initials]WD_SkillReview_0-1_Me* document, but leave Word open to continue working:

a. Click the **File** tab to open Backstage view.

b. Select **Close.**

Now you are going to create a new document by using a template.

10. Search Help:

a. Click the blue question mark to open Word Help again. In the Word Help window, in the search box, type **templates.**

b. Click the **Search** button.

c. A list of results appears.

d. Click a result to display the help topic.

e. Click the back arrow to go back to the results, and choose a different help topic to view.

f. Read several help topics about using existing templates to create documents before you go on with this project.

g. Close the Help window.

11. Create a new document using a template:

a. Click the **File** tab and select **New.**

b. In the *Available Templates* section, click **Sample Templates.**

c. Click the **Black Tie Resume** template.

d. Click the **Create** button to create the document.

12. Save your résumé document as follows:
   a. Click the **Save** button on the Quick Access Toolbar.
   b. The *Save As* dialog box appears.
   c. Navigate to the location where you will be saving your completed documents.
   d. Click in the *File name:* box and type the new file name: `[your initials]WD_SkillReview_0-1_Resume.`
   e. Click the **Save** button in the *Save As* dialog box.
13. Edit template-provided text:
   a. Select the name at the top of the page and replace it with your full name, *including your first name, middle initial, and last name.*
   b. Continue to enter information about yourself to fill one page, your objectives for this class, your educational goal, your experience with computers, and your current computer skills.
   c. If you don't need part of the template, select that part and delete it. Click the placeholder on the template, click the tab handle with the three dots, and then press the **Delete** key.
   d. As you make each change, pay attention to the results. If you do not like what you have done, click the [Undo] button on the Quick Access Toolbar, and then try something else.

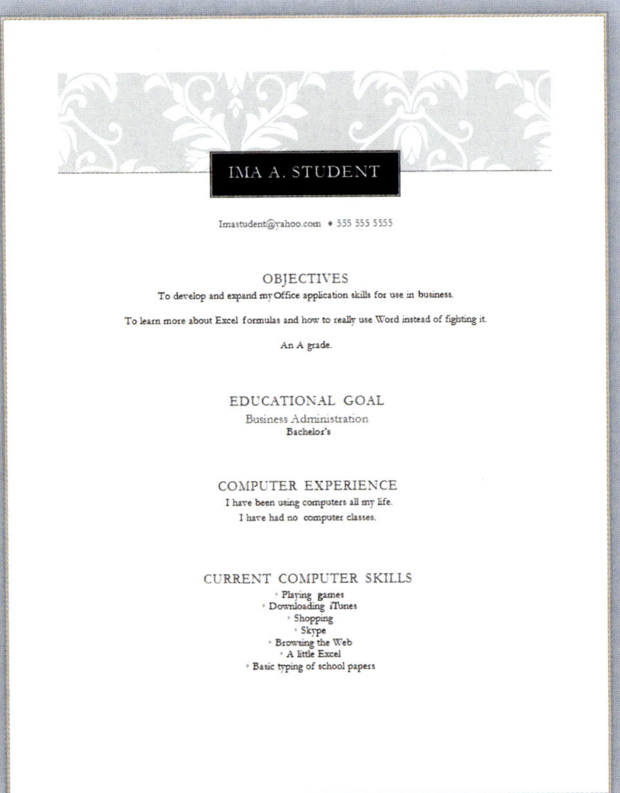
IMA A. STUDENT

Imastudent@yahoo.com • 555 555 5555

OBJECTIVES

To develop and expand my Office application skills for use in business.

To learn more about Excel formulas and how to really use Word instead of fighting it.

An A grade.

EDUCATIONAL GOAL

Business Administration
Bachelor's

COMPUTER EXPERIENCE

I have been using computers all my life.
I have had no computer classes.

CURRENT COMPUTER SKILLS

- Playing games
- Downloading iTunes
- Shopping
- Skype
- Browsing the Web
- A little Excel
- Basic typing of school papers

FIGURE WD 0.33

14. On the Quick Access Toolbar, click the **Save** button to save the changes which you made to *[your initials]WD_SkillReview_0-1_Resume.*
15. Check your *[your initials]WD_SkillReview_0-1_Resume* document for spelling errors:
   a. On the status bar, look for the icon of a book or pencil and for perhaps a red X.
   b. If a box indicating proofing errors were found appears, click it to correct them.
   c. At each error, a shortcut menu will appear with suggestions. Click the appropriate option for each.
16. Use the Ctrl + S keyboard shortcut:

   Hold the Ctrl key and tap the S key to save the proofing corrections to *[your initials]WD_SkillReview_0-1_Resume.*
17. Preview and print the *[your initials]WD_SkillReview_0-1_Resume* file:
   a. Click the **File** tab to open Backstage view, and click **Print.**
   b. Look at the preview of the document.
   c. Click the **Print** button.
   d. Leave the *[your initials]WD_SkillReview_0-1_Resume* document open to continue with the next part of the skills review project.

Now you are going to copy some text from your *[your initials]WD_SkillReview_0-1_Resume* and then link and paste it in your *[your initials]WD_SkillReview_0-1_Me* document.

18. Use the Office Clipboard to copy text from *[your initials]WD_SkillReview_0-1_Resume.*

a. With your *[your initials]WD_SkillReview_0-1_Resume* file still open and active, click the **Clipboard** dialog launcher in the *Clipboard* group on the *Home* tab to open the Office Clipboard.

b. Select one of your skills in the *[your initials]WD_SkillReview_0-1_Resume* file, which you will copy and paste into the *[your initials]WD_SkillReview_0-1_Me* document.

c. On the *Home* tab, click **Copy.** The skill you selected should now be visible on the Clipboard.

d. Select your full name in the *[your initials]WD_SkillReview_0-1_Resume* file.

e. On the *Home* tab, click **Copy.** Your full name should now be a visible item on the Clipboard.

19. Open the *[your initials]WD_SkillReview_0-1_Me* document:

a. Click the **File** tab to open Backstage view.

b. Select the **Open** command.

c. The *Open* dialog box opens. Navigate to location where you saved the file. Select the document name in the large list box: *[your initials]WD_SkillReview_0-1_Me.*

d. Click the **Open** button in the dialog box.

20. Use the *Paste Special* command to link from the *[your initials]WD_SkillReview_0-1_Resume* file to the *[your initials]WD_SkillReview_0-1_Me* file:

a. At the top of your *[your initials]WD_SkillReview_0-1_Me* document, select the word *Introduction.*

b. On the *Home* tab, in the *Clipboard* group, click the **Paste** drop-down list arrow, and choose **Paste Special.**

c. In the *Paste Special* dialog box, click to select the **Paste Link** option.

d. Click **Unformatted Text.**

e. Click **OK.**

f. Press the [←Enter] key, if needed, to break the line.

21. Use the Office Clipboard to paste:

a. Go to the end of your *[your initials]WD_SkillReview_0-1_Me* document by holding the [Ctrl] key and tapping the **End** key. Your insertion point should be at the end of your document.

b. On the Clipboard, click your skill to paste it into your *[your initials]WD_SkillReview_0-1_Me* document.

c. Click the **Paste Options** button which will appear very near the pasted text. Click the drop-down arrow, point at the different options to observe what each does to your pasted text, and choose **Merge Formatting.**

d. Use the [←Enter] key, if needed, to break the line.

22. Use the Ctrl + S keyboard shortcut to save the addition of the pasted text to *[your initials]WD_SkillReview_0-1_Me.*

23. Use the status bar:

Drag the slider at the right side of the status bar to the left to decrease the zoom percentage to display the entire page. Return the zoom percentage to 100%.

24. Move a word using cut-and-paste keyboard shortcuts:

a. In your *[your initials]WD_SkillReview_0-1_Me* document, double-click the word **Outgoing** to select it.

b. While holding the Ctrl key, tap the X key to *cut* (remove) it from the current location.

c. Press Ctrl + End to go to the end of your document.

d. Ensure you are at the beginning of a new line. Press Ctrl + V to paste the cut word at the insertion point.

e. Press the ↵Enter key, if needed, to break the line.

25. Format by using the Mini toolbar, Ribbon, Quick Access Toolbar, and undo and redo:

a. While holding the Ctrl key, tap the A key (**Ctrl + A**) to select all the text in the *[your initials]WD_SkillReview_0-1_Me* document.

b. Right-click the selected text to display the Mini toolbar.

(1) Click the **Font** button to list fonts, and click one to change the font of the selected text.

(2) Click the **Undo** button on the Quick Access Toolbar to remove the font change.

(3) With all the text still selected, right-click the selection to display the Mini toolbar. Click the **Grow Font** button to increase the font size of the selected text.

(4) Click **Redo** button on the Quick Access Toolbar to repeat the last command, to increase the font size again.

26. On the Quick Access Toolbar, click the **Save** button to save the changes that you made to *[your initials]WD_SkillReview_0-1_Me* on the screen onto the disk as well.

27. Customize Word—turn the Mini toolbar on or off:

a. Click the **File** tab to open Backstage view.

b. Click the **Options** button.

c. In the *User Interface Options,* check or uncheck the **Show the Mini Toolbar on selection** option, as desired.

d. Click **OK** in the *Word Options* dialog box.

28. Print the *[your initials]WD_SkillReview_0-1_Me* document:

a. Click the **File** tab to open Backstage view, and select **Print.**

b. Check the print settings:

(1) Verify that one copy of the document is going to be printed.

(2) Verify that the correct printer name is displayed in the *Printer* section.

c. Click the **Print** button.

29. Modify document properties:

a. Click the **File** tab to open Backstage view.

b. Under *Properties* in the right panel, add the title `Job Skills` to the metadata for the document.

30. Close the *[your initials]WD_SkillReview_0-1_Me* document but leave Word open to continue with this project:

a. In Backstage view, click **Close.**

b. In the message box, click **Save** to save the changes.

Now you are going to see how the linking works. You will see that changing text in the *[your initials]WD_SkillReview_0-1_Resume* source document also changes the linked text in the *[your initials]WD_SkillReview_0-1_Me* destination document.

31. Edit source text:

In the *[your initials]WD_SkillReview_0-1_Resume* file, at the top of the page, delete your middle initial.

32. Close and save the *[your initials]WD_SkillReview_0-1_Resume* document, but leave Word open to continue working on this project:

a. Click the **File** tab to open Backstage view.

b. Select **Close** on the menu.

c. Click **Save** to save the changes.

33. Open the *[your initials]WD_SkillReview_0-1_Me* document:

a. Click the **File** tab to open Backstage view.

b. Select the **Open** command.

c. The *Open* dialog box opens. If necessary, navigate to where you saved the *[your initials]WD_SkillReview_0-1_Me* document.

d. Select the document name in the large list box: *[your initials]WD_SkillReview_0-1_Me.*

e. Click the **Open** button in the dialog box.

f. Word will display a message box, asking if you want to update the document based on the changes made in the linked file. Click **Yes.**

34. Notice updated linked destination text:

Notice because of the link, your middle initial is now removed from the *[your initials]WD_SkillReview_0-1_Me* file too.

35. Exit Word:

a. Click the **File** tab to open Backstage view.

b. Click the **Exit** button.

c. In the message box, click **Save** to save the changes.

Skill Review 2

In this project you will be creating two Microsoft Word 2010 documents. The first will be a simple 8½- by 11-inch page recipe. The second will utilize a template to create a recipe card.

1. Start Microsoft Word 2010 as follows:

Click the **Start** button. If you see **Microsoft Word 2010** on the *Start* menu, you can click it.

If not:

a. Point to **All Programs.**

b. Scroll as needed; click **Microsoft Office.**

c. Click **Microsoft Word 2010.**

After Word 2010 launches, a new blank document is opened. This document starts with the default name *Document1*. From here you can begin typing text for your document.

2. Type the name of the recipe: `Saltine Toffee`

Press the **Enter** key.

3. Save your toffee recipe document as follows:

a. Click the **Save** button on the Quick Access Toolbar.

b. The **Save As** dialog box appears.

c. Navigate to the location where you will be saving your completed documents.

d. Click in the *File name:* box and type the new file name: `[your initials]WD_SkillReview_0-2_Recipe.`

e. Click the **Save** button in the *Save As* dialog box.

You will see that file name *Document1* has been replaced with the new file name.

4. Use the status bar and customize Word:

a. Drag the slider at the right side of the status bar to adjust the zoom percentage to display the entire page.

b. Change views: The view buttons are on the status bar to the left of the zoom. Click the **Draft** view button; it is the rightmost button. Return to Print Layout view when you wish by clicking the leftmost view button. Return zoom view to 100%.

c. View document statistics on the status bar. You should see the number of words. If you do not, customize the status bar as follows:

(1) Right-click anywhere on the status bar.

(2) The *Customize Status Bar* menu appears. Options with check marks next to them are presently turned on. Options with no check mark are off.

(3) Click **Word Count** on the menu to add it to the status bar display.

5. Continue entering recipe text in your toffee recipe document.

a. Type the title `Ingredients` and then press the ←Enter key.

b. Type the ingredients as shown in the figure below. Press ←Enter after each ingredient.

1 sleeve of saltine crackers

1 cup butter

1 cup sugar

1 cup chocolate chips

½ cup chopped nuts

c. Notice the word count on the status bar has increased. Click the **Word Count** button on the status bar to view document statistics, such as number of words, pages, characters, etc. Click the **Close** button to close the *Word Count* dialog box.

d. Continue entering the recipe; press ←Enter to leave a blank line.

e. Type the title `Directoins` and then press the ←Enter key.

f. Type the directions as shown in the figure, and press ←Enter after each direction.

Line one-sided cookie sheet with foil and crackers.
Melt butter and sugar over medium heat until frothy.
Pour butter and sugar over crackers, spreading to cover all.
Bake approximately 10 minutes at 400 degrees.
Take out of oven and sprinkle chocolate chips on top.
Once chips are soft, spread to cover all crackers.
Sprinkle chopped nuts on top of soft chocolate.

g. Notice the word count on the status bar has increased.

(1) Select just the ingredient text.

(2) On the status bar, you will see the number of words selected, a slash, and then the number of words in the document.

(3) Select just the direction text to see how many words are included in the directions.

(4) Deselect the text.

6. Use the Quick Access Toolbar:

On the Quick Access Toolbar, click the **Save** button to save the recipe information which you added to the screen into the toffee recipe file on the disk as well.

7. Check your toffee recipe document for spelling errors:

a. Click the *Review* tab on the Ribbon.

b. Click the **Spelling & Grammar** button in the *Proofing* group.

c. Ignore any grammar errors found.

d. Change the misspelled word *Directoins* to *Directions.* Correct any other misspellings in the document.

e. A message appears to tell you that the spelling and grammar check is complete; click **OK.**

f. Click the **Home** tab.

8. Use Word Help:

a. Click the Microsoft Word **Help** button. It is a blue circle with a question mark, located at the far right of the Ribbon.

b. Type `bullets and numbering` in the *Search* box at the top of the *Help* window and click the **Search** button.

c. Click the **Create a bulleted or numbered list** topic to display that article.

d. Under *In this article,* click **Create a one-level bulleted or numbered list.**

e. Minimize the Help window.

9. Use bullets and numbering:

a. Select the recipe directions.

b. Add numbers to the list of directions. Do not add a number to the title *Directions.*

10. Use the Mini toolbar and Ribbon:

a. While holding the Ctrl key, tap the A key (**Ctrl + A**) to select all the text in the document.

b. Right-click the selection to display the Mini toolbar.

(1) Click the **Font Color** button, and click to change the color of the selected text.

(2) Click the **Grow Font** button to increase the font size of the selected text.

(3) Click **Undo** on the Quick Access Toolbar to undo the grow font. Click it again to undo the color.

(4) Now changing your mind, click **Redo** on the Quick Access Toolbar to restore the undone color. Click **Redo** again to restore the font size.

c. Continue to format your document by using the Ribbon and Live Preview:

(1) Click the arrow next to the *Font* box in the *Font* group on the *Home* tab. Scroll the list, observing the preview of how your recipe looks with various fonts. Click the font you find most readable and pleasing.

Saltine Toffee

Ingredients

1 sleeve of saltine crackers

1 cup butter

1 cup sugar

1 cup chocolate chips

½ cup chopped nuts

Directions

1. Line one-sided cookie sheet with foil and crackers.
2. Melt butter and sugar over medium heat until frothy.
3. Pour butter and sugar over crackers, spreading to cover all.
4. Bake approximately 10 minutes at 400 degrees
5. Take out of oven and sprinkle chocolate chips on top.
6. Once chips are soft, spread to cover all crackers.
7. Sprinkle chopped nuts on top of soft chocolate.

FIGURE WD 0.34

11. Use Ctrl + S keyboard shortcut:

Hold the Ctrl key and then tap the S key to save the formatting changes to the file.

12. Close the *[your initials]WD_SkillReview_0-2_Recipe* document:

a. Click the **File** tab to open Backstage view.

b. Select **Close.**

You have created a one-page recipe on 8½- by 11-inch paper. This will be nice to three-hole punch and put into binder. But now you are thinking it might also be nice to have this recipe on a recipe card for your recipe box.

13. Create a new document using a template:

a. Click the **File** tab and select **New.**

b. In the *Office.com Templates* section, click the **Search Office.com for templates** search box.

c. Type in: `recipe`. Press **Enter** to begin search.

d. Click the **Recipe card (multiple columns)** template.

e. Click the **Download** button to create a document from this template at Office.com.

f. Read all the template directions on the recipe card. If desired, print them; click the **File** tab, click the **Print** tab, and click the **Print** button.

SALTINE TOFFEE

INGREDIENTS

1 sleeve of saltine crackers
1 cup butter
1 cup sugar
1 cup chocolate chips
½ cup chopped nuts

DIRECTIONS

1. Line sided cookie sheet with foil and crackers.
2. Melt butter and sugar over medium heat until frothy.
3. Pour butter and sugar over crackers, spreading to cover all.
4. Bake approximately 10 minutes at 400 degrees
5. Take out of oven and sprinkle chocolate chips on top.
6. Once chips are soft, spread to cover all crackers.
7. Sprinkle chopped nuts on top of soft chocolate.

FIGURE WD 0.35

14. Save your *Recipe card (multiple columns)* document as follows:

a. Click the **Save** button on the Quick Access Toolbar.

b. The *Save As* dialog box appears.

c. Navigate to the location where you will be saving your completed documents.

d. Click in the *File name:* box, and type the new file name: ***[your initials]*****WD_SkillReview_0-2_Card.**

e. Click the **Save** button in the *Save As* dialog box.

f. A message box appears, telling you that you are about to save the document in a newer file format. Click **OK** in the message box.

15. Use the template to finish typing the saltine toffee recipe:

   a. Read and follow the helpful directions on the template itself.

   b. Select the template text you want to change and replace it by typing the appropriate text from the saltine toffee recipe.

   c. If you don't need part of the template, select that part and delete it.

16. Preview and print the recipe card file:

   a. Click the **File** tab to open Backstage view, and click **Print.**

   b. Look at the preview of the document.

   c. Click the **Print** button.

17. Close and save the recipe card document:

   a. Click the **File** tab to open Backstage view, and click **Close.**

   b. Click **Save** in the message box.

18. Open the *[your initials]WD_SkillReview_0-2_Recipe* document:

   a. Click the **File** tab to open Backstage view.

   b. Select the **Open** command.

   c. The *Open* dialog box appears; make sure the location in the *Look in:* box is the location where you saved your file.

   d. Select the document name in the large list box: *[your initials]WD_SkillReview_0-2_Recipe.*

   e. Click the **Open** button in the dialog box.

19. Print the recipe document:

   a. Click the **File** tab to open Backstage view, and select **Print.**

   b. Check the print settings:

      (1) Verify that the correct number of copies to print is entered in the *Copies* section.

      (2) Verify that the correct printer name is displayed in the *Printer* section.

   c. Click the **Print** button.

20. Modify document properties:

   a. Click the **File** tab to open Backstage view.

   b. Under *Properties* in the right panel, add the title **`Saltine Toffee Recipe`** to the metadata for the document.

21. Exit Word:

   a. Click the **File** tab to open Backstage view.

   b. Click the **Exit** button.

   c. Word displays a message box asking if you want to save the changes you made before exiting. Click **Save** to save the changes.

challenge yourself 1

In this project you will apply the skills from this chapter to type a medical record release authorization letter. You will also use a template to create a similar document, a medical record release request letter.

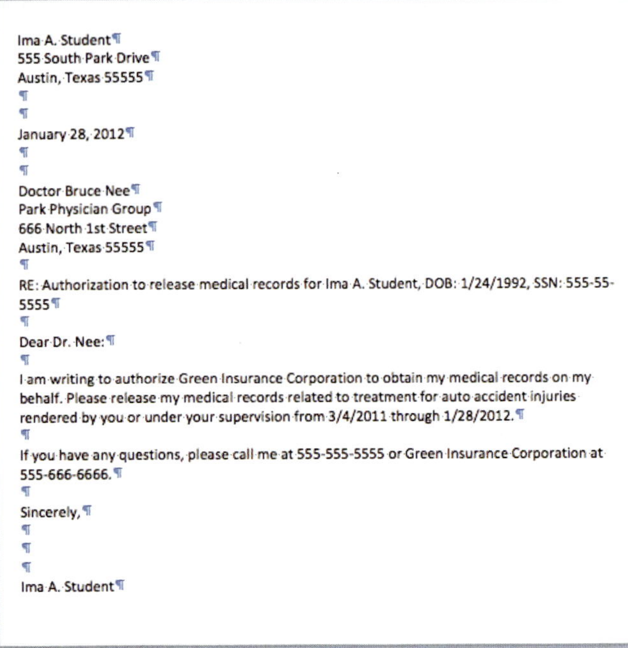
Ima A. Student¶
555 South Park Drive¶
Austin, Texas 55555¶
¶
¶
January 28, 2012¶
¶
¶
Doctor Bruce Nee¶
Park Physician Group¶
666 North 1st Street¶
Austin, Texas 55555¶
¶
RE: Authorization to release medical records for Ima A. Student, DOB: 1/24/1992, SSN: 555-55-5555¶
¶
Dear Dr. Nee:¶
¶
I am writing to authorize Green Insurance Corporation to obtain my medical records on my behalf. Please release my medical records related to treatment for auto accident injuries rendered by you or under your supervision from 3/4/2011 through 1/28/2012.¶
¶
If you have any questions, please call me at 555-555-5555 or Green Insurance Corporation at 555-666-6666.¶
¶
Sincerely,¶
¶
¶
¶
Ima A. Student¶

FIGURE WD 0.36

1. Open Word, but before you begin typing your request letter, change the text style to the **No Spacing Style** from the *Styles* group on the *Home* tab of the Ribbon.
2. Save the document as ***[your initials]*** **WD_Challenge_0-3_Request1.**
3. Type, proof, save, and print the following letter. (Keep in mind that the ¶ symbol shown on the sample indicates each time you should press the [←Enter] key.)
4. Search the Word templates for *medical* templates to locate the *Request for Medical Records* template.
5. Use this template to create a document with the same data for Ima Student as we used for the previous document. You may copy and paste from the one document to the other, if you wish to save yourself retyping. Delete any part of the template you do not need. Use undo as needed.
6. Proof and print this second letter.
7. Save the document as ***[your initials]*** **WD_Challenge_0-3_Request2.**

challenge yourself 2

In this project you will create a new document with planning notes regarding awards for your upcoming school award night. Then you will make five award certificates using Word templates.

1. Browse and search Word templates, looking for templates for different types of certificates.
2. In a new Word document, type up the notes for the award certificates:
   a. Make up and type the name of your school, the principal's name, your name as the teacher, and any other general information that you will need to fill in the certificates.
   b. Make up and type a list of three student names; include first and last names. After each student's name, enter the type of award that student is to receive.
   c. In the same document, make a list of two parents who will receive appreciation awards for their contributions to the class or school.
   d. Proof and print the notes.
   e. Save the document as ***[your initials]*****WD_Challenge_0-4_Notes.**
3. Use templates to create five different certificates.
   a. Make a different certificate for each student and parent whom you are honoring.
   b. If you wish, use copy and paste to save yourself the trouble of retyping.
   c. Proof and print the certificates.
   d. Save the document as ***[your initials]*****WD_Challenge_0-4_Certificates.**

on your own

In this capstone project, you will collect job hunting notes and create a résumé and cover letter using Word templates.

1. Start a new Word document. Save it as
   [your initials]**WD_OnYourOwn_0-5_Notes.**
2. In this document enter the job description for the job you want. Use an actual position description, or brainstorm what you know employers want, and/or combine from various sources into one general job description. Use the Office Clipboard to copy pieces of text, and then paste them back in the document in an organized order. Include a job title, a list of duties, a list of skills needed, educational requirements, and so forth. In this way create a combined job description. Save your job hunting notes.
3. Check the status bar to make sure that there are no proofing errors; if you see the red X indicating proofing errors were found, correct the spelling and grammar errors.
4. In your job hunting notes, type your name, address, e-mail address, and phone number. Save your job hunting notes.
5. In your job hunting notes document, type the name, address, e-mail, and phone number of the first company where you plan to send your résumé. Also note how you heard about the job and the date you applied. Each time you send another résumé, record the date, company name, address, etc., so that you will have a record of your job hunting efforts and contacts. Save your job hunting notes.
6. Explore Word *Templates* to see the résumé and cover letter options available. There are some nice résumé and cover letter examples in the templates. Look for a template to use to create your cover letter and a template for your résumé. They should look similar in style.
7. Use Word Help to search for résumé help. Explore the useful information. Don't miss the help article *Six steps to developing a great résumé.*
8. Enter your personal data and information about your own experience and qualifications for this job into the résumé and the cover letter. Copy your personal information from your notes, and use the *Paste Special* command to insert the information into the résumé. Use undo as needed. Save your résumé as ***[your initials]*****WD_OnYourOwn_0-5_Resume** and the cover letter as ***[your initials]*****WD_OnYourOwn_0-5_Cover.**
9. Check the status bar to make sure that there are no proofing errors. If you see the red X indicating proofing errors were found, correct the spelling and grammar errors. Save your résumé and cover letter.
10. Preview and print your letter and résumé.

fix it

In this project you will be imagining that you are taking an online course. You've completed your first assignment, but your instructor tells you that it needs to be fixed. Thankful for the opportunity to correct the mistakes in your assignment, you will also create a thank-you card for your instructor by using a template.

1. Open the provided file *Introducing yourself letter assignment directions* to review the original assignment directions from your online course. Print the directions file.
2. Open the provided file called *Letter introducing 1st & last name.* This is the file that you will be fixing. Use the status bar to change view and zoom to your preference.

These are the comments from your instructor regarding the *Letter introducing 1st & last name* file you submitted:

Dear Student:

I can see that you have submitted a file for the Introducing Yourself Letter assignment. However, you have submitted a DOCX Word file. I do not have a program that will allow me to read that file type. I will allow you to resubmit this assignment. Please submit your letter in the Microsoft Word 97-2003 file format.

Also, please include your name in the file name instead of 1st & last name.

Hint: If you have combined and split paragraphs as instructed in the directions, you will have four paragraphs: general information, college and career plans, reasons to take the course, and computer information.

Professor Tu Koole

3. You need to find out how to save a file in the Microsoft Word 97-2003 file format.
   a. Use Word Help to look up how to save a file in the Word 97-2003 format.
   b. Use the *Save As* command to save the file in the Word 97-2003 file format with the name ***[your initials]*WD_FixIt_0-6_Letter.**

   Review the assignment directions in the provided file: *Introducing yourself letter assignment directions.*

   Make changes and corrections to your letter file as follows:
4. Do not alter the professor's name in the letter's greeting line.
5. View the properties. Modify the document properties to correctly show your name as author and your college as company.
6. Use cut and paste and the Office Clipboard to rearrange the letter content to match the assignment requirements. Use undo and redo as needed.
7. Where appropriate, change the letter information to reflect yourself instead of the fictitious student *Bree Ediger.* Use the word count on the toolbar to ensure your letter contains the required number of words.
8. The font formatting in a letter should all be the same throughout. Use the Ribbon, Mini toolbar, and keyboard shortcuts to clean up the formatting. The font should be a sans serif font, 10 to 12 pt., and black.
9. Add the *Spell Check* button to the Quick Access Toolbar. If you can't find a button by trial and error, use Word Help to find out how.

   You are so thankful for the opportunity to resubmit this assignment that you decide to make your instructor a thank-you card.
10. Fix spelling and grammar mistakes in your document. Save the letter.
11. Use an appropriate Word template of your choice to create, a thank-you card for your instructor. Proofread the card and then save it with the name ***[your initials]*WD_FixIt_0-6_thankyou.**
12. You are interested in trying to link from one file to another.
    a. Use *Copy* and *Paste Special* commands to *link* your instructor's name from the letter to the thank-you card. Save the thank-you card.
    b. Now, correct the spelling of the professor's name in the letter. Close and save the letter file.
    c. In the thank-you card, the linked professor's name should also be updated. If it does not update automatically, use Word Help to find out how to make the link update.
13. Preview and print the thank-you card and the letter.

word 2010

chapter 1

Getting Started with Word 2010

In this chapter, you will learn the following skills:

- Enter, select, and delete text
- Use the AutoCorrect feature
- Use the spelling, grammar, and Thesaurus features
- Find and replace text in a document
- Change the way the document is viewed in the user interface

Skill **1.1** Introduction to Word 2010

Skill **1.2** Entering, Selecting, and Deleting Text

Skill **1.3** Using AutoCorrect

Skill **1.4** Checking Spelling and Grammar as You Type

Skill **1.5** Using the Thesaurus

Skill **1.6** Finding Text

Skill **1.7** Replacing Text

Skill **1.8** Using Views

Skill **1.9** Zooming a Document

skills

introduction

This introductory chapter will introduce students to some of the basic editing features of Microsoft Word 2010, and demonstrate changing how a document is displayed in the user interface. Students will learn how to save and edit documents, use the spell and grammar checker, use the Thesaurus, change the view and size of a document, use Find and Replace, and add AutoCorrect entries.

1.1 Introduction to Word 2010

Microsoft Office Word 2010 is a word processing program that enables you to create many types of documents including letters, résumés, reports, proposals, Web pages, blogs, and more. Word's advanced editing capabilities allow you to quickly and easily perform tasks such as checking your spelling and finding text in a long document. Robust formatting allows you to produce professional-looking documents with stylized fonts, layouts, and graphics. Building Blocks and Quick Styles allow you to insert complex desktop publishing elements to your document. Printing and file management can be managed directly from the Word window. In short, everything you need to create polished professional and personal documents is available in Microsoft Word.

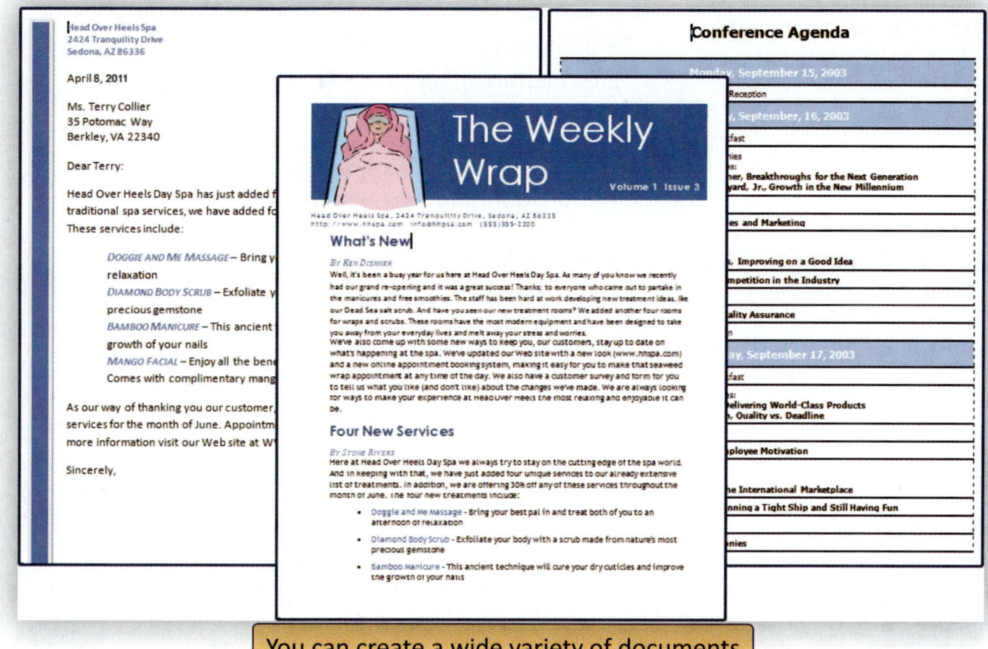

You can create a wide variety of documents with Microsoft Office Word 2010.

FIGURE WD 1.1

Here are some basic elements of a Word document:

Font—also called the typeface, refers to a set of characters of a certain design. You can choose from several pre-installed fonts available.

Paragraph—groups of sentences separated by a hard return. A hard return refers to pressing the (←Enter) key to create a new paragraph. You can assign a paragraph its own style to help it stand out from the rest of the document.

Styles—complex formatting, including font, color, size, and spacing, that can be applied to text. Use consistent styles for headings, body text, notes, and captions throughout your document. Styles also can be applied to tables and graphics.

Tables—used to organize data into columns and rows.

Graphics—photographs, clip art, SmartArt, or line drawings that can be added to documents.

tips & tricks

Microsoft Office 2010 includes many other features that can help further enhance your documents. If you would like to learn more about these features, click the **Help** icon in the upper-right corner of the Word interface or visit Microsoft Office online through your Web browser.

tell me more

Some basic features of a word processing application include

Word wrap—places text on the next line when the right margin of the page has been reached.

Find and replace—searches for any word or phrase in the document. Also, allows all instances of a word to be replaced by another word.

Spelling and grammar—checks for errors in spelling and grammar and offers solutions to the problem.

1.2 Entering, Selecting, and Deleting Text

The basic function of a word processing application like Microsoft Word is to create written documents. Whether the documents are simple, such as a letter, or complex, such as a newsletter, one of the basic tasks you will perform in Word is entering text. **Word wrap** is a feature in Microsoft Word that automatically places text on the next line when the right margin of the document has been reached. There is no need to press [←Enter] to begin a new line in the same paragraph. Only press [←Enter] when you want to create a break and start a new paragraph.

To enter text in a document:

1. Place the cursor where you want the new text to appear.
2. Begin typing.
3. When the cursor reaches the end of the line, do not press [←Enter]. Keep typing and allow word wrap to move the text to the next line.
4. If you make a mistake when entering text, you can press the [←Backspace] key to remove text to the left of the cursor, or press the [Delete] key to remove text to the right of the cursor.

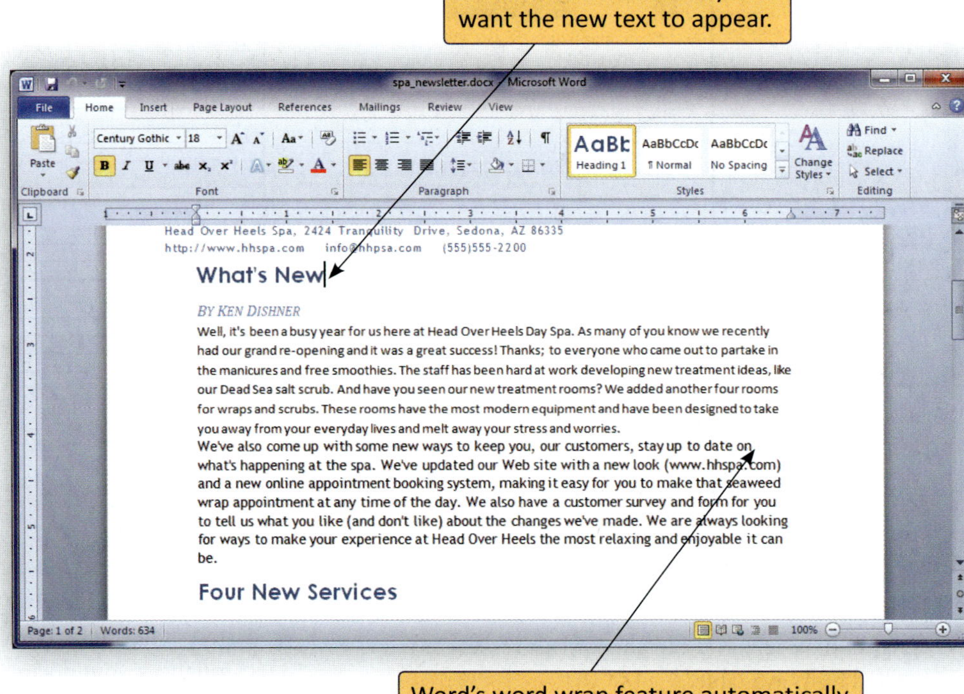

FIGURE WD 1.2

To select text in a document, click and drag the cursor across the text. A shaded background appears behind the selected text. Once the text is selected, you can apply commands, such as changing the font or applying the bold effect, to the text as a group.

tips & tricks

If you want to edit text you have typed, click in the text to place the cursor anywhere in the document. When you begin typing, the new text will be entered at the cursor point, pushing any existing text out to the right. You also can use the arrow keys to move the cursor around in the document and then begin typing.

tell me more

The cursor indicates the place on the page where text will appear when you begin typing. There are a number of cursors that display, but the default text cursor is a blinking vertical line.

try this

To select all the text in the document, you can press [Ctrl] + [A] on the keyboard.

1.3 Using AutoCorrect

While you are typing, Word's **AutoCorrect** feature analyzes each word as it is entered. Each word you type is compared to a list of common misspellings, symbols, and abbreviations. If a match is found, AutoCorrect automatically replaces the text in your document with the matching replacement entry. For example, if you type "teh," AutoCorrect will replace the text with "the."

You can create your own AutoCorrect entries, as well as modify preexisting ones. AutoCorrect also allows you to check for common capitalization errors. If you find yourself making spelling errors that are not recognized by AutoCorrect, you can add your own entries to the AutoCorrect replacement list.

To add a new entry to the AutoCorrect list:

1. Click the **File** tab.
2. Click the **Options** button.
3. In the *Word Options* dialog box, click the **Proofing** button.
4. Click the **AutoCorrect Options . . .** button.
5. Type your commonly made mistake in the *Replace:* box.
6. Type the correct spelling in the *With:* box.
7. Click **OK** in the *AutoCorrect* dialog box.
8. Click **OK** in the *Word Options* dialog box.

The next time you type the error, Word will automatically correct it for you.

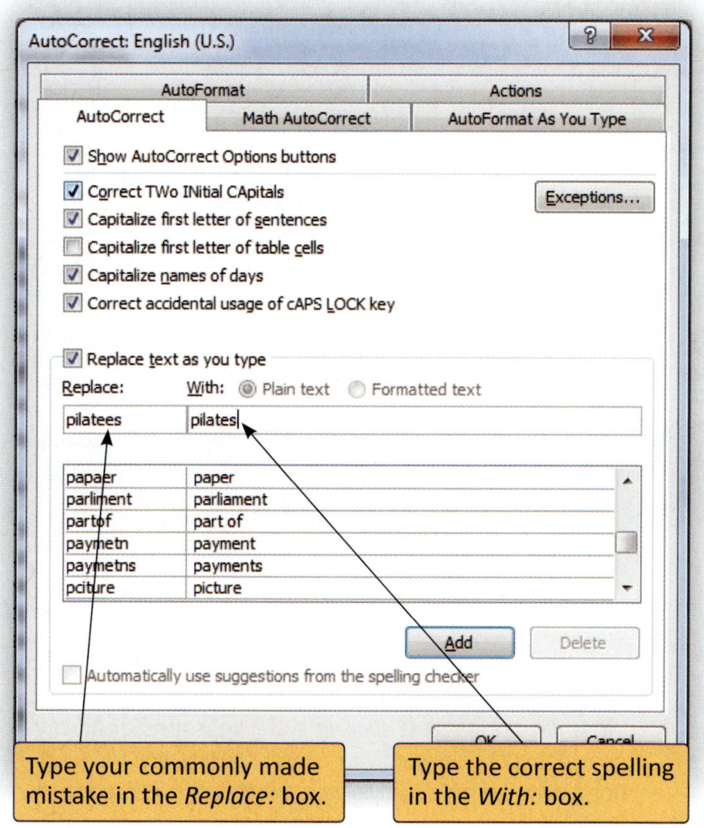

Type your commonly made mistake in the *Replace:* box.

Type the correct spelling in the *With:* box.

FIGURE WD 1.3

tips & tricks

If you find yourself typing certain long phrases over and over again, you can use the AutoCorrect feature to replace short abbreviations with long strings of text that you don't want to type. For example, you could replace the text *hhspa* with *Head Over Heels Day Spa*. This will not only save you time when typing, but more importantly ensure accuracy in your documents.

tell me **more**

AutoCorrect does more than just fix spelling errors. From the *AutoCorrect* dialog box you can set options to

- Correct accidental use of the Caps Lock key.
- Automatically capitalize the first letter in a sentence or the names of days.
- Automatically apply character formatting such as bold and italic, and format lists and tables.

Explore the *AutoCorrect* dialog box on your own to discover all the options available.

1.4 Checking Spelling and Grammar as You Type

Microsoft Word can automatically check your document for spelling and grammar errors while you type. Misspelled words, words that are not part of Word's dictionary, are indicated by a wavy red underline. Grammatical errors are similarly underlined in green, and are based on the grammatical rules that are part of Word's grammar checking feature. When you right-click either type of error, a shortcut menu appears with suggestions for correcting the error and other options.

To correct a misspelled word underlined in red:

1. Right-click the misspelled word.
2. Choose a suggested correction from the shortcut menu.

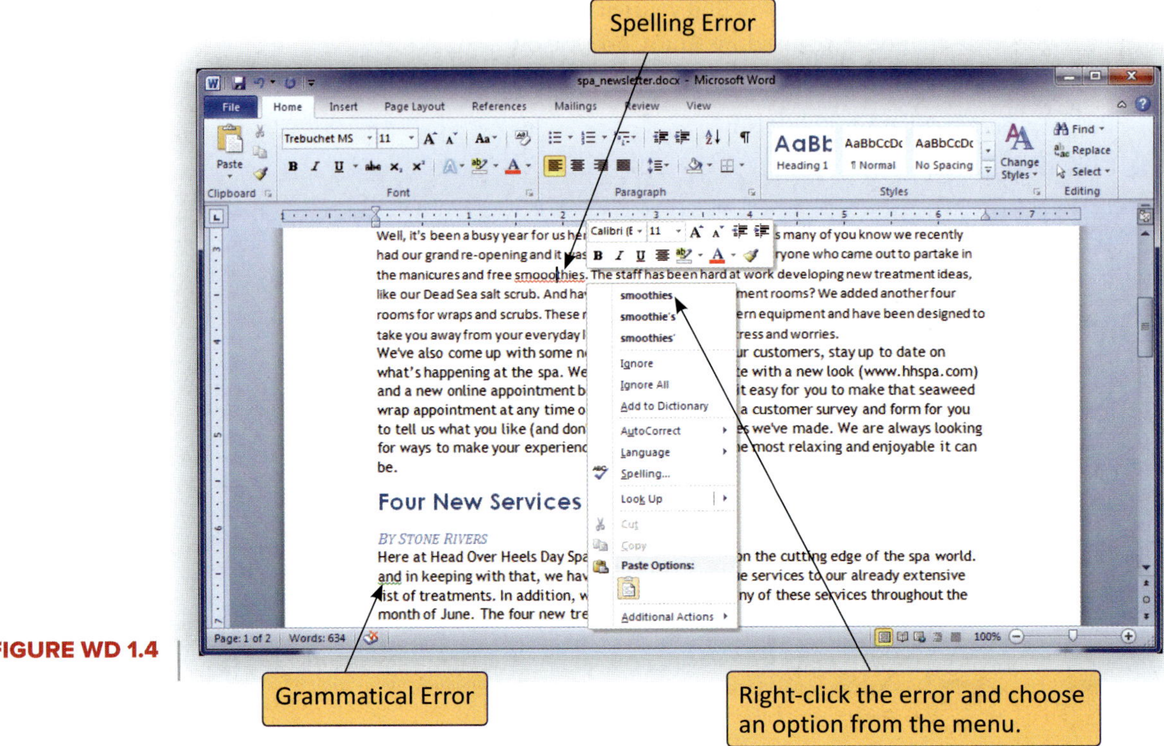

FIGURE WD 1.4

tips & tricks

Although checking spelling and grammar as you type is a useful tool when creating documents, there are times when you may find it distracting. You can choose to turn off checking spelling errors or grammar errors as you type. To turn the *Check Spelling as you type* and *Check Grammar as you type* features on and off:

1. Click the **File** tab.
2. Click the **Options** button.
3. In the *Word Options* dialog box, click the **Proofing** button.
4. In the *When correcting spelling and grammar in Word* section, deselect the *Check spelling as you type* option for spelling errors or the *Mark grammar errors as you type* option for grammatical errors.

tell me **more**

Word will not suggest spelling corrections if its dictionary does not contain a word with similar spelling, and Word will not always be able to display grammatical suggestions. In these cases, you must edit the error manually.

If the word is spelled correctly, you can choose the *Add to Dictionary* command on the shortcut menu. When you add a word to the dictionary, it will no longer be marked as a spelling error.

1.5 Using the Thesaurus

When writing documents, you may find that you are reusing a certain word over and over again, and that you would like to use a different word that has the same meaning. Microsoft Word's **Thesaurus** tool provides you with a list of synonyms (words with the same meaning) and antonyms (words with the opposite meaning).

To replace a word using the Thesaurus:

1. Place the cursor in the word you want to replace.
2. Click the **Review** tab.
3. In the *Proofing* group, click the **Thesaurus** button.
4. The selected word appears in the *Search for:* box of the *Research* task pane with a list of possible meanings below it. Each possible meaning has a list of synonyms (and, in some cases, antonyms).
5. Point to a synonym (or antonym) and click the arrow that appears to display a menu of options.
6. Click **Insert** on the menu to replace the original word with the one you selected.

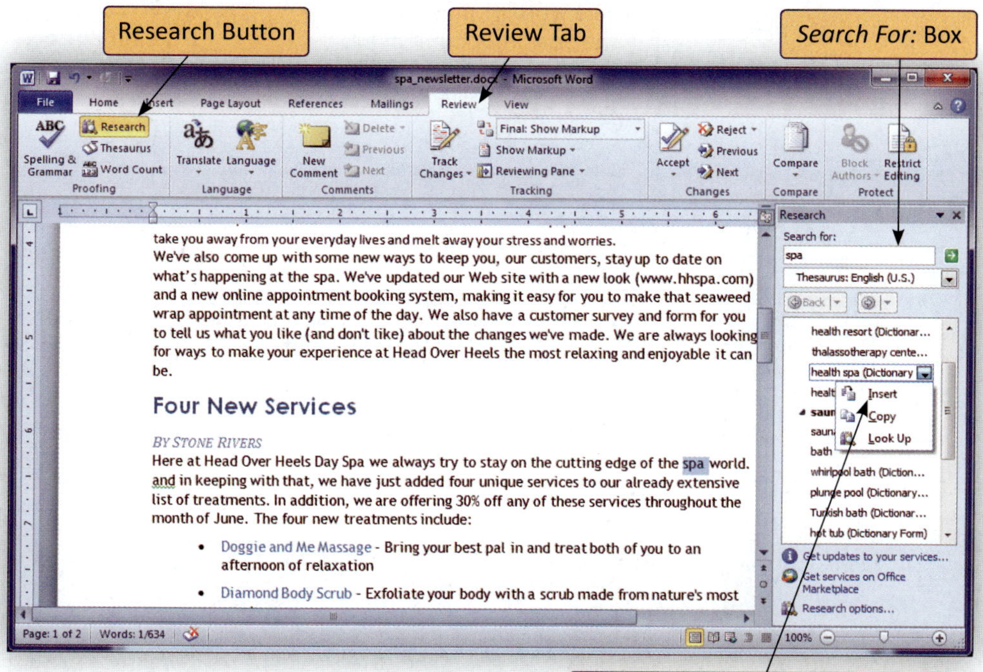

FIGURE WD 1.5

tips & tricks

If one of the synonyms is close to what you want, but not quite right, you can select **Look Up** from the menu to see a list of alternatives for the synonym. You also can click the synonym (without displaying the menu) to see the list of alternative synonyms.

tell me more

The *Research* task pane is a robust tool that contains more than just the English Thesaurus. The *Research* task pane also contains links to research Web sites, translation tools, and the Encarta Dictionary. Click the arrow next to *Thesaurus: English (US)* to select a different research tool.

try this

To look up a word using the Thesaurus, you also can

- Right-click the word, point to *Synonyms,* and select **Thesaurus . . .**
- With the cursor in the word you want to look up, press ⇧Shift + F7 on the keyboard.

1.6 Finding Text

In past versions of Microsoft Word, searching for text in a document was performed through the *Find and Replace* dialog box. In Word 2010, the default method for searching for text in a document is to use the *Navigation* task pane. When you search for a word or phrase using the *Navigation* task pane, Word will highlight all instances of the word or phrase in your document and display each instance as a separate result in the task pane.

To find a word or phrase in a document:

1. Start on the *Home* tab.
2. In the *Editing* group, click the **Find** button.
3. The *Navigation* task pane appears.
4. Type the word or phrase you want to find in the *Search Document* box at the top of the task pane.
5. As you type, Word automatically highlights all instances of the word or phrase in the document and displays any results in the task pane.
6. Click a result to navigate to that instance of the word or phrase in the document.

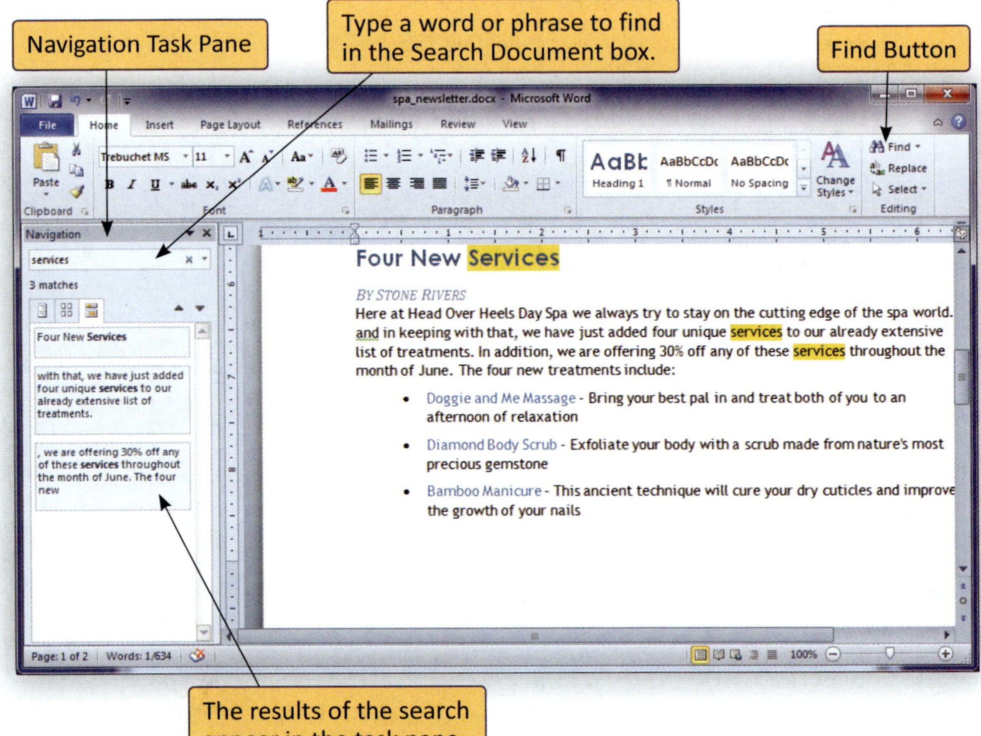

FIGURE WD 1.6

tips & tricks

If you are more comfortable using the *Find and Replace* dialog box, you can still use it to search for text in your document. To open the *Find and Replace* dialog box, start on the *Home* tab. In the *Editing* group, click the **Find** button arrow and select **Advanced Find . . .** The *Find and Replace* dialog box opens with the *Find* tab displayed. Use the dialog to search for text just as you would in previous versions of Word.

tell me more

- The magnifying glass in the *Search Document* box gives you access to more search options. You can choose to only search specific elements in your document, such as tables, graphics, or footnotes.
- Clicking the **X** next to a search word or phrase will clear the search, allowing you to perform a new search.

try this

To display the *Navigation* task pane with the *Search* tab displayed, you also can

- Click the **Find** button and select **Find** on the menu.
- Press Ctrl + F on the keyboard.

1.7 Replacing Text

The **Replace** command in Word allows you to locate specific instances of text in your document and replace them with different text. With the *Replace* command, you can replace words or phrases one instance at a time or all at once throughout the document.

To replace instances of a word in a document:

1. On the *Home* tab, in the *Editing* group, click the **Replace** button.
2. Type the word or phrase you want to change in the *Find what:* box.
3. Type the new text you want in the *Replace with:* box.
4. Click **Replace** to replace just that one instance of the text.
5. Click **Replace All** to replace all instances of the word or phrase.
6. Word displays a message telling you how many replacements it made. Click **OK** in the message that appears.
7. To close the *Find and Replace* dialog, click the **Cancel** button.

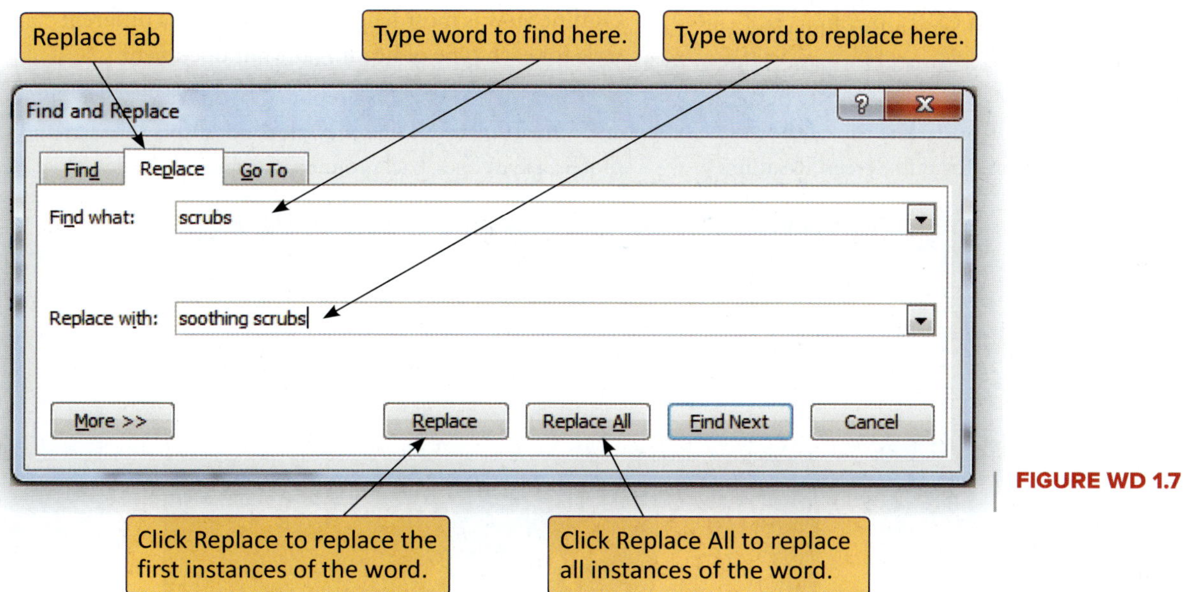

FIGURE WD 1.7

tips & tricks

In addition to text, the *Replace* command also can operate on formatting characters such as italicized text and paragraph marks. The *More >>* button in the *Find and Replace* dialog box displays additional options, including buttons that allow you to select formatting and other special characters in the document.

tell me more

The *Go To* tab in the *Find and Replace* dialog box allows you to quickly jump to any page, line, section, comment, or other object in your document.

try this

To open the *Find and Replace* dialog box with the *Replace* tab displayed, you also can press Ctrl + H on the keyboard.

1.8 Using Views

By default, Microsoft Word displays documents in Print Layout view, but you can display your documents in a number of other ways. Each view has its own purpose, and considering what you want to do with your document will help determine which view is most appropriate to use. To switch between different views, click the appropriate icon located in the lower-right corner of the status bar next to the zoom slider.

Word 2010 allows you to view your documents five different ways:

Print Layout view—Use this view to see how document elements will appear on a printed page. This view will help you edit headers and footers, and adjust margins and layouts.

Full Screen Reading View—Use this view when you want to review a document. Full Screen Reading view presents the document in an easy-to-read format. In this view, the Ribbon is no longer visible. To navigate between screens, use the navigation buttons at the top of the window. To change the options for Full Screen Reading view, click the **View Options** button. To return to the Print Layout view, click the **Close** button in the upper-right corner of the window.

Web Layout View—Use this view when designing documents that will be viewed on-screen, such as a Web page. Web Layout view displays all backgrounds, drawing objects, and graphics as they will appear on-screen. Unlike Print Layout view, Web Layout view does not show page edges, margins, or headers and footers.

Outline View—Use this view to check the structure of your document. In Outline view, you can collapse the document's structure to view just the top-level headings or expand the structure to see the document's framework. Outline view is most helpful when you use a different style for each type of heading in your document.

Draft View—Use this simplified layout view when typing and formatting text. Draft view does not display headers and footers, page edges, backgrounds, or drawing objects.

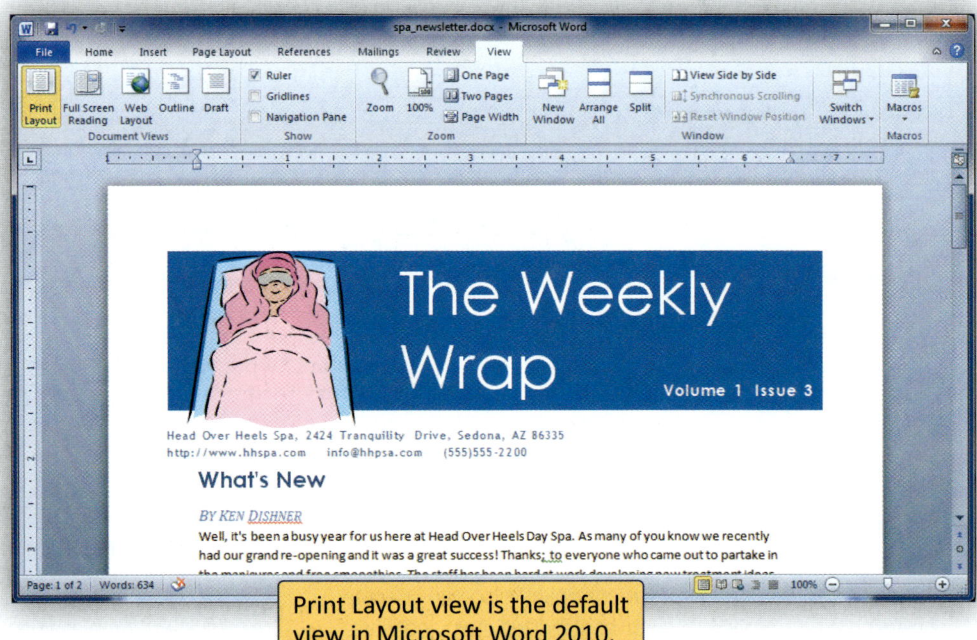

FIGURE WD 1.8

tips & tricks

Draft view is useful for checking the placement of page and section breaks in your document. You can easily remove a break in Draft view by selecting the break and pressing Delete on the keyboard.

tell me more

In Word 2003, the default view for documents was called *Normal* view and was the same as *Draft* view. In Word 2007 and Word 2010, Microsoft changed the default view for documents to *Print Layout* view.

try this

To switch views, you also can click the **View** tab on the Ribbon and select a view from the *Document Views* group.

1.9 Zooming a Document

When you first open a document, you may find that the text is too small to read, or that you cannot see the full layout of a page. Use the **zoom slider** in the lower-right corner of the window to zoom in and out of a document, changing the size of text and images on-screen. Zooming a document only affects how the document appears on-screen. It does not affect how the document will print.

To zoom in on a document, making the text and graphics appear larger:

- Click and drag the zoom slider to the right.
- Click the **Zoom In** button (the button with the plus sign on it) on the slider.

To zoom out of a document, making the text and graphics appear smaller:

- Click and drag the zoom slider to the left.
- Click the **Zoom Out** button (the button with the minus sign on it) on the slider.

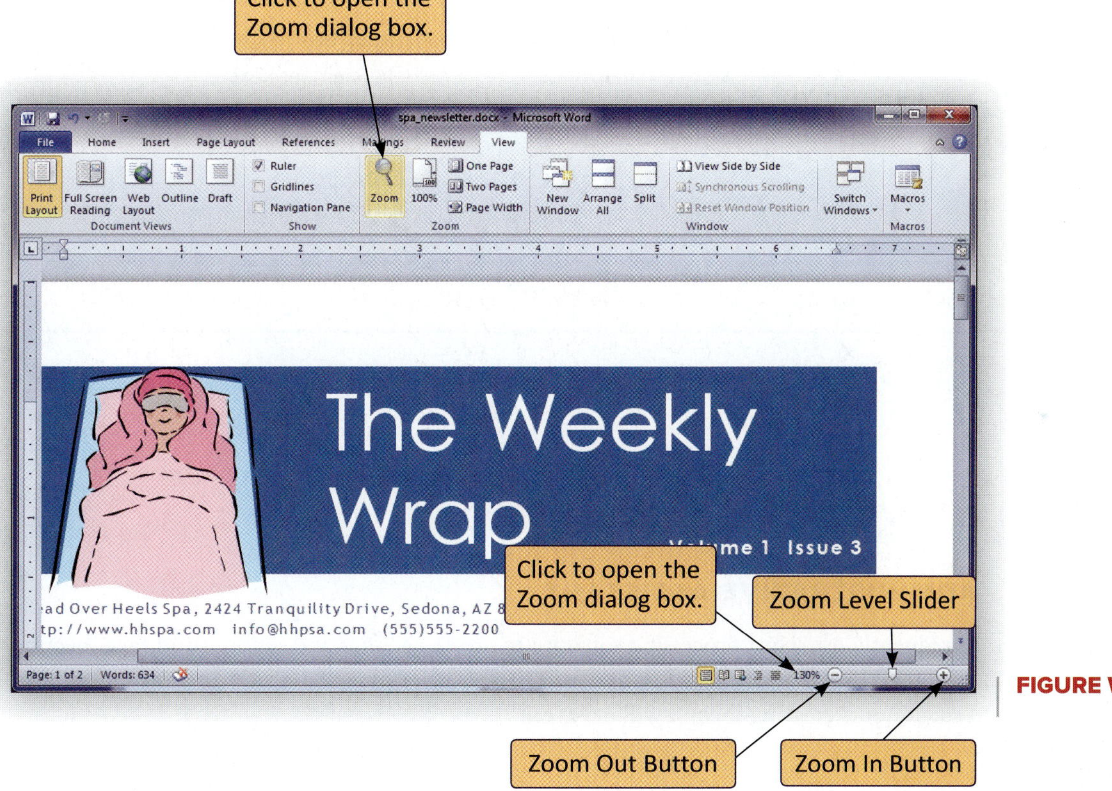

FIGURE WD 1.9

tips & tricks

As you move the slider, the zoom level displays the percentage the document has been zoomed in or out. When zooming a document, 100% is the default zoom level. If you change the zoom percentage and then save and close the document, the next time you open the document, it will display at the last viewed zoom percentage. If you work on a large monitor at a high resolution and need to display your document at a higher zoom percentage, it is a good idea to return the document back to 100% before sending it out to others.

tell me more

You can use the *Zoom* dialog box to apply a number of display presets:

Page width—changes the zoom so the width of the page including margins fills the screen.

Text width—changes the zoom so the width of the page not including margins fills the screen.

Whole page—changes the zoom so the entire page, both vertically and horizontally, displays on the screen. This is a helpful view when working with a page's layout.

Many pages—changes the zoom to display anywhere from one to six pages on the screen at once.

try this

You also can change the zoom level through the *Zoom* dialog box:

1. To open the *Zoom* dialog box:
   a. Click the zoom level number next to the zoom slider OR
   b. Click the **View** tab. In the *Zoom* group, click the **Zoom** button.
2. Click a zoom preset or type the zoom percentage in the *Percent:* box.
3. Click **OK**.

from the perspective of . . .

ADMINISTRATIVE ASSISTANT

I frequently use word processing software to create agendas and reports, and take meeting minutes. Using document, color, and font themes saves time and makes documents look like I spent hours creating them. I will never tell.

Data files for projects can be found on
www.mhhe.com/office2010skills

projects

Skill Review 1.1

In this project you will be editing the *Values Statement_01* document from Sierra Pacific Community College District.

1. Open Microsoft Word 2010.

2. Open the *Values Statement_01* document.

a. Click the **File** tab. The Backstage view will open.

b. Click the **Open** button. The *Open* dialog box will open.

c. Browse to the location of your student data files for Chapter 1.

d. Click the **Values Statement_01** document.

e. Click the **Open** button (or double-click the document). The *Values Statement_01* document will open.

3. Save your document with a different file name.

a. Click the **File** tab.

b. Click the **Save As** button. The *Save As* dialog box will open.

c. Navigate to the location where you will be saving your completed documents.

d. In the *File name:* box, type: ***[your initials]*WD_SkillReview_1-1.**

e. Click **Save.** Notice how the name of the document is now changed at the top of your Word window.

4. Change how the document is displayed on your computer.

a. Click the **View** tab.

b. In the *Zoom* group, click the **Page Width** button. The document will be displayed according to the width of your Word window.

5. Add an entry to the AutoCorrect feature of Word 2010.

a. Click the **File** tab to open the Backstage view.

b. Click the **Options** button. The *Word Options* dialog box will open.

c. Click the **Proofing** button.

d. Click the **AutoCorrect Options** button. The *AutoCorrect* dialog box will open.

e. The *AutoCorrect* tab should be displayed. If not, click the **AutoCorrect** tab.

f. In the *Replace:* box type: SPCCD

g. In the *With:* box type: Sierra Pacific Community College District

h. Click the **Add** button. Notice how this AutoCorrect entry has been added and it is displayed in alphabetical order in the list of AutoCorrect entries.

i. Click **OK** to close the *AutoCorrect* dialog box.

j. Click **OK** to close the *Options* dialog box.

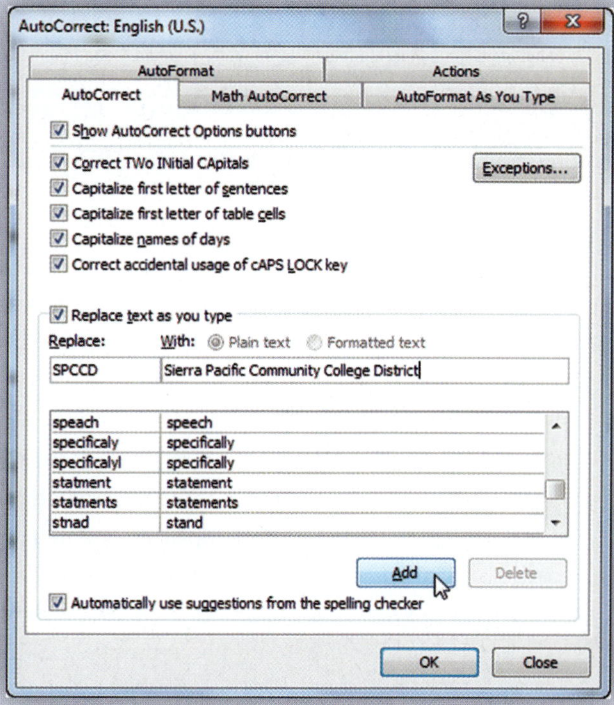

FIGURE WD 1.10

6. Add text to the document.

a. Click in front of the *Student Learning Outcome* heading in the first column.

b. Press **Enter.**

c. Press the *up arrow* key on your keyboard to move your cursor to the blank line you just inserted. Or click on the blank line you just inserted.

d. Type the following heading: `Leadership`

e. Press **Enter.**

f. Type the following text: `Responsible leadership and service among all SPCCD faculty, staff, and students are nurtured and encouraged so the college will be a leader for positive change, growth, and transformation in student-oriented educational practices.`

Notice how *SPCCD* was changed to *Sierra Pacific Community College District.*

g. Press **Enter.**

h. In the *Communication* paragraph in the second column, click directly in front of the word *mission* and type: `SPCCD` (be sure to space after). Notice how *SPCCD* was changed to *Sierra Pacific Community College District.*

i. Click before the word *Values* in the title of the document.

j. Type: `SPCCD` and space after.

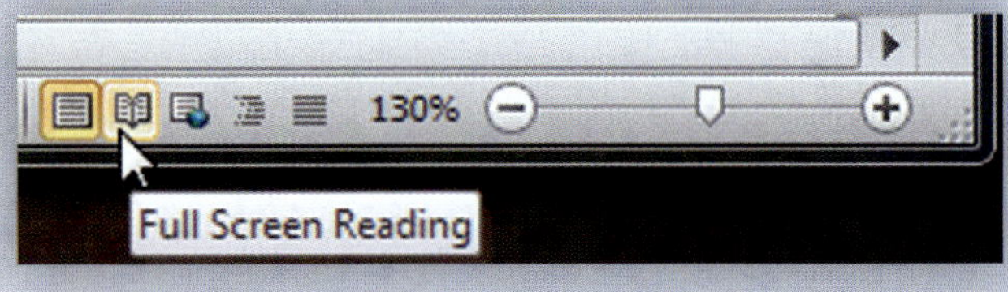

FIGURE WD 1.11

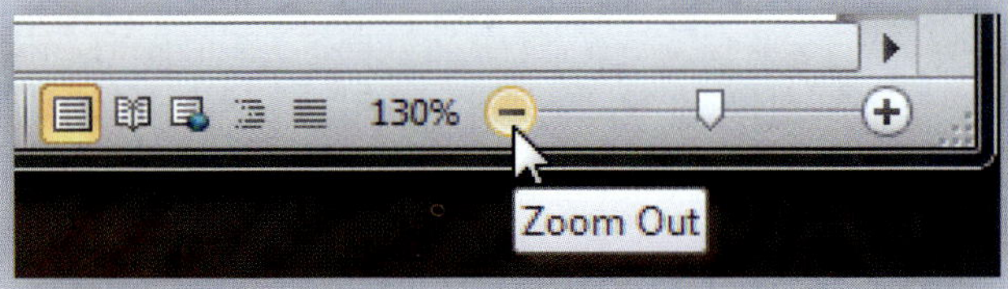

FIGURE WD 1.12

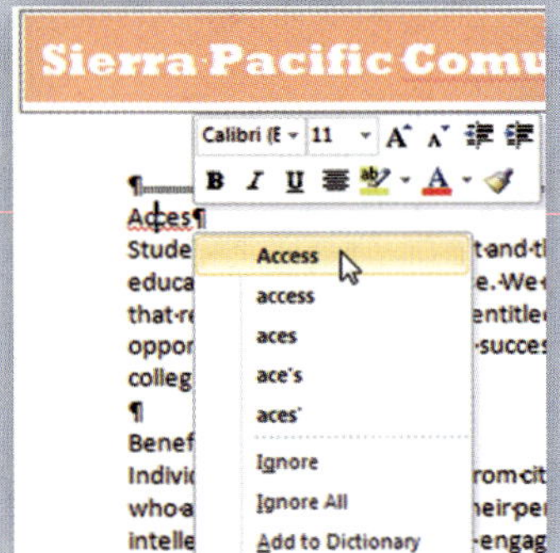

FIGURE WD 1.13

7. Change how your document is viewed in the window.

a. At the bottom-right corner of your Word window, click the **Full Screen Reading** icon (second icon) to change the display view. This also can be done by clicking the **View** tab and clicking the **Full Screen Reading** button in the *Document Views* group.

b. Click the **Close** button in the upper right to close this view and return to *Print Layout* view (the default view in Word).

c. In the *Zoom Out* and *Zoom In* area at the bottom-right corner of your Word window, click the **Zoom Out** button until your document is displayed at 100%. This also can be done by clicking the **View** tab and clicking the **100%** button in the *Zoom* group.

8. Check spelling and grammar as you type. Notice how words that Word does not recognize are underlined in red and potential grammar errors are underlined in green.

a. Right-click the heading *Access* at the top of the first column. A list of suggested changes is shown.

b. Click **Access.** Word corrects the spelling of this word.

c. Right-click the word *Of* in the heading *Benefits Of Education.*

d. Click on **of** (lowercase).

9. Spell and grammar check the entire document with the *Spelling and Grammar* dialog box.

a. Click the **Review** tab.

b. In the *Proofing* group, click the **Spelling & Grammar** button. The *Spelling and Grammar* dialog box will open.

c. The word *assesment* is indicated as *Not in Dictionary.*

d. Click **assessment** in the *Suggestions* area.

e. Click the **Change All** button. Both misspelled instances of this word are changed.

f. The next word not in the dictionary is *ageis.*

g. Click **age is.**

h. Click the **Change** button.

i. Continue to check the spelling and grammar on the remainder of the document. If Word prompts you to continue at the beginning of the document, click **Yes.**

j. Click **OK** when finished.

10. Save and close the document.

a. Click the **File** tab and click **Save.** You also can save your document by pressing **Ctrl+S** or clicking the **Save** icon on the *Quick Access* toolbar.

b. To close the document, click the **File** tab and click **Close.** You also can close a document by pressing **Ctrl+W.**

11. Close Microsoft Word.

a. Click the **File** tab and click **Exit.** You also can click the **X** button in the upper-right corner of the Word window.

b. If you have any unsaved documents, you will be prompted to save them.

Skill Review 1.2

In this project you will be editing the *Employment Offer_01* document from Central Sierra Insurance.

1. Open Microsoft Word 2010.

2. Open the *Employment Offer_01* document.

a. Click the **File** tab. The Backstage view will open.

b. Click the **Open** button. The *Open* dialog box will open.

c. Browse to the location of your student data files for Chapter 1.

d. Click the **Employment Offer_01** document.

e. Click the **Open** button (or double-click the document). The *Employment Offer_01* document will open.

3. Save your document with a different file name.

a. Click the **File** tab.

b. Click the **Save As** button. The *Save As* dialog box will open.

c. Navigate to the location where you will be saving your completed documents.

d. In the *File name:* box, type: ***[your initials]*WD_SkillReview_1-2.**

e. Click **Save.** Notice how the name of the document is now changed at the top of your Word window.

4. Turn on the Show/Hide feature so you can view the paragraph marks and other formatting characters.

a. Click the **Home** tab.

b. In the **Paragraph** group, click the **Show/Hide** button. The formatting characters will be revealed in the document.

c. The *Show/Hide* button can be toggled on or off. *Ctrl+** also will toggle on/off this feature.

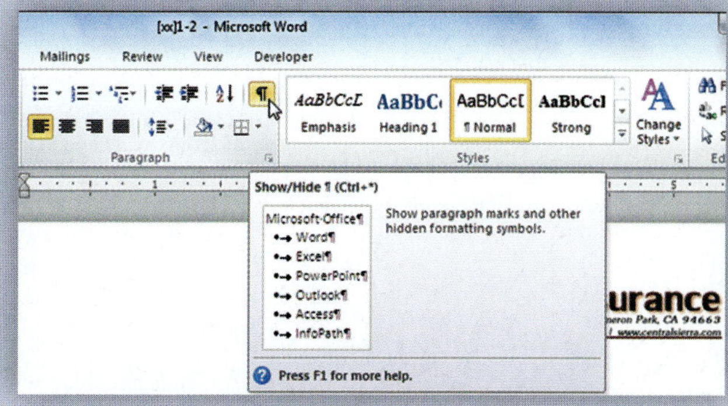

FIGURE WD 1.14

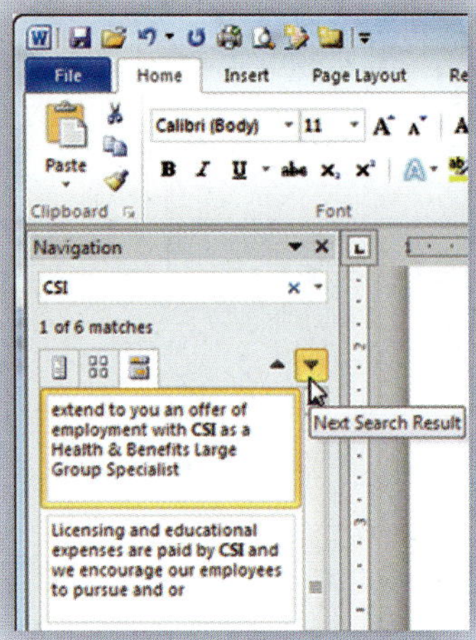

FIGURE WD 1.15

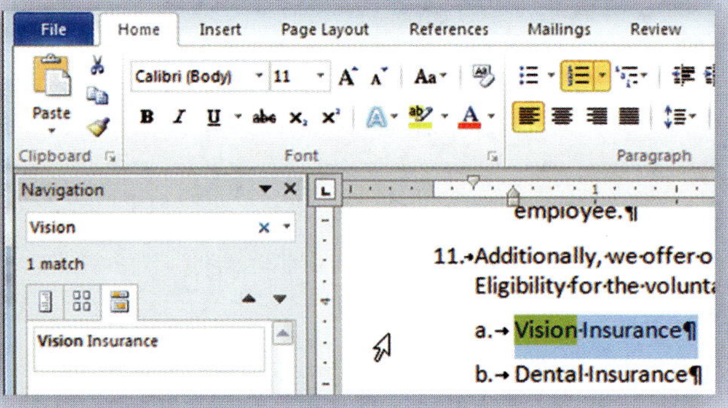

FIGURE WD 1.16

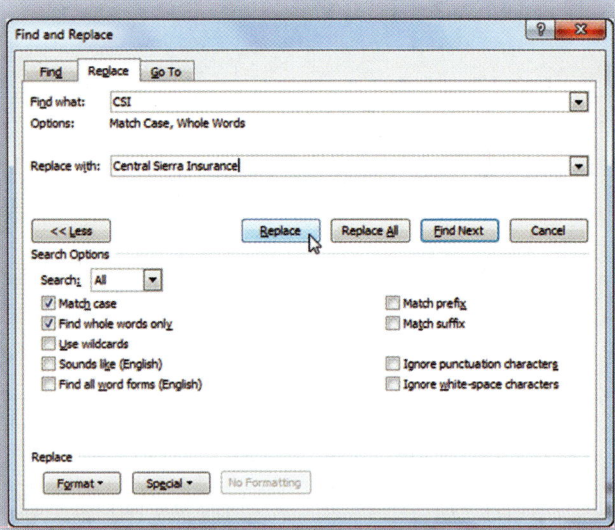

FIGURE WD 1.17

5. Find words in the document and display in the *Navigation* pane.

a. On the *Home* tab, in the *Editing* group, click the **Find** button. The *Navigation* pane is displayed on the right side of the Word window. *Ctrl+F* also will open the *Find* feature in the *Navigation* pane.

b. Click in the *Search Document* box and type: `CSI`

c. Press **Enter.** Each occurrence of this word is displayed in the *Navigation* pane.

d. Click the **Next Search Result** arrow to move to the next matching occurrence.

e. Click the **X** button in the *Search Document* box to clear the current search.

f. In the *Search Document* box type: `Vision`

g. Press **Enter.** Only one occurrence is found.

h. In the document select this entire line by clicking to the left of the lettered item outside of the left margin. The entire line will be selected.

i. Press **Delete** to delete this line.

j. Click the **X** in the upper-right corner of the *Navigation* pane to close it.

6. Use the *Find and Replace* feature to replace *CSI* with *Central Sierra Insurance.*

a. Press **Ctrl+Home** to move to the top of the document.

b. On the *Home* tab, in the *Editing* group, click the **Replace** button. The *Find and Replace* dialog box will open. *Ctrl+H* also will open the *Find and Replace* dialog box.

c. In the *Find what:* box type: `CSI`

d. In the *Replace with:* box type: `Central Sierra Insurance`

e. Click the **More** button to view *Search Options.*

f. Click the **Match case** check box.

g. Click the **Find whole words only** check box.

h. Click the **Replace** button. The first occurrence of this word is selected in the document.

i. Click **Replace** to replace *CSI* with *Central Sierra Insurance.* The next occurrence will be selected.

j. Click **Replace All** to replace all occurrences in the document.

k. Click **OK** to finish the find and replace process.

l. Click **Close** to close the *Find and Replace* dialog box.

7. Use *Find and Replace* with wildcards to replace *percent* with *%.*

a. Press **Ctrl+Home** to move to the top of the document.

b. Click the **Replace** button.

c. In the *Find what:* box type: `?percent` (The ? is a wildcard representing one character.)

d. In the *Replace with:* box type: `%`

e. Click the **Use wildcards** check box in the *Search Options* box.

f. Click the **Replace All** button to replace all occurrences of *percent* with *%.*

g. Click **OK** to finish the find and replace process.

h. Click **Close** to close the *Find and Replace* dialog box.

8. Spell and grammar check the entire document.

a. Click the **Review** tab.

b. Click the **Spelling & Grammar** button in the *Proofing* group. The *Spelling and Grammar* dialog box will open.

c. Click the **Ignore All** button to skip the personal names not recognized by Word (for example *Skaar*).

d. Choose **days' vacation** when you come to this phrase.

e. Continue to check the spelling and grammar on the remainder of the document. If Word prompts you to continue at the beginning of the document, click **Yes.**

f. Click **OK** when finished.

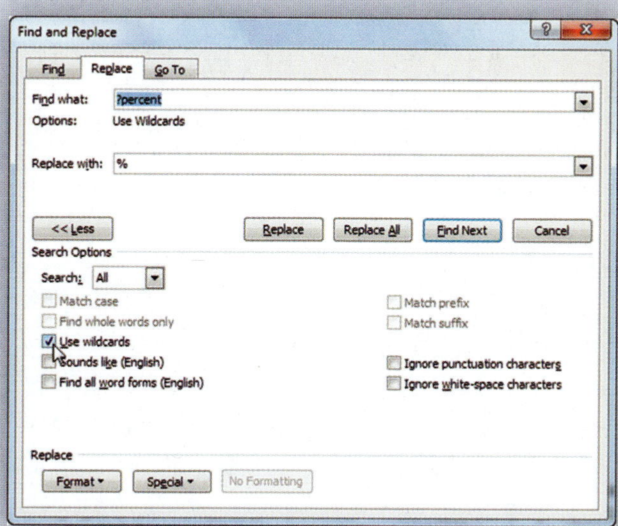

FIGURE WD 1.18

9. Find the words in the document, and use the *Thesaurus* to find an appropriate synonym.

a. On the *Home* tab, in the *Editing* group, click the **Find** button. The *Navigation* pane is displayed on the right side of the Word window.

b. Click in the *Search Document* box and type: `accrual`

c. Press **Enter.** One occurrence is found.

d. Click the **Review** tab.

e. In the *Proofing* group, click the **Thesaurus** button. The *Research* pane will open at the right side of the Word window.

f. Click the **arrow** to the right of the word *accumulation.*

g. Click **Insert.** The word *accumulation* replaces *accrual.*

h. Click the **X** to close the *Research* pane.

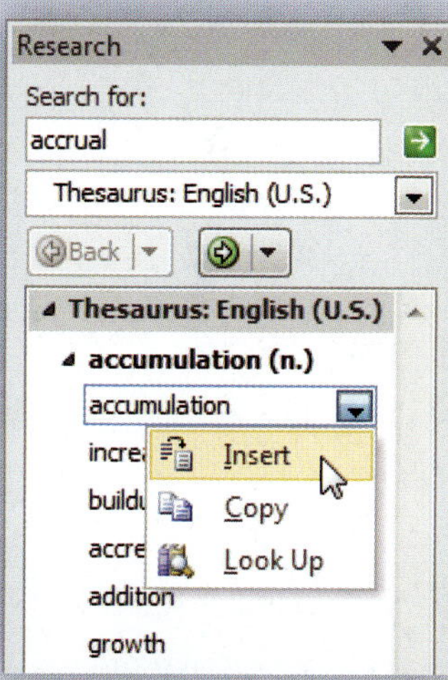

FIGURE WD 1.19

i. In the *Navigation* pane, clear the current search.

j. Click in the **Search Document** box and type: `construed`

k. Press **Enter.** One occurrence is found.

l. Right-click the word *construed* in the document.

m. Point to **Synonyms** and then click **understood.**

n. Close the *Navigation* pane.

10. Save and close the document.

a. Click the **File** tab and click **Save.** You also can save your document by pressing **Ctrl+S** or clicking the **Save** icon on the *Quick Access* toolbar.

b. To close the document, click the **File** tab and click **Close.** You also can close a document by pressing **Ctrl+W.**

11. Close Microsoft Word.

a. Click the **File** tab and click **Exit.** You also can click the **X** button in the upper-right corner of the Word window.

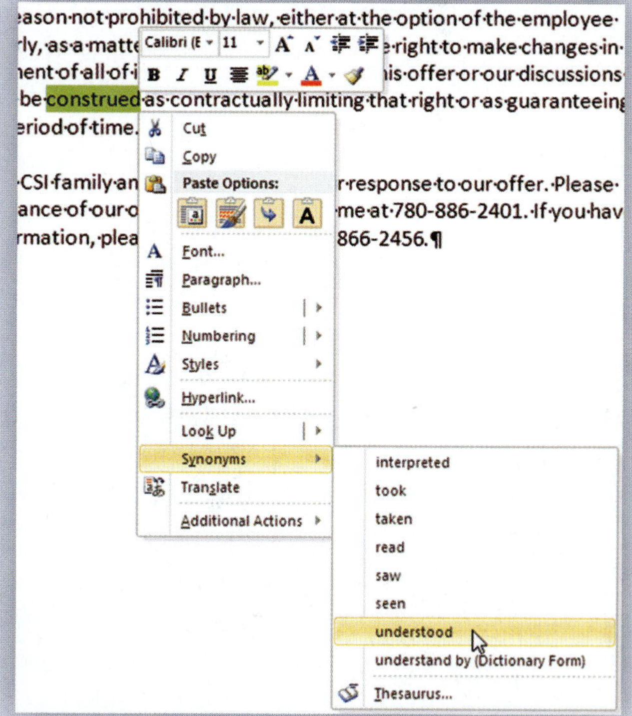

FIGURE WD 1.20

challenge yourself 1

In this project you will be editing the *Notice of Privacy_01* document from Courtyard Medical Plaza.

1. Open Microsoft Word 2010.
2. Open the *Notice of Privacy_01* document.
3. Save this document as **`[your initials]WD_Challenge_1-3.`**
4. Turn on the *Show/Hide* feature so you can view the paragraph marks and other formatting characters.
5. Change the zoom level to view the document in *Page Width.*
6. Add an *AutoCorrect* entry to change *CMP* to *Courtyard Medical Plaza.* Close the *AutoCorrect* dialog box and the *Options* dialog box.
7. On the second line on the first page, select *Courtyard Medical Plaza* and delete this entire line including the paragraph mark at the end.
8. Click in front of *Notice of Privacy Practices* on the first line of the document, and type `CMP` and press **Enter.**
9. Click at the end of the sentence of the first numbered item on the first page.
10. Press **Enter.**
11. Type the following text: `tell you about your rights and our legal duties with respect to your protected heath information, and`
    a. If Word automatically capitalized *tell,* change it back to lowercase.
12. Press **Enter.**
13. Click at the end of the second bulleted item.
14. Replace the period with a semicolon, space once, and type `and`
15. Press **Enter** and type the following text: `Information about your relationship with CMP such as medical services received, claims history, and information from your benefits plan sponsor or employer about group health coverage you may have.`
    a. *CMP* will automatically be replaced with *Courtyard Medical Plaza.*
16. Use *Find and Replace* to replace *protected health information* with *PHI.*
    a. In the *Search Options* area, select **Match case.**
    b. Do not change this occurrence.
    c. Ignore any occurrences of this information in headings (bolded text). Click **Find Next** to skip an occurrence.
17. Use *Find and Replace* to replace *Privacy and Compliance Office* with *Office of Privacy & Compliance.*
18. Use the *Find* feature to find the word *utilization.*
19. Use the *Thesaurus* to change the word to *employment.*
20. Check the spelling and grammar on the entire document.
    a. Ignore the section heading text that is marked as a potential grammatical error (e.g., *Your*).
    b. Ignore all proper nouns.
    c. Ignore the lowercase letters at the beginning of the numbered list.

21. Delete the *AutoCorrect* entries you created in this exercise and *Skill Review 1.1* exercise.
    a. Open the *AutoCorrect* dialog box. The *AutoCorrect* tab should be displayed. If not, click the **AutoCorrect** tab.
    b. In the *Replace* box type: `CMP`
    c. Select this *AutoCorrect* entry.
    d. Click the **Delete** button.
    e. Repeat this process to delete the entry for *SPCCD.*
    f. Close the open dialog boxes.
22. Save and close this document.

challenge yourself 2

In this project you will be editing the *Personal Training Program_01* document from American River Cycling Club.

1. Open the *Personal Training Program_01* document.
2. Save this document as ***[your initials]*WD_Challenge_1-4.**
3. Change the zoom level to view the document at 120%.
4. Turn on the *Show/Hide* feature so you can view the paragraph marks and other formatting characters.
5. In the *Training Intensity and Heart Rate* section, delete the second paragraph.
6. In the *Training Intensity and Heart Rate* section, add bulleted items.
    a. Press **Enter** after the second bulleted item and add the following bulleted items:
    `Recover back to 65%-75% (4-6 minutes)`
    `Pedal at 90% for 3-5 minutes`
    `Recover back to 65%-75% (4-6 minutes)`
    `Repeat this cycle 5-8 times depending on the duration of your training ride`
    `Warm down at 50-60% for the last 10 minutes`
7. Delete the *Tracking Training—Miles versus Hours* heading and the paragraph following the heading.
8. Replace all occurrences of *heartrate* (one word) with *heart rate* (two words).
9. Replace all occurrences of *personal training program* with *PTP.*
    a. Skip the occurrences in the title and section headings.
10. Replace all occurrences of the word *percent* with *%.*
    a. Be sure to use a single-character wildcard before percent so there will not be a space between the number and the percent symbol (e.g., 90%).
11. Use *Find* to locate the word *Incorporate.*
12. Use the *Thesaurus* to find an appropriate synonym to replace this word.
13. Use *Find* to locate the word *effectiveness.*
14. Use the *Thesaurus* to find an appropriate synonym to replace this word.
15. Find *40K* in the document and change it to `25 mile`
16. Find *BMI* in the document and change it to `body mass index (BMI)`
17. Check the spelling and grammar on the entire document.
    a. Ignore the word *criterium.*

18. View the document in *Draft* view.
19. Change the view to *Full Screen Reading* view.
20. Close the *Full Screen Reading* view, which will return you to *Print Layout* view.
21. Save and close the document.

on your own

In this project you will be editing the *Distance Education Plan_01* document from Sierra Pacific Community College District.

1. Open the *Distance Education Plan_01* document.
2. Save this document as **`[your initials]WD_OnYourOwn_1-5.`**
3. Change the zoom level to your preference.
4. Replace occurrences of *online learning* with *OL.*
   a. Make sure you look at the context of the sentence to make sure the replacement is appropriate.
   b. Do not make this replacement in headings.
5. Replace all % with *percent.*
   a. Make sure the replacement includes a space between the number and *percent* (e.g., 100 percent).
6. Replace *SPCCD* with *Sierra Pacific.*
   a. Make sure you look at the context of the sentence to make sure the replacement is appropriate.
   b. Do not make this replacement in headings.
7. In the *Planning Process* section, delete the last paragraph and the four bulleted items beneath it.
8. Locate *learning management system* in the body of the document and put the acronym in parentheses after these words. Use proper spacing.
9. Locate *Planning Coordination Council* in the body of the document and put the acronym in parentheses after these words. Use proper spacing.
10. Add an *AutoCorrect* entry to change *SPCCD* to *Sierra Pacific Community College District.*
11. In the *PURPOSE OF THIS PLAN* section, type the following as the first sentence in the paragraph: `The Online Learning Task Force was formed in February 2005 to develop an Online Learning Strategic Plan for the SPCCD.`
12. In the *Online Learning Offerings and Programs* section, type the following as the second paragraph: `SPCCD currently has no complete degree programs being offered entirely by distance methods, but there are several certificate programs which are available online. At least one course in each General Education area has been approved for online learning delivery, but not all of these courses are currently being offered. There are other graduation requirements that cannot currently be met through online learning methods.`
13. View the document in *Draft* view.
14. Delete an extra *Enters* (paragraph marks) in the document to ensure consistent spacing between paragraphs and sections.

15. Return to *Print Layout* view.
16. Use appropriate synonyms to replace the following words: *dramatic* and *strategically.*
17. The first fully online course offered at SPCCD was in *1997,* not *1998.* Find and make this change.
18. The current success rate for online courses is *72* percent. Find and make this change.
19. Delete the *AutoCorrect* entry you created in this exercise.
20. Check the spelling and grammar on the entire document and make appropriate changes.
21. Save and close the document.

In this project you will be editing the *Disclosure Letter_01* document from Placer Hills Real Estate.

1. Open the *Disclosure Letter_01* document.
2. Save this document as ***[your initials]*****WD_FixIt_1-6.**
3. Change the zoom level to your preference.
4. Change the inside address of this block format business letter to:

   David and Sharon Wing

   4685 Orange Grove

   Rocklin, CA 97725
5. Make the necessary change to the salutation of the letter.
6. Find and replace all occurrences of *release* with *disclosure.*
7. The word *disclosure/disclose* is used too often in this document. Find the word *disclose* and use an appropriate synonym to replace it.
8. Find the word *transference* and use an appropriate synonym to replace it.
9. Change the date of the letter to the *current date.* Use proper date format.
10. Add the following sentence as the first sentence in the last body paragraph.

    Please complete the enclosed disclosure statement by [*insert a date five days from today*] and return it to me.
11. Whenever a letter refers to an attached or enclosed document, it is proper to include an *Enclosure* notation. Type the word Enclosure on the line directly below the reference initials.
12. On a block format business letter, all lines should begin at the left margin. Using the Word 2010 default line and paragraph spacing, there should be a blank line (two Enters) after the date line and after the complimentary close (Best regards). There should be one Enter after other parts of the letter. The inside address and the writer's name, title, and company are kept together using line breaks (Shift + Enter). Turn on Show/Hide and make any necessary changes to ensure the document has proper and consistent spacing between parts. This document will fit on one page.
13. Use *mixed punctuation* on this business letter. Mixed punctuation requires a *colon* after the salutation and a *comma* after the complimentary close.
14. Proofread the document carefully and make any necessary spelling and grammar changes.
15. There should be approximately the same amount of white space at the top and bottom of the document. Use *Enter(s)* before the date line to balance the letter on the page.
16. Save and close the document.

chapter 2

Formatting Text and Paragraphs

In this chapter, you will learn the following skills:

- Apply fonts and styles to text
- Incorporate different types of lists to organize information
- Use Quick Styles to enhance readability
- Change paragraph alignment and spacing to effectively use white space
- Set and use tabs and indents to improve document layout

Skill **2.1** Applying Character Effects
Skill **2.2** Changing Fonts
Skill **2.3** Changing Font Sizes
Skill **2.4** Changing Text Case
Skill **2.5** Changing Font Colors
Skill **2.6** Applying Highlights
Skill **2.7** Using Format Painter
Skill **2.8** Clearing Formatting
Skill **2.9** Creating Bulleted Lists
Skill **2.10** Creating Numbered Lists
Skill **2.11** Creating Multilevel Lists
Skill **2.12** Using Quick Styles
Skill **2.13** Changing Paragraph Alignment
Skill **2.14** Changing Paragraph Spacing
Skill **2.15** Revealing Formatting Marks
Skill **2.16** Changing the Space between Paragraphs
Skill **2.17** Changing Indents
Skill **2.18** Using Tab Stops
Skill **2.19** Using Tab Leaders

skills

introduction

This chapter will cover character and paragraph formatting and alignment to enhance the presentation, professionalism, and readability of documents. Students will apply fonts and styles, incorporate lists, use Quick Styles, change paragraph alignment and spacing, and use tabs and indents.

2.1 Applying Character Effects

Character effects are special formatting you can apply to text that alters the text's appearance. You can call attention to text in your document by using the **bold,** *italic,* or underline effects. Remember that these effects are used to emphasize important text, and should be used sparingly—they lose their effect if overused.

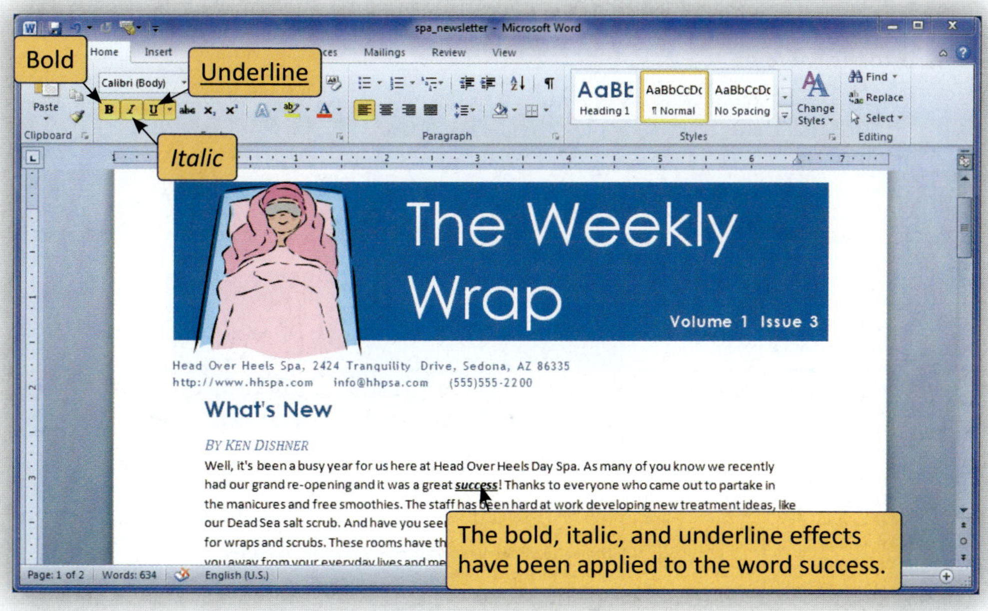

FIGURE WD 2.1

You can apply these effects using similar steps:

1. Select the text you want to emphasize.
2. On the *Home* tab, in the *Font* group click the button of the effect you want to apply:

B **Bold**—gives the text a heavier, thicker appearance.

I **Italic**—makes text slant to the right.

U **Underline**—draws a single line under the text.

Some of the other character effects available from the Ribbon include:

abc **Strikethrough**—draws a horizontal line through the text.

x_2 **Subscript**—draws a small character below the bottom of the text.

x^2 **Superscript**—draws a small character above the top of the text.

Aa **Change Case**—changes the capitalization on selected text.

tips & tricks

The *Font* dialog box contains other character formatting options not available from the Ribbon. These effects include **Shadow** and **Outline** among others. To open the *Font* dialog box, on the *Home* tab, in the *Font* group, click the dialog launcher. Select an option in the *Effects* section and click **OK** to apply the character effect to the text.

tell me more

When text is bolded, italicized, or underlined, the button appears highlighted on the Ribbon. To remove the effect, click the highlighted button, or press the appropriate keyboard shortcut.

try this

- The following keyboard shortcuts can be used to apply the bold, italic, and underline effects:
  - Bold = Ctrl + B
  - Italic = Ctrl + I
  - Underline = Ctrl + U
- To access the bold or italic commands, you can also right-click the selected text and click the **Bold** or **Italic** button on the Mini toolbar.
- To apply an underline style, click the **Underline** button arrow and select a style.

2.2 Changing Fonts

A **font**, or typeface, refers to a set of characters of a certain design. The font is the shape of a character or number as it appears on-screen or in a printed document.

To change the font:

1. Select the text to be changed.
2. On the *Home* tab, click the arrow next to the *Font* box.
3. As you roll over the list of fonts, the Live Preview feature in Word changes the look of the text in your document, giving you a preview of how the text will look with the new font applied.
4. Click a font name from the menu to apply it to the text.

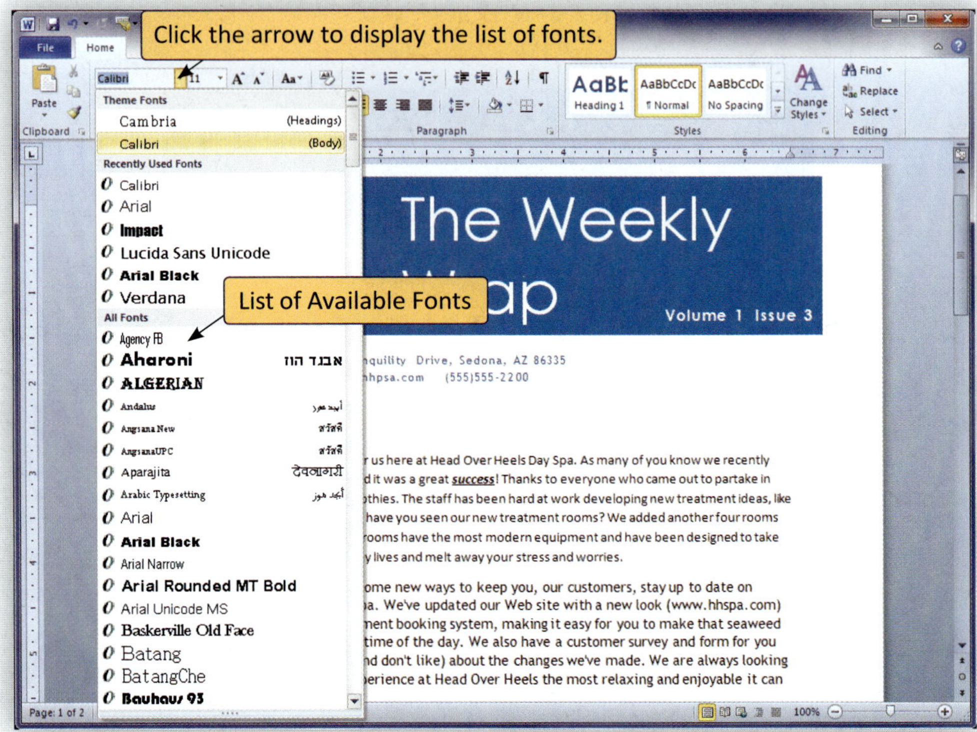

FIGURE WD 2.2

Word offers many fonts. **Serif fonts**, such as Cambria and Times New Roman, have an embellishment at the end of each stroke. **Sans serif fonts**, such as Calibri and Arial, do not have an embellishment at the end of each stroke.

Cambria is a serif font.

Calibri is a sans serif font.

FIGURE WD 2.3

tips & tricks

If you want to change the font of an individual word, you can place your cursor in the word you want to modify then select the new font.

try this

To change the font you can also right-click the text, click the arrow next to the *Font* box on the Mini toolbar, and select a font from the list.

tell me more

Using different fonts can enhance your document, giving it a polished look, but when writing a document it is best to limit the number of fonts you use. Using multiple fonts in one document can give it a cluttered and unprofessional appearance. It is good practice to use the same font for body text and the same font for headings in your document. Sans serif fonts are easier to read onscreen and should be used for the main body text for documents that will be delivered and read electronically, such as a blog. Serif fonts are easier to read on the printed page and should be used for documents that will be printed such as a report.

2.3 Changing Font Sizes

When creating a document it is important to not only choose the correct font, but also to use the appropriate font size. Fonts are measured in **points**, abbreviated "pt." On the printed page, 72 points equal one inch. Different text sizes are used for paragraphs and headers in a document. Paragraphs typically use 10 pt., 11 pt., and 12 pt. fonts. Headers often use 14 pt., 16 pt., and 18 pt. fonts.

To change the size of the text:

1. Select the text to be changed.
2. On the *Home* tab, in the *Font* group, click the arrow next to the *Font Size* box.
3. Scroll the list to find the new font size.
4. Click the size you want.

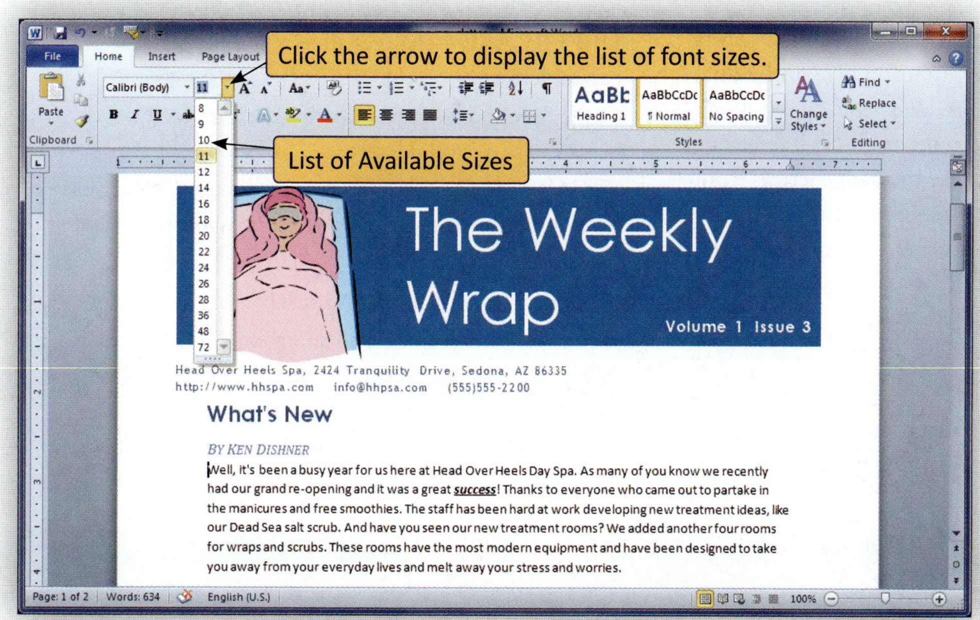

FIGURE WD 2.4

tips & tricks

Sometimes when you are formatting text, you may not be sure of the exact size you want your text to be. You can experiment with the look of text in your document by incrementally increasing and decreasing the size of the font. Use the *Grow Font* or *Shrink Font* button, available in the *Font* group, to change the font size by one increment.

tell me more

The *Font* dialog box gives you access to all the attributes for text fonts. In the *Font* dialog box, you can not only change the size of the font, but also the type, color, and effects applied to the font. To open the *Font* dialog box, click the dialog launcher in the *Font* group.

try this

To change the font you can also right-click the text, click the arrow next to the *Font Size box* on the Mini toolbar, and select a font size from the list.

from the perspective of . . .

COLLEGE GRADUATE

Word processing software is perfect to create my résumé. With fonts, themes, styles, and a spelling and grammar checker, my résumé is eye-catching and professional.

2.4 Changing Text Case

When you type on a keyboard you use the Shift key to capitalize individual letters and the Caps Lock key to type in all capital letters. Another way to change letters from lowercase to uppercase, and vice versa, is to use the *Change Case* command. When you use the **Change Case** command in Word, you are manipulating the characters that were typed, changing how the letters are displayed. There are five types of text case formats you can apply to text:

Sentence case—formats text as a sentence with the first word being capitalized and all remaining words beginning with a lowercase letter.

lowercase—changes all letters to lowercase.

UPPERCASE—changes all letters to uppercase, or capital letters.

Capitalize Each Word—formats text so each word begins with a capital letter.

tOGGLE cASE—formats text in the reverse of the typed format, converting uppercase letters to lowercase and lowercase letters to uppercase.

To apply text case formatting to text:

1. Select the text you want to change.
2. On the *Home* tab, in the *Font* group, click the **Change Case** button.
3. Select a text case option from the menu to apply it to the text.

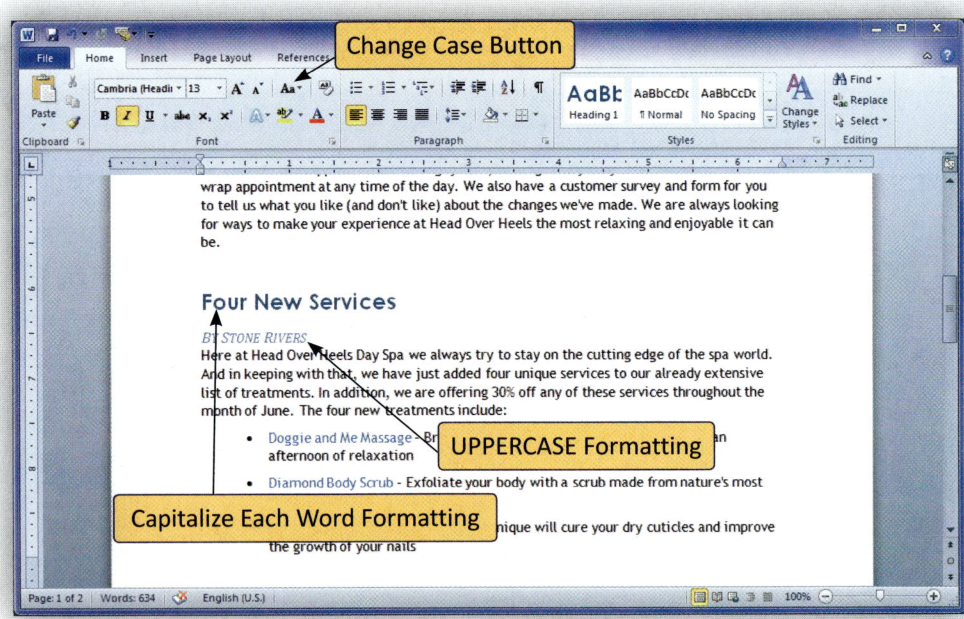

FIGURE WD 2.5

tips & tricks

Headers and titles often use the *Capitalize Each Word* format. One way to ensure that your headers and titles are consistent in text case is to use the *Change Case* command.

tell me more

From the *Font* dialog box, you can apply the *All caps* or *Small caps* character formatting to text. Although the *All caps* command has the same effect as the *UPPERCASE* case command, *All caps* applies character formatting, while *UPPERCASE* changes the underlying text that was typed.

2.5 Changing Font Colors

In the past, creating black and white documents was the standard for most business purposes. This was mostly because printing color documents was cost prohibitive. Today, color printing is more affordable and accessible. Business documents often include graphics, illustrations, and color text. Adding color to text in your document adds emphasis to certain words and helps design elements, such as headers, stand out for your reader. It is important to be selective when adding color to your document. Using too many colors can often be distracting to the reader.

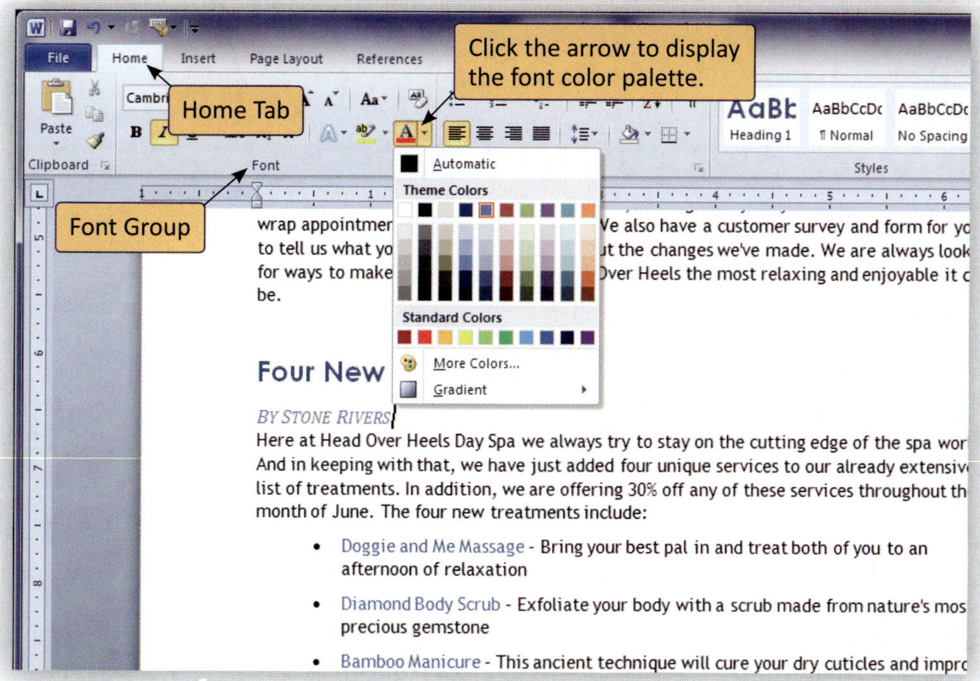

FIGURE WD 2.6

To change the color of the text:

1. Select the text to be changed.
2. On the *Home* tab, in the *Font* group, click the arrow next to the *Font Color* button.
3. Click the color you want from the color palette.

tips & tricks

When you change the color of text, the *Font Color* button changes to the color you selected. Click the **Font Color** button to quickly apply the same color to other text in the document.

tell me **more**

A color theme is a group of predefined colors that work well together in a document. You can apply a color theme to change the color of a number of elements at once. When you change the color theme, the color palette changes and displays only colors that are part of the color theme.

try **this**

You can change the font color from the Mini toolbar. To display the Mini toolbar, right-click in the text you want to change. Click the arrow next to the *Font Color* button and select the color you want.

2.6 Applying Highlights

Text in a Word document can be highlighted to emphasize or call attention to it. The effect is similar to that of a highlighting marker. When text is highlighted, the background color of the selected area is changed to make it stand out on the page.

Highlighting is very useful when you are sharing a document with coworkers or reviewers. It calls the other person's attention to elements that most need his or her attention. However, highlighting can sometimes be distracting as well. Be careful when using the highlighter in Word; only use it for small amounts of text.

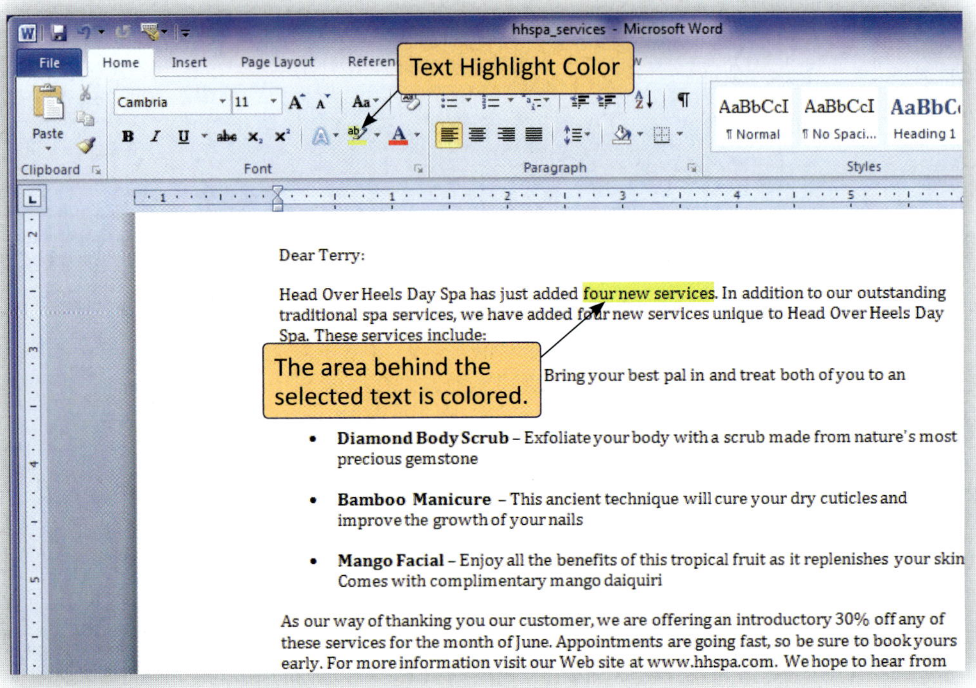

FIGURE WD 2.7

To highlight text in a document:

1. Select the text to be highlighted.
2. On the *Home* tab, in the *Font* group, click the arrow next to the *Text Highlight Color* button.
3. Click the color you want to use.

tips & tricks

Be careful when selecting colors to use for highlighting. If both the color of the text and the highlight color are dark, the text will be hard to read. If the highlight color is too light, it may not give the text enough emphasis.

tell me more

Rather than applying highlighting to text you have already selected, you can use the highlighter to apply highlighting to text throughout your document. Click the **Text Highlight Color** button without selecting any text first. Your cursor changes to a highlighter shape. Click and drag across text with the highlighter cursor to highlight text. To change your cursor back, click the **Text Highlight Color** button again.

try this

You can highlight text from the Mini toolbar. First, select the text you want to highlight; right-click the selected text to display the Mini toolbar. Click the arrow next to the *Text Highlight Color* button and select the color you want.

2.7 Using Format Painter

When you want to copy text from one part of your document to another, you use the copy and paste commands. What if you don't want to copy the text but instead copy all the formatting from text in one part of your document to text in another part of your document? The **Format Painter** tool allows you to copy formatting styles that have been applied to text. You can then "paste" the formatting, applying it to text anywhere in the document.

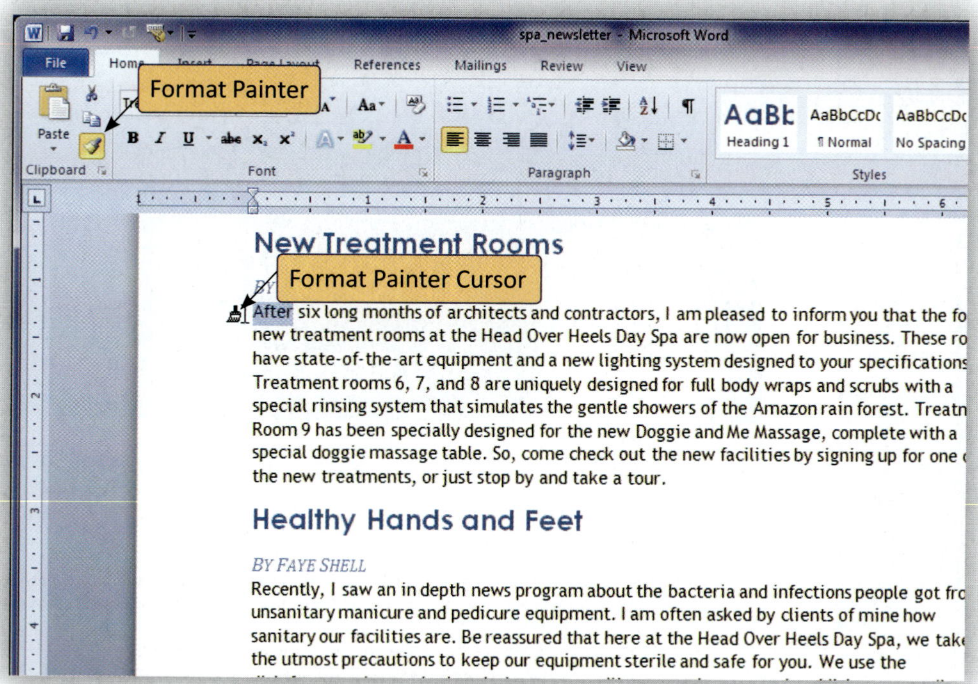

FIGURE WD 2.8

To use Format Painter:

1. Select the text that has the formatting you want to copy.
2. On the *Home* tab, in the *Clipboard* group, click the **Format Painter** button.
3. Select the text that you want to apply the formatting to.
4. The formats are automatically applied to the selected text.

tips & tricks

If the text you are copying the formatting from is formatted using a paragraph *style,* then you don't need to select the entire paragraph. Just place the cursor anywhere in the paragraph and click the **Format Painter** button. To apply the same paragraph style formatting to another paragraph, click anywhere in the paragraph to which you want to apply the formatting.

tell me more

If you want to apply the formats more than once, double-click the **Format Painter** button when you select it. It will stay on until you click the **Format Painter** button again or press Esc to deselect it.

try this

To activate *Format Painter,* you can right-click the text with formatting you want to copy and click the **Format Painter** button on the Mini toolbar.

2.8 Clearing Formatting

After you have applied a number of character formats and effects to text, you may find that you want to return your text to its original formatting. You could perform multiple undo commands on the text, or you could use the *Clear Formatting* command. The **Clear Formatting** command removes any formatting that has been applied to text, including character formatting, text effects, and styles, and leaves only plain text.

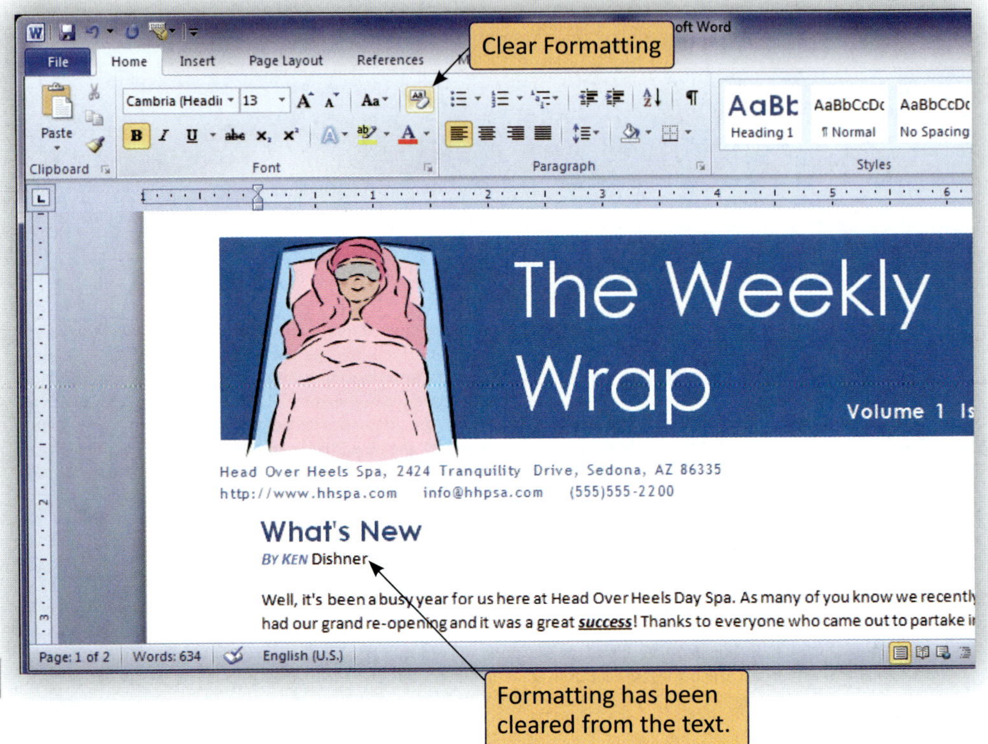

FIGURE WD 2.9

To remove formatting from text:

1. Select the text you want to remove the formatting from.
2. On the *Home* tab, in the *Font* group, click the **Clear Formatting** button.

tips & tricks

If you clear the formatting from text and then decide that you want to keep the formatting that was removed, you can use the undo command to apply the previous formatting to the text.

tell me more

The *Clear Formatting* command does not remove highlighting that has been applied to text. In order to remove highlighting from text, you must click the **Text Highlighting Color** button and select **No Color.**

try this

To clear the formatting from text, you can also:

1. On the *Home* tab, in the *Styles* group, click the **More** button.
2. Click **Clear Formatting.**

2.9 Creating Bulleted Lists

When typing a document you may want to include information that is best displayed in list format rather than paragraph format. If your list does not include items that need to be displayed in a specific order, use a bulleted list to help information stand out from surrounding text. A **bullet** is a symbol that is displayed before each item in a list. When a bullet appears before a list item, it indicates that the items in the list do not have a particular order to them.

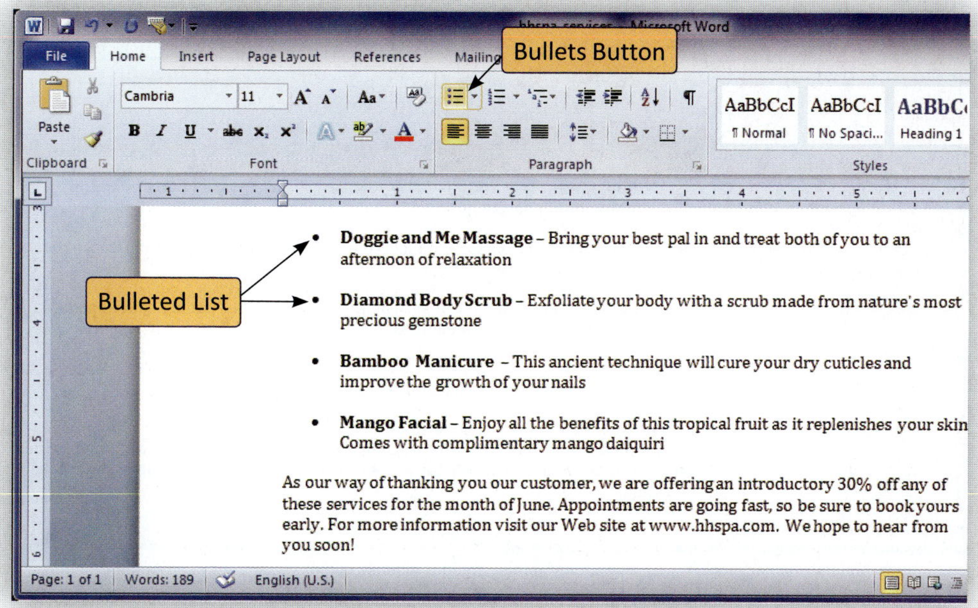

FIGURE WD 2.10

To create a bulleted list:

1. Select the text you want to change to a bulleted list. In order to appear as separate items within a bulleted list, each item must be followed by a hard return (press Enter).
2. On the *Home* tab, in the *Paragraph* group, click the **Bullets** button.
3. Click outside the list to deselect it.

tips & tricks

- Sometimes you will want to add more items to an existing list. Place your cursor at the end of a list item and press Enter to start a new line. A bullet will automatically appear before the list item.
- You can turn off the bullets formatting feature by pressing Enter twice.

tell me more

To change the bullet type, click the **Bullets** button arrow and select an option from the *Bullet Library*. You can create new bullets by selecting **Define New Bullet . . .**

try this

You can start a bulleted list by

- Typing an asterisk, a space, and your list item, then pressing the Enter key.
- Clicking the **Bullets** button, typing your list item, then pressing the Enter key.

You can convert text to a bulleted list by right-clicking the selected text, pointing to **Bullets**, and selecting an option.

2.10 Creating Numbered Lists

Some lists, such as directions to complete a task, need to have the items displayed in a specific order. **Numbered lists** display a number next to each list item and display the numbers in order. Numbered lists help you organize your content and display it in a clear, easy-to-understand manner.

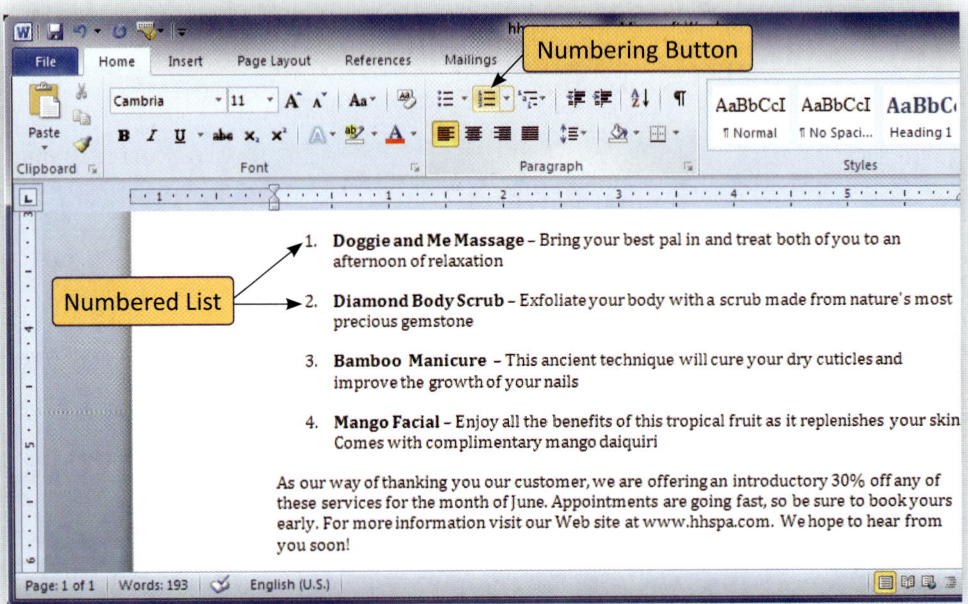

FIGURE WD 2.11

To create a numbered list:

1. Select the text you want to change to a numbered list. As with bulleted lists, in order to appear as separate items within a numbered list, each item must be followed by a hard return (press ←Enter).
2. On the *Home* tab, in the *Paragraph* group, click the **Numbering** button.
3. Click outside the list to deselect it.

tips & tricks

› Sometimes you will want to add more items to an existing list. To add another item to the list, place your cursor at the end of an item and press ←Enter to start a new line. The list will renumber itself to accommodate the new item.

› You can turn off the numbering feature by pressing ←Enter twice.

tell me more

To change the numbering list type, click the **Numbering** button arrow and select an option from the *Numbering Library*. You can create new numbered list styles by selecting **Define New Number Format . . .**

try this

You can start a numbered list by:

› Typing a 1, a space, and your list item, then pressing the ←Enter key.

› Clicking the **Numbering** button, typing your list item, then pressing the ←Enter key.

› You can convert text to a numbered list by right-clicking the selected text, pointing to **Numbering,** and selecting an option.

2.11 Creating Multilevel Lists

A **multilevel list** divides your content into several levels of organization.

1. For example, your top level organization might start with 1.
   a. The next level appears indented, and the numbering scheme restarts at the beginning.
2. When you return to the first outline level, the numbering scheme picks up with the next number.
   a. But the sublevels restart each time.

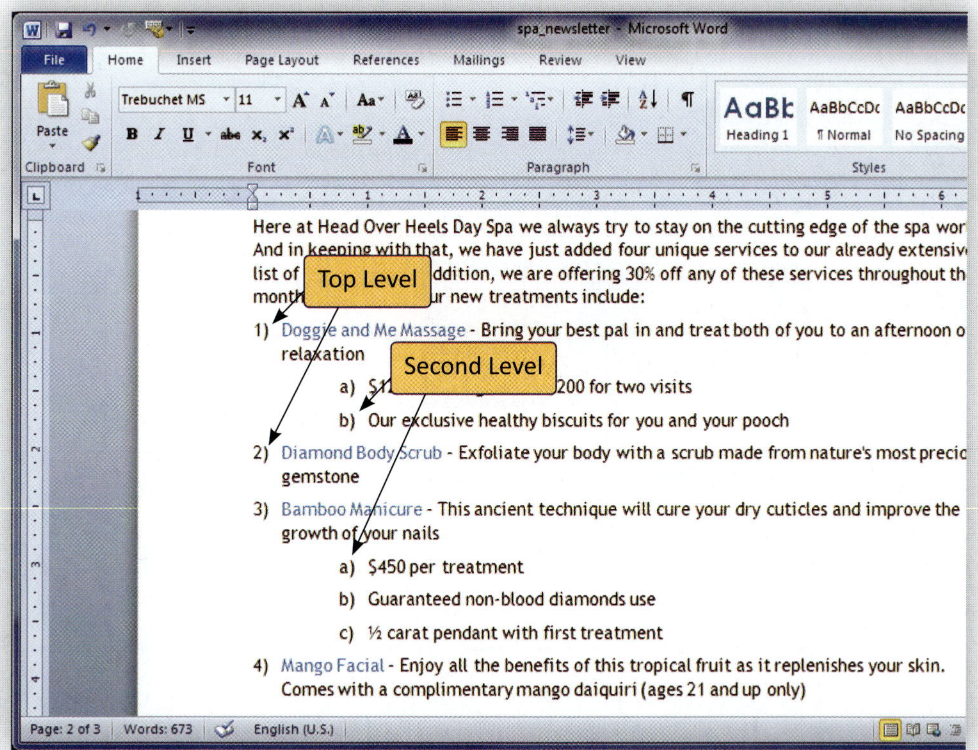

FIGURE WD 2.12

A multilevel numbered list can have up to nine levels of organization. The numbering for sublevels can be displayed in a variety of formats, available from the *Multilevel List* gallery.

To create a multilevel list:

1. Select the text you want to change into a list.
2. On the *Home* tab, in the *Paragraph* group, click the **Multilevel List** button.
3. The list has been created with each item at the same level.
4. To demote an item in the list, select the text, and click the **Increase Indent** button.
5. To promote an item in the list, select the text, and click the **Decrease Indent** button.

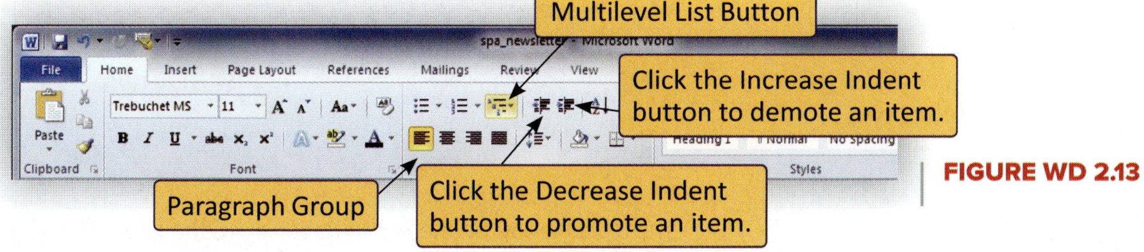

FIGURE WD 2.13

tips & tricks

Word comes with a number of predesigned multilevel list styles, but you also can choose to create your own multilevel list style. To create a custom multilevel list format, click the **Define New List Style . . .** item at the bottom of the *Multilevel List* gallery.

tell me more

Some multilevel lists show headings, which are based on predefined styles. Heading 1 text is placed at the topmost level of the list, followed by Heading 2 text, followed by Heading 3, etc.

2.12 Using Quick Styles

A **Quick Style** is a group of formatting, including character and paragraph formatting, that you can easily apply to text in your document. Quick Styles can be applied to body text, headers, quotes, or just about any type of text you may have in your document.

It is a good idea to use Quick Styles to format your documents. When you use Quick Styles to format text in your document, you can quickly change the look of that style across your document by changing the document's theme. Certain Quick Styles, such as headings, are also used by other features in Word, such as creating a table of contents and the Navigation task pane.

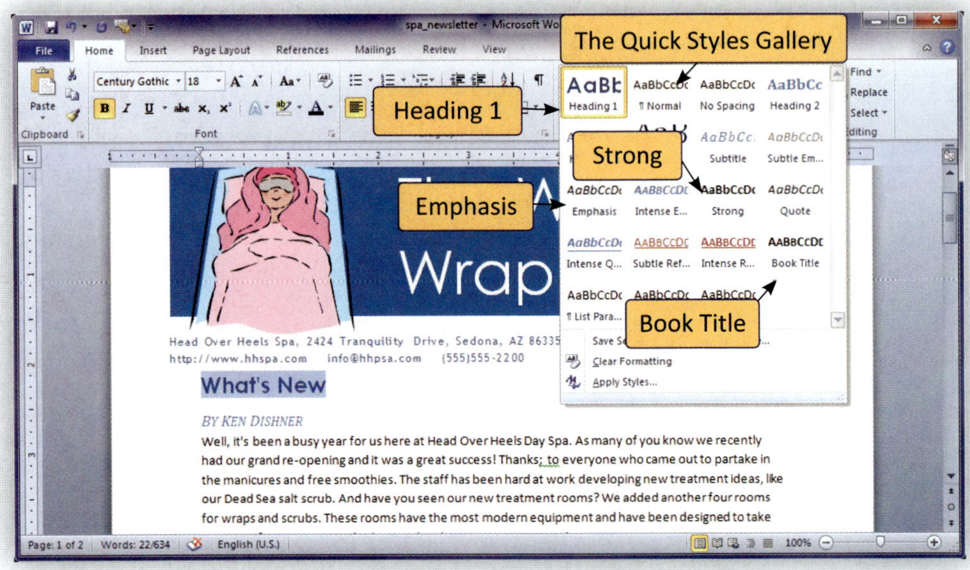

FIGURE WD 2.14

To apply a Quick Style to text:

1. Select the text you want to change.
2. On the *Home* tab, in the *Styles* group, click the **More** button.
3. Select a **Quick Style** from the *Quick Styles* gallery.

tips & tricks

If you modify a Quick Style, you can save the style with a new name and then use it throughout your document. To save a new text Quick Style, open the *Quick Styles* gallery and select **Save Selection as a New Quick Style . . .**

tell me more

When you select a new Quick Style, it replaces the style for the text. If you want to clear all the formatting for text, open the *Quick Styles* gallery and select **Clear Formatting.**

try this

The *Styles* group on the *Home* tab displays the latest Quick Styles you have used. If you want to apply a recently used Quick Style, you can click the option directly from the Ribbon without opening the *Quick Styles* gallery.

2.13 Changing Paragraph Alignment

Paragraph alignment refers to how text is aligned with regard to the left and right margins.

Left alignment aligns the text on the left side, leaving the right side ragged.

Center alignment centers each line of text relative to the margins.

Right alignment aligns the text on the right side, leaving the left side ragged.

Justified alignment evenly spaces the words, aligning the text on the right and left sides of the printed page.

It is important to understand common uses of different alignments. Paragraph text and headers are typically left aligned, but titles are often centered. Newspaper columns are often justified, and columns of numbers are typically right aligned.

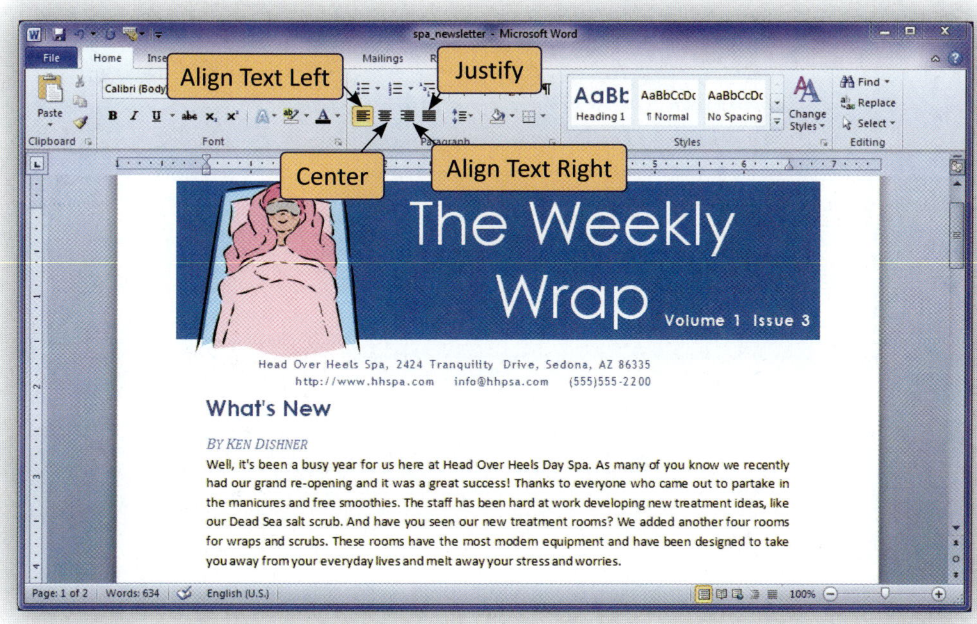

FIGURE 2.15

To change the alignment of text:

1. Click in the paragraph you want to change.
2. On the *Home* tab, in the *Paragraph* group, click an alignment button:

- **Align Text Left**
- **Center**
- **Align Text Right**
- **Justify**

tips & tricks

If you want to center text, you can right-click the text and select the **Center** button on the Mini toolbar. The Mini toolbar includes the *Center* button. However, it does not include any of the other alignment buttons. To apply other horizontal alignment, use the Ribbon or the keyboard shortcut.

try this

The following keyboard shortcuts can be used to apply horizontal alignment:

- **Align left** = Ctrl + L
- **Center** = Ctrl + E
- **Align Right** = Ctrl + R
- **Justify** = Ctrl + J

2.14 Changing Paragraph Spacing

Line spacing is the white space between lines of text. The default line spacing in Microsoft Word 2010 is 1.15 spacing. This gives each line the height of single spacing with a little extra space at the top and bottom. This line spacing is a good choice to use for the body of a document. Other commonly used spacing options include single spacing, double spacing, and 1.5 spacing.

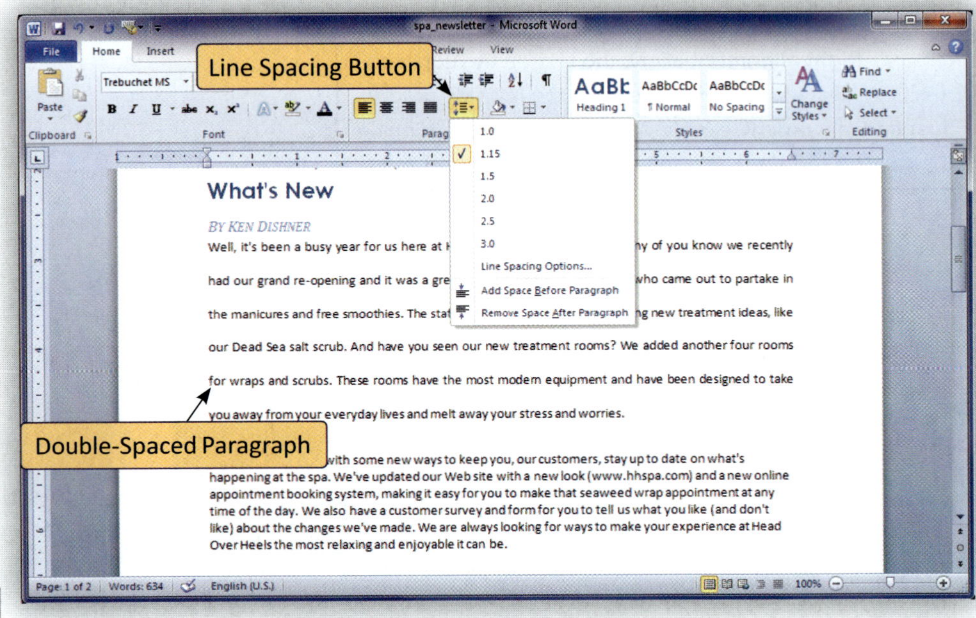

FIGURE WD 2.16

To change line spacing:

1. Select the text you want to change.
2. On the *Home* tab, in the *Paragraph* group, click the **Line Spacing** button.
3. Select the number of the spacing you want.

tips & tricks

You can add and remove space before and after your paragraphs by selecting the **Add Space Before Paragraph** and **Remove Space After Paragraph** options on the *Line Spacing* drop-down menu.

tell me more

Formatting marks control the appearance of your document and can be displayed by clicking the **Show/Hide** button ¶ on the *Home* tab.

A paragraph mark, ¶, is created every time the ←Enter key is pressed. Although these marks are hidden by default, revealing them can help you check your document for errors.

try this

- To apply single spacing, you can also press Ctrl + 1 on the keyboard.
- To apply double spacing, you can also press Ctrl + 2 on the keyboard.

2.15 Revealing Formatting Marks

When creating a document it is important to use consistent formatting, such as a single space after the period at the end of a sentence. As you create a document, Word adds formatting marks that are hidden from view. You can quickly check the formatting of your document by displaying these hidden formatting marks.

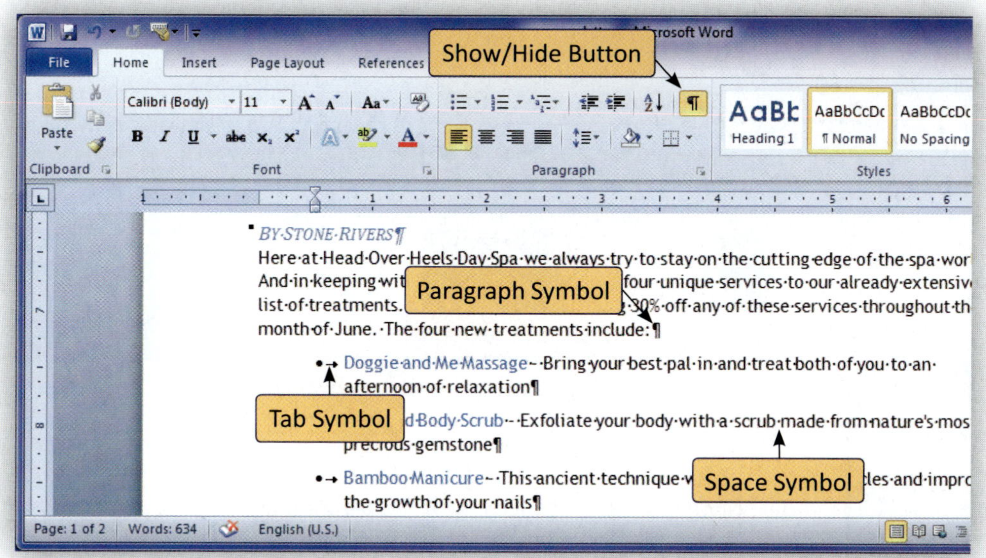

FIGURE WD 2.17

To display formatting marks in a document:

1. On the *Home* tab, in the *Paragraph* group, click the **Show/Hide** button.
2. The formatting marks are displayed in the document.
3. Click the **Show/Hide** button again to hide the formatting marks. Formatting marks include symbols that represent spaces, nonbreaking spaces, tabs, and paragraphs. The following table shows examples of formatting marks:

CHARACTER	FORMATTING MARK
Space	·
Nonbreaking Space	°
Tab	→
Paragraph	¶

tips & tricks

You can choose to always show specific formatting marks on-screen even when the *Show/Hide* button is inactive. To show specific formatting marks:

1. Click the **File** tab and select **Options.**
2. In the *Word Options* dialog box, click the **Display** category.
3. Select the formatting marks you want to display in the *Always show these formatting marks on the screen* section.
4. Click **OK.**

tell me more

- Formatting marks appear on-screen, but they do not appear in the printed document.
- A nonbreaking space is a space between two words that keeps the words together and prevents the words from being split across two lines.

try this

To show formatting marks, you can press Ctrl + Shift + 8.

2.16 Changing the Spacing between Paragraphs

When you set line spacing for a paragraph, Word creates new paragraphs based on that line height. This results in a very evenly spaced document, but also one where it can be difficult to differentiate between paragraphs, especially if your document is single spaced. To help differentiate between paragraphs in a document, you can change the spacing before and after paragraphs.

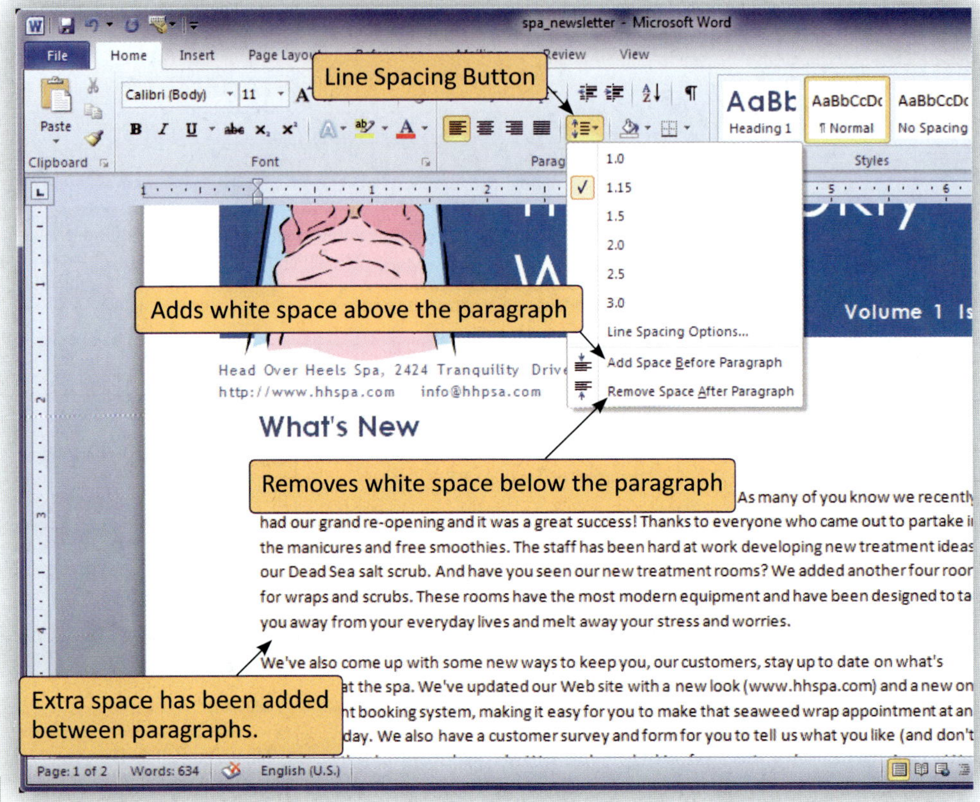

FIGURE WD 2.18

To increase and decrease the space before and after paragraphs:

1. Click in the paragraph you want to change.
2. On the *Home* tab, in the *Paragraph* group, click the **Line Spacing** button.
3. Choose one of the following options:

Click **Add Space Before Paragraph** to add space above the first line of the paragraph.

Click **Add Space After Paragraph** to add space below the last line of the paragraph.

Click **Remove Space After Paragraph** to remove space from below the last line of the paragraph.

Click **Remove Space Before Paragraph** to remove space from above the first line of the paragraph.

tips & tricks

You can control how much spacing appears before and after paragraphs.

1. Click the **Page Layout** tab.
2. In the *Paragraph* group, type a number in the *Before:* or *After:* box and press Enter to adjust the spacing between paragraphs. You can also click the arrows next to the boxes to adjust the spacing.

tell me more

Many of the Quick Styles available in the *Styles* group on the *Home* tab include spacing before and after paragraphs. Use Quick Styles to add text that includes text and paragraph formatting.

2.17 Changing Indents

When you create a document, the margins control how close the text comes to the edge of a page. But what if you don't want all your paragraphs to line up? Indenting paragraphs increases the left margin for a paragraph, helping it stand out from the rest of your document.

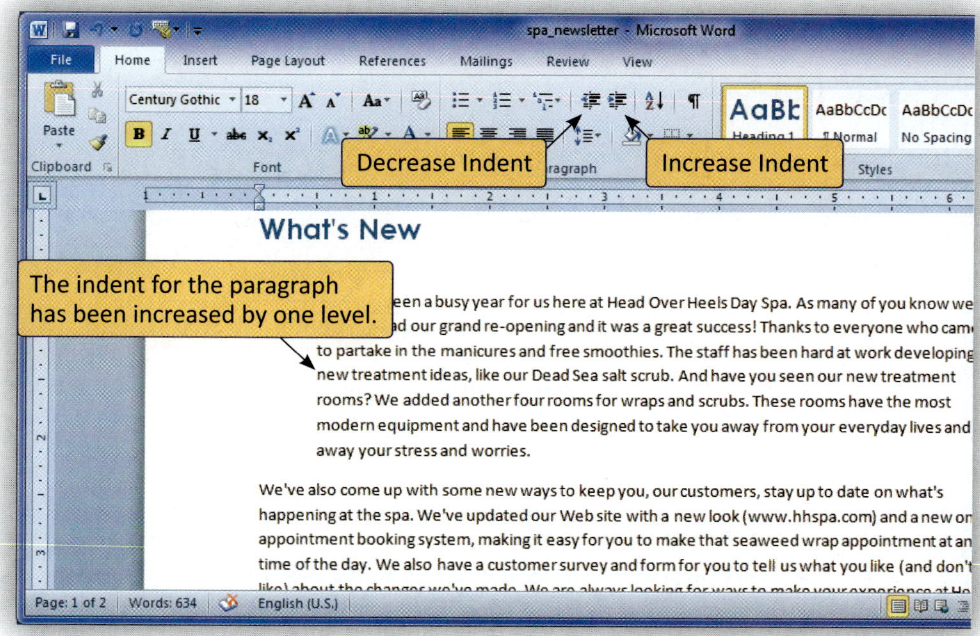

FIGURE WD 2.19

To change the indentation of a paragraph:

1. Place the cursor anywhere in the paragraph you want to change.
2. To increase the indent of the paragraph by one level, on the *Home* tab, in the *Paragraph* group, click the **Increase Indent** button.
3. To reduce the indent of the paragraph and bring it closer to the edge of the page by one level, click the **Decrease Indent** button.

tips & tricks

You can increase indents by one increment rather than by one level:

1. Click the **Page Layout** tab.
2. In the *Paragraph* group, click the arrows next to *Left:* and *Right:* to move paragraphs by one increment for each click.

try this

To change the indentation of a paragraph, you can right-click the paragraph and click the **Increase Indent** button or **Decrease Indent** button on the Mini toolbar.

tell me more

The *Indent* commands indent all lines in a paragraph the same amount. If you want only the first line of a paragraph to be indented and the remainder of the paragraph to be left-aligned, use a **First Line** indent. If you want the first line of a paragraph to be left-aligned and the remainder of the paragraph to be indented, use a hanging indent. In the *Format Paragraph* dialog box, you can precisely set options for first line indents and hanging indents. To open the *Format Paragraph* dialog box, click the **Dialog Launcher** in the *Paragraph* group on the *Home* tab or in the *Paragraph* group on the *Page Layout* tab.

2.18 Using Tab Stops

A **tab stop** is a location along the horizontal ruler that indicates how far to indent text when the Tab key is pressed.

There are five types of tab stops:

Left —Displays text to the right of the tab stop

Center —Displays text centered over the tab stop

Right —Displays the text to the left of the tab stop

Decimal —Aligns the text along the decimal point

Bar —Displays a vertical line through the text at the tab stop

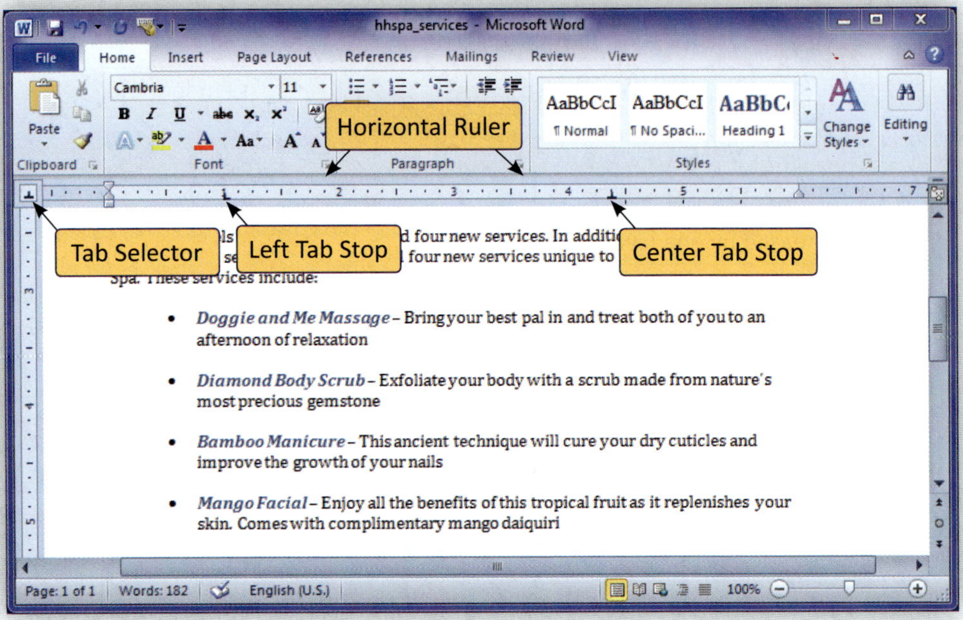

FIGURE WD 2.20

To set a tab stop:

1. Select the paragraph in which you want to set a tab stop.
2. Click the **tab selector** at the far left of the horizontal ruler until it changes to the type of tab you want.
3. Click the horizontal ruler where you want to set a tab stop.

tips & tricks

To clear a tab stop:

› Drag the tab marker down from the horizontal ruler to remove it.

To move a tab stop:

› Drag the tab marker to the right or left along the horizontal ruler to its new position.

If the ruler is not displayed, click the **View** tab and select the **Ruler** check box in the *Show* group.

tell me more

The tab selector also includes two options for adding indents to your document. The **First Line Indent** controls where the first line of a paragraph begins. The **Hanging Indent** controls where the remainder of the paragraph is indented.

try this

You can set tab stops in the *Tabs* dialog box:

1. Double-click the ruler to open the *Tabs* dialog box.
2. In the *Tab stop position:* box, type the number of where you want the tab stop to appear.
3. Click a radio button in the *Alignment* section.
4. Click **OK.**

2.19 Using Tab Leaders

Adding tab leaders can make data even easier to read. **Tab leaders** fill in the space between tabs with solid, dotted, or dashed lines. Using tab leaders helps associate columns of text by leading the reader's eye from left to right.

INSIDE THIS ISSUE

WHAT'S NEW . . . 1

FOUR NEW SERVICES 1

NEW TREATMENT ROOMS 2

HEALTHY HANDS AND FEET 2

Tab Leader

FIGURE WD 2.21

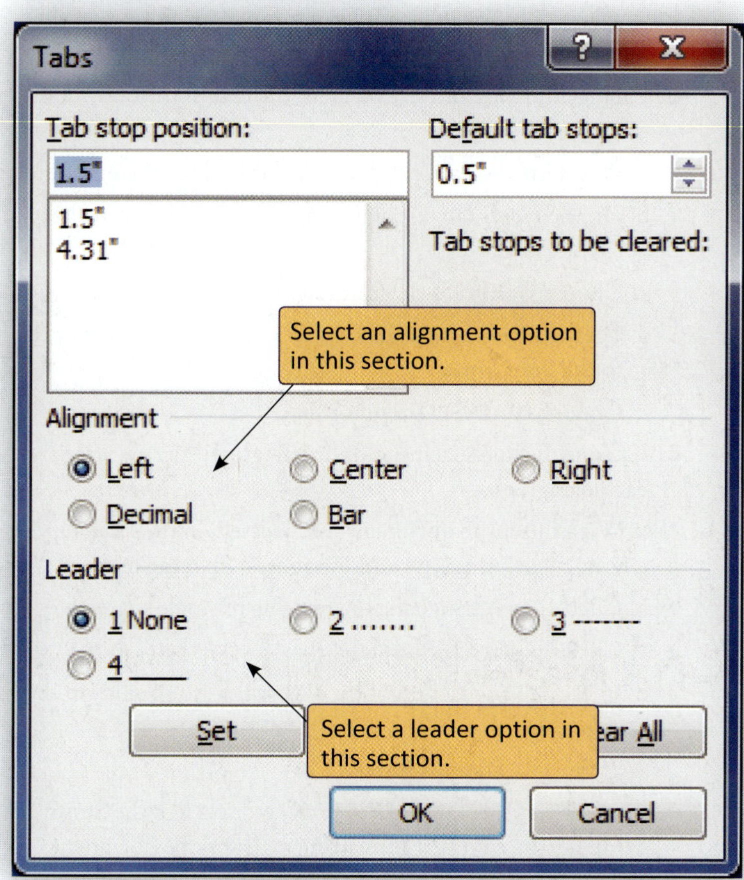

FIGURE WD 2.22

To add tab leaders:

1. Select the text to which you want to add the leader.
2. On the *Home* tab, in the *Paragraph* group, click the dialog launcher.
3. In the *Paragraph* dialog box, click the **Tabs . . .** button.
4. In the *Leader* section of the *Tabs* dialog box, select the leader option you want.
5. Click **OK.**

tips & tricks

When creating a table of contents for your document, use tab leaders to visually link section headings with page numbers.

try this

To open the *Tabs* dialog box, you can double-click a tab stop on the ruler.

projects

Data files for projects can be found on www.mhhe.com/office2010skills

Skill Review 2.1

In this project you will be editing the *Brochure_02* document from Placer Hills Real Estate.

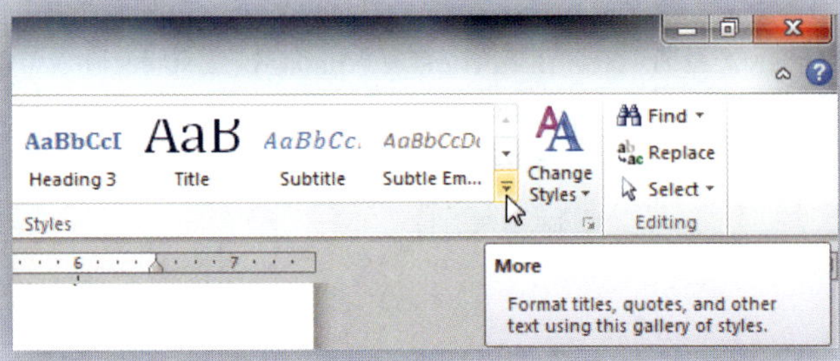

FIGURE WD 2.23

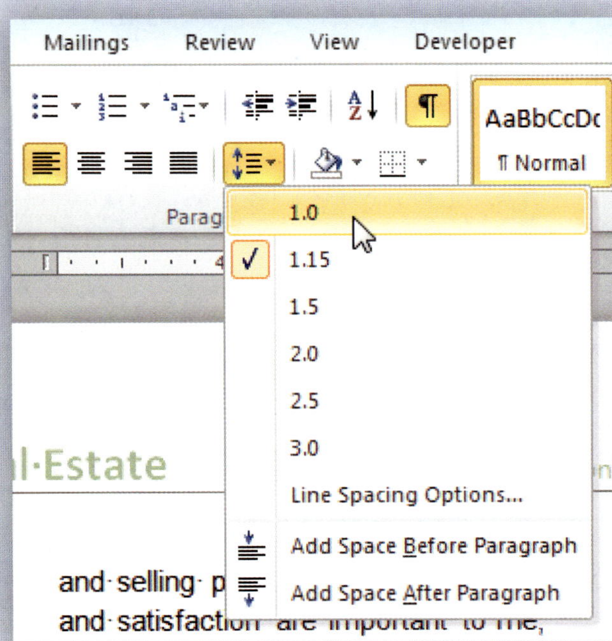

FIGURE WD 2.24

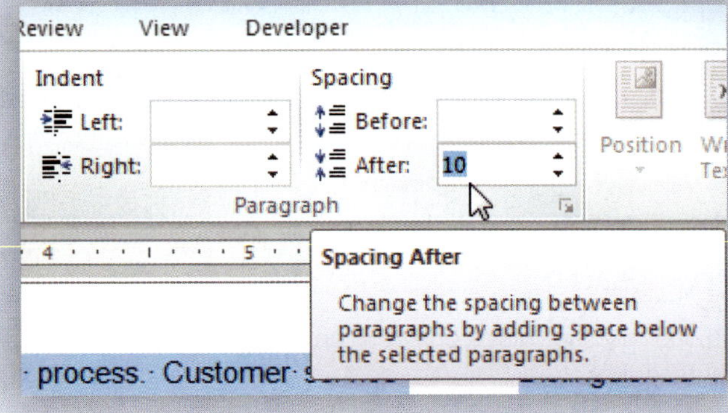

FIGURE WD 2.25

1. Open Microsoft Word 2010.
2. Open the *Brochure_02* document.
3. Save this document as `[your initials]WD_Projects_2-1`.
4. Clear the formatting on the first two lines of text in the first column.
   a. Select the first two lines of text in the first column.
   b. On the *Home* tab, in the *Styles* group, click the **More** button to expand the *Styles* gallery.
   c. Click the **Clear Formatting** selection below the *Styles* gallery. This will clear all current formatting and reset these lines to the default format from the Normal template.
5. Change the font and size on all of the text in the body of the document.
   a. Press **Ctrl+A** to select all text in the body of the brochure.
   b. On the *Home* tab, in the *Font* group, click the arrow next to the **Font** box.
   c. Choose **Calibri** as the font to use on the selected text.
   d. On the *Home* tab, in the *Font* group, click the arrow next to the **Font** box.
   e. Choose **10** as the font point size.
6. Change the line spacing and the paragraph spacing after each paragraph.
   a. With the entire document still selected, in the *Paragraph* group, click the **Line and Paragraph Spacing** button.
   b. Click **1.0** to change the line spacing to single space.
   c. Click the **Page Layout** tab.
   d. In the *Spacing* section of the *Paragraph* group, click in the **After** box.
   e. Type: `10` and press **Enter.**
7. On the *Home* tab, in the *Paragraph* group, click the **Show/Hide** button to reveal formatting marks in the document.
8. Delete all of the extra blank lines between paragraphs in the document.
9. Change after paragraph spacing to keep lines together.
   a. Select the lines of text containing the *Phone* and *Email* in the first column.
   b. Click on the **Page Layout** tab.
   c. In the *Paragraph* group, change the *After* spacing to **0 pt.**

10. Use *Quick Styles* to apply a heading format to a section heading in the document.

a. Select the **Mission Statement** heading in the first column.

b. Click the **Home** tab.

c. In the *Styles* group, click the **Heading 1** style. The *Heading 1* style is applied to the selected section heading.

11. Change the spacing before paragraph on the selected heading.

a. Make sure the *Mission Statement* heading is still selected.

b. Click on the **Page Layout** tab.

c. In the *Spacing* section of the *Paragraph* group, change *Before* to **0 pt.** You can either type **0 pt** or click on the down arrow to decrease the paragraph spacing to **0 pt.**

12. Use the *Format Painter* to change the format on all of the section headings to match the style and spacing of the first section heading.

a. Select the **Mission Statement** heading in the first column.

b. On the *Home* tab, in the *Clipboard* group, click the **Format Painter** button.

c. Select the entire line of the next heading (*Real Estate Experience*). The formatting is applied to this heading and the *Format Painter* is turned off.

d. With the *Real Estate Experience* heading selected, double-click the **Format Painter** button. Double-clicking the *Format Painter* button will allow you to use the *Format Painter* on more than one selection.

e. Select each of the remaining headings one at a time. The format will be applied to each heading. Be careful not to click on or select any other text during this process or the style will be applied to that selection.

f. Click the **Format Painter** button to turn it off after you have finished applying this style to all of the headings.

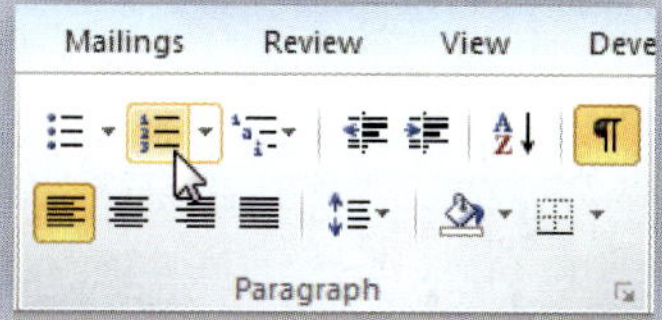

FIGURE WD 2.26

13. Add a numbered list to and decrease the indent on a section of the brochure.

a. In the *Why I Am a Real Estate Agent* section, select all of the text.

b. On the *Home* tab, in the *Paragraph* group, click the **Numbering** button. Numbering is applied to this section and it is indented.

c. Click the **Decrease Indent** button once to change the left indent to 0″.

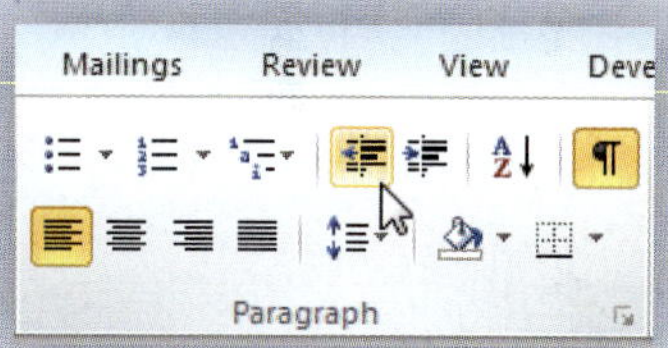

FIGURE WD 2.27

14. Add a bulleted list to and decrease the indent on a section of the brochure.

a. In the *Professional Credentials* section, select all of the text.

b. On the *Home* tab, in the *Paragraph* group, click the **Bullets** button. Bullets are applied to this section and it is indented.

c. Click the **Decrease Indent** button once to change the left indent to 0″.

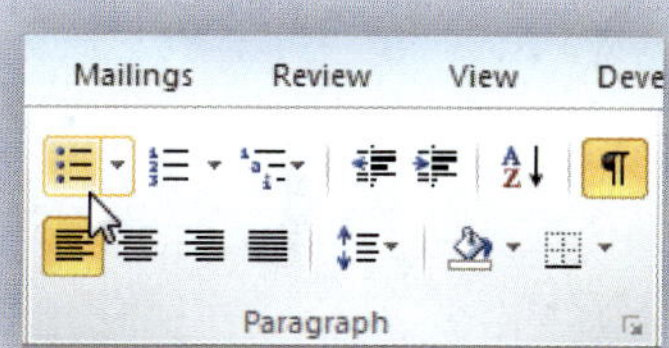

FIGURE WD 2.28

15. Change the paragraph spacing on selected text and use the *Format Painter.*

a. Select all of the text in the *Education & Training* section. Do not include the heading.

b. Click the **Page Layout** tab.

c. In the *Paragraph* group, change the *After* spacing to *3 pt.*

d. Select one line of the text in this section.

e. Click the **Format Painter.**

f. Select all of the text in the *The Placer Hills Belief System* section. Do not include the heading. The format will be applied to this section.

16. Apply a *Quick Style* to and change the paragraph spacing on selected text.

a. In the *What Clients Are Saying* section, select the first quote and include the quotation marks.

b. Click the **Home** tab.

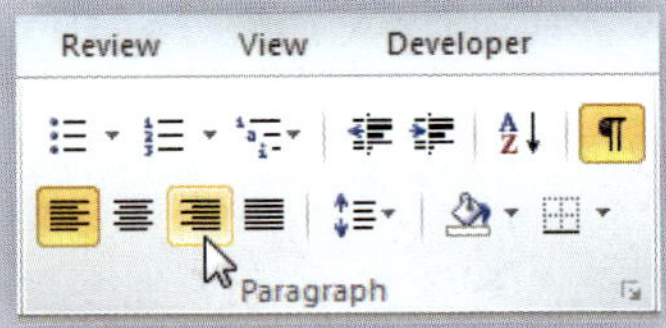

FIGURE WD 2.29

c. In the *Styles* group, apply the **Quote** style. You might have to click the **More** button to locate this style.

d. Click the **Page Layout** tab.

e. In the *Paragraph* group, change the *After* spacing to *3 pt.*

f. Use the *Format Painter* to apply this format to the second quote in this section.

g. Select **–Rod & Luisa Ellisor, Rocklin, CA.**

h. Click the **Home** tab.

i. In the *Paragraph* group, click the **Align Text Right** button or press **Ctrl+R.**

j. Select and right align **–Jon & Robin Anderson, Roseville, CA.**

17. Change font size, style, effects, and color on selected text.

a. Select **Emma Cavalli** and **Realtor Consultant** at the top of the first column.

b. On the *Home* tab, in the *Font* group, change the font to **Cambria.**

c. Click the **Bold** button in the *Font* group.

d. Change the *Font Size* to **14 pt.**

e. Click on the *Font Color* button, and change the color to **Dark Blue, Text 2.**

f. On the *Home* tab in the *Font* group, click the **Dialog Launcher.**

g. Click on **Small Caps** in the *Effects* area, and click **OK** to close the *Font* dialog box.

h. Select **Realtor Consultant.**

i. Click the **Italic** button in the *Font* group or press **Ctrl+I.**

j. Select the word **Commitment** in the *The Placer Hills Belief System* section.

k. Click on **Bold** in the *Font* group.

l. On the *Home* tab in the *Font* group, click the **Dialog Launcher.**

m. Click **Small Caps** in the *Effects* area, and click **OK** to close the *Font* dialog box.

n. Use the *Format Painter* to apply this format to all of the other introductory words in this section (Communication, Trust, Integrity, Customers, Teamwork, Success, Creativity, Win-Win).

18. Save and close the document.

Skill Review **2.2**

In this project you will be editing the *Seller Escrow Checklist_02* document from Placer Hills Real Estate.

1. Open the *Seller Escrow Checklist_02* document.
2. Save this document as ***[your initials]*WD_SkillReview_2-2.**
3. Change font, font size, and line spacing on the entire document.

   a. Press **Ctrl+A** to select the entire document.

   b. On the *Home* tab, in the *Font* group, change the font to **Calibri** and the font size to **12 pt.**

   c. In the *Paragraph* group, change the line spacing to **2.0.**
4. Click the **Show/Hide** button in the *Paragraph* group to reveal formatting marks in the document.
5. Delete all of the extra blank lines between paragraphs in the document.

6. Add tabs and leaders to selected lines using the *Tabs* dialog box.
   a. Select the **Seller** and **Escrow Company** lines.
   b. Click on the **Dialog Launcher** button in the bottom-right corner of the *Paragraph* group. The *Paragraph* dialog box will open.
   c. Click the **Tabs** button. The *Tabs* dialog box will open.
   d. Click **Clear All** to clear all existing tabs on these lines.
   e. Click in the *Tab stop position* box; type: `3`
   f. In the *Alignment* area click **Right.**
   g. In the *Leader* area click **4** (solid underline leader).
   h. Click the **Set** button to set this 3″ right tab with a solid underline leader.
   i. Set another tab with the following settings: 3.5″, Left alignment, no leader. Be sure to press **Set** to add the tab.
   j. Set another tab with the following settings: 6.5″, Right alignment, solid underline leader (4).
   k. Click **OK** to close the *Tabs* dialog box.

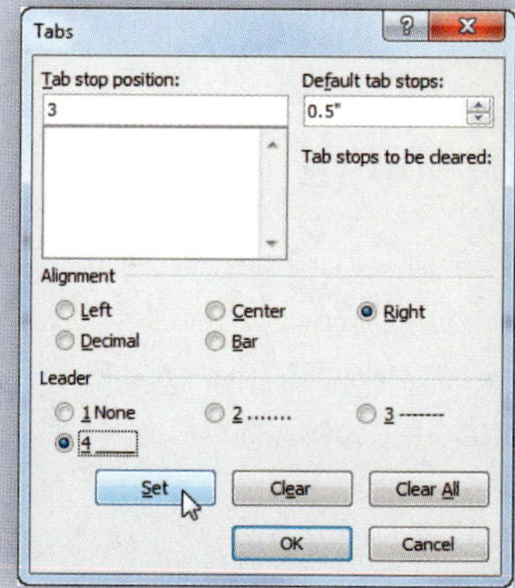

FIGURE WD 2.30

7. Add text and use tabs.
   a. Click after the word *Seller.*
   b. Press **Tab.** A solid underline will appear.
   c. Press **Tab** to move to 3.5″
   d. Type: `Property Address`
   e. Press **Tab.**
   f. Click after the words *Escrow Company.*
   g. Press **Tab.** A solid underline will appear.
   h. Press **Tab** to move to 3.5″
   i. Type: `Escrow #`
   j. Press **Tab.**
8. Add a center tab on the ruler and add text.
   a. Select the **Task to Be Completed** line.
   b. Click on the **Tab** selector to change the tab to a *Center Tab.* If the ruler is not visible below the ribbon, click on the **View Ruler** icon above the vertical scroll bar on the right side of the Word window. The ruler can also be turned on by clicking on the **View** tab and clicking on the **Ruler** check box in the *Show* group.
   c. Click on the Ruler at 5.5″ to set a center tab.
   d. Click after *Task to Be Completed.*
   e. Press **Tab.**
   f. Type: `Date Completed`**.** This text should be centered at 5.5″.

FIGURE WD 2.31

9. Set tabs on the remaining lines of the document.
   a. Select the remaining lines of text **Open Escrow with Escrow Company** through **Fax/Email Clear Pest Report.**
   b. Click the **Dialog Launcher** button in the bottom-right corner of the *Paragraph* group. The *Paragraph* dialog box will open.
   c. Click the **Tabs** button. The *Tabs* dialog box will open.
   d. Set a left tab at 4.5″.
   e. Set a right tab with a solid underline leader at 6.5″.

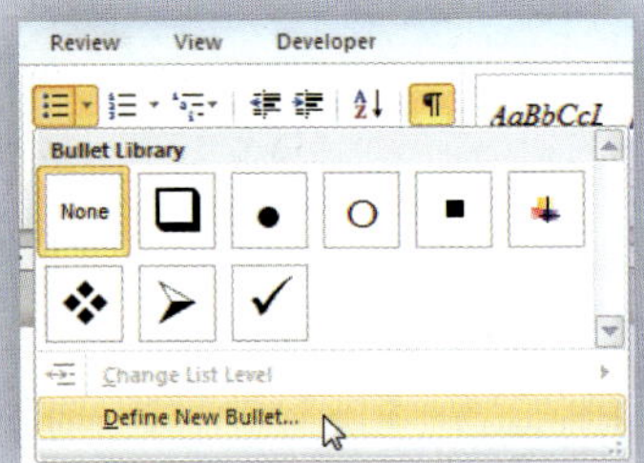

FIGURE WD 2.32

f. Click **OK** to close the *Tabs* dialog box.

g. Click after *Open Escrow with Escrow Company.*

h. Press **Tab** to move to 4.5″.

i. Press **Tab** to insert a solid underline leader to 6.5″.

j. Repeat this process after each of the remaining lines through *Fax/Email Clear Pest Report.*

10 Add bullets to selected lines of text.

a. Select the lines of text **Open Escrow with Escrow Company** through **Fax/Email Clear Pest Report.**

b. Click on the **arrow** to the right of the *Bullets* button in the *Paragraph* group to open the *Bullets* menu.

c. Select one of the bullets in the *Bullet Library* area. The selected lines will have this bullet applied.

d. In the *Paragraph* group, click on the **Decrease Indent** button once to move the bulleted list to the left margin.

11. Customize the bulleted list and add text.

a. Press **Ctrl+End** to move to the end of the document.

b. Press **Enter.**

c. Type: `Title` and press **Tab** twice.

d. Press **Enter.**

e. Type: `Lender` and press **Tab** twice.

f. Press **Enter.**

g. Type: `Buyer's Agent` and press **Tab** twice.

h. Click at the end of the *Fax/Email Clear Pest Report* line (after the underline tab).

i. Press **Backspace** twice to delete the two tabs.

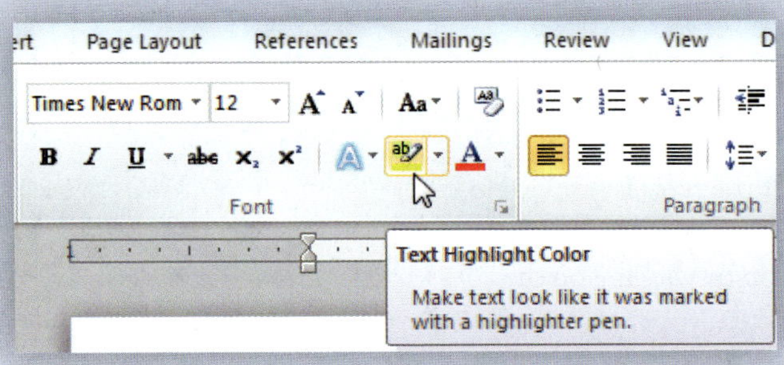

FIGURE WD 2.33

j. Click the **Bullets** button to turn off the bullet on this line.

k. Change the line spacing to **1.0** on this line.

l. Click the **Page Layout** tab.

m. Change the **After** spacing in *Paragraph* group to **6 pt.**

n. Select the word **Clear** on this line of text.

o. Click the **Home** tab.

p. Click the **Text Highlight Color** button in the *Font* group to highlight this text with yellow.

12. Change font case and style on selected text.

a. Select the entire line beginning with **Task to Be Completed.**

b. In the *Font* group, click on the **Change Case** button and select **UPPERCASE.**

c. Click the **Bold** button in the *Font* group.

d. In the *Font* group, click the **arrow** to the right of the *Font Color* button.

e. Select **Dark Blue.**

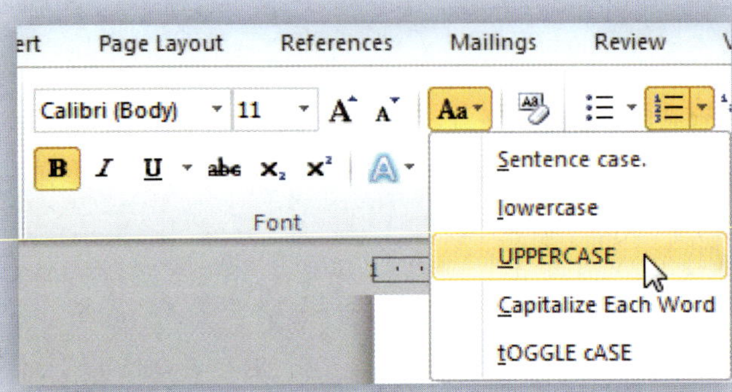

FIGURE WD 2.34

13. Apply a *Quick Style* to selected text.

a. Select the first line of the document (**Seller Escrow Checklist**).

b. In the *Styles* group, click the **Title** style.

c. Click the **Center** button in the *Paragraph* group, or press **Ctrl+E** to center the selected text.

14. Save and close the document.

challenge yourself 1

In this project you will be editing the *Staying Active_02* document from Courtyard Medical Plaza.

1. Open the *Staying Active_02* document.

2. Save this document as `[your initials]WD_Challenge_2-3.`

3. Change font, font size, line spacing, and paragraph spacing on entire document.

a. Change the font to Calibri and the size to 11 pt.

b. Change the line spacing to single (1.0).

c. Change the before paragraph spacing to 6 pt.

4. Delete all of the extra blank lines between paragraphs in the document.

5. Customize the title of the document.

a. Apply the **Intense Reference** *Quick Style* to the title of the document.

b. Change the font size to 18 pt.

c. Change the before paragraph spacing to 36 pt. and the after spacing to 12 pt.

d. Center the title.

6. Customize the first section heading in the document (*Try some of the following suggestions:*).

a. Apply the **Subtle Reference** *Quick Style.*

b. Change the font size to 14 pt.

c. Change the before paragraph spacing to 12 pt. and the after paragraph spacing to 6 pt.

7. Use the *Format Painter* to apply the formatting of the first section heading to the second section heading (*To keep exercise fun and interesting:*).

8. Change the case of both section headings to **Capitalize Each Word.**

9. Add a multilevel list to the four paragraphs after the first section heading.

a. Select all four paragraphs after the first section heading.

b. Apply numbered and lettered [1), a), i), etc.] multilevel list to selected text.

10. The first sentence in each paragraph will be a first-level numbered item. You will change the remaining sentences to be either a second- or third-level entry.

a. Click before the second sentence in the first paragraph of this multilevel list.

b. Press **Enter** and then press **Tab** (or **Increase Indent**). This sentence is now listed as *a).*

c. Click before the next sentence (*For example . . .*) and press **Enter.**

d. Press **Tab** (or **Increase Indent**) to change this sentence to *i)* (a third-level entry).

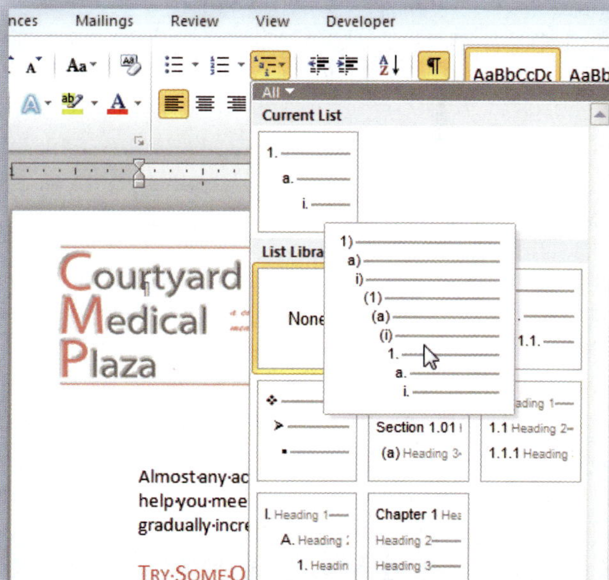

FIGURE WD 2.35

e. Click before the next sentence (*The more physical activity . . .*) and press **Enter.**

f. Press **Shift+Tab** (or **Decrease Indent**) to change this sentence to *b)* (a second-level entry).

11. In the second paragraph (*If you don't like counting calories . . .*), change the second and third sentences to second-level entries.

12. In the third paragraph (*Use both aerobic and strengthening . . .*), change the second and third sentences to second-level entries.

13. Press **Enter** after the fourth paragraph and add the following second- and third-level entries.

`Household chores` (second level)

`Cleaning windows` (third level)

`Vacuuming` (third level)

`Doing laundry` (third level)

`Yard work and gardening` (second level)

`Using stairs rather than an elevator` (second level)

`Getting up and moving regularly at work` (second level)

14. Customize the font style, effects, and paragraph spacing in the multilevel list.

a. Select the first line in the multilevel list.

b. Use bold and small caps on this line (Hint: Use the *Font* dialog box).

c. Open the *Paragraph* dialog box and deselect the *Don't add space between paragraphs of the same style* check box so the 6 pt. before paragraph spacing is applied to this selection.

d. Use the Format Painter to apply this formatting to the other first-level entries in this multilevel list.

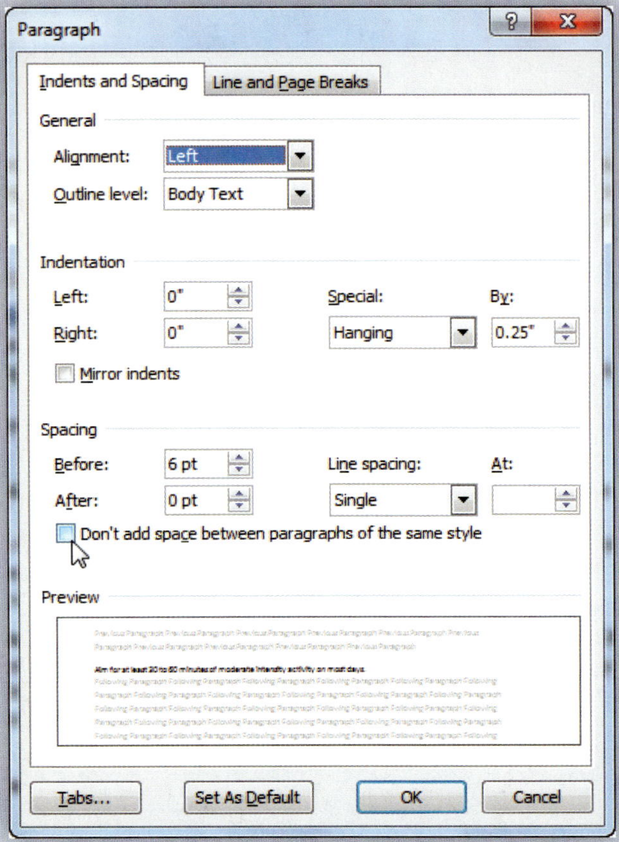

FIGURE WD 2.36

15. Add a bulleted list to the four paragraphs after the second section heading (*To keep exercise fun and interesting:*).

a. Select all four paragraphs in this section and apply a bullet of your choice.

b. Decrease the indent of the bulleted list so the bullets are at the left margin.

c. Open the *Paragraph* dialog box and deselect the *Don't add space between paragraphs of the same style* check box so the 6 pt. before paragraph spacing is applied to this bulleted list.

16. Change the first sentence on each of the bulleted items to bold and small caps.

17. Save and close the document.

challenge yourself 2

In this project you will be editing the *Emergency Procedures_02* document from Sierra Pacific Community College District.

1. Open the *Emergency Procedures_02* document.

2. Save this document as ***[your initials]*** **`WD_Challenge_2-4`.**

3. Change the font on the entire document to Times New Roman and 12 pt.

4. Customize the title of the document.
   a. Apply the **Heading 1** *Quick Style* to the title of the document.
   b. Change the case to UPPERCASE.
   c. Change the before paragraph spacing to 18 pt.
5. Customize the section headings of the document.
   a. Apply the **Heading 2** *Quick Style* to the first section heading [*Emergency Telephones (blue phones)*] in the document.
   b. Underline this heading and change to small caps.
   c. Change the before paragraph spacing to 14 pt.
   d. Use the *Format Painter* to apply this formatting to the remaining headings in the document.
6. Customize the section headings of the document.
   a. Apply the **Heading 2** *Quick Style* to the first section heading [*Emergency Telephones (blue phones)*] in the document.
   b. Underline this heading and change to small caps.
   c. Use the *Format Painter* to apply this formatting to the remaining headings in the document.
7. Delete all of the extra blank lines in the document.
8. Change the bulleted list in the *Emergency Telephones* section to a numbered list.
   a. Change the left indent to 0.25″ (use the *Paragraph* group on the *Page Layout* ribbon).
9. Apply this numbered list formatting to the text in the following sections (do not include the section headings): *Assaults, Fights, or Emotional Disturbances; Power Failure; Fire; Earthquake; Bomb Threat.*
10. In the *Emergency Telephone Locations* section, change the left indent of the locations to 0.25″ (do not include the heading).
11. Bold each of the emergency telephone locations in this section (**Stadium Parking Lot, Barton Hall,** etc.).
12. In the *Emergency Phone Numbers* section, change the left indent of these lines to 0.25″ (do not include the heading).
13. Select the text in the *Emergency Phone Numbers* section and set a 6.5″ right tab with a dot leader (leader selection 2).
14. Press **Tab** before each of the phone numbers in this section to line up the numbers at the right margin. A dot leader will be inserted before each phone number.
15. Select the text in the *Accident or Medical Emergency* section and apply a bullet of your choice.
    a. Make sure the left indent is at 0.25″.
16. Use the *Format Painter* to apply this bulleted list format to the text in the following sections (do not include the section headings): *Tips to Professors and Staff, Response to Students.*
17. In the *Accident or Medical Emergency* section, bold, italicize, and underline **Life-threatening emergencies** and **Minor emergencies.**
18. Find all occurrences of *Phone 911* in the document. On each occurrence, change to red font color, bold, and all caps.
19. Save and close the document.

on your own

In this project you will be editing the *Central Sierra Questionnaire_02* document from Central Sierra Insurance.

1. Open the *Central Sierra Questionnaire_02* document.
2. Save this document as `[your initials]WD_OnYourOwn_2-5`.
3. Select the entire document and make the following formatting changes:
   a. Clear all formatting.
   b. Change the font to Calibri and 10 pt.
   c. Change the line spacing to single space.
   d. Change the after paragraph spacing to 6 pt.
   e. Set left tabs at 0.25″ and 0.5″.
   f. Set a right tab with a solid underline leader at 6.5″.
4. Delete all extra blank lines in the document.
5. Select the first line of the document and make the following changes:
   a. Apply the *Title* style.
   b. Change the case to *Capitalize Each Word.*
   c. Bold text and use small caps.
6. Select the next line of the document (*Please carefully read . . .*) and apply *Intense Reference* style, uppercase, no underline, and 12 pt. font size.
7. Select the next line of the document (*Applicant's Instructions*) and make the following changes:
   a. Apply the *Intense Quote* style.
   b. Change the left and right indents to 0″.
   c. Change the after paragraph spacing to 6 pt.
8. Apply the formatting from *Applicant's Instructions* heading to *Insurance Application Disclaimer* (on the second page).
9. Select all of the text after the *Insurance Application Disclaimer* heading to the end of the document and change the after paragraph spacing to 12 pt.
10. Click at the end of the *Name and Title of Insured* line and press **Tab** to insert a solid underline leader.
11. Add a tab after the *Signature of Insured* and *Date of Application* lines.
12. Add a multilevel list to all of the lines between the *Applicant's Instructions* and *Insurance Application Disclaimer* headings.
   a. Use the following multilevel style: 1), a), i)
   b. With the text still selected, open the *Paragraph* dialog box and deselect the *Don't add space between paragraphs the same style* check box.
   c. Use either *Tab* or *Increase Indent* to change each line that begins *If "yes, ". . .* to a second-level item.
   d. Click at the end of each paragraph in the multilevel list and press **Tab** to insert a solid underline leader after each question.
13. Click after the *Applicant's Instructions* heading and press **Enter.**
14. Add the following paragraph: `Answer ALL questions. If the answer to any is NONE, please write NONE. Questionnaire must be signed and dated by owner, partner, or officer.`

15. In the paragraph you just typed, use a text highlight color of your choice to highlight the words *ALL* and the second occurrence of *NONE*.
16. Select the entire document and change the paragraph alignment to *Justify*.
17. Save and close the document.

In this project you will be editing the *Conference Registration Form_02* document from Central Sierra Insurance.

1. Open the *Conference Registration Form_02* document.
2. Save this document as ***[your initials]*** **WD_FixIt_2-6.**
3. Using the Microsoft Word 2010 features you have learned and practiced in this chapter, you will edit and customize this conference registration form to enhance readability and produce a more professional-looking document. *Note: You do not need to fill in the information requested in the registration form; you are just customizing this form.*
4. Use *Quick Styles* to attractively and professionally format the opening and closing lines of the document.
5. Delete unnecessary blank lines, tabs, indents, and spaces.
6. Change font, size, color, style, effects, and case as necessary.
7. Use line and paragraph spacing and alignment as necessary to consistently format this form.
8. Use an appropriate bullet for a check box.
9. Use indents as needed to align bulleted items.
10. Use tabs and solid underline leaders to provide fill-in areas on this form.
11. Change indents as necessary to attractively, professionally, consistently format this document.
12. Use the *Format Painter* as necessary to ensure consistent formatting.
13. Make all occurrences of *Agriculture Insurance Conference* bold and small caps.
14. On all occurrences of *Westfield Hotel & Spa* change the font color and make bold and italicize.
15. Highlight the due date of the conference registration form.
16. The document should be formatted to fit on one page.
17. Proofread and spell check the document carefully.
18. Save and close the document.

chapter 3

Formatting Documents

In this chapter, you will learn the following skills:

- Add consistency to document fonts and colors by using themes
- Use headers and footers to display page numbering and date/time
- Control document layout by adjusting margins and using page and section breaks
- Enhance document formatting and readability by using borders, watermarks, and hyperlinks
- Use building blocks, Quick Parts, and property controls to save time and provide consistency for commonly used information

Skill **3.1** Applying Document Themes
Skill **3.2** Using Color Themes and Font Themes
Skill **3.3** Adding Page Borders
Skill **3.4** Creating Watermarks
Skill **3.5** Inserting Building Blocks
Skill **3.6** Adding Headers and Footers
Skill **3.7** Adding the Date and Time to the Header
Skill **3.8** Inserting Page Numbers
Skill **3.9** Inserting Property Controls
Skill **3.10** Saving Quick Parts as Building Blocks
Skill **3.11** Inserting Hyperlinks
Skill **3.12** Adjusting Margins
Skill **3.13** Inserting Page Breaks and Section Breaks
Skill **3.14** Adding a Cover Page
Skill **3.15** Viewing Documents Side by Side

skills

introduction

This chapter will cover additional features of document formatting to enhance the consistency of fonts and colors, to control margins and pagination, and to increase user efficiency by creating and storing commonly used information. Students will be using themes, borders, watermarks, headers and footers, building blocks and Quick Parts, margins, and page and section breaks to improve document readability.

3.1 Applying Document Themes

A **theme** is a group of formatting options that you apply to an entire document. Themes include font, color, and effect styles that are applied to specific elements of a document. Theme colors limit the colors available from the color palette for fonts, borders, and backgrounds. Theme fonts change the fonts used for built-in styles—such as Normal style and headings. Theme effects control the way graphic elements in your document appear. Applying a theme to your document is a quick way to take a simple piece of text and change it into a polished, professional-looking document.

To apply a theme to a document:

1. Click the **Page Layout** tab.
2. In the *Themes* group, click the **Themes** button.
3. Click an option in the *Built-In* section to apply it to your document.

FIGURE WD 3.1

tips & tricks

To reset the theme to the original theme that came with the document's template, click the **Themes** arrow and select **Reset to Theme from Template.**

tell me more

You can modify any of the existing themes and save it out as your own custom theme. The file will be saved with the *.thmx* file extension. The theme will be saved in the *Document Themes* folder and will be available from Excel, PowerPoint, and Outlook as well as Word.

3.2 Using Color Themes and Font Themes

When creating a document, it can sometimes be difficult to choose colors that work well together. Documents can end up monochromatic or with too many colors that don't work well together. A **color theme** is a set of colors that are designed to work well together in a document. A color theme will change the color of text, tables, and drawing objects in a document. When you apply a theme to a document it includes a color theme, which has default theme colors for document elements. You can change the color theme without affecting the other components of the theme.

To apply a color theme to a document:

1. Verify you are on the *Home* tab.
2. In the *Styles* group, click the **Change Styles** button.
3. Point to **Colors** and select a color theme.

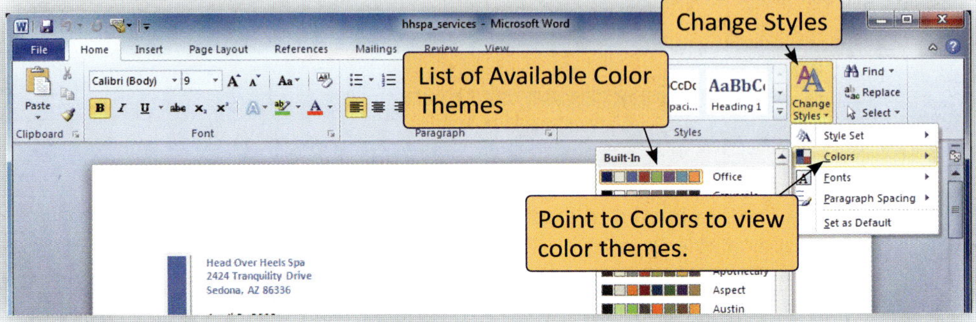

FIGURE WD 3.2

There are thousands of fonts for you to choose from to use in your documents. Some fonts are designed to work well as header text, such as Cambria, and others are designed to work well as body text, such as Calibri. When you apply a theme to a document, this includes a **font theme**, which includes default fonts for body text and header text. As with color themes, you can change the font theme without affecting the other components of the theme.

To apply a font theme to a document:

1. On the *Home* tab, in the *Styles* group, click the **Change Styles** button.
2. Point to **Fonts** and select a font theme.

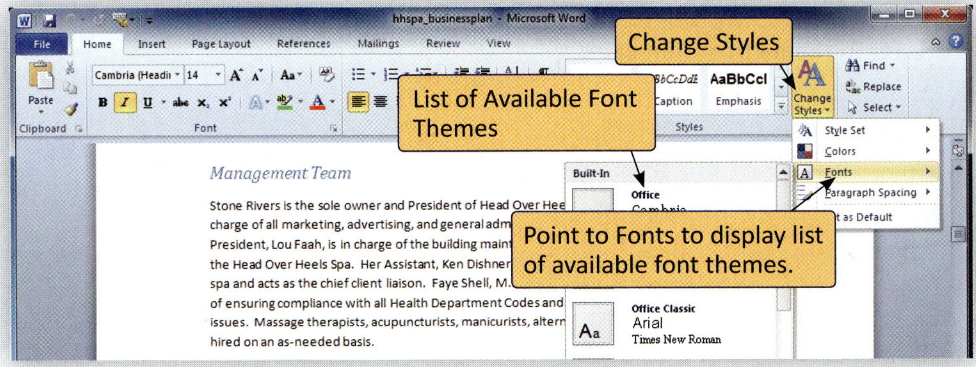

FIGURE WD 3.3

tell me **more**

- When you change the color theme for a document, the color options for document elements will change. The theme colors will appear in the *Font Color* menu, as well as in the *Table Styles* and *Shape Styles* galleries. Choose your colors from these preset theme colors to ensure your document has a consistent color design.
- The font theme menu displays a preview of the header font (on top) and the body font (on bottom). Notice that some themes include two different fonts, but others include the same font, only in different sizes. The default font theme for Word 2010 is the Office Cambria/Calibri font theme.

try **this**

- To apply a color theme, you can click the **Page Layout** tab, click the **Theme Colors** button, and select a color theme.
- To apply a font theme, you can click the **Page Layout** tab, click the **Theme Fonts** button, and select a font theme.

3.3 Adding Page Borders

Page borders are graphic elements that can give your document a more polished look. **Page borders** draw a decorative graphic element along the top, right, bottom, and left edges of the page. Borders can be simple lines or include 3-D effects and shadows. You can modify borders by changing the style and color. You can apply a border to the entire document or parts of a section.

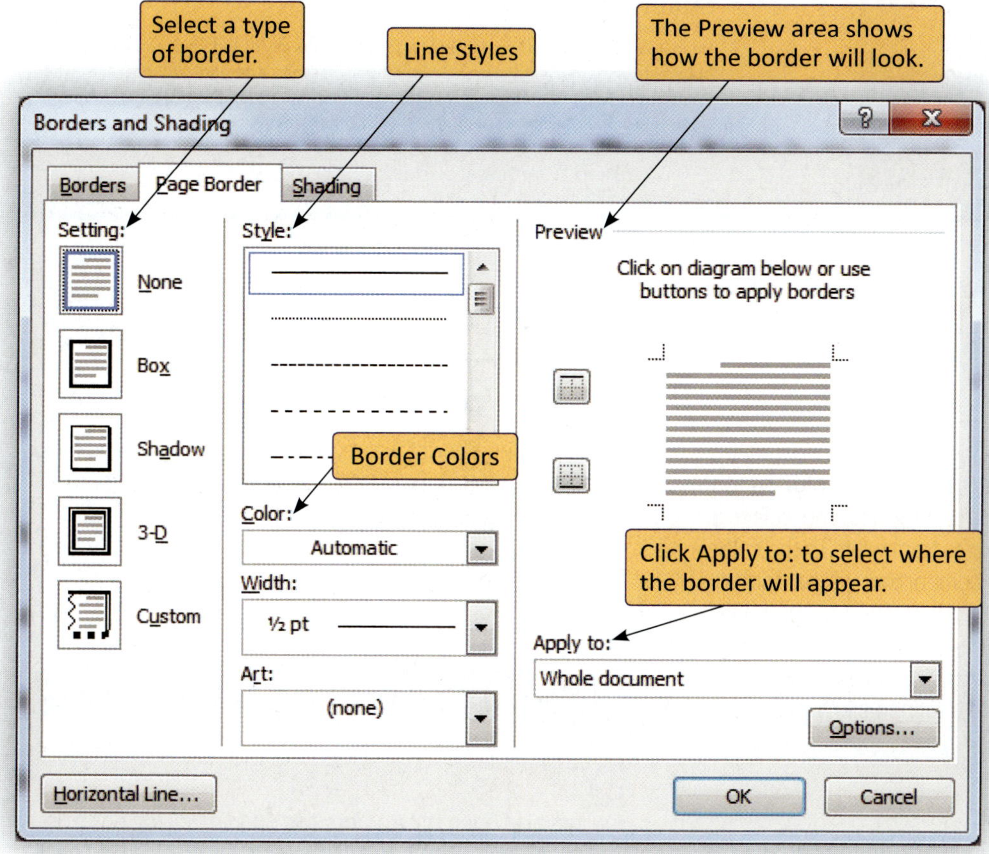

FIGURE WD 3.4

To add a border to a document:

1. Click the **Page Layout** tab.
2. In the *Page Background* group, click the **Page Borders** button.
3. The *Borders and Shading* dialog box opens with the *Page Border* tab displayed.
4. Click a setting for the border.
5. Select a style, color, and width for the page border.
6. The *Preview* area shows how the border will look.
7. Click the **Apply to:** arrow and select the part of the document to add the page border to.
8. Click **OK** to accept your changes and add the page border to the document.

FIGURE WD 3.5

tips & tricks

If you want to add further visual interest to your document, you can change the page color. Click the **Page Color** button [Page Color] in the *Page Background* group and select a color. The page background changes from white to the color you chose. If you have a large document that will be printed, you may not want to add a color background to the entire document. Printing color takes longer than printing in black and white and is more expensive in the end. However, adding color to a cover page can add a refined element to your document.

tell me more

There are a number of ways you can further adjust the look of page borders from the *Borders and Shading* dialog box:

- Click on the *Preview* area diagram to add or remove parts of the border.
- Click the **Art:** drop-down menu to select graphic elements for the border.
- Click the **Horizontal Line . . .** button to add a graphic horizontal line element to your document.

try this

You can also open the *Borders and Shading* dialog box from the *Home* tab. In the *Paragraph* group, click the arrow next to the *Borders* button and select **Borders and Shading . . .**

3.4 Creating Watermarks

A **watermark** is a graphic or text that appears as part of the page background. Watermarks appear faded so that the text that appears on top of the watermark is legible when the document is viewed or printed.

There are three categories of watermarks:

- **Confidential**—Include the text "Confidential" or "Do Not Copy" in different layouts.
- **Disclaimers**—Include the text "Draft" or "Sample" in different layouts.
- **Urgent**—Include the text "ASAP" or "Urgent" in different layouts.

To add a watermark to a document:

1. Click the **Page Layout** tab.
2. Click the **Watermark** button and select an option from the gallery.

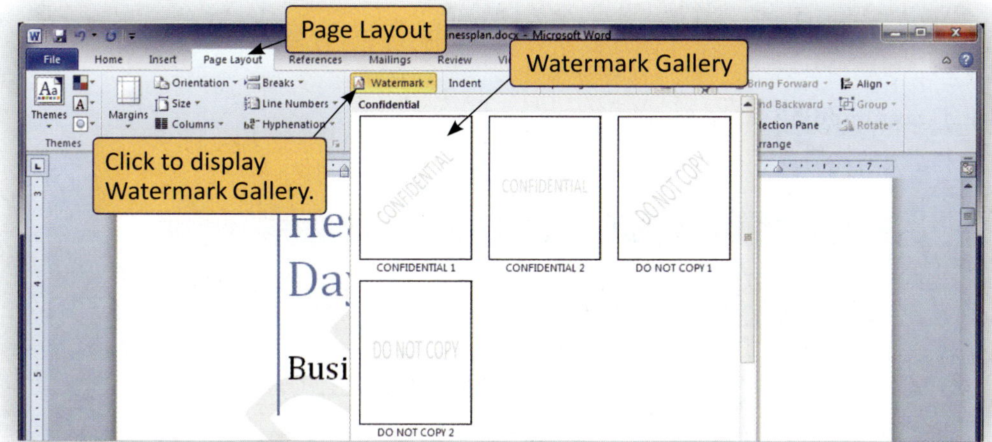

FIGURE WD 3.6

tips & tricks

You do not have to use one of the built-in watermarks from the *Watermark* gallery. You can create your own custom watermark, displaying whatever text or image you like. Click the **Custom Watermark . . .** command to open the *Printed Watermark* dialog box and choose different options for the text watermark. You can add pictures as watermarks from this dialog box. When you add a picture as a watermark, it appears faded so any text on top of it is still legible.

tell me more

To remove a watermark, click the **Watermark** button and select **Remove Watermark.**

try this

You can add watermarks through the *Building Blocks Organizer.*

3.5 Inserting Building Blocks

A **building block** is a piece of content that is reusable in any document. Building blocks can be text, such as AutoText, or they can include graphics, such as a cover page. You can insert building blocks from specific commands on the Ribbon or from the **Building Blocks Organizer**. The *Building Blocks Organizer* lists the building blocks in alphabetical order by which gallery they appear in and includes Bibliographies, Cover Pages, Equations, Footers, Headers, Page Numbers, Table of Contents, Tables, Text Boxes, and Watermarks.

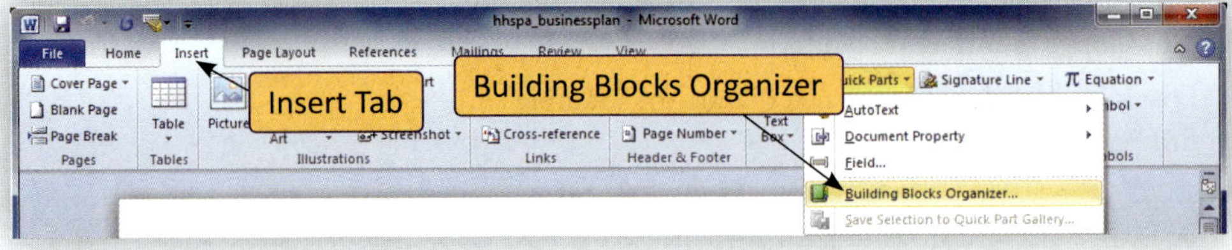

FIGURE WD 3.7

To insert a building block from the *Building Blocks Organizer:*

1. Click the **Insert** tab.
2. Click the **Quick Parts** button and select **Building Blocks Organizer . . .**
3. Select a building block in the list and click the **Insert** button.

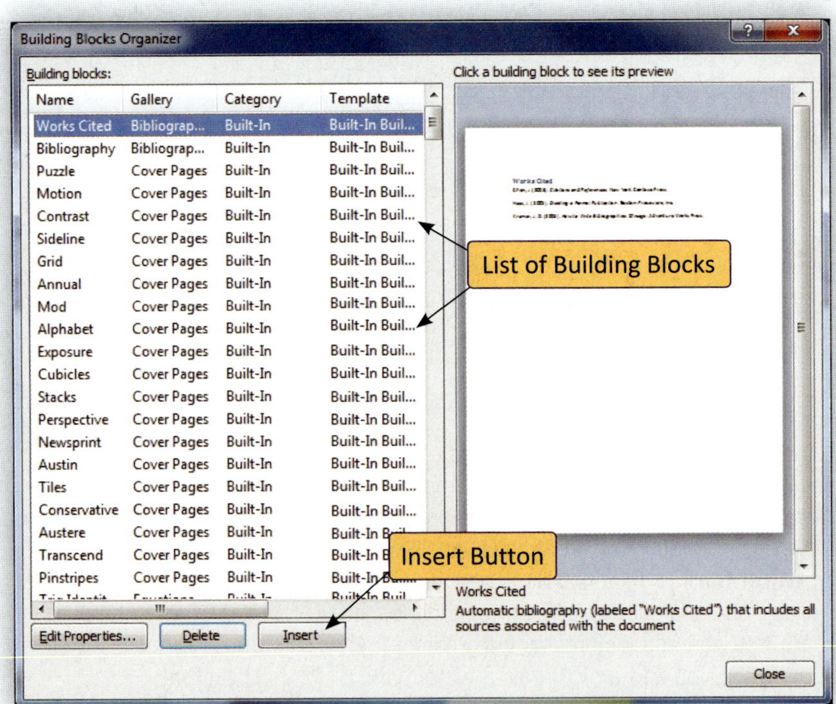

FIGURE WD 3.8

tips & tricks

If you find that the list of building blocks is too long, you can remove building blocks you don't use. To remove a building block from the *Building Blocks Organizer,* select a building block and click the **Delete** button. Be aware that the *Building Blocks Organizer* is used across all of Word 2010. If you delete a building block from the *Building Blocks Organizer,* it will no longer be available when you are working on other documents.

tell me more

You can sort the list of building blocks by clicking the *Name, Gallery, Category,* or *Template* button at the top of the *Building Blocks Organizer.* You can also modify the properties of a building block, changing properties such as the name or which gallery the building block appears in.

3.6 Adding Headers and Footers

A **header** is text that appears at the top of every page, just below the top margin; a **footer** is text that appears at the bottom of every page, just above the bottom margin. Typically, headers and footers display dates, page numbers, document titles, or authors' names. Word 2010 comes with a number of predesigned headers and footers that you can add to your document and then modify to suit your needs.

To add a header to a document:

1. Click the **Insert** tab.
2. In the *Header & Footer* group, click the **Header** button and select a header design from the gallery.
3. Word displays the *Header & Footer Tools* contextual tab and inserts a header with content controls for you to enter your own information. Click a content control and enter the information for your header.
4. To close the header and return to your document, click the **Close Header and Footer** button on the contextual tab.

To add a footer to a document:

1. Click the **Insert** tab.
2. In the *Header & Footer* group, click the **Footer** button and select a footer design from the gallery.
3. Word displays the *Header & Footer Tools* contextual tab and inserts a footer with content controls for you to enter your own information. Click a content control and enter the information for your footer.
4. To close the header and return to your document, click the **Close Header and Footer** button on the contextual tab.

If the first page of your document is a title page, you won't want the header text to display on the page. To display a different header on the first page of the document than the rest of the document, display the *Header & Footer Tools* contextual tab. In the *Options* group, click the **Different First Page** check box so it is selected.

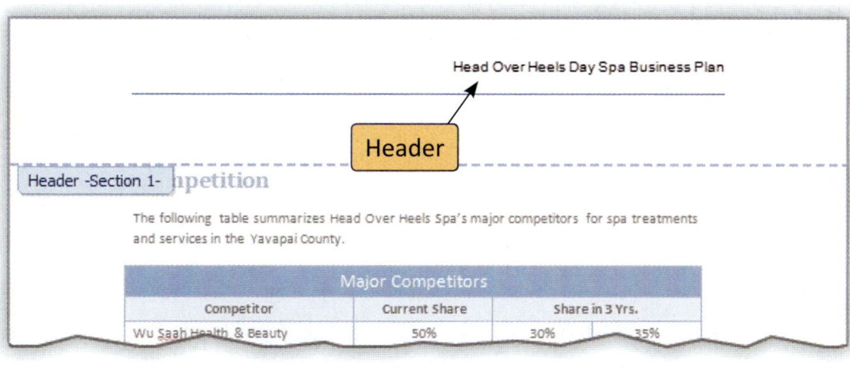

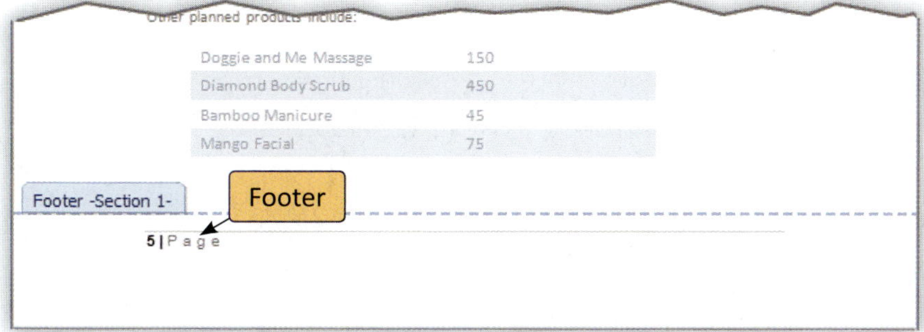

FIGURE WD 3.9

tips & tricks

Headers and footers appear faded out in Print Layout view. If you want to edit a header or footer, double-click it and make your changes. Click the **Close Header and Footer** button to return to the document.

tell me more

When you add a header or footer to your document, the *Design* tab under *Header & Footer Tools* displays. This tab is called a contextual tab because it only displays when a header or footer is the active element. Click the **Design** tab to modify the header or footer properties.

try this

You can add headers and footers through the *Building Blocks Organizer.*

3.7 Adding the Date and Time to the Header

In addition to information such as the company name and page numbers, headers and footers typically include the current date. You could manually type the date in the header or footer and then update the date every time you work on the document, or you could add an **automatic date stamp**. An automatic date stamp pulls the current date from the computer's system clock and displays the date in the document. The date is then automatically updated when the computer's date changes.

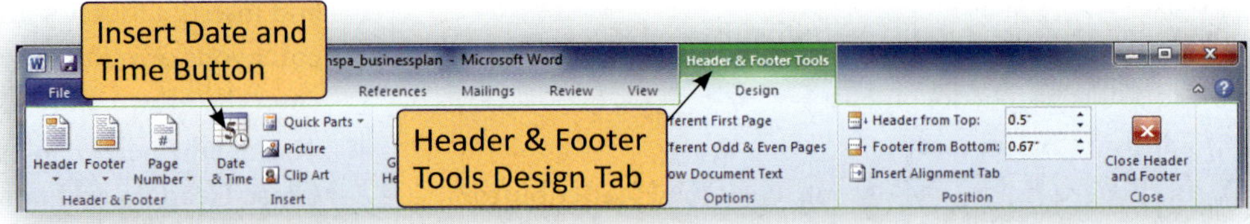

FIGURE WD 3.10

To add an automatic date stamp to the header of a document:

1. Double-click the header to switch to header view.
2. Under the *Header & Footer Tools,* in the *Insert* group, click the **Insert Date and Time** button.
3. In the *Date and Time* dialog box, click a date format in the *Available formats:* box.
4. Select the **Update automatically** check box.
5. Click **OK.**

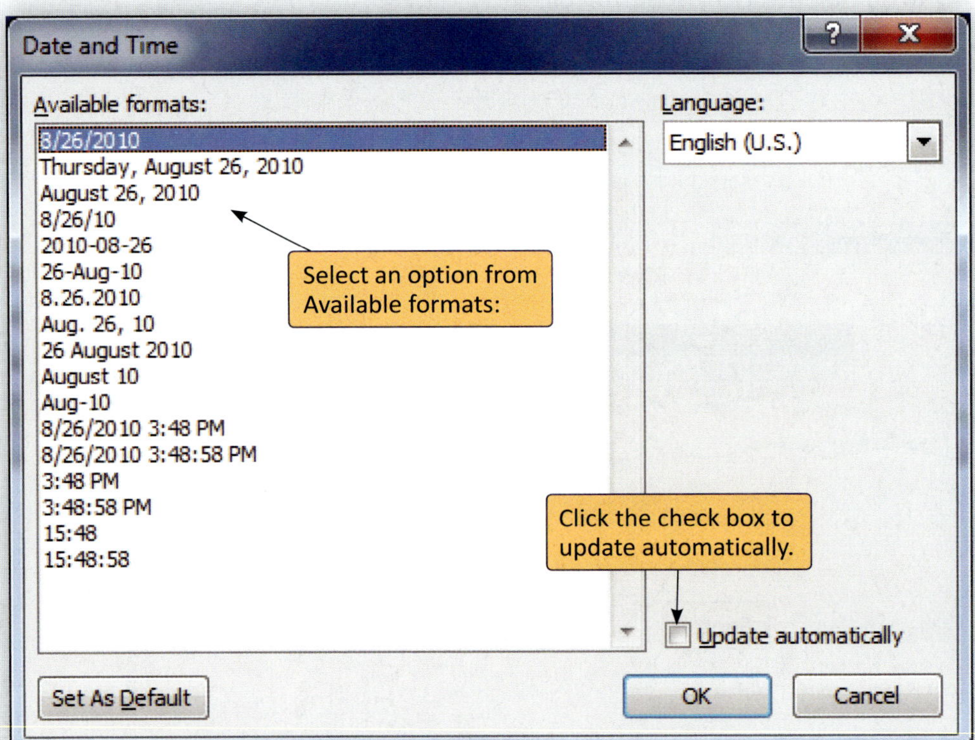

FIGURE WD 3.11

tips & tricks

To update the date in your document, click the date and then click the **Update** button. Word will automatically display the computer's current date. If you did not select the *Update automatically* check box when you inserted the date, the computer will not automatically update the date in your document.

try this

You can also use *Quick Parts* to add the date and time to the header or footer of your document:

1. Under the *Header & Footer Tools,* in the *Insert* group, click the **Quick Parts** button and select **Field . . .**
2. In the *Field* dialog box, click the **CreateDate** or the **Date** field.
3. Select a format for the date.
4. Click **OK.**

3.8 Inserting Page Numbers

Headers and footers often include page numbers, but they also include other information, such as author name, date, and document title. If all you want to do is add page numbers to a document, you don't need to use the header and footer feature. Instead, you can insert simple page numbers to a document through the *Page Number* gallery.

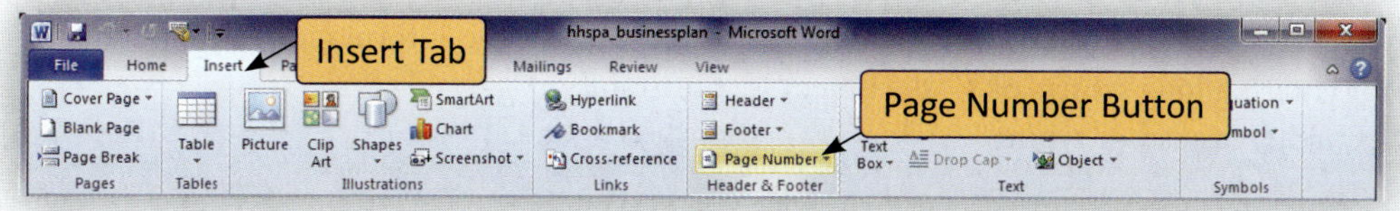

FIGURE WD 3.12

To add page numbers to the bottom of pages of a document:

1. Click the **Insert** tab.
2. In the *Header & Footer* group, click the **Page Number** button. Point to *Bottom of Page,* and select an option.
3. To remove a page number, click the arrow next to the *Page Number* button and select **Remove Page Numbers.**

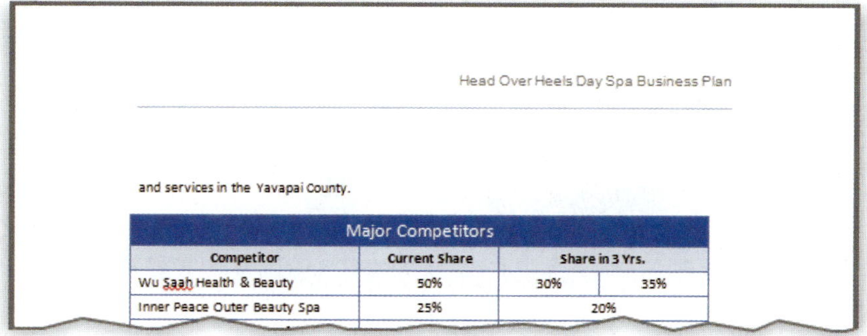

Competitor	Current Share	Share in 3 Yrs.	
Wu Saah Health & Beauty	50%	30%	35%
Inner Peace Outer Beauty Spa	25%	20%	

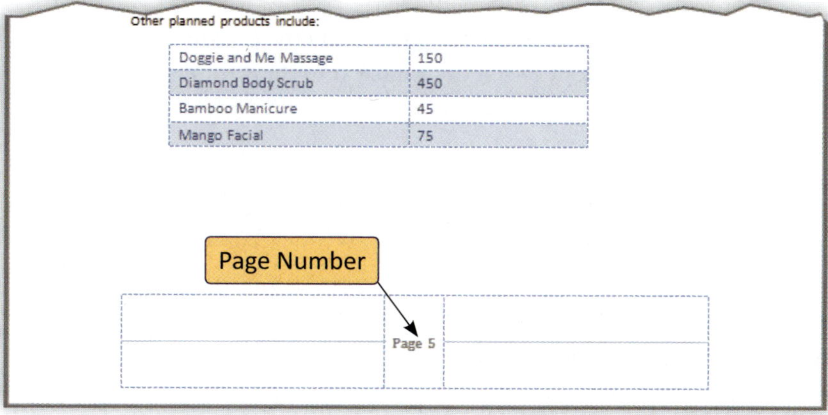

Doggie and Me Massage	150
Diamond Body Scrub	450
Bamboo Manicure	45
Mango Facial	75

FIGURE WD 3.13

tips & tricks

When adding page numbers to a document, you should always use Word's built-in building block. If you type page numbers into your document manually, they will not update when you add or remove pages.

tell me more

Traditionally, page numbers appear in the header or footer of the document. However, you can choose to display page numbers in the margin or at the current location of the cursor in the document.

try this

You can also add a page number through the *Building Blocks Organizer.*

3.9 Inserting Property Controls

A **property control** is an element you can add to your document to save time entering the same information over and over again. When you insert a property control and then replace the text with your own information, any time you add that control again it will include your custom text. Property controls can be used as shortcuts for entering long strings of text that are difficult to type. For example, instead of typing the company name Head Over Heels Day Spa, you can insert the *Company* property control. Word will add the text to the document and update the text automatically if any changes are made to the property control. By using property controls, you can be assured that all the information throughout the document is consistent.

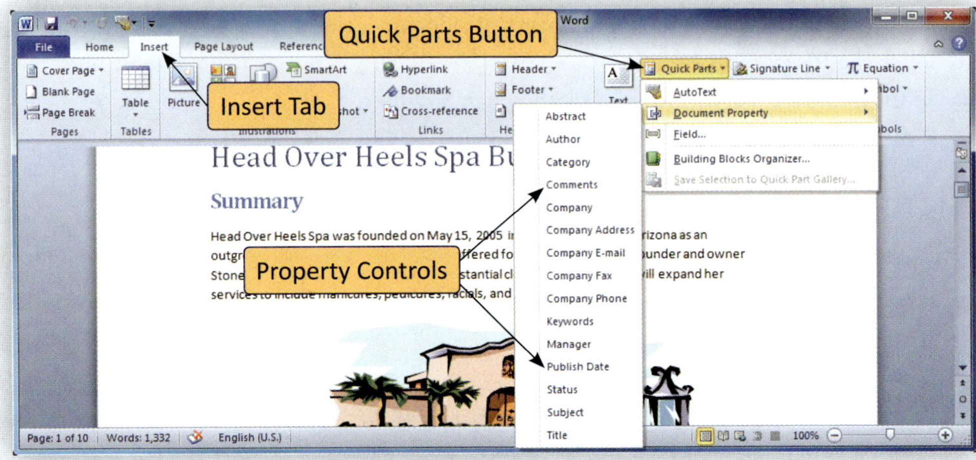

FIGURE WD 3.14

To add a property control to a document:

1. Click the **Insert** tab.
2. In the *Text* group, click the **Quick Parts** button, point to **Document Property,** and select a control.
3. Type your text in the control.
4. Select the same control from the *Document Property* menu to add the same text to the document.

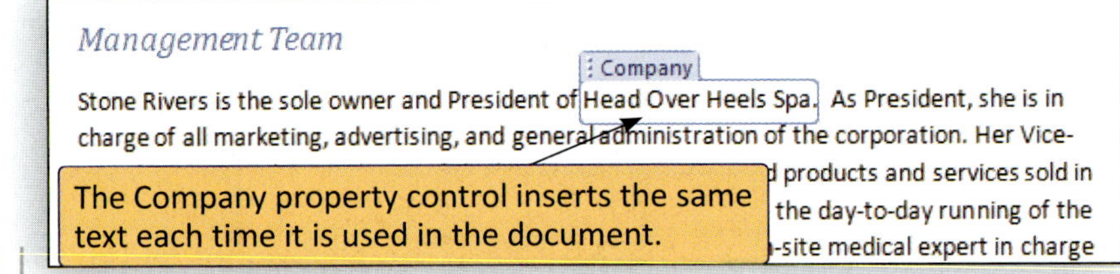

FIGURE WD 3.15

tips & tricks

If you need to update a property control, you only need to type the change once in the document. As you update any property control, all the other controls created from the same property control will update.

tell me more

Many of the built-in property controls, such as company name and author, pull their information from the document's properties. If you add a property control and modify the information, the document's related property will be updated as well.

3.10 Saving Quick Parts as Building Blocks

Quick Parts are snippets of text that you can save and then add to any document. They include the text and all the formatting that has been applied to it. Use Quick Parts when you want text to appear a certain way throughout your documents, such as a company's tag line.

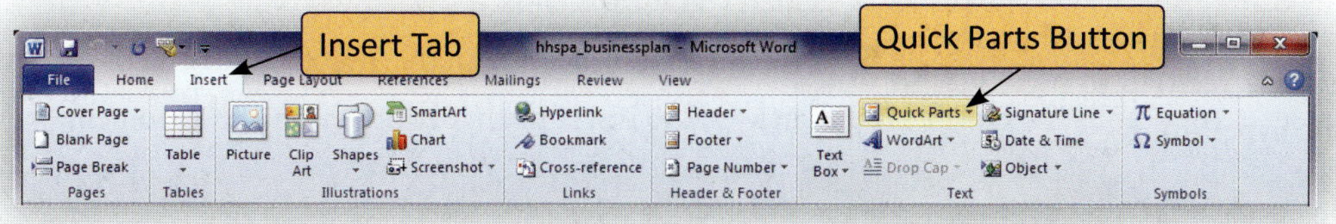

FIGURE WD 3.16

To add text to the *Quick Parts* gallery:

1. Select the text to add to the gallery.
2. Click the **Insert** tab.
3. In the *Text* group, click the **Quick Parts** button and select **Save Selection to Quick Part Gallery . . .**
4. The *Create New Building Block* dialog box opens.
5. Review the information for the Quick Part and make any changes.
6. Click **OK.**

To add a Quick Part to a document from the *Quick Part* gallery:

1. Click the **Insert** tab.
2. Click the **Quick Parts** button and select the Quick Part to add.

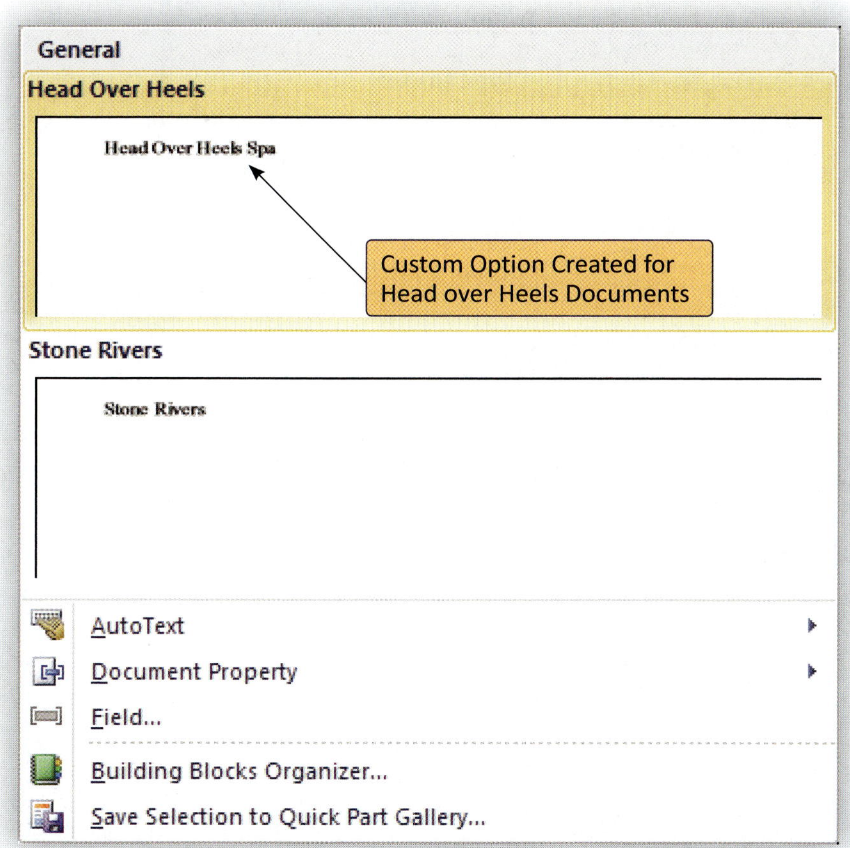

FIGURE WD 3.17

tips & tricks

When you save text to the *Quick Parts* gallery, you are actually creating a building block. The Quick Part you created appears in the *Building Blocks Organizer* under the category *Quick Parts.*

tell me more

To edit or delete a Quick Part, open the *Building Blocks Organizer,* select the Quick Part building block in the list, and click the **Edit Properties . . .** or **Delete** button.

3.11 Inserting Hyperlinks

A **hyperlink** is text or a graphic that, when clicked, opens another page or file. You can use hyperlinks to link to a section in the same document, to a new document, or to an existing document, such as a Web page. Some hyperlinks include ScreenTips. A **ScreenTip** is a bubble that appears when the mouse is placed over the link. Add a ScreenTip to include a more meaningful description of the hyperlink.

To insert a hyperlink:

1. Select the text or graphic you want to use as the link.
2. Click the **Insert** tab.
3. In the *Links* group, click the **Hyperlink** button to open the *Insert Hyperlink* dialog box.
4. Select an option under *Link to:* and select the file to which you want to link.
5. Type the text of the link in the *Text to display:* box.
6. Click **OK** to insert the hyperlink into your document.

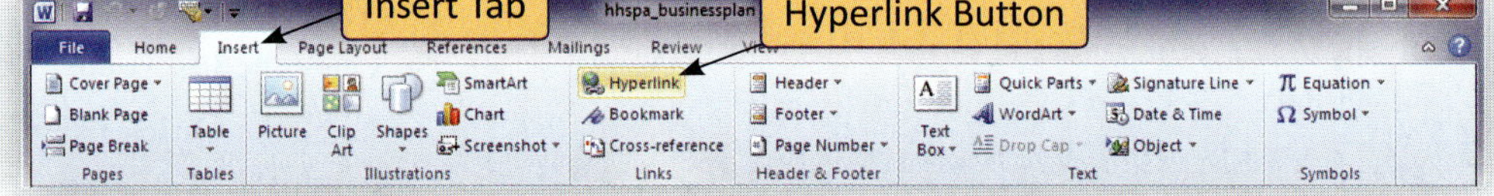

FIGURE WD 3.18

FIGURE WD 3.19

To edit a hyperlink, right-click the link and select **Edit Hyperlink . . .** from the menu. Make any changes in the *Edit Hyperlink* dialog box.

To remove a hyperlink, right-click the link and select **Remove Hyperlink** from the menu.

tell me **more**

You can add bookmarks to a long document to help you easily return to a specific place in the document. To add a bookmark:

1. Click the **Insert** tab.
2. In the *Links* group, click the **Bookmark** button. The *Bookmark* dialog box opens.
3. Type a name for the bookmark in the *Bookmark name:* box.
4. Click the **Add** button.

To return to a place in a document using bookmarks:

1. First open the *Bookmark* dialog box.
2. Click the name of the bookmark you want to navigate to.
3. Click the **Go To** button.

try **this**

To open the *Insert Hyperlink* dialog box, you can:

- Right-click the text or object you want as the link and select **Hyperlink . . .** from the shortcut menu.
- Press Ctrl + K on the keyboard.

from the perspective of . . .

POLICE OFFICER

I use word processing software to write my reports. I keep notes regarding complaints, disturbances, and accidents.

3.12 Adjusting Margins

Margins are the blank spaces at the top, bottom, left, and right of a page. Word's default margins are typically 1 inch for the top and bottom and 1 inch for the left and right. Word 2010 comes with a number of predefined margin layout options for you to choose from, including normal, narrow, wide, and mirrored.

To adjust the margins for a document:

1. Click the **Page Layout** tab.
2. In the *Page Setup* group, click the **Margins** button and select an option for the page layout.

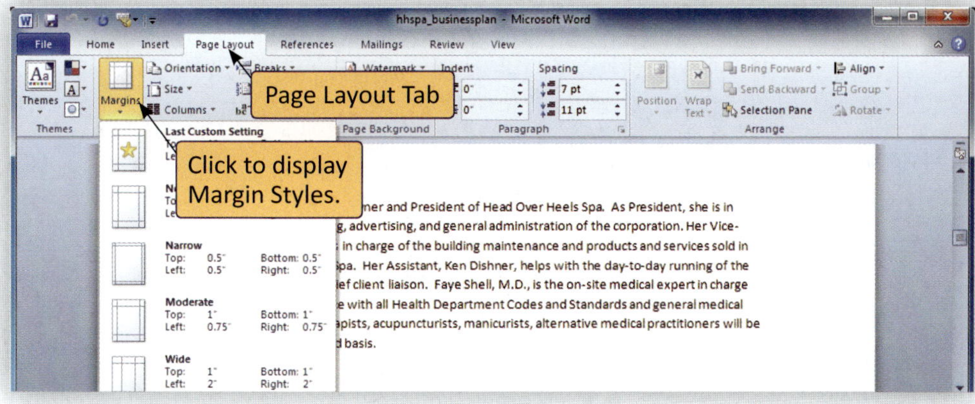

FIGURE WD 3.20

tips & tricks

While most documents you create will use the Normal or Moderate settings for margins, some documents will require either less or more space around the text. If you have a large exhibit or table, you may want to make the margins narrow so the content will still fit in portrait orientation. On the other hand, if you are writing a letter, you may want to increase your margins to accommodate preprinted stationery.

tell me more

The default settings for margins in Word 2003 used to be 1 inch for the top and bottom and 1.25 inches for the left and right. Starting in Word 2007, Microsoft changed this default setting to be 1 inch for all four margins.

try this

If you don't want to use one of Word's preset margins, you can set your own margin specifications in the *Page Setup* dialog box. To open the *Page Setup* dialog box, at the bottom of the *Margins* gallery, select **Custom Margins . . .**

3.13 Inserting Page Breaks and Section Breaks

When text or graphics have filled a page, Word inserts a soft page break and goes on to a new page. However, at times you may want to manually insert a **hard page break**—forcing the text to a new page no matter how much content is on the present page. Typically hard page breaks are used to keep certain information together—for instance, sections of a document.

To insert a hard page break:

1. Click the **Page Layout** tab.
2. In the *Page Setup* group, click the **Breaks** button, and select **Page.**

When you insert a page break, any remaining content in the document appears at the top of the next page. If you want an empty page to appear after the break, you can insert a blank page. When you insert a blank page, Word places a hard break, followed by a blank page, followed by the remaining content of the document.

To insert a blank page:

1. Click the **Insert** tab.
2. In the *Pages* group, click the **Blank Page** button.

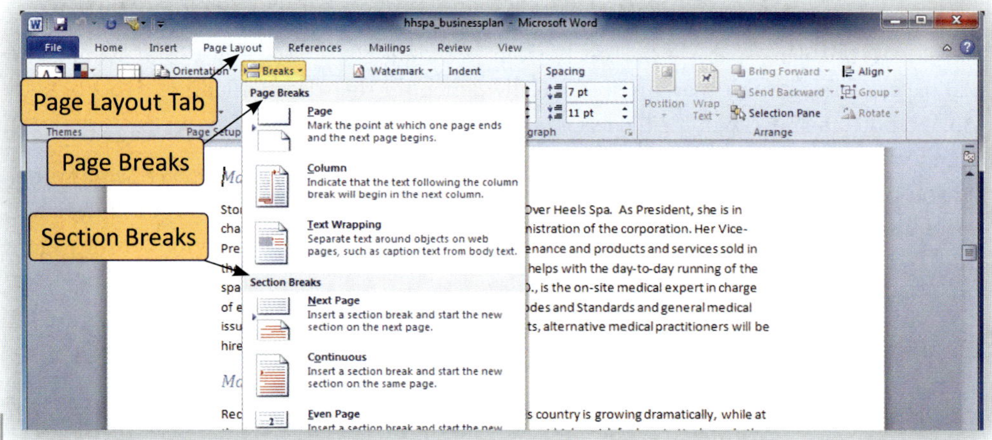

FIGURE WD 3.21

tips & tricks

If you want to remove a hard page break, switch to Draft view so you can see where the break is. Place your cursor below the break and press Delete on the keyboard.

tell me more

There are two basic types of breaks you can add to a document:

- **Page Break**—These breaks create visual breaks in your document but keep the content in the same section. Page breaks include Page, Column, and Text Wrapping.
- **Section Breaks**—These breaks create new sections in your document. Section breaks include Next Page, Continuous, Even Page, and Odd Page.

try this

To insert a hard page break, you can:

- On the *Insert* tab, in the *Pages* group, click the **Page Break** button Page Break.
- Press Ctrl + Enter on the keyboard.

3.14 Adding a Cover Page

When creating documents such as proposals or business plans, it is a good idea to include a cover page that contains the title of the document and the date. You can also add other information such as a subtitle, a short description of the document, and company information. Word 2010 comes with a number of prebuilt cover pages that you can quickly and easily add to your documents.

To add a cover page:

1. Click the **Insert** tab.
2. In the *Pages* group, click the **Cover Page** button and select an option.
3. Word inserts a cover page with content controls for you to enter your own information. Click a content control and enter the information for your document.

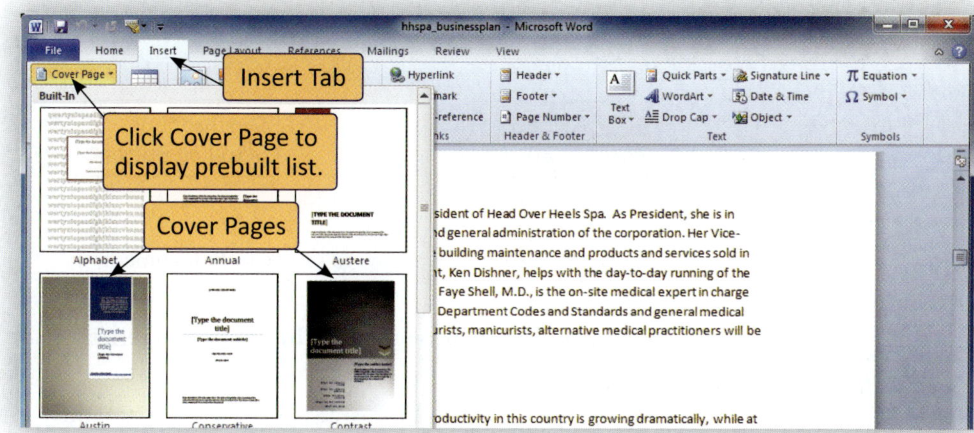

FIGURE WD 3.22

tips & tricks

Most content controls include instructions for adding text to the cover page. However, some content controls, such as the author, do not include text and are hidden from view. One way to see all the fields available in a cover page is to use the Select All command by pressing Ctrl + A on the keyboard.

tell me more

When you click a date content control, you will notice a calendar icon next to the text area. Click the icon to display the calendar to select a date to add to the cover page.

try this

You can also add cover pages through the *Building Blocks Organizer.*

3.15 Viewing Documents Side by Side

If you have two documents that are similar, you may want to compare them to each other. Word's **Compare Side by Side** feature allows you to compare two documents at the same time. When you compare documents, the **Synchronous Scrolling** feature is on by default. This feature allows you to scroll both documents at once. If you scroll the active document, the other document will scroll at the same time, allowing you to carefully compare documents.

FIGURE WD 3.23

To compare two documents side by side:

1. Open the documents you want to compare.
2. Click the **View** tab.
3. In the *Window* group, click the **View Side by Side** button.
4. The two documents are displayed next to each other.
5. Scroll the active window to scroll both documents at once.
6. Click the **Synchronous Scrolling** button to turn the feature off and scroll each document separately.
7. Click the **View Side by Side** button again to turn this feature off.

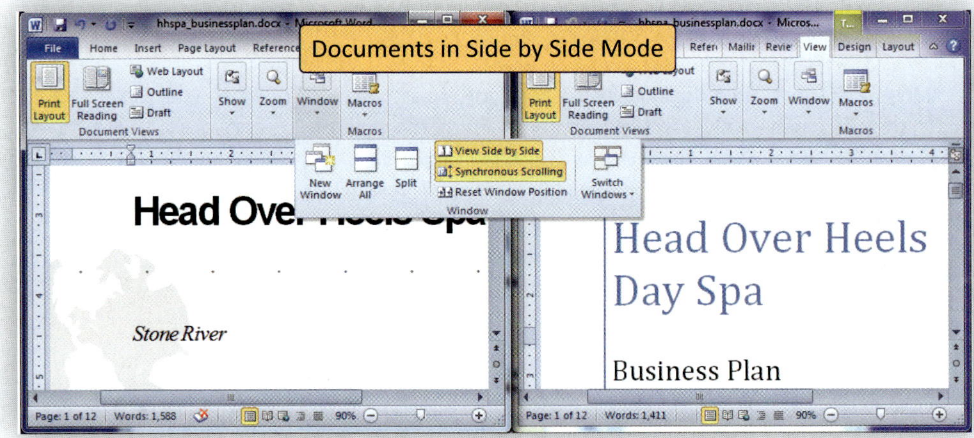

FIGURE WD 3.24

tips & tricks

When you click the *View Side by Side* button, both documents may not display equally on-screen. Click the **Reset Window Position** button to reset the windows so they share the screen equally.

tell me more

If you have more than two documents open, the *Compare Side by Side* dialog box will open when you click the **View Side by Side** button. Select a document in the dialog box to compare with the current document and click **OK.**

Data files for projects can be found on
www.mhhe.com/office2010skills

projects

Skill Review 3.1

Note for student data files: If a document opens in *Protected View,* click on the **Enable Editing** button to allow document to be edited in Word.

In this project you will be editing the *Disclosure Statement_03* document from Placer Hills Real Estate.

1. Open Microsoft Word 2010.
2. Open the *Disclosure Statement_03* document.
3. Save this document as
   ***[your initials]*WD_SkillReview_3-1.**
4. Change line and paragraph spacing and apply a document theme.
   a. Press **Ctrl+A** to select the entire document.
   b. Change line spacing to single space.
   c. Click the **Page Layout** tab.
   d. Change before and after paragraph spacing to **0 pt**.
   e. Click the **Themes** button in the *Themes* group.
   f. Select **Metro** as the theme. This document theme will apply a set of fonts and colors to the document.

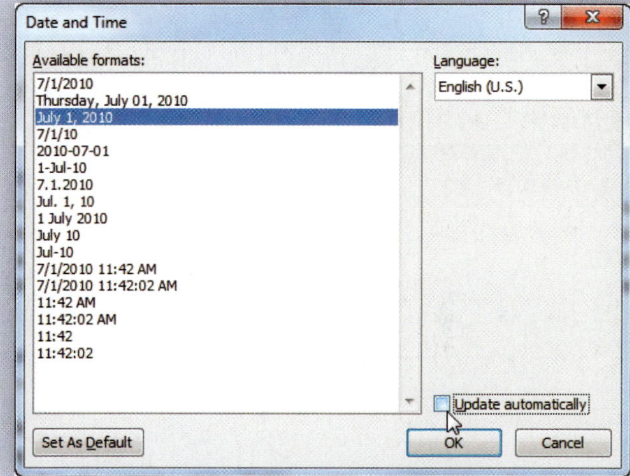

FIGURE WD 3.25

5. Add a date line at the top of the document and change the before paragraph spacing.
   a. Click in front of the first line of the document and press **Enter** four times.
   b. Double-click the header area to activate the header and footer.
   c. The *Header & Footer Tools* contextual tab displays.
   d. On the *Design* tab, in the *Insert* group, click the **Date & Time** button. The *Date and Time* dialog box will open.
   e. In the *Available formats:* area, select the third option (e.g., February 28, 2012).
   f. Deselect the **Update automatically** check box so the date is not automatically updated each time the document is opened.
   g. Click **OK** to close the *Date and Time* dialog box.
   h. Close the header and footer and return to the main document.
6. Change margins on the document.
   a. Click the **Page Layout** tab.
   b. In the *Page Setup* group, click the **Margins** button.
   c. Select the **Wide** setting.

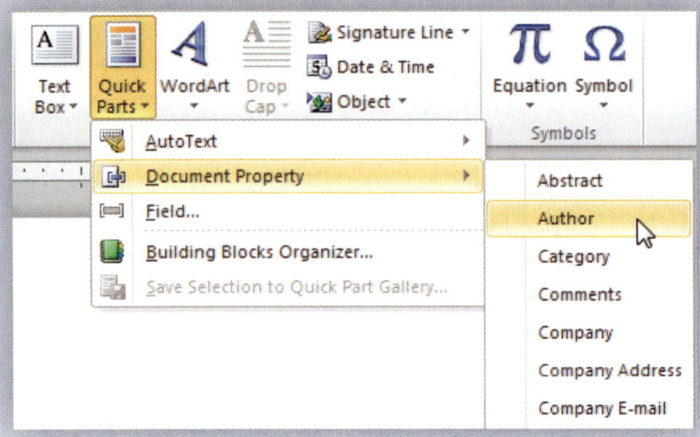

FIGURE WD 3.26

FIGURE WD 3.27

7. Customize *Property Controls.*

a. Click at the end of the document or press **Ctrl+End** to move the cursor to the end of the document.

b. Press **Enter** twice.

c. Click the **Insert** tab.

d. In the *Text* group, click the **Quick Parts** button.

e. Put your mouse pointer on *Document Property* and select **Author.** The *Author* property control will be inserted into your document.

f. If there is text in this property control, delete it and type `Emma Cavalli`.

g. Click after this property control to deselect it and press **Enter**. You also can use the *right arrow key* to deselect a property control.

h. Repeat the above steps to add the following property controls:

Company: `Placer Hills Real Estate`

Company Address: `7100 Madrone Road, Roseville, CA 95722`

Company E-mail: `ecavalli@phre.com`

Company Phone: `916-450-3333`

i. Select all five lines and text you just entered and delete them.

j. Delete any blank lines at the end of the document.

8. Insert text and *property controls* into the document to create the closing lines of the document.

a. Click at the end of the document or press **Ctrl+End** to move the cursor to the end of the document. Your cursor should be at the end of the last paragraph in the document.

b. Press **Enter** twice.

c. Type: `Best Regards` and press **Enter** four times.

d. Click on the **Quick Parts** button in the *Text* group on the *Insert* tab.

e. Put your mouse pointer on *Document Property* and select **Author**. The *Author* property control will be inserted into your document.

f. Click after *Emma Cavalli* and press **Enter**.

g. Type: `Realtor Consultant` and press **Enter**.

h. Insert the **Company** property control into your document.

9. Insert a paragraph of text and include property controls.

a. Click at the end of the last body paragraph in your document and press **Enter** twice.

b. Type the following paragraph inserting property controls where indicated: `As always, if you have any questions or concerns, please call me at` *[Company Phone]* `or e-mail me at` *[Company E-mail].* `Best wishes and thank you for choosing` *[Company].*

(Note: you might have to use the ***right arrow*** *key to deselect the property control fields after inserting them.)*

10. Create a *Quick Part* and save as a *Building Block.*

a. Select the closing lines of the document (*Best Regards* through *Placer Hills Real Estate*).

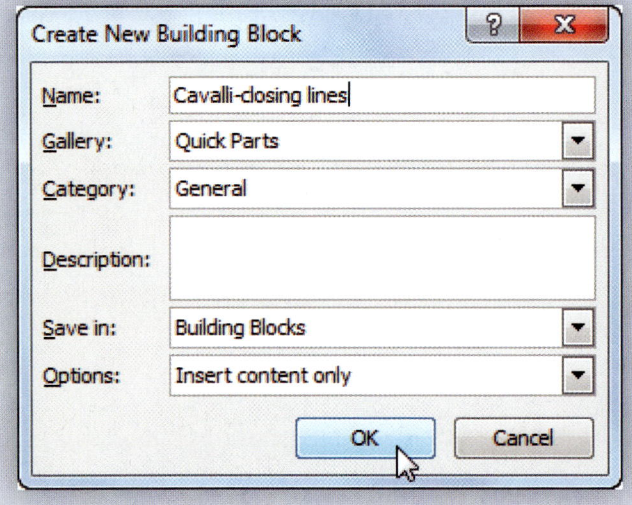

FIGURE WD 3.28

b. On the *Insert* tab, in the *Text* group, click the **Quick Parts** button.

c. Select **Save Selection to Quick Part Gallery.** The *Create New Building Block* dialog box will open.

d. In the *Name* box type: `Cavalli-closing lines`

e. Click **OK** to close the *Create New Building Block* dialog box. The selection will be saved and available to be used from Quick Parts.

f. Select the closing lines of the document (*Best Regards* through *Placer Hills Real Estate*) and press **Backspace** to delete these lines.

g. On the *Insert* tab, in the *Text* group, click the **Quick Parts** button.

h. Select **Cavalli-closing lines** to insert this *Quick Part* into the document.

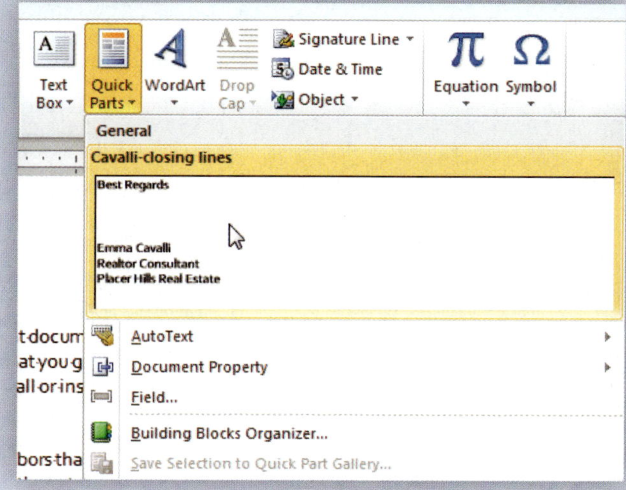

FIGURE WD 3.29

11. Use property controls and text to create information which will later be used as a footer.

a. Go to the end of the document and press **Enter** twice.

b. Set a right tab at 6″. You can use either the ruler or the *Tabs* dialog box.

c. Insert the **Author** property control, click at the end of this control, and press **Tab** to move to the right margin.

d. Insert the **Company** property control, click at the end of this control, and press **Enter** to move to the next line.

e. Insert the **Company Phone** property control, click at the end of this control, and press **Tab** to move to the right margin.

f. Insert the **Company Address** property control, click at the end of this control, and press **Enter** to move to the next line.

g. Insert the **Company E-mail** property control, click at the end of this control, and press **Tab** to move to the right margin.

h. Type: `www.phre.com`

i. Select and bold the first line of this text you just entered.

j. Select the second and third lines of text you just entered and change the font size to **10 pt**.

12. Add a border to text and save text as a *Quick Part.*

a. Select the first line of text entered in the step above (11).

b. Click the **Home** tab.

c. Click the **small arrow** to the right of the *Border* button in the *Paragraph* group.

d. Click **Top Border** to insert a border above the selected line of text.

e. Select all three lines of text.

f. On the *Insert* tab, in the *Text* group, click the **Quick Parts** button.

g. Select **Save Selection to Quick Part Gallery**. The *Create New Building Block* dialog box will open.

h. In the *Name* box type: `Cavalli-footer`

i. Click **OK** to close the *Create New Building Block* dialog box.

j. Select and delete these three lines of text.

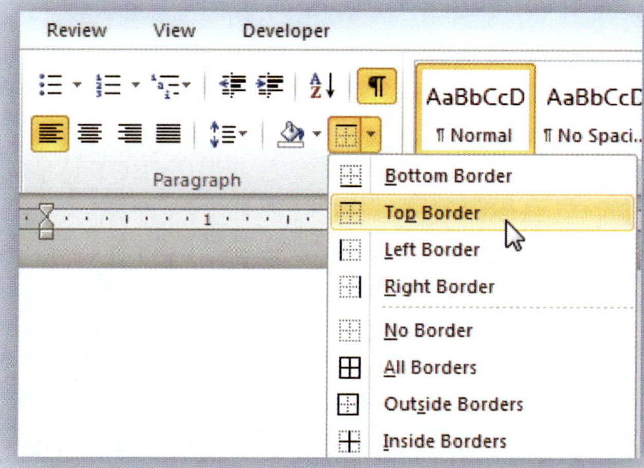

FIGURE WD 3.30

13. Insert a footer into the document.

a. Click the **Insert** tab.

b. Click the **Footer** button in the *Header & Footer* group.

c. Click **Edit Footer**. The footer will open at the bottom of the page.

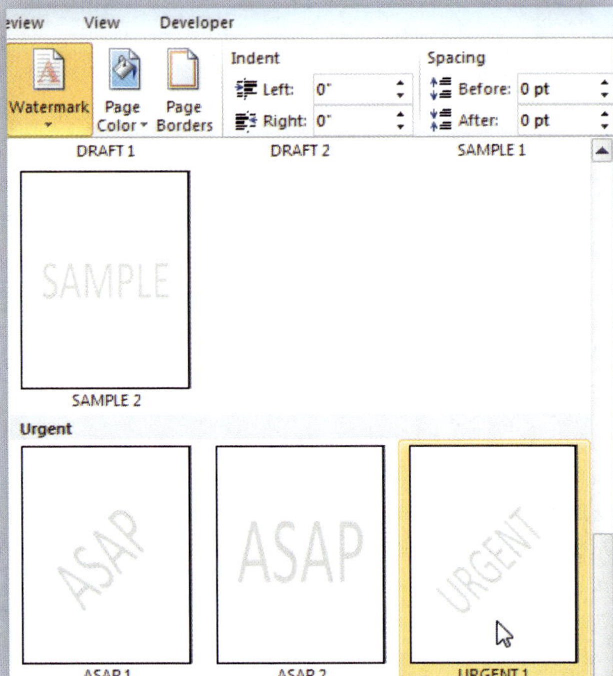

FIGURE WD 3.31

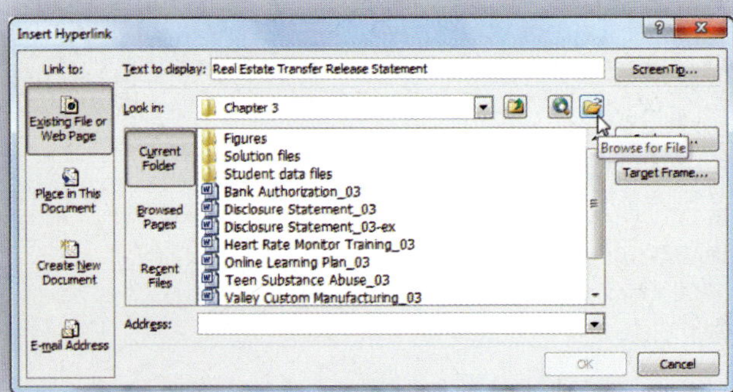

FIGURE WD 3.32

d. Click the **Insert** tab.

e. Click the **Quick Parts** button in the *Text* group.

f. Select **Cavalli-footer** to insert this *Quick Part* into the document.

g. Press **Backspace** to delete the blank line below the footer.

h. Click the **Design** tab and click the **Close Header and Footer** button in the *Close* group. Double-clicking in the body of the document will also close the *Header/Footer.*

14. Insert a watermark on the document.

a. Click the **Page Layout** tab.

b. Click the **Watermark** button in the *Page Background* group.

c. Click **Urgent 1** to insert this watermark into the document. You might have to scroll down to locate this watermark.

15. Insert hyperlinks into the document.

a. Find and select **Real Estate Transfer Release Statement** in the body of the letter.

b. Click the **Insert** button.

c. Click the **Hyperlink** button in the *Links* group. The *Insert Hyperlink* dialog box will open.

d. In the *Link to:* area click **Existing File or Web Page** if it is not already selected.

e. Click the **Browse for File** button. The *Link to File* dialog box will open.

f. In the menu to the right of the *File name:* box, click **Office Files** and select **All Files** to display all of the files in the selected folder.

g. Browse to the folder containing your student data files and select the **Form 521** .pdf file.

h. Click **OK** to close the *Link to File* dialog box.

i. Click **OK** to insert the hyperlink and close the *Insert Hyperlink* dialog box. The selected text now appears as a hyperlink.

16. Modify a property control.

a. Click the phone number (*Company Phone* property control) in the last body paragraph of the letter.

b. Change the phone number to **916-450-3334** and click outside of the property control. Notice that the phone number in the footer is also changed.

17. Use *View Side by Side* to view the edited document with the original document.
    a. Click the **File** tab to open the Backstage.
    b. Click the **Open** button. The *Open* dialog box will open.
    c. Browse to find the *Disclosure Statement_03* document from your student data files.
    d. Select the file and click the **Open** button. This document will open.
    e. Click the **View** tab.
    f. Click the **View Side by Side** button in the *Window* group. The two documents will be displayed side by side. Examine the two documents.
    g. Scroll down in one of the documents. Notice how they scroll down together.
    h. Click the **View Side by Side** button in the *Window* group to close this viewing option.
18. Close each document, saving the `[your initials]WD_SkillReview_3-1` file. Do not save the *Disclosure Statement_03* file.

Skill Review 3.2

In this project you will be editing the *Heart Rate Monitor Training_03* document from American River Cycling Club.

1. Open the *Heart Rate Monitor Training_03* document.
2. Save this document as `[your initials]WD_SkillReview_3-2`.
3. Change the document margins, theme fonts, and theme colors.
    a. Click the **Page Layout** tab.
    b. Click the **Margins** button in the *Page Setup* group.
    c. Choose **Normal** (1″ top, bottom, left, and right margins).
    d. On the *page layout* tab, in the *Themes* group, click the **Colors** button.
    e. Choose **Grid** as the theme colors.
    f. On the *page layout* tab, in the *Themes* group, click the **Fonts** button.
    g. Choose **Austin** as the theme fonts.
    h. Select the entire document and change the font size to **10 pt**.
4. Apply *Quick Styles* to title and section headings.
    a. Select the title of the document.
    b. Apply the **Title** style to the title.
    c. Use the *Font* dialog box to make the title **22 pt.**, **small caps**, and **bold**.
    d. **Center** the title.
    e. Change the before paragraph spacing on the title to **24 pt**.
    f. Select the first bold heading (*Know Your Resting Heart Rate*).
    g. Apply the **Heading 1** style.
    h. Change the before paragraph spacing to **12 pt**.
    i. Use the *Format Painter* to apply this format to all of the other bolded headings. Remember to double-click the *Format Painter* button to apply to multiple selections and click the button again when finished applying formats.
    j. Select the first italicized heading (*Comparing Heart Rate Values with Others*).
    k. Apply the **Heading 2** style.
    l. Use the *Format Painter* to apply this format to all of the other italicized headings.

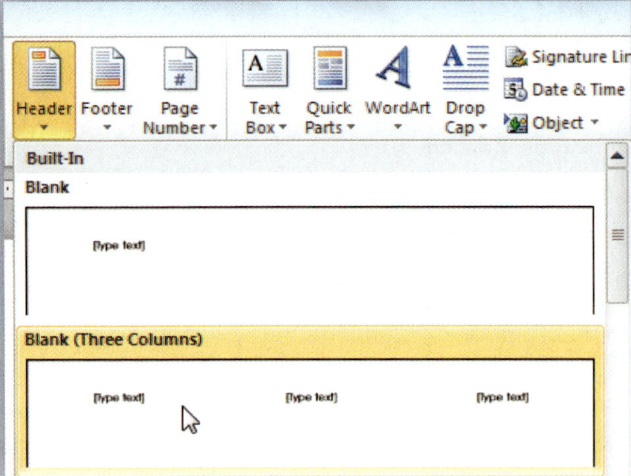

FIGURE WD 3.33

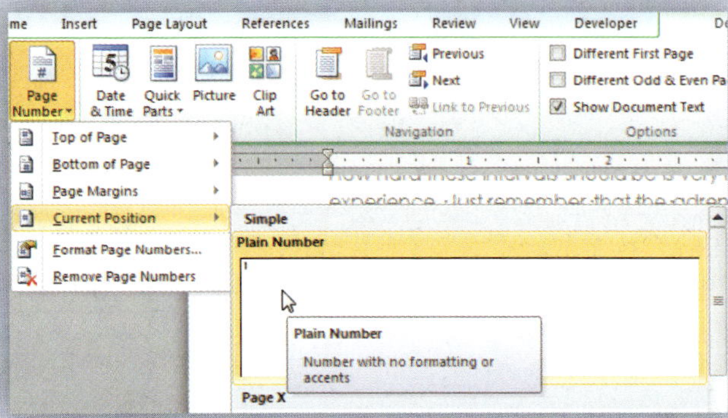

FIGURE WD 3.34

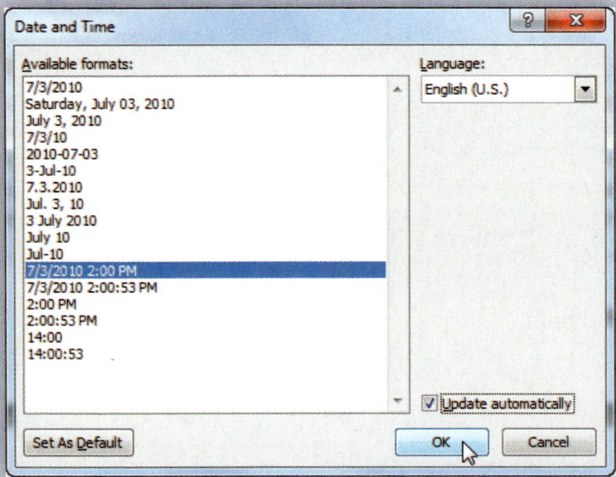

FIGURE WD 3.35

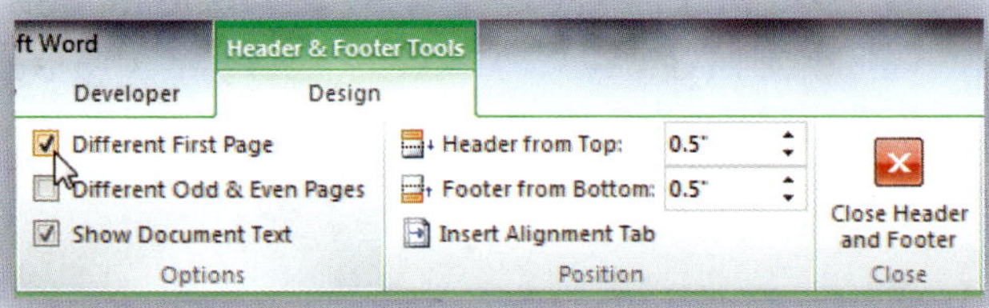

FIGURE WD 3.36

5. Insert a header in the document.

a. Click the **Insert** tab.

b. Click the **Header** button in the *Header & Footer* group.

c. Select **Blank (Three Columns)**. The header of the document will open with three *Type text* fields available.

d. Click in the first *Type text* field and type: `American River Cycling Club`

e. Click in the second *Type text* field and press **Delete** to remove this field.

f. Click in the last *Type text* field and type **your name**.

g. Select the entire line in the header.

h. Press **Ctrl+B** to make bold.

i. Click the **Home** tab.

j. Click the small arrow to the right of the *Border* button in the *Paragraph* group and select **Bottom Border**.

6. Insert a footer in the document.

a. With the header still open, scroll down to the bottom of the page to view the footer.

b. Click in the footer of the document and type `Page` and space once after the word.

c. Click the **Design** tab.

d. Click the **Page Number** button in the *Header & Footer* group.

e. Put your cursor on **Current Position** and then select **Plain Number**. The page number is inserted after the word *Page*.

f. Press **Tab** twice.

g. Type: `Last Modified` and space once after.

h. Click the **Date & Time** button in the *Insert* group. The *Date and Time* dialog box will open.

i. Select the format with the date and time (e.g., *7/3/2010 2:00 PM*).

j. Select the **Update automatically** check box.

k. Click **OK** to insert the date/time and close the *Date and Time* dialog box.

l. Select the entire footer.

m. Click the **Home** tab.

n. Change the font to **9 pt.** and add a **Top Border**.

o. Click the **Design** tab.

p. Click on the **Different First Page** check box. This will turn off the header/footer on the first page so the header/footer will only be displayed on second and continuing pages.

q. Click on the **Close Header and Footer** button in the *Close* group.

7. Add a page border and color to the document.

a. Press **Ctrl+Home** to move to the top of the document.

b. Click the **Page Layout** tab.

c. Click the **Page Borders** button in the *Page Background* group. The *Borders and Shading* dialog box will open.

d. In the *Setting:* area, click **Shadow**.

e. In the *Style:* area, select the solid line.

f. In the *Color:* area, the theme color should already be selected. If it is not, choose **Tan**, **Accent 1**.

g. In the *Width:* area, choose **2¼ pt**.

h. In the *Apply to:* area, choose **Whole document** if it is not already selected.

i. Click **OK** to apply the page border and close the *Borders and Shading* dialog box.

j. Click the **Page Color** button in the *Page Background* group.

k. Select **Tan**, **Accent 2**, **Lighter 80%** for the page color.

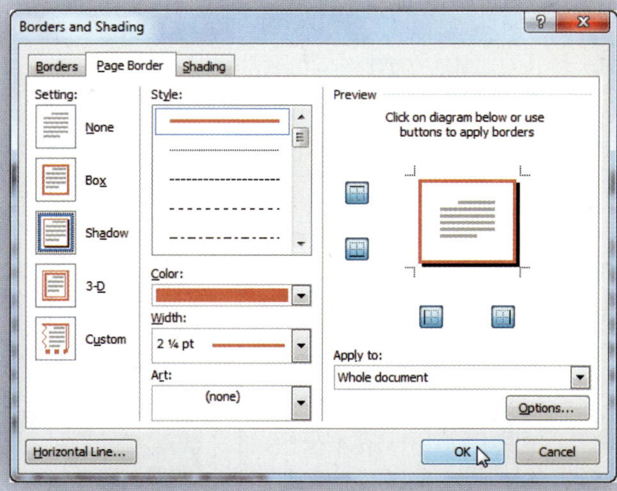

FIGURE WD 3.37

FIGURE WD 3.38

8. Insert page breaks.

a. Click in front of the *Analyze Your Heart Rate Data* heading near the bottom of the first page.

b. Click the **Page Layout** tab.

c. Click the **Breaks** button in the *Page Setup* group.

d. Select **Page** to insert a page break before the heading. The heading and text following are moved to the top of the second page.

e. Click in front of the *Not Being Aware of Factors Affecting Heart Rate* heading near the bottom of the second page.

f. Press **Ctrl+Enter** to insert a page break before this heading.

9. Add a cover page to the document.

a. Press **Ctrl+Home** to move to the top of the document.

b. Click the **Insert** tab.

c. Click the **Cover Page** button in the *Pages* group.

d. Select **Austin** as the cover page. The cover page is inserted before the first page of the document.

e. Click in the **Abstract** area and type: `In this document are some tips to help you use your heart rate monitor to improve the effectiveness of your training rides.`

f. Click in the **Title** area and type: `Tips For Better Heart Rate Monitor Training`

g. Select the text in the *Title* area and change the font size to **24 pt**. and **bold** the text.

h. Click in the **Subtitle** area and type: `American River Cycling Club`

i. Select the text in the *Subtitle* area and change the font size to **14 pt**. and **bold** the text.

j. Click in the **Author** area and type **your name**.

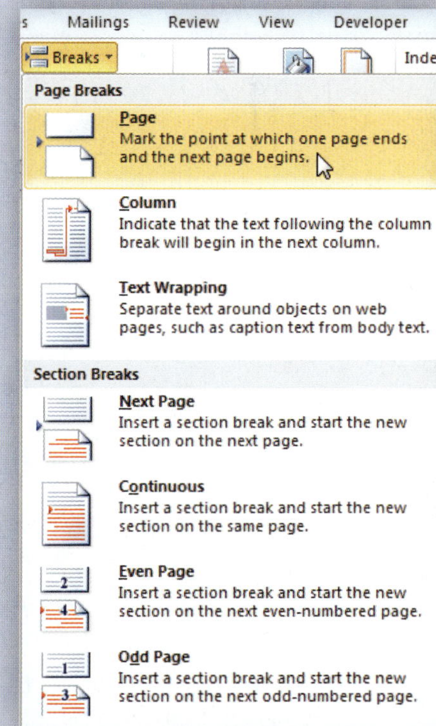

FIGURE WD 3.39

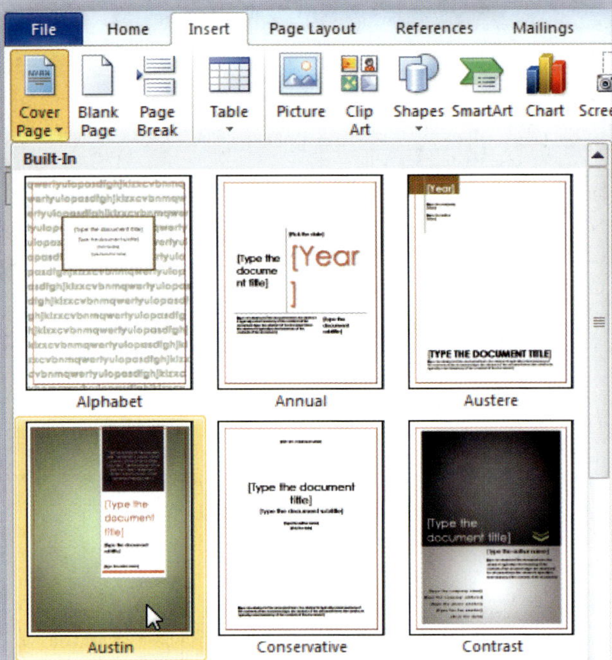

FIGURE WD 3.40

10. Insert a hyperlink into the document.
    a. Locate and select **American River Cycling Club** in the first body paragraph of the document.
    b. Click the **Insert** tab.
    c. Click the **Hyperlink** button in the *Links* group (or press **Ctrl+K**) to open the *Insert Hyperlink* dialog box.
    d. In the *Link to:* area click the **Existing File or Web Page** button.
    e. In the *Address:* area type: `http://www.americanrivercyclingclub.org`
    f. Click **OK** to insert the hyperlink and close the *Insert Hyperlink* dialog box. The selected text now appears as a hyperlink.
11. Save and close the document.

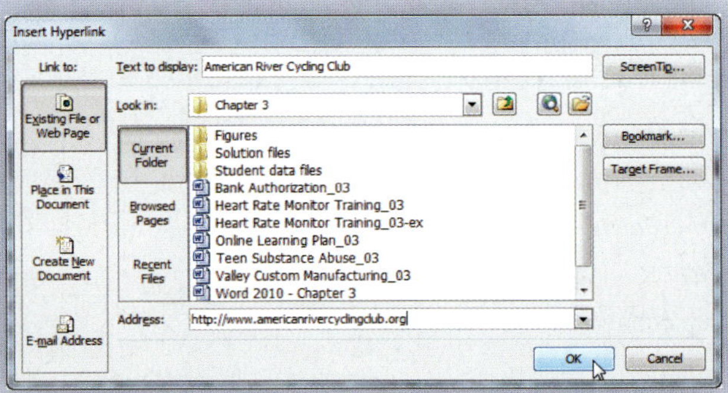

FIGURE WD 3.41

challenge yourself 1

In this project you will be editing the *Bank Authorization_03* document from Placer Hills Real Estate.

1. Open the *Bank Authorization_03* document.
2. Save this document as ***[your initials]*WD_Challenge_3-3.**
3. Change the margins to the **Office 2003 Default** setting.
4. Apply the **Thatch** theme to the document.
5. Select the entire document and make the following changes.
    a. Change the font size to **12 pt**.
    b. Change the after paragraph spacing to **18 pt**.
    c. Change the line spacing to single space.
6. Delete the extra blank lines in the document.

7. Click at the top of the document and insert the date in the proper business letter format (January 1, 2012). Make sure the date updates automatically.
8. Press **Enter** after the date.
9. Select **Authorization Letter to Lender**.
10. Apply the **Book Title** style and change the font size to **12 pt**.
11. Click at the end of the document and press **Enter**.
12. Add/modify the following property controls:

    Author: `Emma Cavalli`

    Company: `Placer Hills Real Estate`

    Company Address: `7100 Madrone Road, Roseville, CA 95722`

    Company E-mail: `ecavalli@phre.com`

    Company Phone: `916-450-3334`
13. Select and delete all of the property controls you just inserted and make sure there are no extra Enters after *Sincerely*.
14. Click after *Sincerely* and press **Enter** twice.
15. Insert the **Author, Company,** and **Company Phone** property controls. Use a line break (*Shift+Enter*) after each property control to place each on a separate line.
16. Open the footer (*Edit Footer*) of the document and insert the **Cavalli-footer** *Quick Part* created in *Skill Review 3.1*. Use **Backspace** to delete the extra line at the end of the footer and then close the footer.
17. Click at the end of the *Borrower Name(s)* line, press **Enter,** and type the following sentence inserting property controls where indicated: `Please consider this my/our authorization to you to provide any and all information regarding our above referenced loan to` *[Author], [Company]* `as per my/our request.`
18. Press **Enter** at the end of the sentence you just entered.
19. Select the lines **Bank/Financial Institution** through **Borrower Name(s)**.
    a. Apply the **Small caps** font effect.
    b. Set a **5.5″** right tab with a solid underline leader.
    c. Press **Tab** at the end of each of these lines to insert the solid underline leader.
20. Select the first **Seller/Borrower Signature(s)** line.
21. Use the *Borders and Shading* dialog box to insert a **solid 1½ pt. top border** to the selection to create a line for a signature(s).
22. Insert a blank line above the date and insert the **Company** property control .
23. Apply the **Title** style to this line and make it **all caps**.
24. Select this line and save it to the *Quick Part* gallery. Save it as **PHRE**.
25. Insert the **Confidential 1** watermark into the document.
26. Open the original document (*Bank Authorization_03*) and compare it to the modified document.
27. Close both documents. When prompted, save the document you modified.

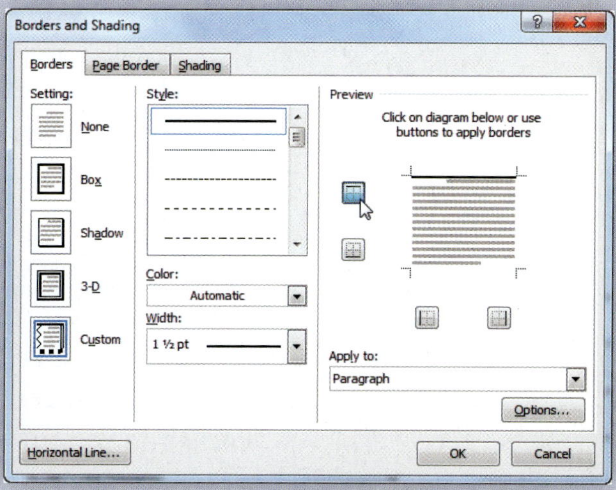

FIGURE WD 3.42

challenge yourself 2

In this project you will be editing the *Teen Substance Abuse_03* document from Courtyard Medical Plaza.

1. Open the *Teen Substance Abuse_03* document.
2. Save this document as `[your initials]WD_Challenge_3-4`.
3. Change the margins to use the **Normal** setting.
4. Select the entire document and make the following changes.
   a. Change the font size to **12 pt**.
   b. Change the line spacing to single space.
   c. Change the after paragraph spacing to **10 pt**.
5. Change the theme font to **Waveform** and the theme color to **Opulent**.
6. Select the title of the document and apply the **Title** style, and use **bold** and **small caps**.
7. Select the first section heading (*What Is Teen Substance Abuse?*) and apply the **Intense Reference** style.
8. Change the font size of this heading to **13 pt**.
9. Use the *Format Painter* to apply this style to the remaining headings in the document.
10. In the *What Are The Signs of Substance Abuse?* section, select the second through fifth paragraphs in this section.
11. Apply a bullet of your choice. Using the *Paragraph* dialog box, deselect the **Don't add space between paragraphs of the same style** check box so the after paragraph spacing remains consistent.
12. Use the *Format Painter* to apply this bullet format to the last five paragraphs in the *Can Teen Substance Use and Abuse Be Prevented?* section.
13. Insert a header and footer into your document.
    a. Use the **Austere (Odd Page)** for the header.
    b. In the *Title* property control field, type `Courtyard Medical Plaza`
    c. In the *Date* property control field, select the **current date** and then center this field.
    d. Use the **Page Number** button to insert the **Bold Numbers 3** page number at the bottom right of the page. Use **Backspace** to remove the blank line after the page number in the footer.
    e. Set the header/footer to display only on second and continuing pages.
    f. Scroll through your document to ensure that the header and footer only appear on the second and continuing pages of the document.
14. Select the header and add it to the *Quick Part* gallery. Save this building block as **CMP-header**.
15. Select the footer and add it to the *Quick Part* gallery. Save this building block as **CMP-footer**.
16. Apply a page border and page color of your choice to the document. Make sure the colors match the theme of your document and the page color is light enough so that the text is readable.
17. Use page breaks where necessary to keep sections together.
18. Insert a cover page of your choice.
    a. Use **Courtyard Medical Plaza** as the *Title* property control. If you change this property control, it will also be changed in the header of the document.

b. Fill in other property controls as needed.

c. Change font size, alignment, and style as needed to make the cover page informative, attractive, and professional.

19. Go to the end of the document and press **Enter** twice.

20. Enter the following text: `For more information visit the Courtyard Medical Plaza Web site (www.cmp.com).`

21. Create a hyperlink to **Courtyard Medical Plaza,** use `www.cmp.com` as the URL.

22. Select this last line of text, center it, and apply a border of your choice to this paragraph.

23. Save and close the document.

on your own

In this project you will be editing the *Valley Custom Manufacturing_03* document from Central Sierra Insurance.

1. Open the *Valley Custom Manufacturing_03* document.
2. Save this document as ***[your initials]*WD_OnYourOwn_3-5.**
3. Insert a **Page break** before the *Liability* heading.
4. Change the margins to use the **Normal** setting.
5. Click after the last of the first page and press **Enter** twice.
6. Type `Sincerely,` and press **Enter** four times.
7. Insert the **Author** property control and change the author to **Jennie Owings, Vice President.**
8. On the next line, insert the **Company** property control and change the company to **Central Sierra Insurance**.
9. Press **Enter** twice after the company name and type `Enclosure`.
10. Select the closing lines you just inserted and add it to the *Quick Part* gallery. Save this building block as **Owings-closing**.
11. Insert the current date at the top of the letter on the first page and press **Enter** four times after. Set the date so it does not update automatically.
12. Choose and apply a document theme of your choice. The letter should fit on the first page. If it does not, change the font size or theme as necessary. Make sure there is a consistent font and size throughout the document.
13. Select the first section heading (**Liability**:) and apply a Quick Style of your choice. Make this heading look professional by making changes to size, style, effects, and/or paragraph spacing.
14. Apply this style to the other section headings in the document (**Property** and **Autos & Trailers**).
15. Select the six building paragraphs in the *Property* section (**Manufacturing Building** through **Sales Building**) and apply numbering to these paragraphs. **Bold** each of the building names (e.g., **Manufacturing Building**).
16. Insert a header and footer and include the following information:

    a. On the first line of the header at the left, type: `Valley Custom Manufacturing`

b. On the next line insert the current date. Set the date so it does not update automatically.

c. On the next line insert the current page number.

d. Press **Enter** twice after the page number.

e. Insert a bottom border on the page number line.

f. In the footer, insert the **Author** property control field at the left and the **Company** property control field at the right. Adjust the right tab if necessary.

g. Insert a top border above the information in the footer.

h. Set the header and footer so they do not appear on the first page, but appear on the second and continuing pages.

17. Add the **Confidential 1** watermark to the document.
18. On the first page adjust the before paragraph spacing on the date line to balance the letter on the page.
19. Select **Central Sierra Insurance** in the first paragraph of the letter and insert a hyperlink. Use `www.centralsierra.com` as the URL.
20. If necessary, change the font and size of the text in the header and footer to match the font and size of the text in the body of the document.
21. Use page breaks where necessary to keep information together.
22. Save and close the document.

fix it

In this project you will be editing the *Online Learning Plan_03* document from Sierra Pacific Community College District. Use the Word features you have learned in this and previous chapters to enhance this report.

1. Open the *Online Learning Plan_03* document.
2. Save this document as ***[your initials]*WD_FixIt_3-6.**
3. Choose a color theme and font theme of your choice.
4. Change the margins to use the **Office 2003 Default** setting.
5. On the entire document, change the font size to **12 pt.**, the line spacing to **1.15**, and the after paragraph spacing to **10 pt**.
6. Delete any extra blank lines in the document.
7. On the bulleted list at the end of the document, edit the list so all of the bullets are at the same level and change the left indent so the bullets line up at the left margin.
8. Insert the **Company** property control at the top of the document. Change the company name to **Sierra Pacific Community College District**.
9. On the next line insert the **Title** property control. Change the title to **Online Learning Plan.** Press **Enter** after this property control field so it is on a line by itself.
10. Apply the **Title** style to the first line of the document. Decrease the size as necessary to make it fit on one line and center this line.
11. Apply the **Subtitle** style to the next line of the document (*Online Learning Plan*) and increase the size of this line, bold it, and make it small caps.
12. Apply the **Heading 1** style to each of the four main headings in the document.
13. Apply the **Heading 2** style to each of the subheadings in the *Where Are We Now with Online Learning* section.

14. Apply the **Heading 3** style to each of the course types in the *Definition of Online Learning Modes* section.
15. Apply a **1 pt.** bottom border to each of the *Heading 1* style headings. The color of the border should be consistent with the color theme of the document.
16. Modify the footer and header.
    a. Insert the current date after **Last Modified:**, and set the date to update automatically.
    b. Insert the **Title** property control field between the company name and *Last Modified.*
    c. Adjust the font size of the text in the footer so all of the information fits and there is space between each of the different items.
    d. Adjust the tabs so the center tab is in the middle of the typing line and the right tab is at the right margin.
    e. Remove the existing page number and insert a right-aligned page number in the header. Use a format that includes both the page number and the number of pages (e.g., 1 of 4).
    f. Set the header and footer so they do not appear on the first page.
17. Remove the page color from the document and add a page border of your choice.
18. Insert a cover page of your choice. Customize the control property fields as needed.
19. Include a watermark with the word **Draft.**
20. Use page breaks as necessary to control pagination.
21. Insert a hyperlink on **Sierra Pacific Community College District** in the first paragraph of the body of the report. Use `www.spccd.edu` as the URL.
22. Save and close the document.

Note to student: If you are using a public computer, you will want to delete the saved Quick Parts from this computer after you have completed these exercises. In the *Building Blocks Organizer,* select and delete the Quick Parts you have created in these exercises.

chapter 4

Working with Tables and Graphics

In this chapter, you will learn the following skills:

- Create, enter text, and edit tables
- Merge cells, align data within cells, and sort data
- Apply borders and Quick Styles to tables
- Insert pictures, resize graphics, and organize graphics around text
- Insert clip art, WordArt, SmartArt, shapes; apply styles to graphics; and add captions to graphics.

skills

introduction

This introductory chapter will show students how to enhance the appearance and readability of a document by including tables and graphics within Word documents, editing these objects, and applying styles to these objects. Students will learn how to create and edit tables; use borders and Quick Styles on tables; insert and edit pictures, Clip Art, WordArt, SmartArt, and shapes; and apply styles and formatting to tables and graphics.

4.1 Creating a Table

A **table** helps you organize information for effective display. Tables are organized by rows, which display horizontally, and columns, which display vertically. The intersection of a row and column is referred to as a **cell**. Tables can be used to display everything from dates in a calendar to sales numbers to product inventory.

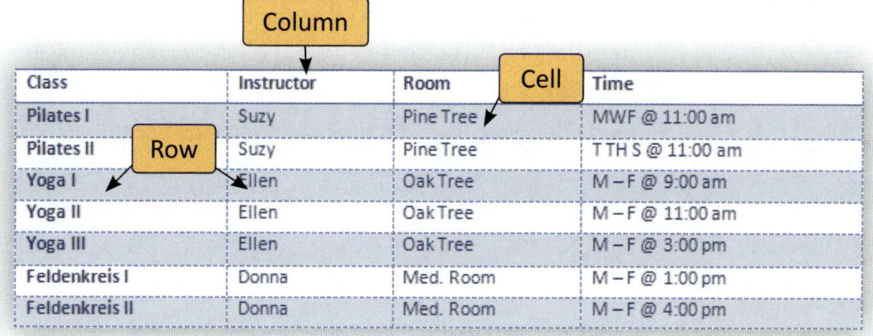

Class	Instructor	Room	Time
Pilates I	Suzy	Pine Tree	MWF @ 11:00 am
Pilates II	Suzy	Pine Tree	T TH S @ 11:00 am
Yoga I	Ellen	Oak Tree	M – F @ 9:00 am
Yoga II	Ellen	Oak Tree	M – F @ 11:00 am
Yoga III	Ellen	Oak Tree	M – F @ 3:00 pm
Feldenkreis I	Donna	Med. Room	M – F @ 1:00 pm
Feldenkreis II	Donna	Med. Room	M – F @ 4:00 pm

FIGURE WD 4.1

To create a simple table:

1. Click the **Insert** tab.
2. Click the **Table** button.
3. Select the number of cells you want by moving the cursor across and down the squares.
4. When the description at the top of the menu displays the number of rows and columns you want, click the mouse.
5. The table is inserted into your document.

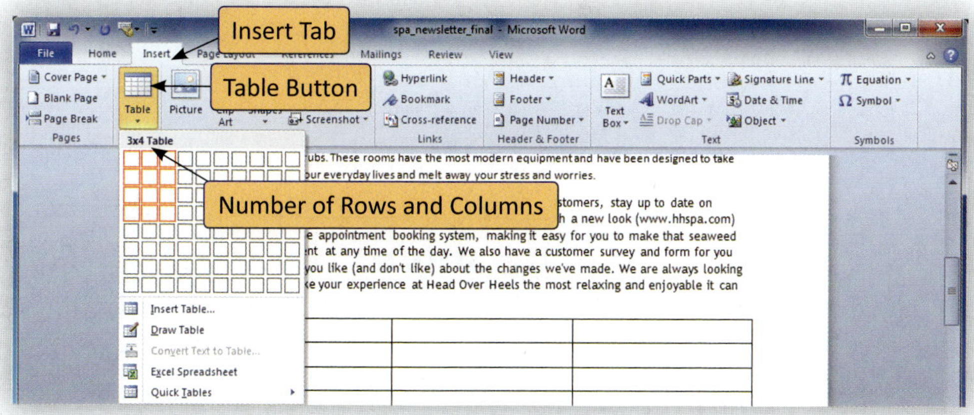

FIGURE WD 4.2

tips & tricks

Rather than inserting a table and then adding data, you can convert existing text into a table. After selecting the text to be converted, click the **Table** button and click **Insert Table . . .** The number of rows and columns will automatically be determined by the tabs and paragraphs in the selection.

tell me more

Word 2010 comes with a number of Quick Tables building blocks. These templates are preformatted for you and include sample data. To insert a Quick Table, click the **Tables** button, point to **Quick Tables,** and select a building block option from the gallery. After you insert a Quick Table, just replace the sample data with your own.

try this

To insert a table, you can:

1. Click the **Table** button and select **Insert Table . . .**
2. In the *Insert Table* dialog box, enter the number of rows and columns for your table.
3. Click **OK.**

4.2 Entering Data in a Table

Once you have inserted a blank table, you will need to enter data. When entering data in a table, it is a good idea to use the first row as a heading row by typing a short description of the content for the column in each cell. After you have labeled each column, continue entering the data into your table.

To enter data in a table:

1. Place the cursor in the cell where you want to enter the data.
2. Type the data just as you would in normal text.
3. Press Tab to move to the next cell and enter more data.
4. When you reach the last cell in the last row of a table, pressing Tab on the keyboard will create a new row in the table.
5. Continue pressing Tab until all data are entered.

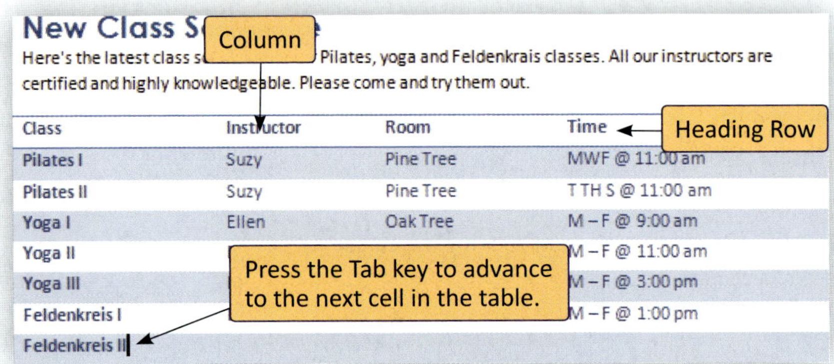

FIGURE WD 4.3

tips & tricks

Each cell is set up as one line, but if you type more data than will fit in one line, Word will automatically wrap and create another line within the cell, making the row taller. If this happens, all the cells in that row will be affected. You also can press ←Enter to force a new line within the cell.

tell me more

When working with tables, the conventional way to identify a cell is by column and row. Columns are typically referred to by letters, and rows by numbers. Thus, the first cell in the third row would be identified as "cell A3" and the third cell in the first row would be identified as "C1."

try this

To move to another cell, you can click in the cell or use the keyboard arrow keys to move across the rows and up and down the columns.

4.3 Inserting Rows, Columns, and Cells

Once you have created a table, you often find you need more rows or columns. With Word, you can easily insert additional rows and columns from the *Table Tools* contextual tabs.

When you place the cursor in a table, the *Table Tools* contextual tabs display. These tabs are called contextual tabs because they only display when a table is the active element. The *Design* tab contains tools to change the look of the table, such as shading and borders. The *Layout* tab contains tools to change how information is displayed in the table, such as row and column commands.

To insert an additional row and column:

1. Click the **Layout** tab under *Table Tools.*
2. To insert a new row, click the **Insert Above** button or the **Insert Below** button.
3. To insert a new column, click the **Insert Left** button or the **Insert Right** button.

To delete a row or column:

1. Click in the row or column you want to delete.
2. Click the **Layout** tab under *Table Tools.*
3. Click the **Delete** button and select an option.

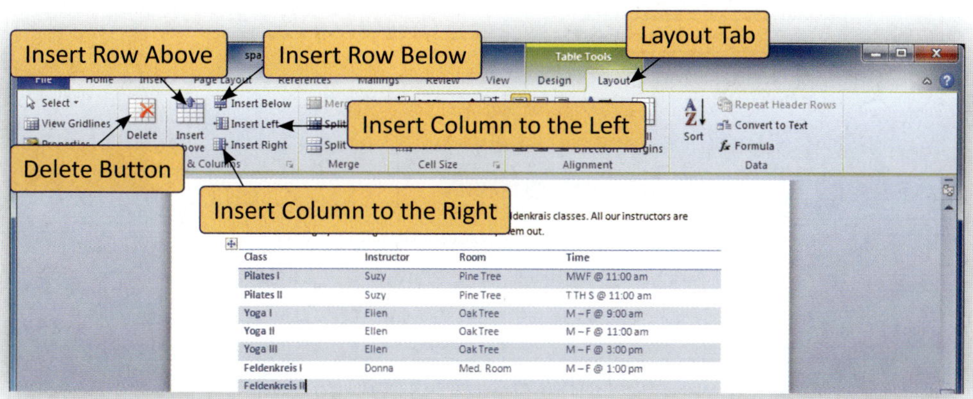

FIGURE WD 4.4

tips & tricks

A quick way to insert a new row at the end of a table is to place the cursor in the last cell in the last row and then press the Tab key. A new row is automatically added to the table, with your cursor in its first cell.

tell me more

Another way to add rows and columns to tables is to copy an existing row or column and then paste it into the table. To copy and paste a row, first select the row you want to copy and click the **Copy** button. Next, place your cursor in the first cell of the row below where you want the copied row to appear. Click the **Paste** button to insert the copied row. You can use the same method to copy and paste columns in tables as well.

try this

To insert rows and columns, you can right-click in a cell, point to **Insert,** and select **Insert Rows Above, Insert Rows Below, Insert Columns to the Left,** or **Insert Columns to the Right.**

4.4 Sizing Tables, Columns, and Rows

When you insert a table, it covers the full width of the page and the columns and rows are evenly spaced. Once you have entered your data, you will probably find that the table is larger than it needs to be and the columns and rows need adjusting. You can resize your table using Word's AutoFit commands.

To adjust the width and height of cells using the AutoFit command:

1. Click in the table you want to resize.
2. Click the **Layout** tab under *Table Tools.*
3. In the *Cell Size* group, click the **AutoFit** button.
4. Select **AutoFit Contents** to resize the cell to fit the text of the table.

To resize all the rows in a table so they have the same height, in the *Cell Size* group click the **Distribute Rows** button. Click the **Distribute Columns** to resize all the columns in a table so they have the same width.

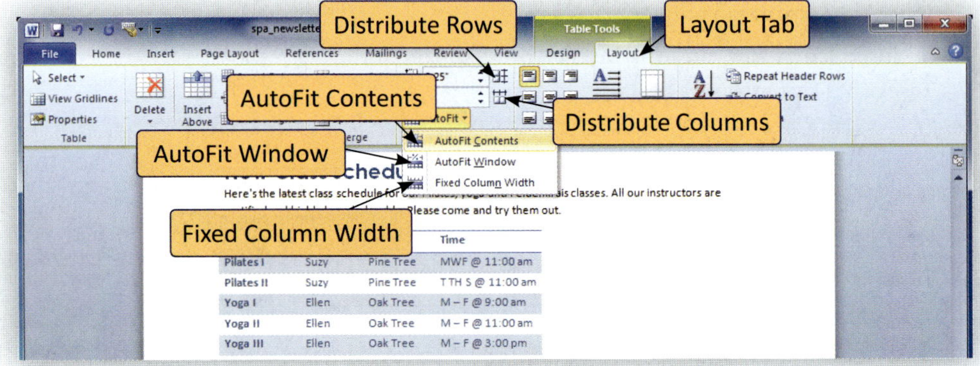

FIGURE WD 4.5

tips & tricks

Once you have resized a table, you will probably want to position it better on the page. You can do this by using the **move handle** tool that appears at the top-left corner of the table when the mouse pointer is placed over the table. Click the move handle and drag the table to where you want it.

tell me more

You can resize a table manually two different ways:

- Rest the mouse pointer anywhere over the table. When the **resize handle** appears at the bottom-right corner of the table, click and drag it until you achieve the desired size. This method can also be used to resize columns and rows.
- Click in the row or column you want to resize. In the *Cell Size* group, adjust the numbers for the **Table Row Height** and **Table Column Width** by clicking the up and down arrows in the control box.

try this

To use the AutoFit command to resize a table, you can right-click in the table, point to **AutoFit,** and select **AutoFit Contents.**

4.5 Merging and Splitting Cells

When you first create a table, it is a grid of rows and columns. But what if you want to display your content across columns or across rows? For instance, if the first row of your table includes the title for the table, then you will probably want to display the title in a single cell that spans all the columns of the table. In this case, you will want to ***merge*** the cells in the first row into one cell. On the other hand, if you have a cell that contains multiple values, you may want to ***split*** the cell so it can display each value in a separate row or column. Use the **merge cells** and **split cells** commands to customize the layout of tables. Merging cells entails combining multiple cells into one, whereas splitting a cell divides the cell into multiple cells.

To merge cells in a table:

1. Select the cells you want to merge into one.
2. Under *Table Tools,* click the **Layout** tab.
3. In the *Merge* group, click the **Merge Cells** button.

To split a cell in a table:

1. Select the cell you want to split.
2. In the *Merge* group, click the **Split Cells** button.
3. In the *Split Cells* dialog box, enter the number of columns and rows.
4. Click **OK** to split the cell.

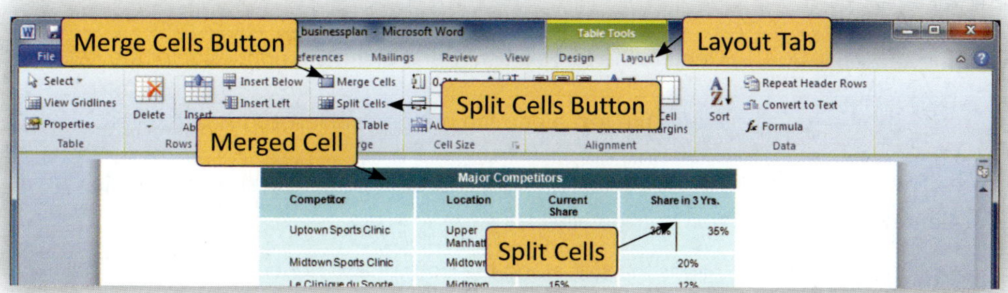

FIGURE WD 4.6

tips & tricks

In addition to splitting cells, you also split a table, creating two tables from one. To split a table into two tables:

1. Place the cursor in the row where you want to split the table.
2. In the *Merge* group, click the **Split Table** button.

tell me more

When you place the cursor in a table, the *Table Tools* tabs display. These tabs are called contextual tabs because they only display when a table is the active element.

try this

- To merge cells, you can right-click the selected cells and select **Merge Cells** from the menu.
- To split cells, you can right-click a cell and select **Split Cells . . .** from the menu.

4.6 Aligning Text in Tables

When entering data in tables, there will be times when you want to change the position of text within a particular cell. While most text in cells is left-aligned, titles and column headings are often center-aligned, and most columns of numbers are right-aligned. You can control both the vertical and horizontal alignment in cells.

To change the alignment of cells:

1. Click the cell you want to change.
2. Under *Table Tools,* click the **Layout** tab.
3. In the *Alignment* group, click one of the nine alignment options:

	Align Top Left	Aligns the text along the top and left edges of the cell.
	Align Top Center	Aligns the text along the top of the cell and centers the text horizontally in the cell.
	Align Top Right	Aligns the text along the top and right edges of the cell.
	Align Center Left	Centers the text vertically and along the left edge of the cell.
	Align Center	Centers the text vertically and horizontally in the cell.
	Align Center Right	Centers the text vertically and along the right edge of the cell.
	Align Bottom Left	Aligns the text along the bottom and left edges of the cell.
	Align Bottom Center	Aligns the text along the bottom of the cell and centers the text horizontally in the cell.
	Align Bottom Right	Aligns the text along the bottom and right edges of the cell.

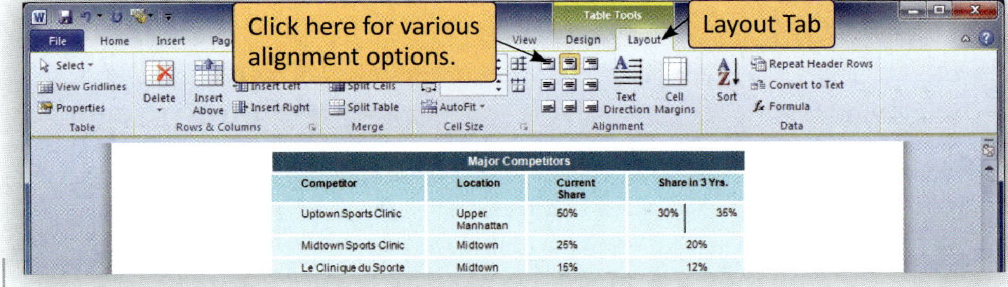

FIGURE WD 4.7

tips & tricks

To manually change the size of margins within cells, click the **Cell Margins** button in the *Alignment* group. The *Table Options* dialog box opens. Here you can adjust the left, right, top, and bottom margins of cells.

tell me **more**

You can change the direction of text in table cells by clicking the **Text Direction** button in the *Alignment* group on the *Layout* tab. The text rotates and is displayed vertically. Click the button again to flip the text the other direction. Click the button a third time to return the text to its original position.

try **this**

- To change the alignment of a cell, you can right-click in the cell, point to **Cell Alignment,** and select an alignment option.
- You can change the horizontal alignment of cells by clicking one of the alignment buttons in the *Paragraph* group on the *Home* tab.

4.7 Sorting Data in Tables

After you have entered data in a table, you may decide it needs to be displayed in a different order. **Sorting** rearranges the rows in your table by the text in a column or columns. Word allows you to sort data based on the first character of each entry. You can sort in alphabetical or numeric order, in either ascending (A–Z) or descending (Z–A) order.

To sort a column alphabetically:

1. Under *Table Tools,* click the **Layout** tab.
2. In the *Data* group, click the **Sort** button.
3. The *Sort* dialog box opens.
4. Click the **Sort by** arrow and select a field to sort by.
5. The *Ascending* radio button is selected by default.
6. Click **OK** to sort the text in the table.

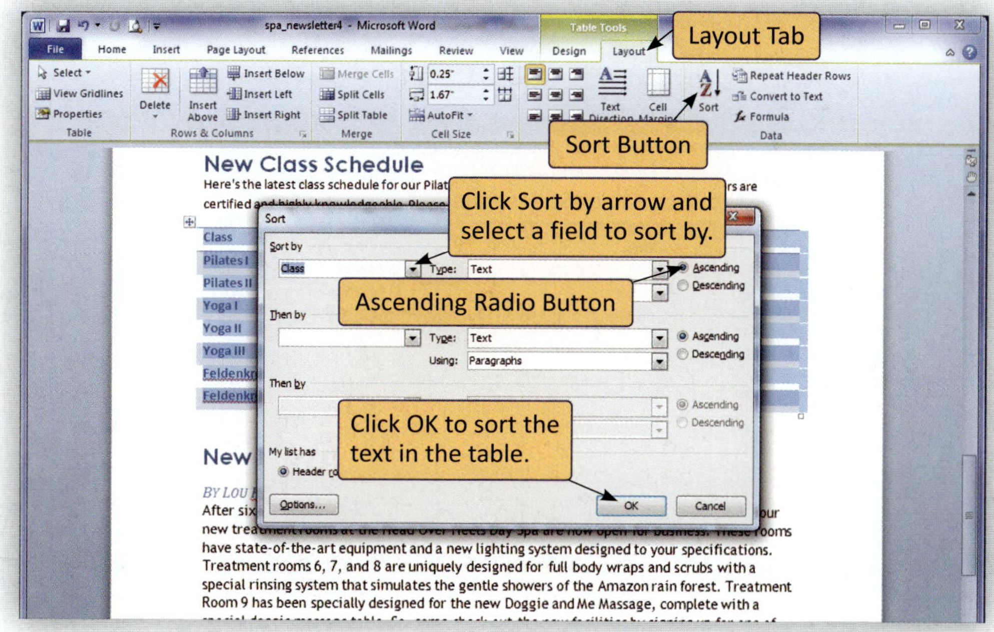

FIGURE WD 4.8

tips & tricks

You can sort by text, number, or date. You can refine the sort by choosing additional fields to sort by:

- If you want to sort the text in reverse order, from Z to A, click the **Descending** radio button.
- Word can sort upper- and lowercase letters differently. Click the **Options . . .** button in the *Sort* dialog box and then click the **Case sensitive** check box in the *Sort Options* dialog box.

try this

To open the *Sort* dialog box, from the *Home* tab, in the *Paragraph* group, click the **Sort** button.

4.8 Adding Table Quick Styles

Just as you can apply complex formatting to paragraphs using Quick Styles for text, you can apply complex formatting to tables using Quick Styles for tables. Using Quick Styles for tables, you can change the text color along with the borders and shading for a table, giving it a professional, sophisticated look without a lot of work.

To apply a Quick Style to a table:

1. Under *Table Tools,* click the **Design** tab.
2. In the *Table Styles* group, click the **More** button.
3. Select a Quick Style from the *Quick Styles* gallery.

By default, the Word *Table Styles* gallery displays styles that include header rows, banded rows, and first column layouts. If you want to change the options that display in the gallery, check or uncheck the options in the *Table Styles Options* group.

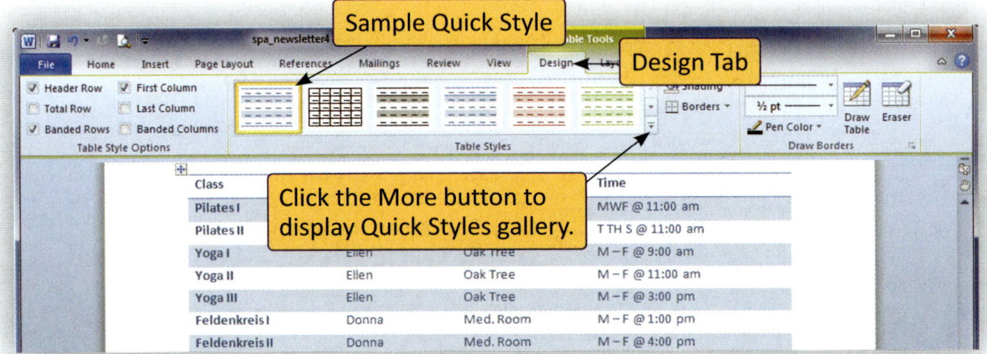

FIGURE WD 4.9

tips & tricks

To create your own table style, click the **More** button and select **New Table Style . . .** In the *Create New Style from Formatting* dialog box, you can create a new table style based on an existing table style, changing options such as grid lines and shading to suit your needs. When you save the style, it will appear in the *Table Styles* gallery.

try this

The *Table Styles* group on the Ribbon displays the latest Quick Styles you have used. If you want to apply a recently used Quick Style, you can click the option directly from the Ribbon without opening the *Quick Styles* gallery.

4.9 Adding Borders to a Table

When you first create a table, it uses the simple grid style. You can apply a Quick Style to your table to quickly add formatting, but what if you want to further adjust the look of a table after applying the Quick Style? You can choose different shading for your table and add and remove borders to change the look of the entire table or just parts of the table.

To change the borders for a table:

1. Select the table you want to change.
2. Under *Table Tools,* click the **Design** tab.
3. In the *Table Styles* group, click the arrow next to the **Borders** button.
4. On the menu that appears, all currently selected options appear active with a background color. Options that are not selected appear without a background color.
5. Click a border option to turn that border on or off in the table.

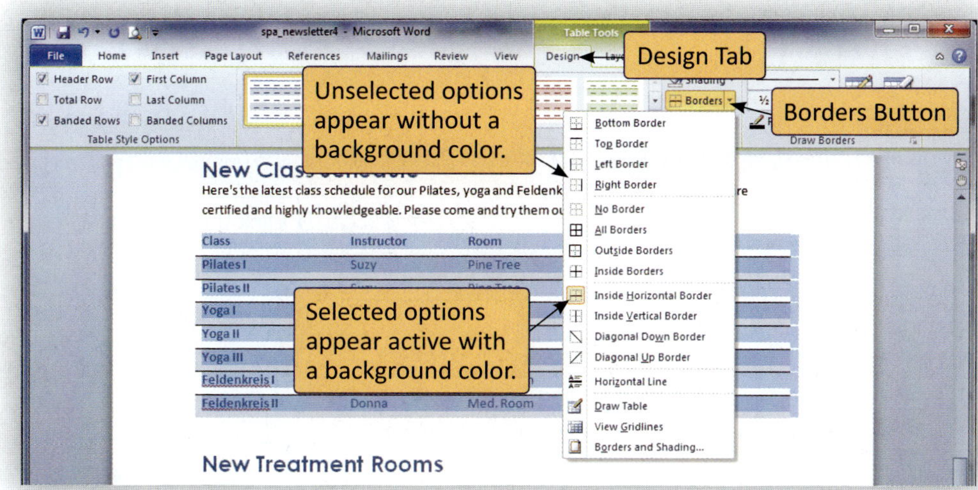

FIGURE WD 4.10

tips & tricks

If your table does not show borders, you can display gridlines to give you a visual guide. The gridlines appear as a dotted line on screen but do not print as part of the final document. To display gridlines, click the **Borders** button and select **View Gridlines.**

tell me more

In addition to changing the borders of a table, you can change the shading, or background color applied to the table. Adding shading to a table helps it stand out on a page. To apply shading to a table, click the **Shading** button in the *Table Styles* group. A palette of colors displays. Select a color to change the background color for the table.

try this

You can change the borders of a table by clicking the *Home* tab. In the *Paragraph* group, click the arrow next to the *Borders* button and select an option.

You can change borders and shading through the *Borders and Shading* dialog box. To open the *Borders and Shading* dialog box:

- From the *Home* tab or from the *Design* tab, click the arrow next to the *Borders* button and select **Borders and Shading . . .**
- Right-click on the table and select **Borders and Shading . . .** from the menu.

4.10 Inserting Clip Art

Word's **clip art** feature allows you to easily insert clips into your document. These **clips** refer to media files from another source. They include images, photographs, scanned material, animations, sound, and video. By default, Word inserts these clips as embedded objects, meaning they become part of the new document (changing the source file will not change them in the new document). The Clip Art task pane allows you to search for different kinds of clips from many different sources.

To insert a clip art image into a document:

1. Click the **Insert** tab.
2. In the *Illustrations* group, click the **Clip Art** button.
3. When the *Clip Art* task pane opens, type a word describing the clip you want in the *Search for:* box.
4. Click the **Go** button.
5. Click the clip you want to insert it into the document

You can narrow your search by media type, only searching for illustrations or photographs or videos or audio clips. Click the **Results should be:** arrow and click the check box in front of a media type to include or exclude those types of files from your search. Click the **All media types** check box to select and deselect all types at once.

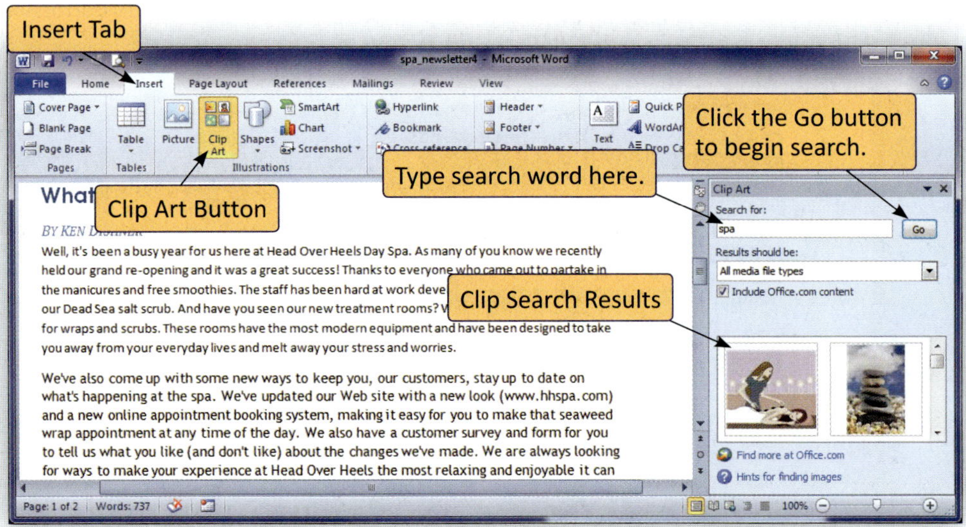

FIGURE WD 4.11

tips & tricks

Microsoft's Web site for office content, *Office.com,* contains more clips for you to use in your documents. If you are connected to the Internet, click the **Include Office.com content** check box to include content from the Web site in your search results.

try this

To insert an image from the *Clip Art* task pane, you can point to the image and click the arrow that appears. A menu of options displays. Click **Insert** on the menu to add the clip to your document.

4.11 Inserting a Picture

You can insert images that you created in another program into your document. By default, Word inserts images as embedded objects, meaning they become part of the new document. Changing the source file will not change or affect the newly inserted image.

To insert an image from a file:

1. Click the **Insert** tab.
2. In the *Illustrations* group, click the **Picture** button.
3. The *Insert Picture* dialog box opens.
4. Navigate to the file location, select the file, and click **Insert.**

To delete a picture, select the picture and press the **Delete** key on the keyboard.

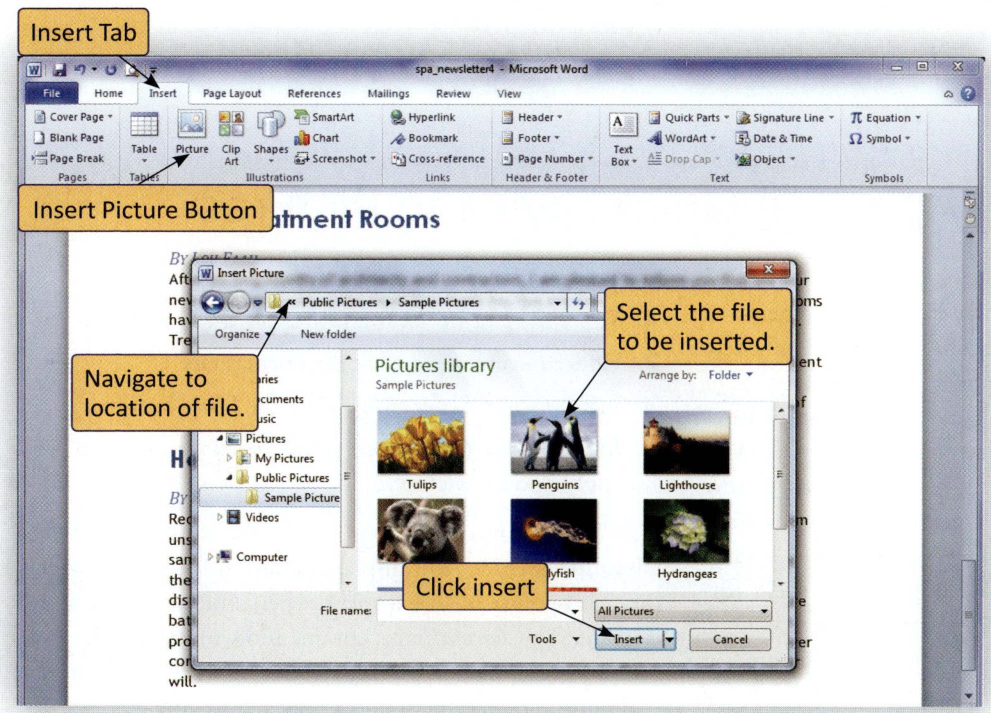

FIGURE WD 4.12

tell me **more**

When you insert a picture to a document, the *Format* tab under *Picture Tools* displays. This tab is called a contextual tab because it only displays when a picture is the active element. The *Format* tab contains tools to change the look of the picture, such as picture style, brightness and contrast, cropping, and placement on the page.

try **this**

To insert the file, you can click the **Insert** button arrow and select **Insert**.

from the perspective of . . .

MEDICAL PROFESSIONAL

Word processing software enables me to record a patient's history, medications, and symptoms. I can easily organize a patient's information using a table, creating an easy-to-read, professional document.

4.12 Applying Quick Styles to Pictures

Quick Styles are a combination of formatting that gives elements of your document a more polished, professional look without a lot of work. Quick Styles for pictures include a combination of borders, shadows, reflections, and picture shapes, such as rounded corners or skewed perspective. Instead of applying each of these formatting elements one at a time, you can apply a combination of elements at one time using a preset Quick Style.

To apply a Quick Style to a picture:

1. Select the picture you want to apply the Quick Style to.
2. Under *Picture Tools,* click the **Format** tab.
3. In the *Picture Styles* group, click the **More** button.
4. In the *Picture Quick Styles* gallery, click an option to apply it to the picture.

When you insert a picture into a document, the *Format* tab under *Picture Tools* displays. This tab is called a contextual tab because it only displays when a picture is the active element. The *Format* tab contains tools to change the look of the picture, such as picture styles, brightness and contrast, cropping, and placement on the page.

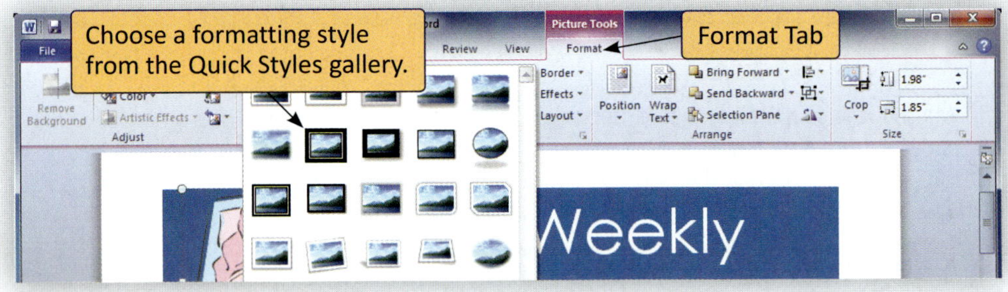

FIGURE WD 4.13

tips & tricks

Once you have applied a Quick Style to a picture, you can further modify the look of the picture using the **Picture Shape, Picture Border,** and **Picture Effects** options.

try this

The *Picture Styles* group displays the latest Quick Styles you have used. If you want to apply a recently used Quick Style, you can click the option directly from the Ribbon without opening the *Quick Styles* gallery.

4.13 Wrapping Text around Graphics

When you first add a graphic to your document, Word inserts the graphic at the insertion point and displays the graphic in line with the text. More often than not, you will want to place the graphic somewhere else on the page. Word comes with a number of preset image positions that include wrapping the text around the image.

To position the image on a page with text wrapping:

1. Under *Picture Tools,* click the **Format** tab.
2. In the *Arrange* group, click the **Position** button.
3. In the *With Text Wrapping* section, select an option.
4. The image is placed on the page according to the option you chose.

	In Line with Text
	Position in Top Left with Square Text Wrapping
	Position in Top Center with Square Text Wrapping
	Position in Top Right with Square Text Wrapping
	Position in Middle Left with Square Text Wrapping
	Position in Middle Center with Square Text Wrapping
	Position in Middle Right with Square Text Wrapping
	Position in Bottom Left with Square Text Wrapping
	Position in Bottom Center with Square Text Wrapping
	Position in Bottom Right with Square Text Wrapping

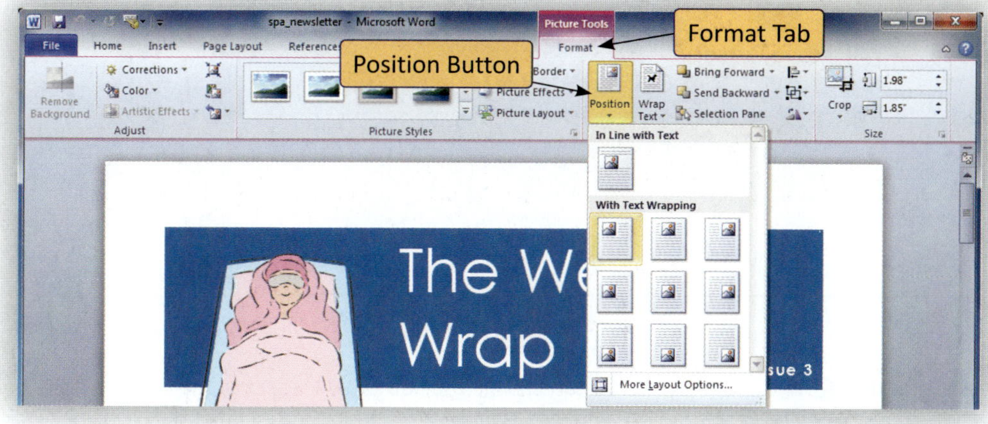

FIGURE WD 4.14

tips & tricks

If you have multiple images, you can layer the images and then arrange them using the **Bring to Front** button [Bring to Front] and **Send to Back** button [Send to Back] in the *Arrange* group.

tell me more

Word's **text wrapping** feature gives you the ability to lay out text and graphics in a number of ways. Other wrapping styles include **Square**, **Tight**, **Behind Text**, **In Front of Text**, **Top and Bottom**, and **Through**. Click the **Wrap Text** button in the *Arrange* group to apply one of these layout options.

try this

You can position images on the page from the *Page Layout* tab. In the *Arrange* group, click the **Position** button and select an option.

4.14 Resizing and Moving Graphics

When you first add an image to a document, you may find it does not appear the way you expected. The image may be too large for the page or it may be in the wrong place on the page. You can change the layout of a document by resizing and moving images.

To resize and move a graphic:

1. Select the graphic you want to change.
2. To resize a graphic, click a **resize handle** and drag toward the center of the image to make it smaller or away from the center of the image to make it larger.
3. To move a graphic, rest your mouse over the graphic. When the cursor changes to the **move cursor**, click and drag the image to the new location.

When an image is selected, you will see two types of resize handles:

	Appears in the middle of one of the sides of the image. Allows you to resize the width or the height, but not both at the same time.
	Appears at the four corners of the image. Allows you to change the width and height of the image at the same time.

FIGURE WD 4.15

tell me **more**

To rotate a graphic, click the **rotate handle** and drag your mouse to the right to rotate the image clockwise or to the left to rotate the image counterclockwise.

try **this**

You can change the size of an image using the *Height:* and *Width:* boxes in the *Size* group on the *Format* tab under *Picture Tools.*

4.15 Adding WordArt to Documents

Sometimes you'll want to call attention to text you have added to your document. You could format the text by using character effects, or if you want the text to really stand out, use **WordArt**.

WordArt Quick Styles are predefined graphic styles you can apply to text. These styles include a combination of color, fills, outlines, and effects.

To add WordArt to a document:

1. Click the **Insert** tab on the Ribbon.
2. In the *Text* group, click the **WordArt** button and select a Quick Style from the gallery.
3. Replace the text "Your Text Here" with the text for your document.

After you have added WordArt to your document, you can modify it just as you would any other text. Use the *Font* box and *Font Size* box on the *Home* tab to change the font or font size of WordArt.

In previous versions of Microsoft Word, WordArt came with a predefined set of graphic styles that could be formatted, but on a very limited basis. In Word 2010, WordArt has been changed to allow a wide range of stylization. When you add WordArt to a document, the *Drawing Tools Format* contextual tab appears. In the *WordArt Styles* group you can apply Quick Styles to your WordArt, or modify it further by changing the text fill, text outline, and text effects.

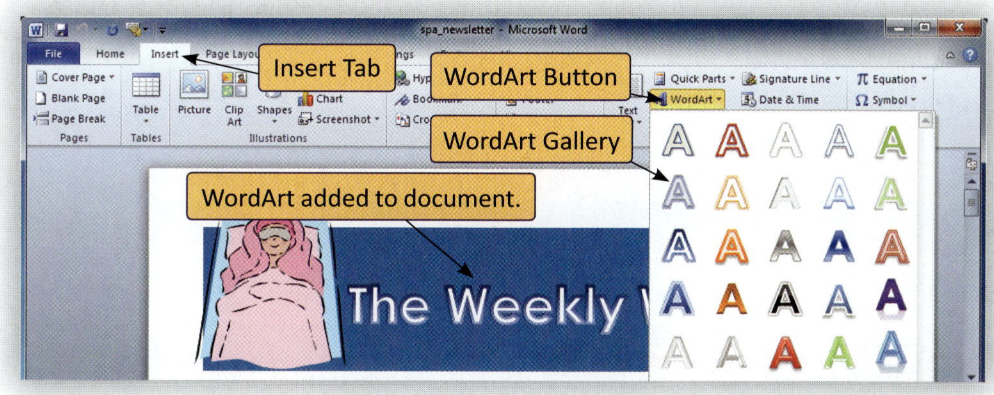

FIGURE WD 4.16

tips & tricks

Be sure to limit the use of WordArt to small amounts of text, such as a newsletter banner. Overuse of WordArt can be distracting to your readers.

tell me more

You can change the look of WordArt using the commands in the *Transform* gallery. You can choose to display the text along a path or to distort the letters creating a warped effect. To transform WordArt, under *Drawing Tools,* click the **Format** tab. In the *WordArt Styles* group, click the **Text Effects** button. Point to **Transform** and select an option from the gallery.

4.16 Inserting SmartArt

SmartArt is a way to take your ideas and make them visual. Where documents used to have plain bulleted and ordered lists, now they can have SmartArt, which are visual diagrams containing graphic elements with text boxes for you to enter your information in. Using SmartArt not only makes your document look better, but it helps convey the information in a more meaningful way.

There are eight categories of SmartArt for you to choose from:

List—Use to list items that do not need to be in a particular order.

Process—Use to list items that do need to be in a particular order.

Cycle—Use for a process that repeats over and over again.

Hierarchy—Use to show branching, in either a decision tree or an organization chart.

Relationship—Use to show relationships between items.

Matrix—Use to show how an item fits into the whole.

Pyramid—Use to illustrate how things relate to each other with the largest item being on the bottom and the smallest item being on the top.

Picture—Use to show a series of pictures along with text in the diagram.

To add SmartArt to a document:

1. Click the **Insert** tab.
2. Click the **SmartArt** button.
3. In the *Choose a SmartArt Graphic* dialog box, click a **SmartArt** option and click **OK.**
4. The Smart Art is added to your document.
5. Click in the first item of the *Text* pane and type your first item.
6. Enter the text for each item.
7. Click outside the SmartArt graphic to hide the *Text* pane.

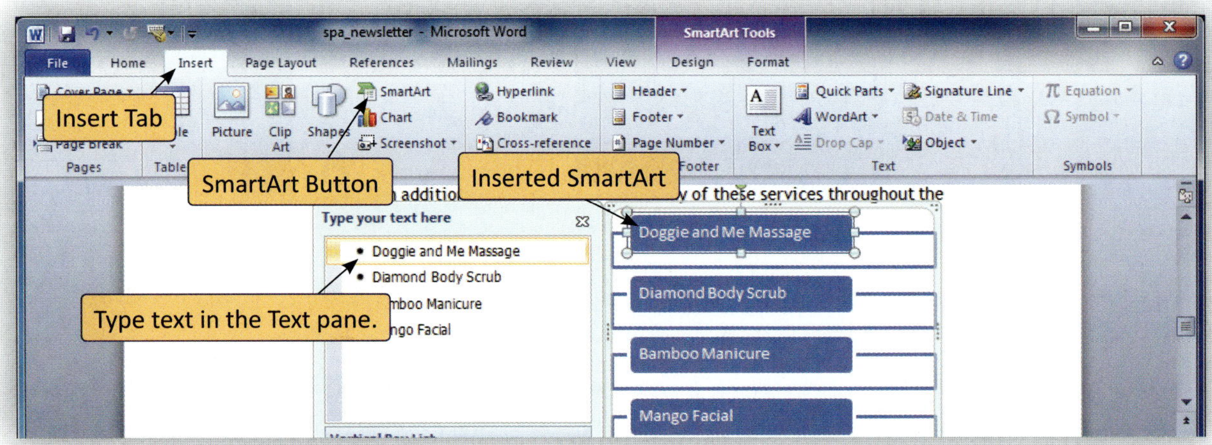

FIGURE WD 4.17

tips & tricks

When choosing a SmartArt diagram, it is important that the diagram type suits your content. In the *Choose a SmartArt Graphic* dialog box, click a SmartArt type to display a preview of the SmartArt to the right. The preview displays not only what the diagram will look like, but also includes a description of the best uses for the diagram type.

try this

To enter text in SmartArt, you can click in the text area of the SmartArt and type your text.

4.17 Inserting a Shape

A **shape** is a drawing object that you can quickly add to your document. Word comes with a number of shapes for you to choose from including lines, block arrows, callouts, and basic shapes such as smiley faces, rectangles, and circles.

To add a shape to a document:

1. Click the **Insert** tab.
2. In the *Illustrations* group, click the **Shapes** button and select an option from the *Shapes* gallery.
3. The cursor changes to a crosshair +.
4. Click anywhere on the document to add the shape.

Once you have added a shape to a document, there are a number of ways you can work with it:

- To resize a graphic: click a resize handle (or) and drag toward the center of the image to make it smaller or away from the center of the image to make it larger.
- To rotate a graphic: click the rotate handle and drag your mouse to the right to rotate the image clockwise or to the left to rotate the image counterclockwise.
- To move a graphic: point to the graphic and when the cursor changes to the move cursor click and drag the image to the new location.

FIGURE WD 4.18

tips & tricks

Some shapes, such as callouts, are designed for displaying text. When you add a callout to a document, a text area automatically appears with the cursor ready for you to enter text. But what if you want to add text to another type of shape? You can add text to any shape you add to a document. To add text, right-click the shape and select **Add Text.** A text area displays in the shape. Type the text and click outside the shape.

tell me more

When you insert a shape into a document, the *Format* tab under *Drawing Tools* displays. This tab is called a contextual tab because it only displays when a drawing object is the active element. The *Format* tab contains tools to change the look of the shape, such as shape styles, effects, and placement on the page.

4.18 Adding a Caption

A **caption** is a brief description of an illustration, chart, equation, or table. Captions can appear above or below the image, and typically begin with a label followed by a number and the description of the image. Captions are helpful when referring to images within paragraphs of text (see Figure 1: An example of a caption).

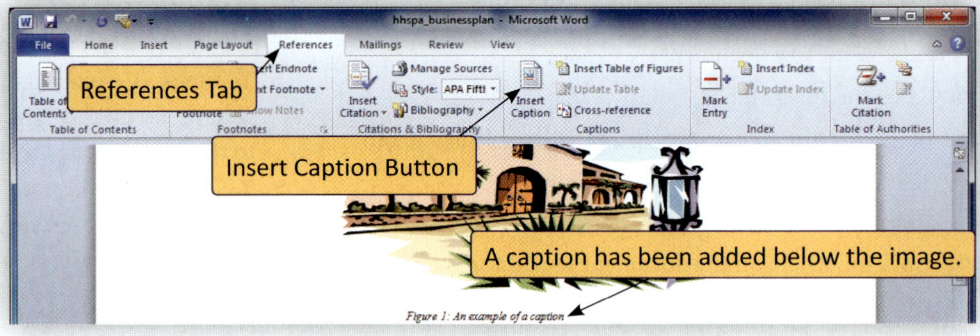

FIGURE WD 4.19

To add a caption to a figure:

1. Select the figure you want to add the caption to.
2. Click the **References** tab.
3. In the *Captions* group, click the **Insert Caption** button.
4. The *Caption* dialog box opens.
5. Click the **Label:** arrow and select a figure type.
6. Click the **Position:** arrow and select where you want the caption to appear.
7. Type any additional text, such as a description of the figure, in the *Caption:* box.
8. Click **OK** to close the dialog box and add the caption.

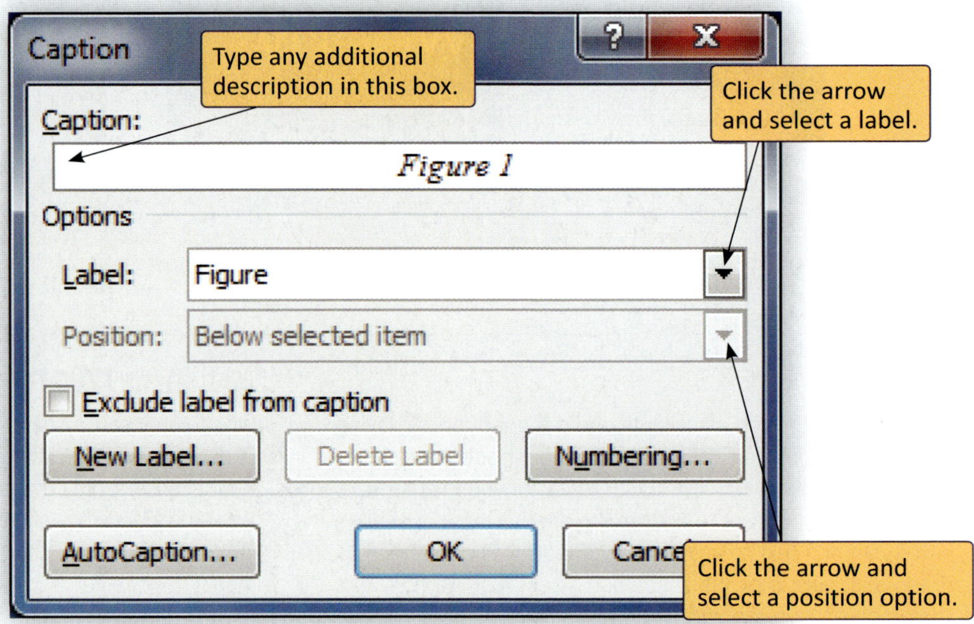

FIGURE WD 4.20

tips & tricks

Word automatically numbers the figures in your document based on the label type. For example, if you have several tables that use the "table" label, those captions will be numbered sequentially. If you have other figures labeled as "figures," those images will be numbered sequentially. If you go back and add a new caption or change the label of an existing caption, Word will renumber the existing captions for you.

tell me more

When you add certain types of images or objects to your document, such as a Microsoft Excel chart or an Adobe Acrobat document, you can have Word automatically add a caption to the figure. In the *Insert Caption* dialog box, click the **AutoCaption . . .** button. In the *AutoCaption* dialog box, select the type of object you want to automatically add captions to and click **OK**.

Data files for projects can be found on
www.mhhe.com/office2010skills

projects

Skill Review 4.1

In this project you will be editing the *Emergency Telephones_04* document from Sierra Pacific Community College District.

1. Open Microsoft Word 2010.
2. Open the *Emergency Telephones_04* document.
3. Save this document as `[your initials]WD_SkillReview_4-1`.
4. Insert and arrange a company logo picture in the document.
   a. Click the **Insert** tab.
   b. In the *Illustrations* group, click the **Picture** button. The *Insert Picture* dialog box will open.
   c. Browse to your student data file location, select the **SPCCD logo** file, and click **Insert**. The logo will be inserted into the document.
   d. On the *Picture Format* tab, in the *Arrange group,* click the **Wrap Text** button and choose **In Front of Text**.

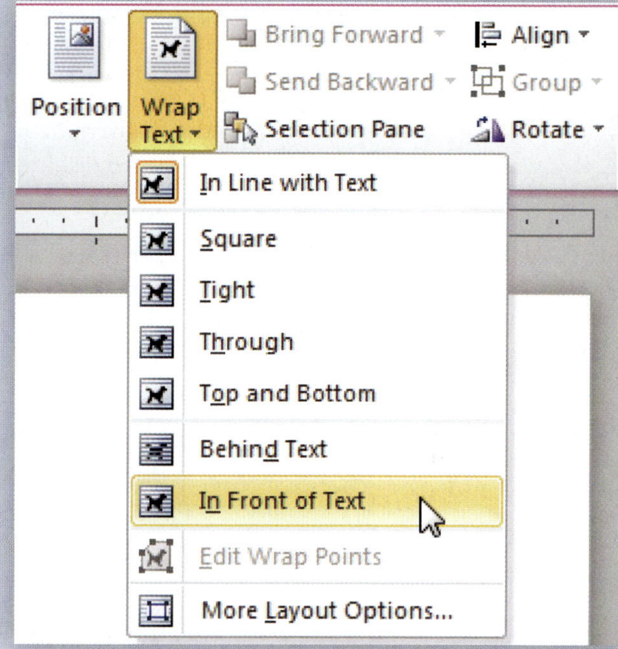

FIGURE WD 4.21

5. Position the company logo in the document.
   a. Click the logo picture and drag it to the upper-left corner of the document.
   b. With the logo still selected, in the *Arrange* group, click the **Position** button and select the top left with square wrapping option.
6. Add a table to the document and enter text into the table.
   a. Move to the end of the document and type `Emergency Phone Numbers` and apply the **Heading 2** style.
   b. Press **Enter** and click the **Insert** tab.
   c. In the *Tables* group, click the **Tables** button and select a **4 × 1** (four columns and one row) table.
   d. Type the information below into the table. Press **Tab** to move forward from cell to cell and press **Shift+Tab** to move back one cell. Press **Tab** at the end of a row to insert a new row. Don't worry about alignment or text wrapping at this point; just enter the data.

Emergency Response System	Fire, Medical, Sheriff	Available 24 hrs.	911
College Police	❯ South Library	❯ M-Su: 7 a.m.-7 p.m.	❯ (209) 658-7777
❯ Health Center	❯ Administration Building	❯ M-F: 7 a.m.-4 p.m.	❯ (209) 658-2239
❯ Information Center	❯ Counseling Building	❯ M-F: 8 a.m.-5 p.m.	❯ (209) 658-4466
❯ Evening Dean	❯ Asst. Dean, Math	❯ M-Th: 5 p.m.-8 p.m.	❯ (209) 658-7700
❯ Site Administrator	❯ VP of Administrative Services	❯ M-F: 8 a.m.-5 p.m.	❯ (209) 658-8501
❯ Weekend College Coordinator	❯ Area Deans	❯ S: 8 a.m.-5 p.m.	❯ (209) 658-6500

7. Delete a column from and insert a row into an existing table.

a. Click somewhere in the second column and click the **Layout** tab under *Table Tools.*

b. In the *Row & Columns* group, click the **Delete** button and select **Delete Columns.** The table should now be three columns and seven rows.

c. Click somewhere in the first row and click the **Insert Above** button in the *Rows & Columns* group.

d. Enter the following information in the first row.

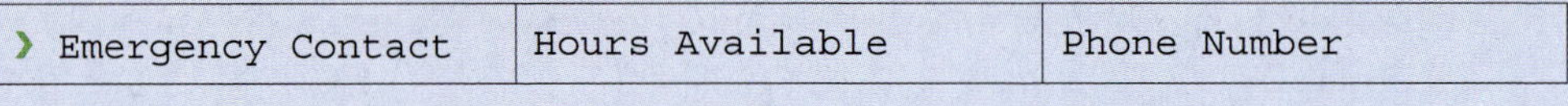

❯ Emergency Contact	Hours Available	Phone Number

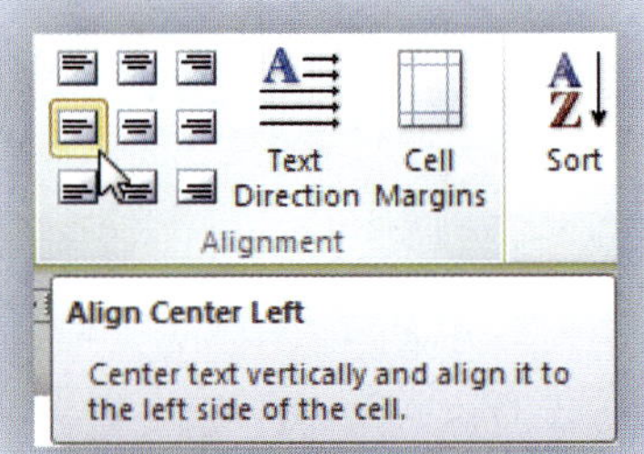

FIGURE WD 4.22

8. Change the size of the columns and rows, sort text within the table, and apply a table Quick Style.

a. On the *Layout* tab, in the *Table* group, click the **Select** button and choose **Select Table** to select the entire table.

b. In the *Cell Size* group, click the **AutoFit** button and choose **AutoFit Contents** to automatically adjust the column width to fit the contents of the table.

c. In the *Cell Size* group, change the *Height* to **0.2″**.

d. In *Alignment* group, click the **Align Center Left** button to vertically center and horizontally left-align the text in each cell.

e. Click the **Sort** button in the *Data* group. The *Sort* dialog box will open.

f. In the *My list has* area, click the **Header row** radio button. This will exempt the first row from being sorted with the rest of the text in the table.

g. In the *Sort by* area, select **Emergency Contact,** which is the first column of the table.

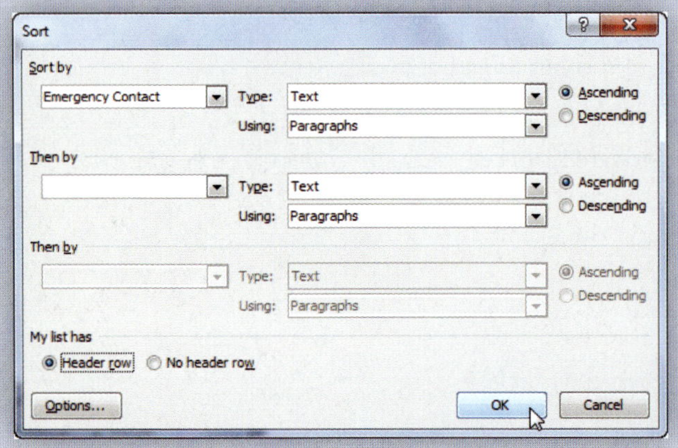

FIGURE WD 4.23

h. Choose **Text** as the *Type,* **Paragraphs** in the *Using* area, and **Ascending** as the sort order.

i. Click **OK** to apply the sort.

j. Click the **Design** tab under *Table Tools.*

k. In the *Table Styles* group, click the **Light Shading – Accent 1** style to apply this style to the table.

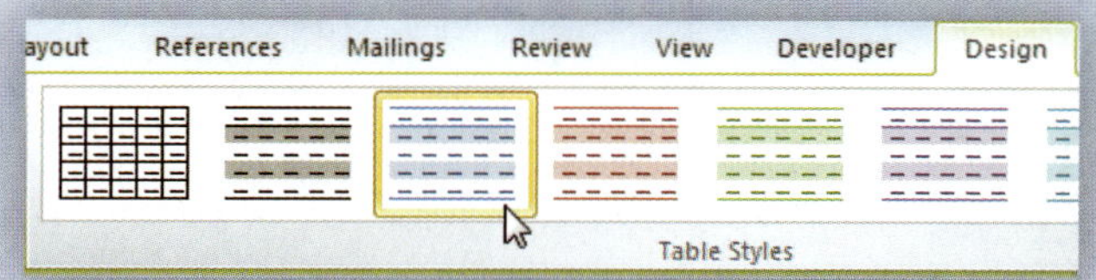

FIGURE WD 4.24

9. Convert existing text to a table.

a. Select the lines of text in the *Emergency Telephone Locations* section (do not include the section heading).

b. Press the **Decrease Indent** button to change the left indent to 0″.

c. On the *Insert* tab, in the *Tables* group, click the **Tables** button. Select **Convert Text to Table**. The *Convert Text to Table* dialog box will open. Word automatically detects the number of columns needed and uses tabs to separate text into cells. (Note: If the *Table size* area does not contain 3 columns and 10 rows, you have incorrectly selected the table.)

d. Click **OK** to convert the text to a table.

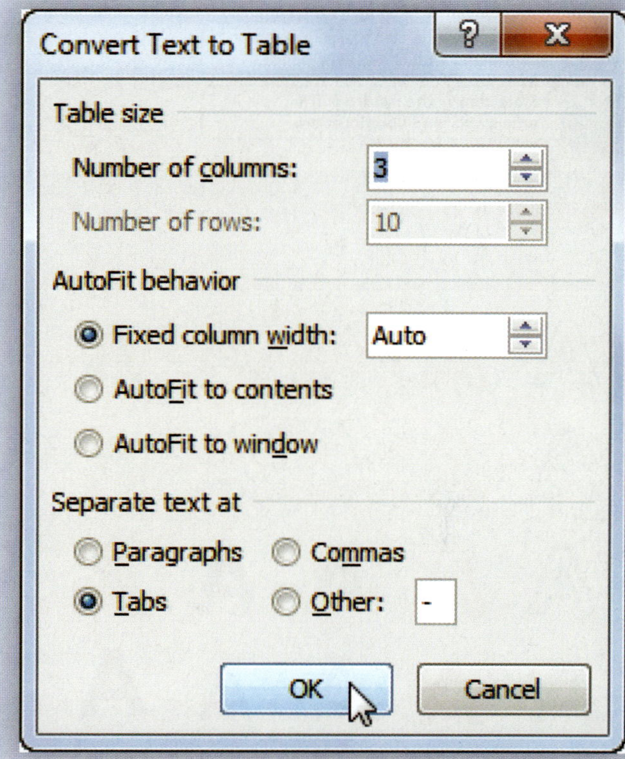

FIGURE WD 4.25

10. Insert a row, merge cells, and insert text in the table.

a. Click somewhere in the first row and click the **Insert Above** button in the *Rows & Columns* group.

b. Click in the first row of the table. On the *Layout* tab, in the *Table* group, click the **Select** button, and choose **Select Row.**

c. Click the **Merge Cells** button in the *Merge* group to merge the three columns in the first row into one column.

d. Enter the following information in the first row: `Blue Emergency Telephones`

11. Change the size of the columns and rows, sort text within the table, and apply a table Quick Style.

a. On the *Layout* tab, in the *Table* group, click the **Select** button and choose **Select Table** to select the entire table.

b. In the *Cell Size* group, click the **AutoFit** button and choose **AutoFit Contents.**

c. In the *Cell Size* group, change the *Height* to **0.2″**.

d. Select all of the rows of the table except for the first row.

e. In the *Alignment* group, click the **Align Center Left** button.

f. Click the **Sort** button in the *Data* group. The *Sort* dialog box will open.

g. In the *Sort by* area choose **Column 1,** and in the *Then by* area choose **Column 2.**

h. Click **OK** to apply the sort.

i. Select the entire table.

j. Click the **Design** tab under *Table Tools.*

k. In the *Table Styles* group, click the **Light Shading – Accent 1** style to apply this style to the table.

l. In the *Table Style Options* group, make sure that both the **Header Row** and **First Column** check boxes are checked.

m. Click in the first row of the table and horizontally center the text in this row.

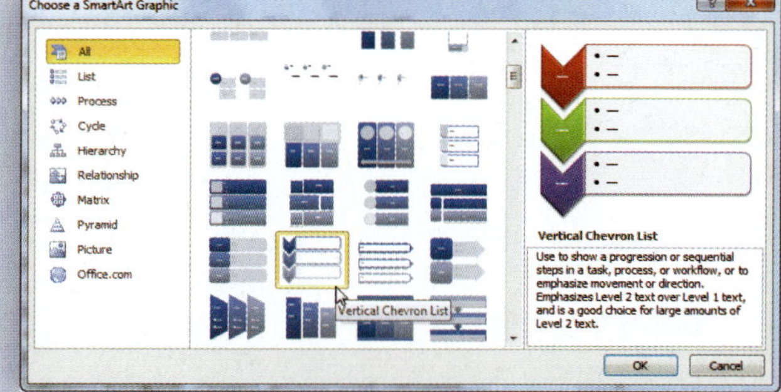

FIGURE WD 4.26

12. Add a SmartArt graphic to the document and resize it.
   a. Select the numbered list in the first section of the document and delete these lines of text.
   b. Click at the end of the first sentence in the first section and press **Enter** twice.

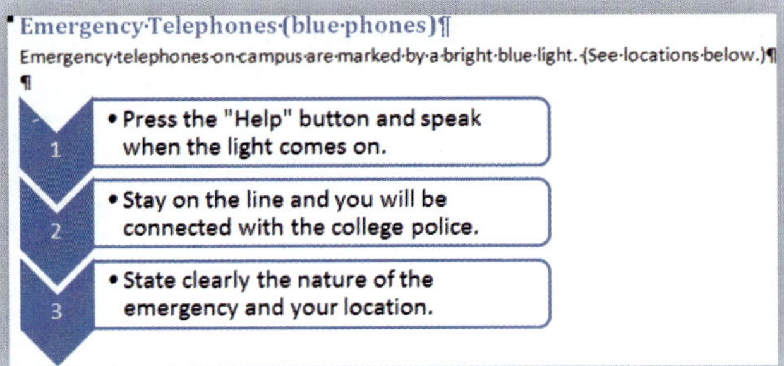

FIGURE WD 4.27

   c. On the *Insert* tab, in the *Illustrations* group, click the **SmartArt** button. The *Choose a SmartArt Graphic* dialog box will open.
   d. Scroll down the graphics options and select **Vertical Chevron List** and press **OK**.
   e. Type the text in the SmartArt graphic as shown in Figure WD 4.28. You will need to delete the extra bulleted *[Text]* field in each of the text areas by clicking it and pressing **Backspace**.
   f. After you have entered the numbers and text into the *SmartArt* graphic, click the outside edge of the graphic to select it.
   g. Click the **Format** tab under *SmartArt Tools.*
   h. In the *Size* group, change the *Height* to **2″** and the *Width* to **4″**.

13. Save and close the document.

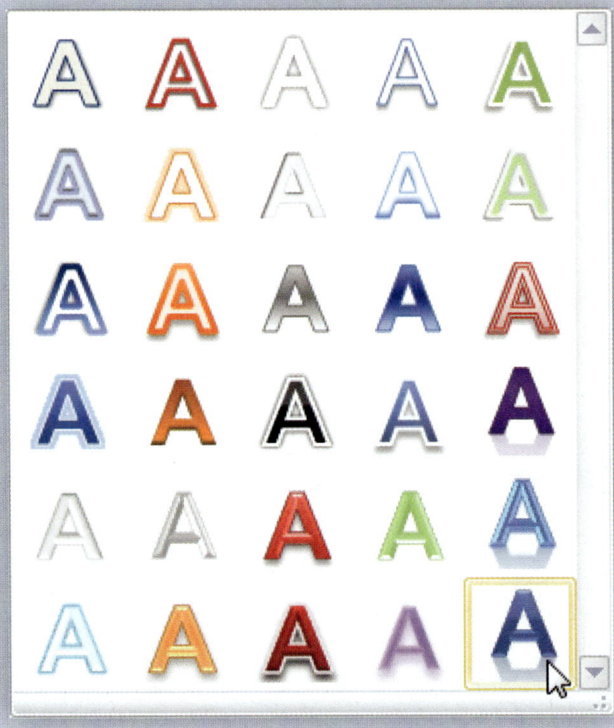
FIGURE WD 4.28

Skill Review 4.2

In this project you will be editing the *Brochure_04* document from Placer Hills Real Estate.

1. Open the *Brochure_04* document.
2. Save this document as **[your initials]WD_SkillReview_4-2.**
3. Insert WordArt into the brochure and resize and reposition it.
   a. Select **Emma Cavalli** at the top of the first column.
   b. Click the **Insert** tab.
   c. In the *Text* group, click the **WordArt** button and select the **Fill – Blue, Accent1, Metal Bevel, Reflection** option (fifth item in the sixth row). The WordArt is inserted into the document.
   d. On the *Format* tab, in the *Size* group, change the *Shape Height* to **0.9″** and the *Shape Width* to **4.5″**.
   e. In the *Arrange* group, click the small arrow to the right of the *Send Backward* button and choose **Send Behind Text**.
   f. Put your mouse pointer on the outside edge of the **WordArt** graphic and drag toward the upper-left corner of the document. Position the graphic so it is approximately 0.2″–0.3″ away from the top and left edge of the brochure.

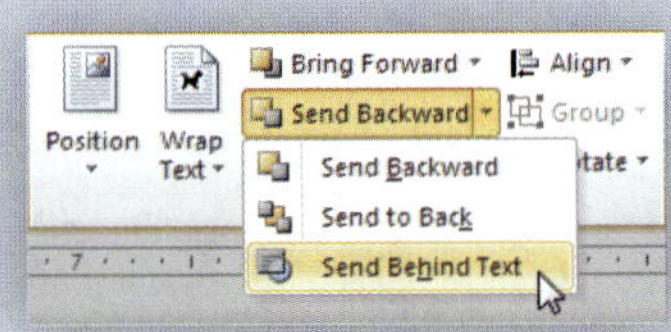

FIGURE WD 4.29

4. Insert a clip art, arrange it in the brochure, and add a caption.
   a. Click at the end of the first column.
   b. On the *Insert* tab, in the *Illustrations* group, click the **Clip Art** button. The *Clip Art* pane will open at the right side of the Word window.

FIGURE WD 4.30

c. Type `House` in the *Search for:* box and click **Go.** *Clip Art* selections will appear below in the *Clip Art* pane.

d. On a clip art selection of your choice, click the small arrow to the right of the graphic and choose **Insert.** The clip art will be inserted into your brochure.

e. In the *Size* group, change the *Height* to **1″** and press **Enter.** The *Width* will automatically be adjusted to keep the graphic proportional.

f. Click on the **Wrap Text** button in the *Arrange* group and choose **Tight.**

g. Drag the graphic to the right of the last numbered item in the first column so the text wraps around the graphic. Make sure the text from the first column does not wrap to the second column.

h. With the clip art still selected, click on the **References** tab.

i. In the *Captions* group, click on the **Insert Caption** button. The *Caption* dialog box will open.

j. Click **OK** to add the caption.

k. Click in the caption below the graphic and delete the text.

l. In the caption area type: `Putting Your Needs First!`

m. Resize the caption by dragging the square sizing handle on the right edge to the right so all the text fits on one line.

n. Move the caption as necessary so it is centered below the clip art.

o. On the *Insert* tab, in the *Illustrations* group, click the **Clip Art** button to close the *Clip Art* pane.

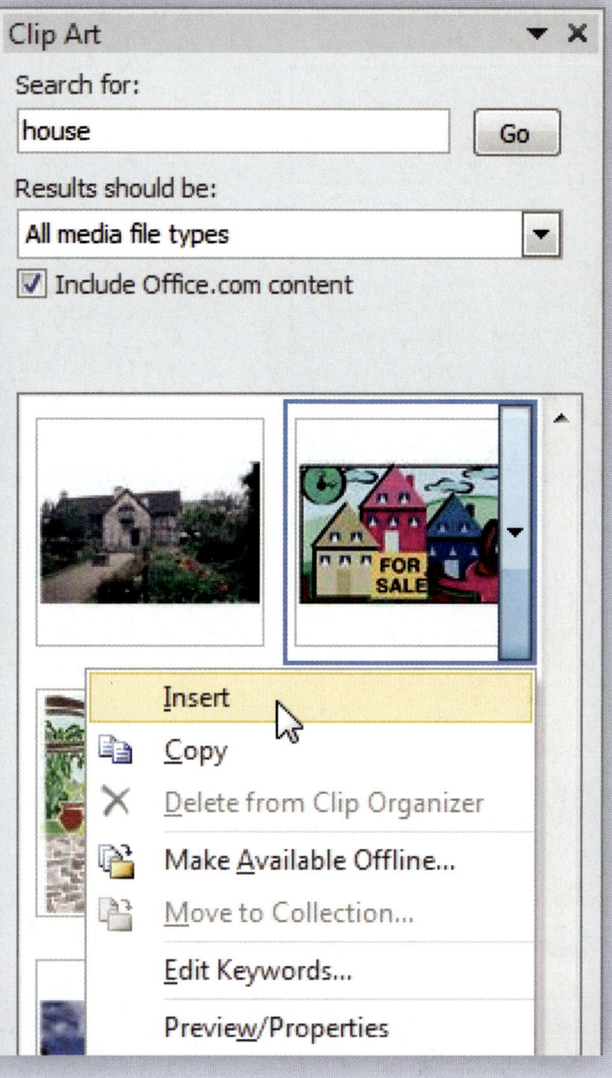

FIGURE WD 4.31

5. Add shapes to the brochure and adjust the fill color and arrangement.

a. Click at the end of the first quote in the second column (*. . . in just 3 days!"*) and put in the line break (**Shift+Enter**). Do the same after the second quote.

b. Click the **Insert** tab.

c. In the *Illustrations* group, click the **Shapes** button and select the first option in the *Callouts* area (**Rectangular Callout**). A drawing cursor will appear (+).

d. Click and drag from the top left of the first quote to the bottom right and then release the mouse button. The callout will appear over the quote. You can resize the callout by dragging one of the sizing handles on the sides and corners.

e. On the *Format* tab, in the *Shape Styles* group, click on the **Shape Fill** button and choose a light blue shade.

f. In the *Arrange* group, click the small arrow to the right of the *Send Backward* button and choose **Send Behind Text.**

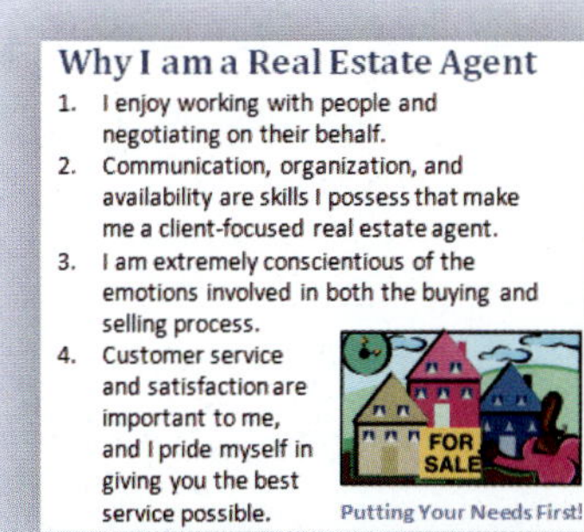

FIGURE WD 4.32

FIGURE WD 4.33

6. Use copy and paste to duplicate a callout. Copying a callout, rather than creating a new one, will allow for consistency in size and features.

a. Click on the callout you just created and press **Ctrl+C** to copy the callout.

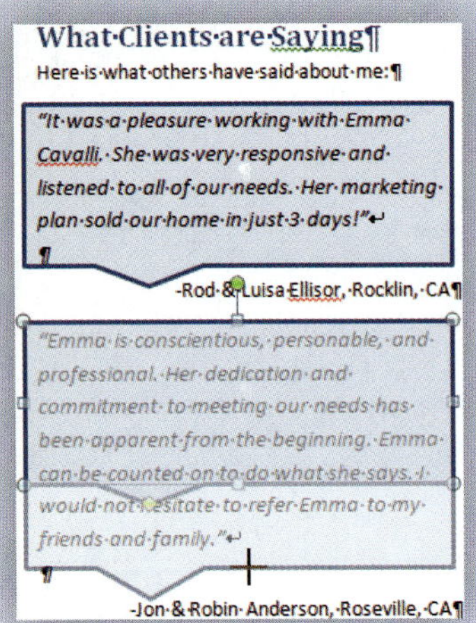

FIGURE WD 4.34

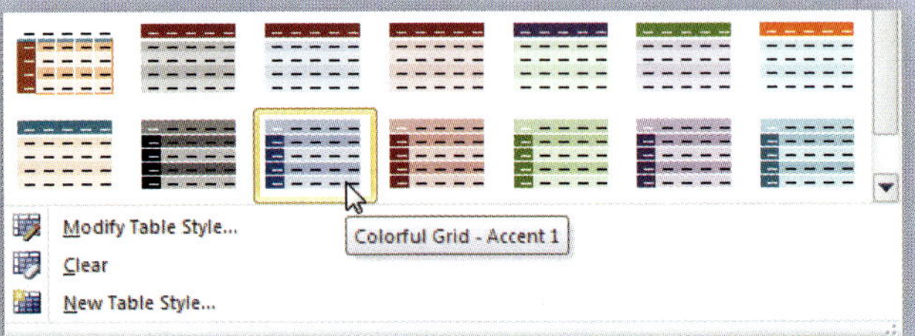

FIGURE WD 4.35

FIGURE WD 4.36

b. Press **Ctrl+V** to paste this item. The callout will be pasted slightly below and to the right of the original callout.

c. Use the left arrow key to drag the new callout so it aligns vertically with the first callout.

d. Use the down arrow key to move the new callout over the second quote.

e. Using the square resizing handle at the bottom of the callout, resize the callout to fit the second quote.

7. Convert text to a table and make formatting changes to the table.

a. Select all of the text in the *The Placer Hills Belief System* section (do not include the heading), and change the font size to **9 pt.** and the after paragraph spacing to **0 pt.**

b. On the *Insert* tab, in the *Tables* group, click the **Table** button and click **Convert Text to Table**. The *Convert Text to Table* dialog box will open.

c. Click **OK** to convert the text to a table.

d. On the *Design* tab in the *Styles* group, choose the **Colorful Grid – Accent 1** style.

e. In the *Table Style Options* group, deselect the **Header Row** check box.

f. On the *Layout* tab in the *Cell Size* group, click the **AutoFit** button and select **AutoFit Contents**.

g. In the *Cell Size* group, change the *Height* to **0.2"**.

h. In the *Alignment* group, click the **Align Center Left** button.

8. Insert a picture, apply a Quick Style, and reposition the picture.

a. Click at the end of the third column of the brochure.

b. On the *Insert* tab in the *Illustrations* group, click the **Picture** button. The *Insert Picture* dialog box will open.

c. Browse to your student data files, select the **PHRE logo** file, and click **Insert.**

d. In the *Arrange* group, click the **Wrap Text** button and choose **In Front of Text.**

e. In the *Picture Styles* group, click the **More** button and select the **Simple Frame, Black** Quick Style (first option in the second row).

f. With the logo still selected, in the *Arrange* group, click the **Position** button and select the bottom right with square wrapping option.

9. Save and close the document.

challenge yourself 1

In this project you will be editing the *Maximum Heart Rate_04* document from American River Cycling Club.

1. Open the *Maximum Heart Rate_04* document.

2. Save this document as `[your initials]WD_Challenge_4-3.`

3. Insert the **ARCC logo** picture into the document. This file is in your student data files.
4. Apply the **Center Shadow Rectangle** (fifth option in the second row; this location might vary depending on the size of your Word window) Quick Style to the logo.
5. Change the height and width of the logo to **120%** of its original size. Use the *Scale* option in the *Layout* dialog box.
6. Use **Square** text wrapping and reposition the logo so it appears in the top left corner of the page.
7. Select the predicted maximum heart rate formula after the first paragraph and insert the **Continuous Block Process** SmartArt (in the *Process* group). The formula will be deleted and the SmartArt inserted.
8. Type in the formula in the text boxes.
9. Change the height and width of the SmartArt graphic to **50%** of its original size.
10. Use the **Position** button to align the graphic at the top right with square text wrapping.

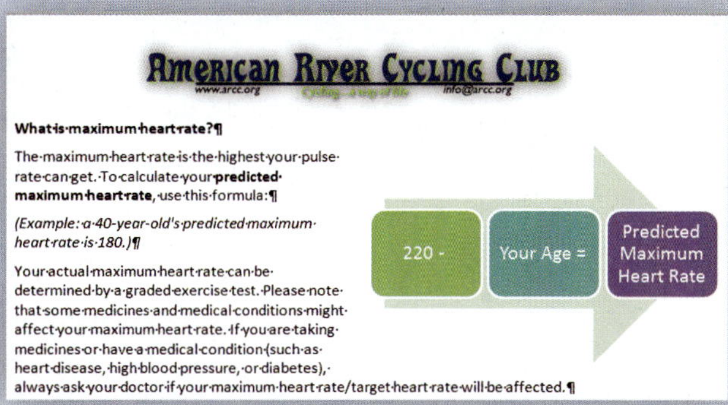
AMERICAN RIVER CYCLING CLUB
www.arcc.org info@arcc.org

What is maximum heart rate?

The maximum heart rate is the highest your pulse rate can get. To calculate your **predicted maximum heart rate**, use this formula:

(Example: a 40-year-old's predicted maximum heart rate is 180.)

Your actual maximum heart rate can be determined by a graded exercise test. Please note that some medicines and medical conditions might affect your maximum heart rate. If you are taking medicines or have a medical condition (such as heart disease, high blood pressure, or diabetes), always ask your doctor if your maximum heart rate/target heart rate will be affected.

FIGURE WD 4.37

11. Change the color of the graphic and apply a *SmartArt Style* of your choice.
12. Select all of the lines of tabbed text at the bottom of the document and convert it to a table.
13. Insert a row above the first row, merge all three columns in this row, and type in bold: `TARGET AND MAXIMUM HEART RATES`
14. Insert a row above the third row (age *25*) and type the following.

20	120-170	200

15. Insert a row after the last row of the table and type:

70	90-128	150

16. Use **AutoFit Window** to distribute the table between the margins.
17. Apply a table Quick Style of your choice. The **Header Row** option should be selected and the **First Column** option should be deselected.
18. Change the row height to **0.25″** and center all the text vertically and horizontally.
19. To the right of the first paragraph in the *Target Heart Rate* section, insert a clip art of a heart.
20. Change the size of the graphic to approximately **1″**, use **Tight** wrapping, and position the graphic to the right of the first paragraph in this section.
21. Apply a *Picture Style* of your choice to this graphic.
22. Insert a caption on the clip art graphic and type: `Know your target heart rate`
23. The document should fit on one page. Adjust the size and/or position of the graphics as necessary.
24. Save and close the document.

challenge yourself 2

In this project you will be editing the *Buyer Escrow Checklist_04* document from Placer Hills Real Estate.

1. Open the *Buyer Escrow Checklist_04* document.
2. Save this document as **`[your initials]WD_Challenge_4-4`.**
3. Apply the **Title** style to the title of the document.
4. Select the five lines of text below the title and change the tab to a **5″** right tab with a solid underline leader.
5. To the right of these lines, insert a Clip Art of a check mark.
6. Resize the graphic so it is approximately **1.5″** and apply a *Picture Style* of your choice.
7. Apply **Tight** text wrapping and position the graphic to the right of these lines.
8. Insert the **PHRE logo** picture.
9. Apply the **Behind Text** text wrapping and position it in the upper-right corner of the document. Make sure the horizontal bottom border from the title is visible below the graphic.
10. Select the lines of text beginning with *Task* through *Verify Preliminary Report with Lender,* and convert this selected text to a table.
11. Insert a column to the right of the first column in the table and type `Initials` in the first row of this column.
12. Insert a column between the existing columns in the table and type `Date Completed` in the first row of this new column (second column).
13. Insert a row above the *Verify Preliminary Report with Buyer* and type `Disclosure Statement to Buyer` in the first column of this new row.
14. Change the row height of the entire table to **0.4″** and align all text vertically centered and left-aligned.
15. Select all of the text in the first column except the first row and apply an open square bullet. Decrease the indent of these bulleted items.
16. **AutoFit** the contents of the table.
17. Use the *Properties* dialog box to center the entire table horizontally (not the text, but the entire table.
18. Select the entire table and use the *Borders and Shading* dialog box to apply a **2¼ pt. Grid** border to the table.
19. On the first row of the table, apply a **2¼ pt**. bottom border and a light gray shading.
20. Insert a column to the right of the last column in the table and type `Notes` in the first row of this column.
21. Change the text alignment of this column so it is consistent with the rest of the table.
22. Change the width of this, the fourth column, to **1.5″**.
23. Change the text alignment in the first row so all text is centered vertically and horizontally.
24. This document should fit on one page.
25. Save and close the document.

In this project you will be creating a training calendar for the American River Cycling Club.

1. Open a new Word document.
2. Save this document as `[your initials]WD_OnYourOwn_4-5`.
3. Change the orientation to **Landscape** and change the margins to use the **Moderate** setting.
4. Insert a table with seven columns and six rows.
5. In the first row type the days of the week beginning with Sunday.
6. In the second through sixth rows type the number for each day of the month.
7. Change widths of all of the columns to **1.3″**.
8. Change the row height of the first row to **0.3″**.
9. Change the row height of rows 2–6 to **0.9″**.
10. Insert a row above the first row, merge all of the cells in this row, and type the current month and year.
11. Change the font size to **48 pt., bold, all caps,** and **centered.**
12. Select the second row and change the text to **14 pt., bold,** and **small caps,** and center the text vertically and horizontally.
13. Select the remaining rows and change the text to **10 pt**. and **bold**, and align the numbers in the upper right of each cell.
14. Horizontally center the entire table on the page (not the text, but the entire table).
15. Apply a Quick Style to the table. Make changes to the *Table Style Options* as necessary.
16. Insert shapes on the calendar and insert text into the shapes.
    a. Insert a shape of your choice on the first Monday of the month. Draw it large enough so it takes up most of the cell and leaves the date visible.
    b. Right-click on the shape and choose **Add Text** and type: `Morning Ride 6-8 a.m.`
    c. Change the font, size, line spacing, and paragraph spacing on the text as necessary. Use a line break (*Shift+Enter*) to wrap text if needed.
    d. Change the shape style, fill, outline, and/or effects to arrange the graphic and text attractively.
    e. Copy this shape and text and paste it on the other Mondays in the month and align to maintain consistency.
17. Use the steps above to create a shape and text on each Wednesday of the month. Use a different shape and add the following text: `River Ride 6-8 p.m.`
18. Use the steps above to create a shape and text on each Friday of the month. Use a different shape and add the following text: `Time Trial 5-6 p.m.`
19. Use the steps above to create a shape and text on each Saturday of the month. Use a different shape and add the following text: `Hilly Ride 8-11 a.m.`
20. Insert WordArt of your choice and type: `American River Cycling Club`. Customize using *WordArt Styles* and align at the top left above the table. (Note: you might have to click below the table to insert items in your document).
21. Insert a clip art of a bicycle and align at the upper right above the table. Resize and arrange as necessary to fit in the upper left. Customize using *Picture Styles.*

22. Insert a SmartArt of your choice (one with three boxes aligned horizontally) and type: EAT, SLEEP, and RIDE! (one word in each box). Center the SmartArt below the table. Resize and arrange as necessary to fit below the table. Customize using *Picture Styles.*
23. The entire document should fit on one page. Make any necessary adjustments to arrange the document attractively.
24. Save and close the document.

fix it

In this project you will be editing the *Vaccination Schedule_04* document from Courtyard Medical Plaza.

1. Open the *Vaccination Schedule_04* document.
2. Save this document as ***[your initials]*WD_FixIt_4-6.**
3. Using the Word features in the chapter, you will be editing and customizing this document to make a professional and readable one-page document.
4. Include in the table the vaccination information that is below the table.
5. A couple of the cells in the table have information about two vaccinations; edit the table so that each vaccination is in a separate row.
6. Delete any extra *Enters* in the table.
7. Sort the table by *Name of Vaccine.*
8. Insert a row at the top of the document and type RECOMMENDED VACCINATION SCHEDULE as the title of the table.
9. Apply a table Quick Style and adjust the *Table Style Options* as necessary.
10. Adjust column widths, row height, borders, shading, and text alignment as necessary.
11. Apply the Quick Style to the title of the document.
12. Insert the **CMP logo** picture into the document and position at the upper left of the document. Use text wrapping as needed and/or adjust the paragraph spacing on the title so the title does not wrap around the company logo.
13. Insert a vaccination clip art to the right of the first two paragraphs of the document. Adjust size and text wrapping as needed. Customize using *Picture Styles.*
14. Insert an appropriate caption on the clip art graphic.
15. Arrange the document so all of the information fits on one page making use of the entire page. Make changes to table row height and graphic(s) size, alignment, and text wrapping as needed to produce a professional-looking document.
16. Save and close the document.

chapter 5
Working with References and Mailings

In this chapter, you will learn the following skills:

Skill 5.1 Inserting a Table of Contents
Skill 5.2 Inserting Footnotes and Endnotes
Skill 5.3 Selecting a Reference Style
Skill 5.4 Adding Citations to Documents
Skill 5.5 Creating a Bibliography
Skill 5.6 Marking Entries for an Index
Skill 5.7 Creating an Index
Skill 5.8 Customizing a Print Job
Skill 5.9 Starting a Mail Merge
Skill 5.10 Inserting Fields and Writing the Mail Merge Document
Skill 5.11 Previewing and Finishing the Mail Merge
Skill 5.12 Creating Envelopes and Labels

- Insert and update table of contents, footnotes, and endnotes
- Use a report reference style and create citations and a bibliography
- Mark words in a document to create an index
- Customize a print job
- Use mail merge to create mailings, labels, and envelopes

skills

introduction

In this chapter, you will be introduced to long reports and the Word features that help users create properly formatted reports, which include table of contents, footnotes and endnotes, reference style, citations, bibliography, and index. You will also be shown how to use Word's mail merge feature to create mailings, envelopes, and labels.

5.1 Inserting a Table of Contents

If you have a long document with many sections and headings, it is a good idea to include a **table of contents** at the beginning of the document. A table of contents lists the topics and associated page numbers, so your reader can easily locate information. The table of contents is created from heading styles in the document. If you want your document's section titles to display in the table of contents, be sure to apply heading styles to that text.

To insert a table of contents:

1. Verify the insertion point is at the beginning of the document.
2. Click the **References** tab.
3. In the *Table of Contents* group, click the **Table of Contents** button and select an option from the gallery.
4. The table of contents is added to the beginning of the document.

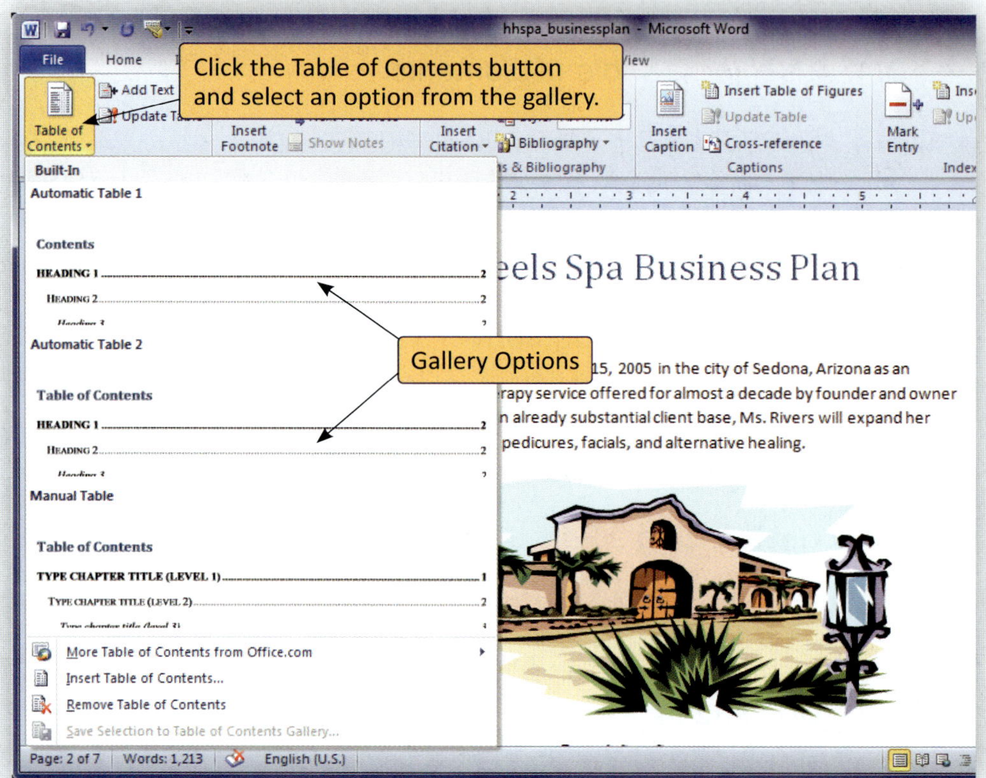

FIGURE WD 5.1

If you make changes to your document after you have inserted a table of contents, you should be sure to update the table of contents to keep the information accurate. To update the table of contents, click the **Update Table** button Update Table in the *Table of Contents* group. You can also update the table of contents by clicking on the table of contents and clicking the **Update Table. . .** button at the top of the control.

tips & tricks

To remove a table of contents, click the **Table of Contents** button and select **Remove Table of Contents** at the bottom of the gallery.

try this

If you want to add your own customized table of contents, click **Insert Table of Contents . . .** at the bottom of the gallery. The *Table of Contents* dialog box opens. Here you can choose different options for the table of contents including tab leaders, formats, and page number formatting.

tell me more

A table of contents is typically based on heading styles, but you can create a table of contents based on custom styles or from marked entries.

A table of contents is a building block that is added to the document. When you select the building block, extra controls appear at the top including the *Table of Contents* and the *Update Table . . .* buttons.

5.2 Inserting Footnotes and Endnotes

Footnotes and **endnotes** provide your reader with further information on a topic in a document. They are often used for source references. Footnotes and endnotes are comprised of two parts: a **reference mark** (a superscript character placed next to the text) and the associated text. Footnotes appear at the bottom of a page, whereas endnotes are placed at the end of the document.

To insert a footnote:

1. Place your cursor where you want the footnote to appear.
2. Click the **References** tab.
3. In the *Footnotes* group, click the **Insert Footnote** button.
4. The superscript number is added next to the text and the cursor is moved to the footnote area at the bottom of the page.
5. Type the text for your footnote. When you are finished, return to your document by clicking anywhere in the main document area.

To insert an endnote:

1. Place your cursor where you want the endnote to appear.
2. Click the **References** tab.
3. In the *Footnotes* group, click the **Insert Endnote** button.
4. The superscript number is added next to the text and the cursor is moved the endnote area at the end of the document.
5. Type the text for your endnote.

To convert footnotes to endnotes or vice versa, click the **dialog launcher** in the *Footnotes* group. In the *Footnote and Endnote* dialog box, click the **Convert. . .** button, choose an option, and click **OK.**

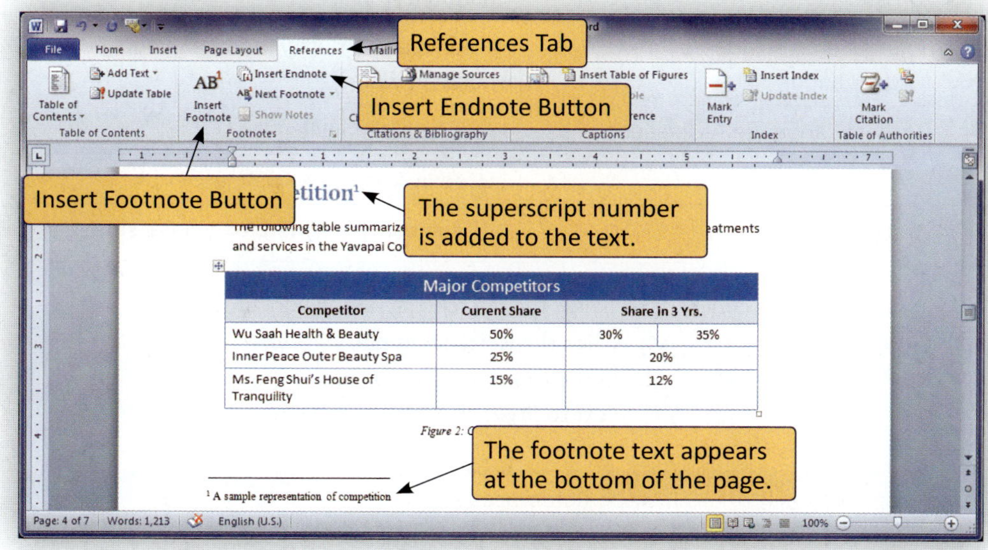

FIGURE WD 5.2

tips & tricks

- Click the **Next Footnote** button to navigate to the next footnote in the document. Click the arrow next to the **Next Footnote** button to display a menu allowing you to navigate to previous footnotes and between endnotes in the document.
- To delete a footnote, you must first select the reference mark in the document and press **Delete** on the keyboard. If you select and delete the text of the footnote, the reference mark will remain and the footnote will not be removed from the document.

tell me more

Once you have inserted and formatted your first footnote or endnote, Word automatically numbers all subsequent notes in your document for you. If you add a new footnote between two existing footnotes, Word will renumber all the footnotes in the document, keeping them in sequential order.

try this

To insert a footnote, you can also click the **dialog launcher** in the *Footnotes* group. In the *Footnote and Endnote* dialog box, verify that the **Footnote** radio button is selected and click **Insert.**

5.3 Selecting a Reference Style

A **reference style** is a set of rules used to display references in a bibliography. These rules include the order of information, when and how punctuation is used, and the use of character formatting, such as italics and bold. The two most common reference styles in use today are *APA* and *Chicago;* however, there are a number of other reference styles you can choose from. It is important that you use the correct reference style for the subject of your document. The following table lists the available styles in Word and when they are most commonly used:

STYLE ABBREVIATION	FULL NAME	PURPOSE
APA Fifth Edition	American Psychological Association	Education, psychology, and social sciences
Chicago Fifteenth Edition	*The Chicago Manual of Style*	Books, magazines, and newspapers
GB7714 2005	NA	Used in China
GOST – Name Sort	Russian State Standard	Used in Russia
GOST – Title Sort	Russian State Standard	Used in Russia
ISO 690 – First Element and Date	International Standards Organization	Patents and industry (both print and nonprint works)
ISO 690 – Numerical Reference	International Standards Organization	Patents and industry (both print and nonprint works)
MLA Sixth Edition	Modern Language Association	Arts and humanities
SIST02	NA	Used in Asia
Turabian Sixth Edition	Turabian	All subjects (designed for college students)

When creating a bibliography, it is important to use a consistent reference style for your citations. Word makes this easy by allowing you to set the reference style for the entire document at once.

To change the reference style for a document:

1. Click the **References** tab.
2. In the *Citations & Bibliography* group, click the arrow next to *Style:* and select a style from the list.

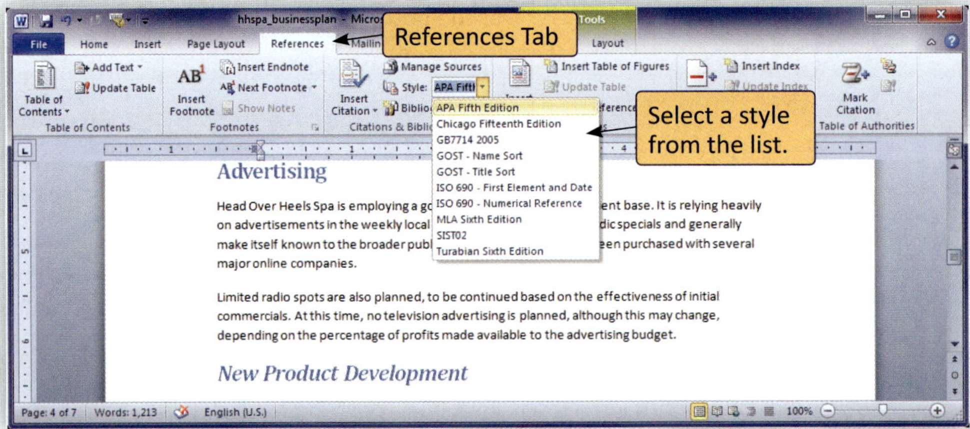

FIGURE WD 5.3

tips & tricks

When you change the reference style for a document, all citations are automatically updated to use the new style.

tell me more

To see a preview of the source style, click the **Manage Sources** button in the *Citations & Bibliography* group. The preview box at the bottom of the *Manage Sources* dialog box shows how the selected reference will appear as a citation and in the bibliography.

5.4 Adding Citations to Documents

When you use materials in a document from other sources, such as a book or a journal article, you need to give credit to the original source material. A **citation** is a reference to such source material. Citations include information such as the author, title, publisher, and the publish date.

To add a citation to a document, you must first create the source:

1. Place the cursor where you want to add the citation.
2. Click the **References** tab.
3. In the *Citations & Bibliography* group, click the **Insert Citation** button and select **Add New Source. . .**
4. In the *Create Source* dialog box, click the arrow next to *Type of Source* and select an option.
5. In the *Author* box, type the name of the author.
6. In the *Title* box, type the title of the book or article.
7. In the *Year* box, type the year the book or article was published.
8. Add other information about the source to the appropriate fields.
9. When you are finished, click **OK** to add the citation to the document.

After you have added a new source, it appears on the **Insert Citation** menu. To add the same source to another part of the document, click the **Insert Citation** button and select the source for the citation.

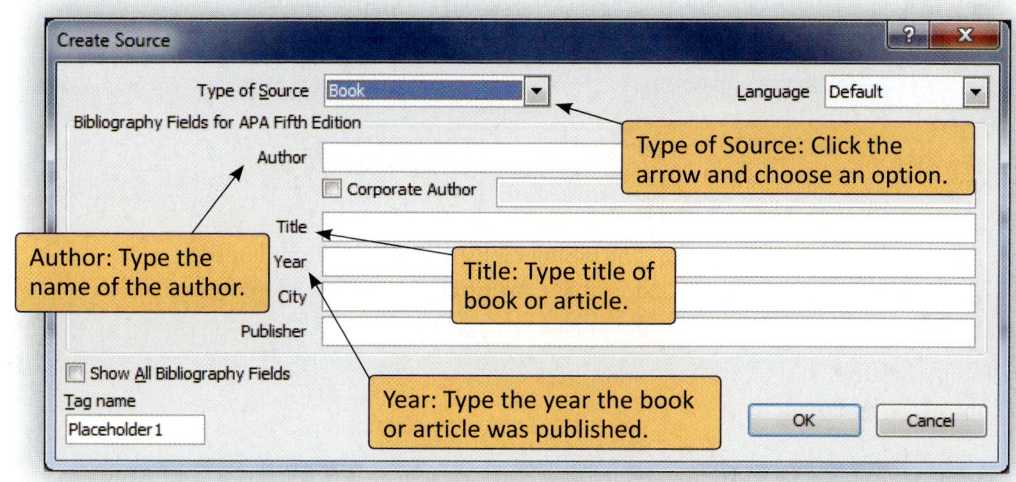

FIGURE WD 5.4

tips & tricks

When you add a citation, the citation appears inside parentheses at the place where you inserted it. A citation includes basic information from the source including the author, year, title, and pages. A bibliography lists all the citations in a document, and includes more of the source information than the citation.

tell me more

Citations appear in the document as a control. When you click the control, you will see an arrow on the right side. Click the arrow to display a menu for editing the source and the citation. In the *Edit Source* dialog box, you can change the information you added when you created the source. In the *Edit Citation* dialog box, you can change information specific to the citation, such as page numbers.

from the perspective of . . .

PARENT

My child uses word processing software to complete assignments and write simple reports. She even enjoys adding interesting clip art to make her work look good while having fun.

5.5 Creating a Bibliography

A **bibliography** is a compiled list of sources you referenced in your document. Typically, bibliographies appear at the end of a document and list all the sources you marked throughout the document. Microsoft Word 2010 comes with a number of prebuilt bibliography building blocks for you to use. When you select one of these building blocks, Word will search the document and compile all the sources from your document and format them according to the style you chose.

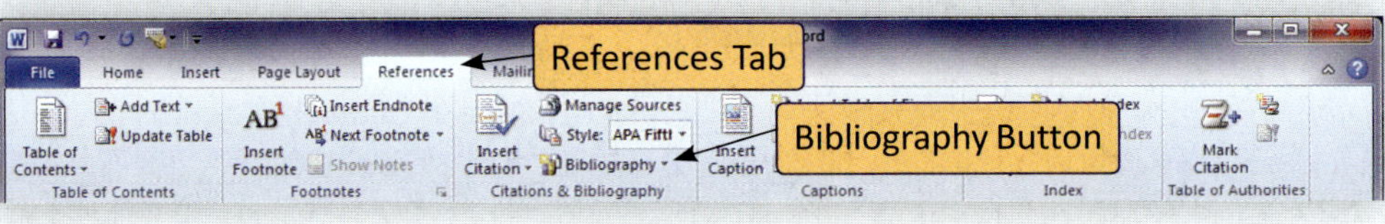

FIGURE WD 5.5

To add a bibliography to a document:

1. Place the cursor at the end of the document.
2. Click the **References** tab.
3. In the *Citations & Bibliography* group, click the **Bibliography** button and select one of the bibliography building blocks.
4. The bibliography is added to the end of the document, listing all the sources referenced in the document.

Bibliography

Rockland Falls Spa v. Ava Codas, IHAV-ENOC-LUE4 (United States Supreme Court May 21, 2009).

Chester, M. (2010). *Avoiding the Pedi-Scare: Health Code Do's and Don'ts.*

Chu, I. W. (2010). *Get Your Ohm On.* St. Louis: McGraw-Hill.

D.U. Tensionmeiser, M. (2009). The Case for Homeopathic Remedies.

Germman, H. (2009). *How to Stand Out in the Booming Health Spa Industry.* Oklahoma City: McGraw-Hill.

Hammerhead, B. (2010). *Alternative Healing Methods Lead to Increased Wellness.* Detroit: McGraw-Hill.

Larson, K. D., Wild, J. J., & Chiappetta, B. (2007). *Fundamental Accounting Principles.* Irwin/McGraw-Hill.

Mallor, J. P., Barnes, A. J., Bowers, T., Phillips, M. J., & Langvardt, A. W. (2010). *Business Law and the Regulatory Environment: Concepts and Cases.* Irwin/McGraw-Hill.

Thompson, R., & Cats-Baril, W. (2008). *Future Trends in Spa Therapies and Meditation.* McGraw-Hill/Irwin.

FIGURE WD 5.6

tell me **more**

The bibliography building blocks include a formatted header for your bibliography. You can choose to have the section titled *Bibliography* or *Works Cited.*

try **this**

To add a simple bibliography, click the **Insert Bibliography** command at the bottom of the *Bibliography* gallery.

from the perspective of . . .

WEDDING CONSULTANT

Using mail merge, I can advertise my business with customized personal letters and send them to my customers. Word processing software makes creating wedding invitations easy too, and I can use mail merge to create the matching envelopes!

5.6 Marking Entries for an Index

When creating long documents, you may want to add an index to the document to help your readers quickly locate specific information. To create an index you must first mark the topics you want to include, and then create the index. When formatting marks are hidden, marked entries look no different from other text in the document. However, when the index is created, Word finds all the marked entries and adds them to the index.

To mark entries:

1. Select the word you want to add to the index.
2. Click the **References** tab.
3. In the *Index* group, click the **Mark Entry** button.
4. The word appears in the *Main entry:* box.
5. Click the **Mark** button to mark the entry.
6. Click the **Close** button to close the *Mark Index Entry* dialog box.

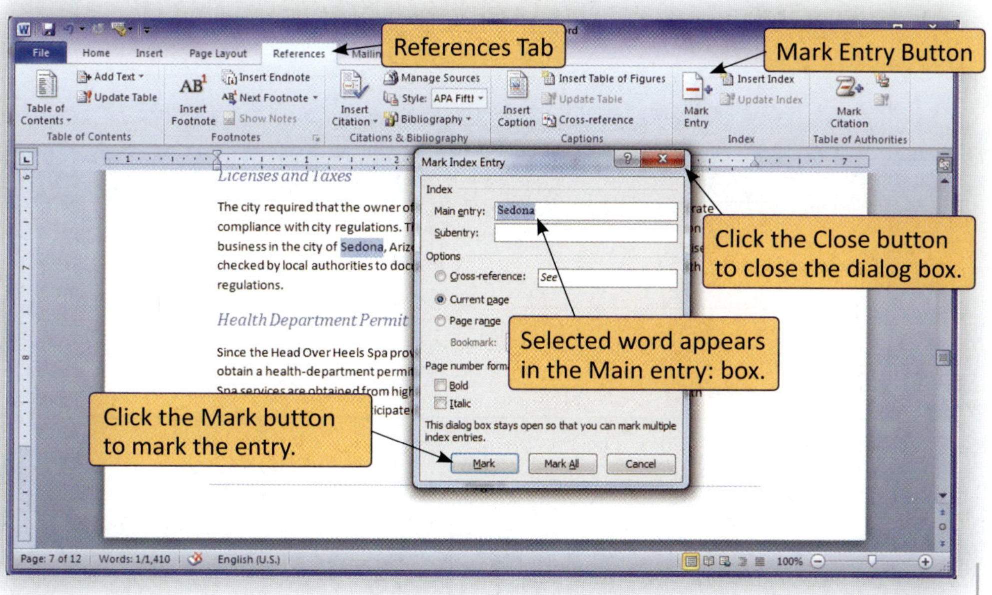

FIGURE WD 5.7

tips & tricks

After you mark an entry, Word adds the *XE (Index Entry)* formatting mark to the word and displays all formatting marks in the document, so you can double-check your page layout. However, formatting marks should be hidden before you create and insert the index to make it easier to view your final document.

tell me more

To add a reference to every instance of a word to the index, click the **Mark All** button in the *Mark Index Entry* dialog box.

try this

To open the *Mark Index Entry* dialog box, you can also click the **Insert Index** button in the *Index* group. In the *Index* dialog box, click the **Mark Entry . . .** button.

5.7 Creating an Index

An **index** is a list of topics and associated page numbers that typically appears at the end of a document. Adding an index to your document can help your readers find information quickly. An index entry can reference a single word, a phrase, or a topic spanning several pages. You can also add cross-references to your index.

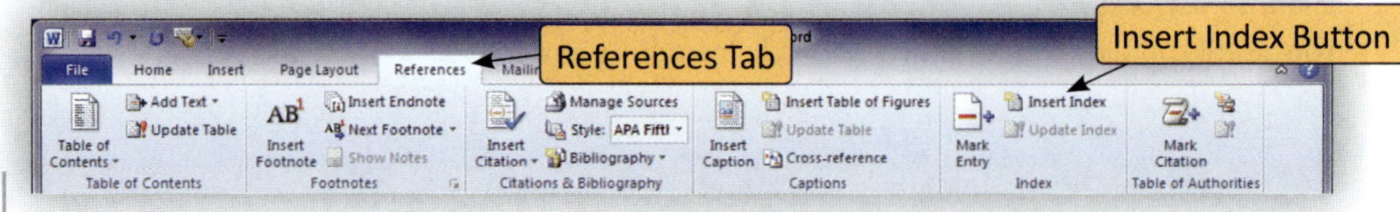

FIGURE WD 5.8

To add an index to a document:

1. Place the cursor at the end of the document.
2. Click the **References** button.
3. In the *Index* group, click the **Insert Index** button.
4. The *Index* dialog box opens.
5. Click the **Formats:** arrow and select a format.
6. Modify the other options until the preview looks the way you want.
7. Click **OK** to insert the index into your document.

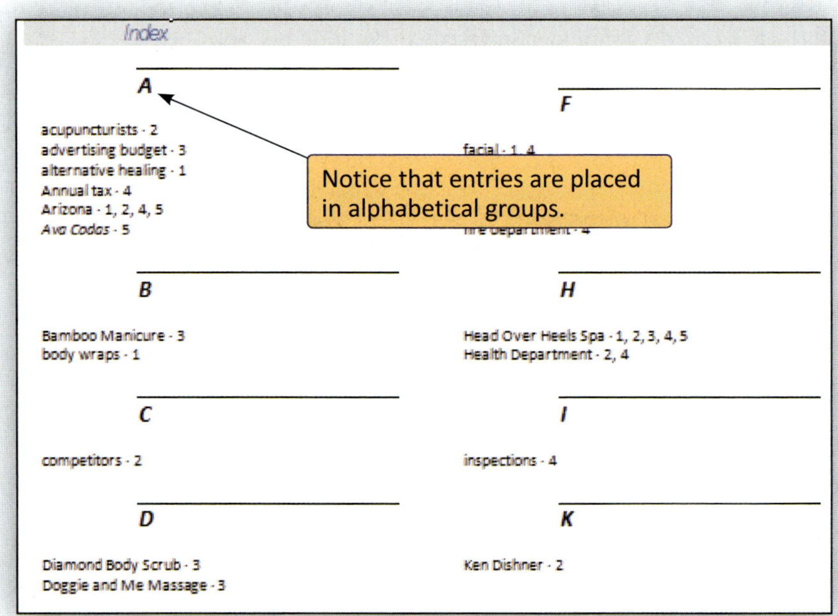

FIGURE WD 5.9

tips & tricks

To add new entries to an index, do not type directly in the index. Instead, mark the entries and then update the index. Any entries typed directly into the index will be deleted when the index is updated. To update an index, first select the index and then click the **Update Index** button in the *Index* group.

tell me more

A cross-reference is an index entry that refers to another entry in the index rather than to a page in the document. Cross-references are often used to direct readers from an uncommon entry to a more frequently used one.

5.8 Customizing a Print Job

The default *Print* command in Word prints one copy of the entire document. But what if you only want to print one section of your document or print five copies of your document at once? From the *Print* tab in Backstage view, you can customize how your document prints, including changing the number of copies and specifying which pages to print.

To modify print settings from Backstage view:

1. Click the **File** tab.
2. Click **Print.**
3. Verify that the correct printer name is displayed in the *Printer* section.
4. In the *Copies:* box, enter the number of copies you want to print.
5. In the *Pages:* box, type the range of pages you want to print.
6. Click **Print.**

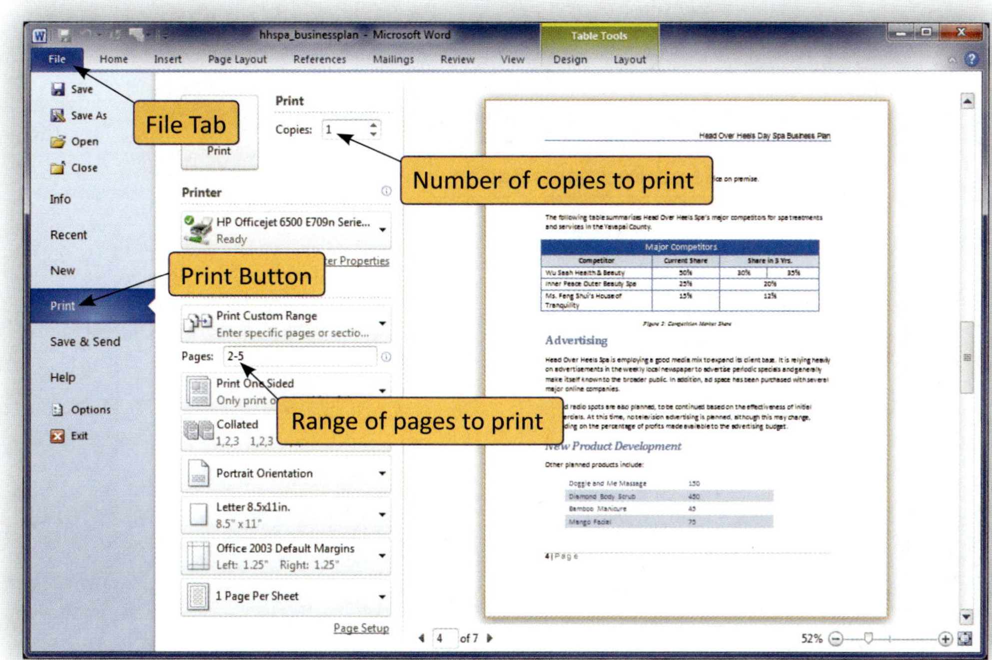

FIGURE WD 5.10

tips & tricks

Past versions of Microsoft Word included a *Print Preview* command that allowed you to see how your document would display on the printed page before printing the document. In Word 2010, *Print Preview* has been integrated into the *Print* tab in Backstage view. As you adjust the settings for printing your document, Word displays a live preview on the right side of the screen of how the document will look when printed.

tell me more

Use a hyphen to print a range of pages. Use a comma between page numbers to print individual pages. For example, if you type `1-5`, page 1 through page 5 will print. If you type `1,5`, page 1 and page 5 will print, but not pages 2, 3, and 4.

try this

To display the *Print* tab in Backstage view, you can also press Ctrl + P on the keyboard.

5.9 Starting a Mail Merge

Suppose you have a letter you want to send out to 20 recipients, but you want each person's name to appear on the letter, giving it a more personal touch. You could write the letter and save 20 versions—one for each recipient—but this is time-consuming and cumbersome. In Word, you can take a list of names and addresses and merge them with a standard document, creating a personalized document for each name on your list. This process is called a **mail merge**.

Before you can create a mail merge, you must first select a main document and select recipients. To set up the main document and select recipients:

1. Click the **Mailings** tab.
2. In the *Start Mail Merge* group, click the **Start Mail Merge** button and select **Letters.**
3. Click the **Select Recipients** button and select **Use Existing List . . .**
4. In the *Select Data Source* dialog box, select a data source and click **Open.**

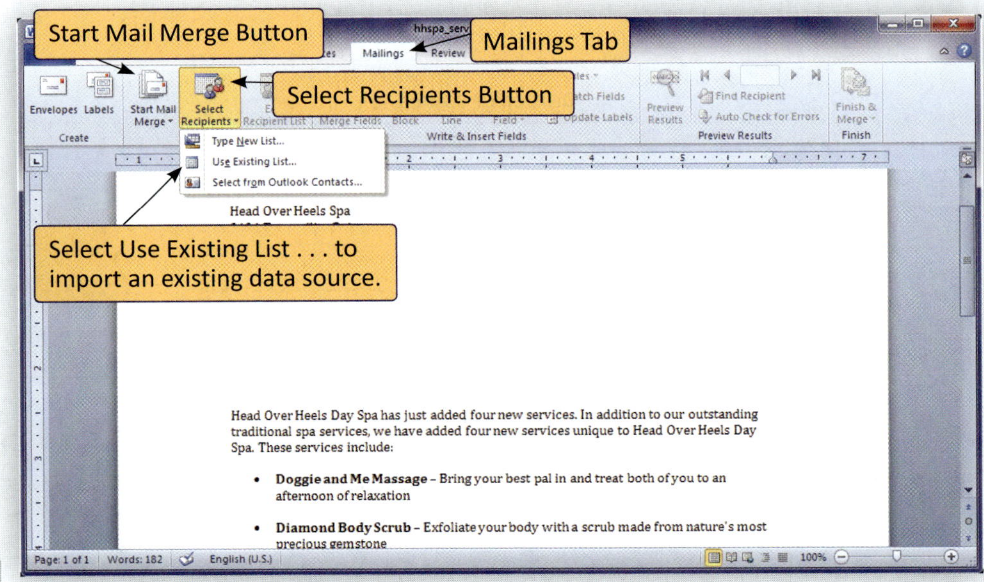

FIGURE WD 5.11

tips & tricks

Use mail merge to automatically create labels, envelopes, directories, and e-mails, as well as form letters.

tell me more

The recipients list for a mail merge can be entered in manually by selecting **Create New List. . .** from the *Select Recipients* menu or can be imported from the list of contacts from Microsoft Outlook. When you import the list of contacts from Outlook, you then have the option to remove any contacts you do not want to include in the merge.

try this

You can also create a mail merge using the *Mail Merge Wizard,* which will take you through creating the mail merge step by step. To display the *Mail Merge Wizard,* click the **Start Mail Merge** button and select **Step by Step Mail Merge Wizard . . .**

5.10 Inserting Fields and Writing the Mail Merge Document

The main document of a mail merge contains the text and merge fields, which appear on every version of the merged document. **Merge fields** are placeholders that insert specific data from the recipients list you created. You can choose to add address blocks, greeting lines, and specific fields such as first names, last names, and e-mail addresses.

The three basic types of merge fields are

Address Block—inserts a merge field with the name and address of the recipient.

Greeting Line—inserts a field with a greeting and the recipient's name.

Merge Fields—allows you to insert merge fields based on your data source, such as first names, last names, addresses, phone numbers, and e-mail addresses.

To add an address block merge field:

1. Click in the document where you want the merge field to appear.
2. On the *Mailings* tab, in the *Write & Insert Fields* group, click the **Address Block** button.
3. In the *Insert Address Block* dialog box, make any changes to the display and click **OK.**

To add a greeting line merge field:

1. Click in the document where you want the merge field to appear.
2. On the *Mailings* tab, in the *Write & Insert Fields* group, click the **Greeting Line** button.
3. In the *Insert Greeting Line* dialog box, make any changes to the display and click **OK.**

To add individual merge fields:

1. Click in the document where you want the merge field to appear.
2. Click the **Insert Merge Field** button and select an option to insert.

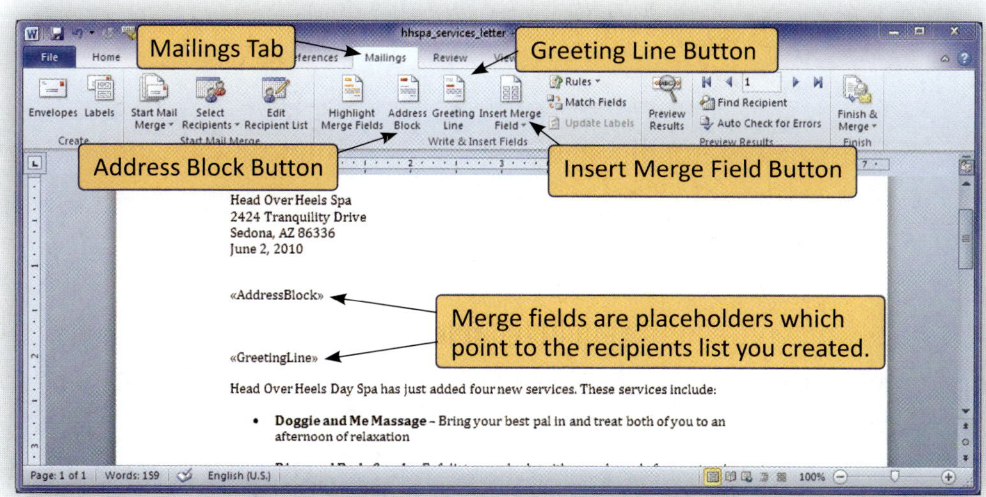

FIGURE WD 5.12

tips & tricks

Both the *Insert Address Block* and the *Insert Greeting Line* dialog boxes include a preview of how the merge fields will display in the document. Click the next and previous buttons to navigate through the list of recipients to see how each one will display before finalizing your choices.

5.11 Previewing and Finishing the Mail Merge

Before you complete the mail merge and print your documents, it is a good idea to review each document created in the merge.

To preview the mail merge:

1. In the *Preview Results* group, click the **Preview Results** button.
2. Click the **Next Record** and **Previous Record** buttons to navigate among different documents.

After you have previewed the mail merge, the last step is to finish the merge by printing the documents.

To print the documents in the mail merge:

1. In the *Finish* group, click the **Finish & Merge** button and select **Print Documents . . .**
2. In the *Merge to Printer* dialog box, click **OK.**

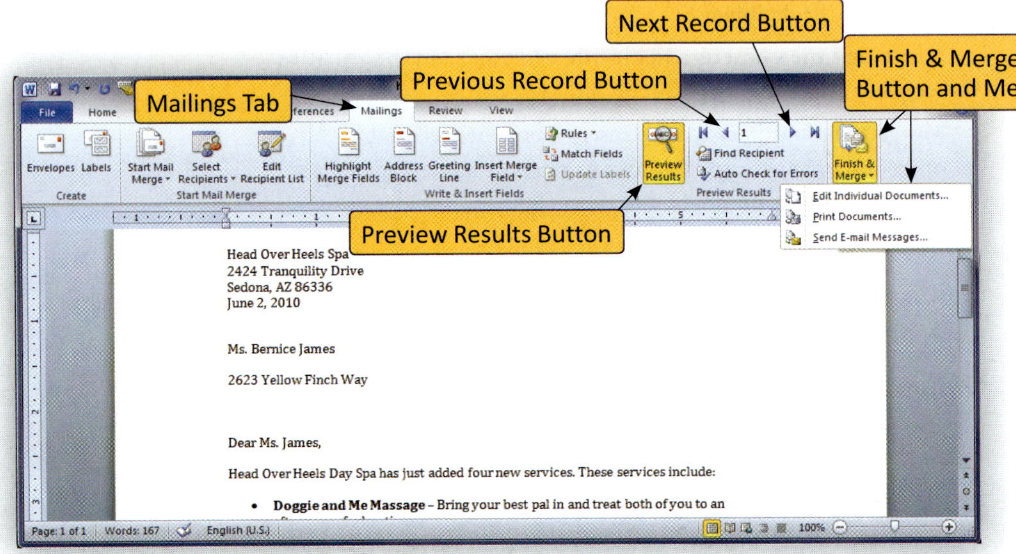

FIGURE WD 5.13

tips & tricks

Before you finish the merge, click the **Auto Check for Errors** button to review your documents for errors.

tell me more

If you want to modify letters individually, click **Edit individual letters . . .** Then, in the *Merge to New Document* dialog box, select the records you want to change and click **OK.** Word opens a new document based on the selected records. Make any changes you want, and then print or save the document just as you would any other file.

If you want to send the document via e-mail, click **Send E-mail Messages . . .** Enter the subject line and mail format. Select the recipients you want to send the document to and click **OK.**

5.12 Creating Envelopes and Labels

With Word you can create an envelope and print it without leaving the document you are working on. Word's preset formats take care of the measuring and layout for you.

To create and print an envelope:

1. Click the **Mailings** tab.
2. In the *Create* group, click the **Envelopes** button.
3. Type the address of the person you are sending the document to in the *Delivery address:* text box.
4. Type your address in the *Return address:* text box.
5. Click the **Options...** button.
6. Click the **Envelope size:** arrow and select an envelope size.
7. Click **OK** in the *Envelope Options* dialog box.
8. Click the **Print** button in the *Envelopes and Labels* dialog box.

Word also comes with a number of preset options for creating mailing labels. To create and print labels, in the *Create* group, click the **Labels** button. From the *Labels* tab, you can create a single label or an entire sheet of labels. You can also choose to send the labels directly to the printer or create a new document of labels to save and print whenever you need them.

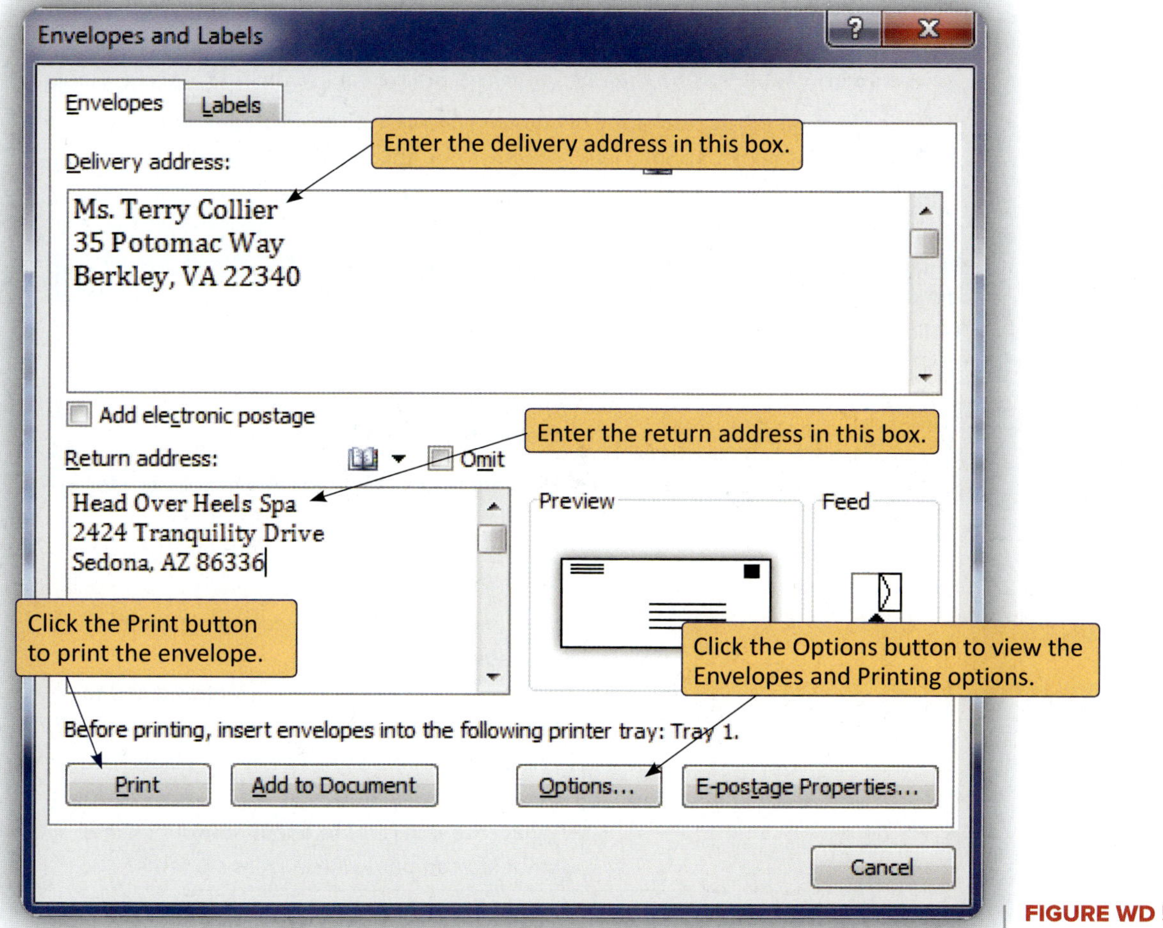

FIGURE WD 5.14

tips & tricks

You may not need to type an address. When you open the *Envelopes and Labels* dialog box, Word searches your document for an address. If it finds what looks like an address, it will copy it directly into the dialog box for you. Of course, you can always change this if it's not what you need.

try this

To open the *Envelopes and Labels* dialog box, you can also click the **Labels** button, and then click the **Envelopes** tab to create an envelope.

projects

Data files for projects can be found on
www.mhhe.com/office2010skills

Skill Review 5.1

In this project you will be editing the *Distance Education Plan_05* document from Sierra Pacific Community College District.

1. Open Microsoft Word 2010.
2. Open the *Distance Education Plan_05* document.
3. Save this document as ***[your initials]*`WD_SkillReview_5-1`**.
4. Apply the **Title** style to the title of the report.
5. Insert a *Table of Contents* at the beginning of the document.
   a. Move to the top of the document and click the **References** tab.
   b. Click the **Table of Contents** button in the *Table of Contents* group and select **Automatic Table 2.** The *Table of Contents* is inserted above the title of the document.
   c. Click in front of the title of the document (*Distance Education Plan*) and insert a **page break** to position the *Table of Contents* on the first page by itself.
6. Apply the **Heading 3** style to the following headings.

SECTION	APPLY HEADING 3 STYLE
Definition of Distance Education Modes	Online course Hybrid course Television or Tele-Web course Web-Enhanced course
Distance Education Offerings and Programs	How are Courses and Programs Selected for Distance Education Delivery? Leadership/Management of Distance Education at SPCCD What student support services are currently available to DE students? How are faculty members currently trained to teach online, hybrid or Web-enhanced courses? What tech support services are available for faculty, staff and students? What research is there about how our online students compare with in-class students?
Specific Goals for Distance Education at SPCCD	Goal #1 Goal #2 Goal #3 Goal #4 Goal #5
Top Priority Action Items for Distance Education	Leadership for DE at SPCCD Technical Infrastructure and Resources Student Services for DE Students Alignment of Instructional Resources Instructor Support and Training

Strategic Issue Areas	Recommendations on Course and Program Development Recommendations on Instructional Quality and Professional Development Recommendations on Student Success and Support Services Recommendations on Funding, Governance and Management

7. Update the *Table of Contents.*

a. Click the *Table of Contents* on the first page of the report.

b. Click the **Update Table** button at the top of the *Table of Contents,* or click the **Update Table** button in the *Table of Contents* group on the *References* tab. The *Update Table of Contents* dialog box will open.

c. Select the **Update entire table** radio button and click **OK.** The *Table of Contents* entries and page numbers will be updated.

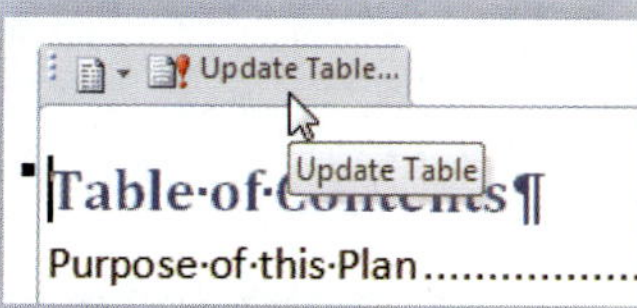

FIGURE WD 5.15

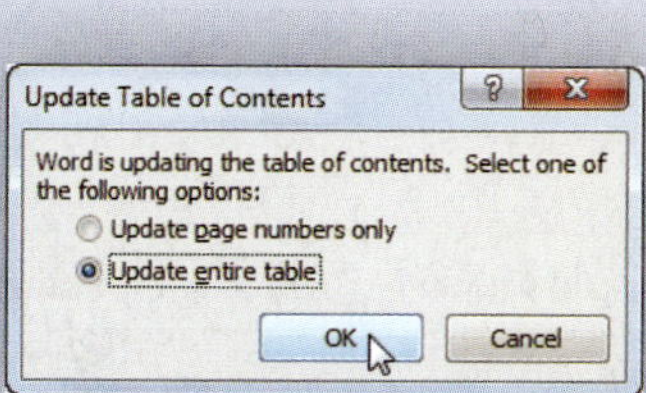

FIGURE WD 5.16

8. Insert footnotes into the report.

a. Click after the *Web-Enhanced course* heading (on page 3).

b. On the *References* tab, in the *Footnotes* group, click the **Insert Footnote** button. The number *1* footnote is inserted into the body of the report, and the footnote area opens at the bottom of the page.

c. Type the following information in the footnote area: `Just for clarification, this is a non-DE course which uses DE tools.`

d. Click at the end of the second paragraph in the *Distance Education Offerings and Programs* section (on page 4), insert a footnote, and type the following: `There are currently two fully online certificate programs going through the curriculum review process.`

e. Click at the end of the *Top Priority Action Items for Distance Education* heading (on page 7), insert a footnote, and type the following: `These DE Action Items were presented to and approved by the Academic Senate during the fall semester.`

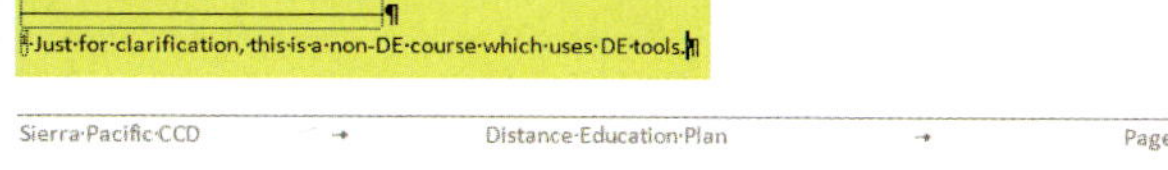

FIGURE WD 5.17

9. Select a *Reference Style* for the document, create a source, and insert a citation.

a. On the *References* tab, in the *Citations & Bibliography* group, click the arrow next to *Style:* and choose **APA Fifth Edition.**

b. Click at the end of the *Web-Enhanced course* paragraph (on page 3).

c. In the *Citations & Bibliography* group, click the **Insert Citation** button and choose **Add New Source.** The *Create Source* dialog box will open.

d. In the *Type of Source* area, choose **Web site.**

e. Continue creating the source with the information shown in Figure WD 5.18.

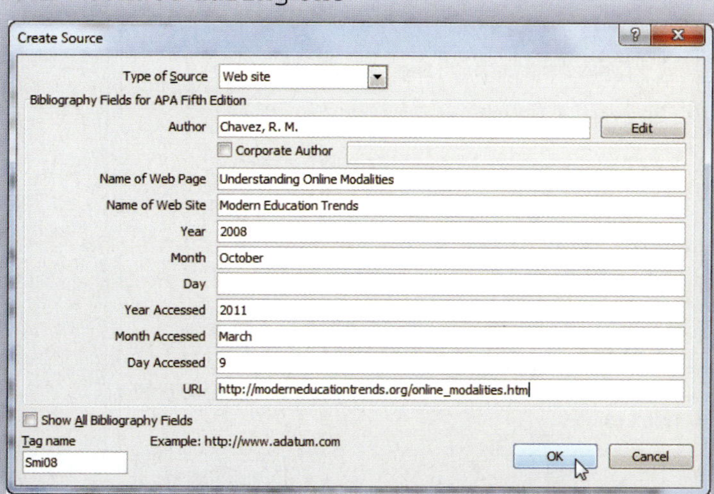

FIGURE WD 5.18

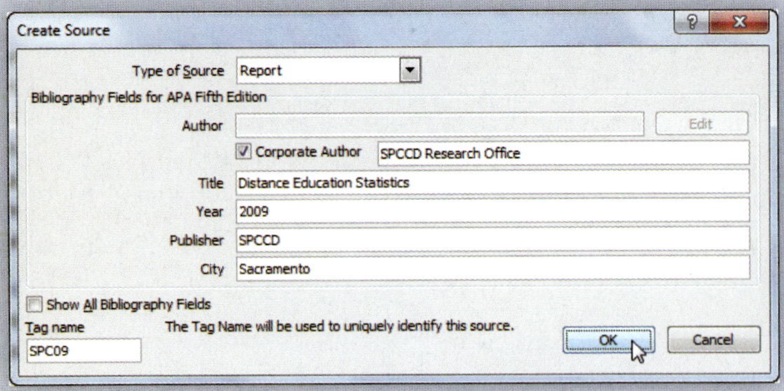

FIGURE WD 5.19

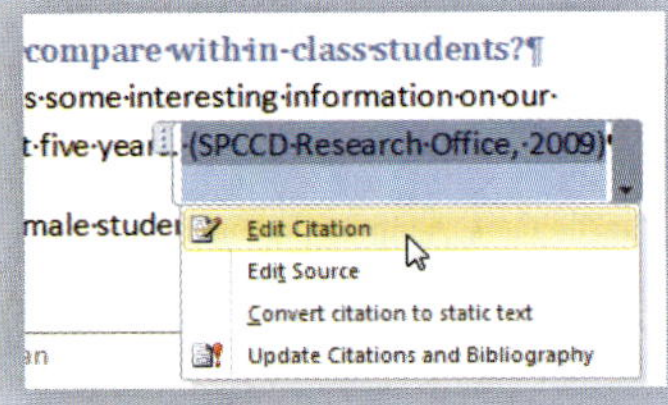

FIGURE WD 5.20

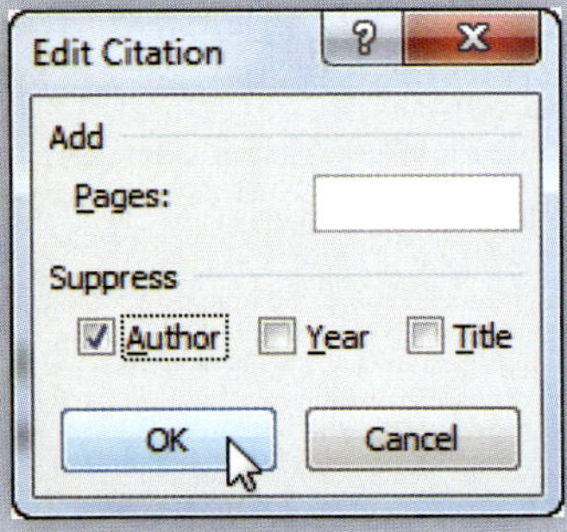

FIGURE WD 5.21

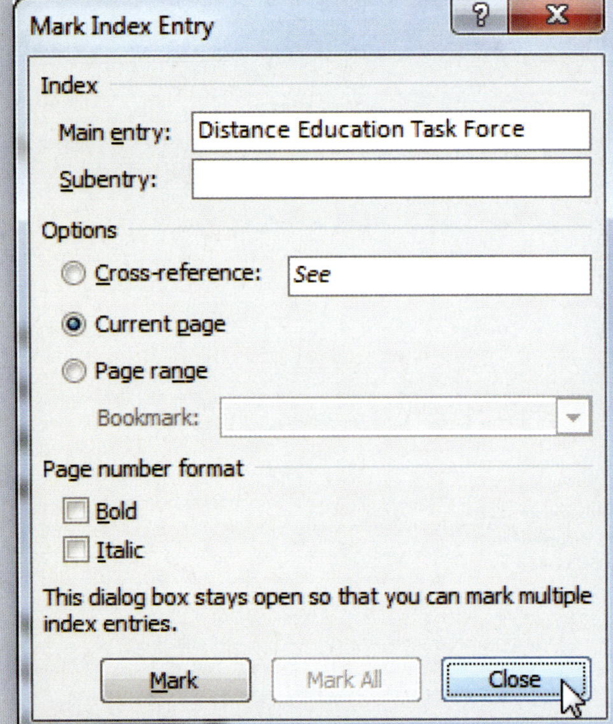

FIGURE WD 5.22

f. Click **OK** to add the source and insert the citation into the document. The parenthetical citation *(Chavez, 2008)* will be inserted into the report.

10. Create another source and edit the citation.

a. Click at the end of the first paragraph in the *What research is there about how our online students compare with in-class students* section (on page 5), click the **Insert Citation** button, click **Add New Source,** and type the source as shown in Figure WD 5.19.

b. Click **OK** to add the source and insert the citation into the document.

c. Click the citation you just inserted.

d. Click the small arrow on the right and choose **Edit Citation.** The *Edit Citation* dialog box will open. Since the author of this source is already mentioned in the paragraph, it does not need to be included in the citation.

e. In the *Suppress* area, click the **Author** check box to suppress this information in the citation.

f. Click **OK** to finish editing this citation. The citation will now contain the title of the report and the date *(Distance Education Statistics, 2009).*

11. Insert a *Works Cited* page at the end of the report and update the *Table of Contents.*

a. Go to the end of the report and insert a page break.

b. On the *References* tab, in the *Citations & Bibliography* group, click the **Bibliography** button and choose **Works Cited.** A works cited page is added to your report with the sources you have added. The *Works Cited* heading is inserted as a *Heading 1* style so it will be included in the *Table of Contents.*

c. Center the *Works Cited* heading.

d. Go to the *Table of Contents* and update the entire table. Notice how the *Works Cited* page is included at the end of the *Table of Contents.*

12. Mark entries in the report to be included in the *Index.*

a. Select **DE Task Force** in the *What student support services are currently available to DE students?* section (on page 3).

b. On the *References* tab, in the *Index* group, click the **Mark Entry** button. The *Mark Index Entry* dialog box will open and the selected text is included in the *Main Entry* area.

c. Confirm that the **Current page** option is selected and click on **Mark.**

d. Click **Close** to close the *Mark Index Entry* dialog box. This index entry is created. When the *Show/Hide* feature is turned on, the index code (*{ XE "Distance Education Task Force" }*) will be visible.

e. Use *Find* to find **online course.**

f. Select the first occurrence of **online course** that is not in the *Table of Contents* or in a heading.

g. Click the **Index** button, click **Mark All,** and click on **Close.** All occurrences of these words in the report should be marked for indexing.

h. Find and mark the following index entries. Do not select a heading or *Table of Contents* entry to mark as an index entry. On each of these choose **Mark All.** (Note: If there is more than one occurrence of an entry in a paragraph, Word will only mark the first occurrence of that entry.)

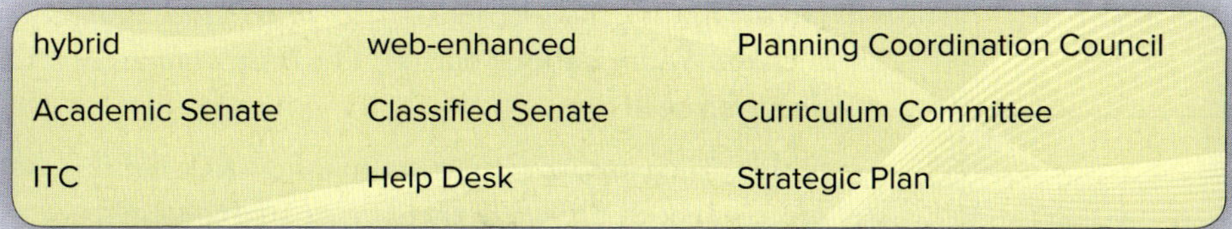

hybrid	web-enhanced	Planning Coordination Council
Academic Senate	Classified Senate	Curriculum Committee
ITC	Help Desk	Strategic Plan

13. Turn off the **Show/Hide** button to hide the index entry codes.

14. Create an *Index* for the report.

a. Go to the end of the report (after the *Works Cited* page) and insert a page break.

b. Type `Index` at the top of the new page, apply the **Heading 1** style to this line, and press **Enter.**

c. On the *References* tab, in the *Index* group, click the **Insert Index** button. The *Index* dialog box will open.

d. In the *Formats:* area, choose **Formal.**

e. The *Type:* should be **Indented** and *Columns:* should be **2.**

f. Click **OK** to insert the *Index.*

g. Center the *Index* title.

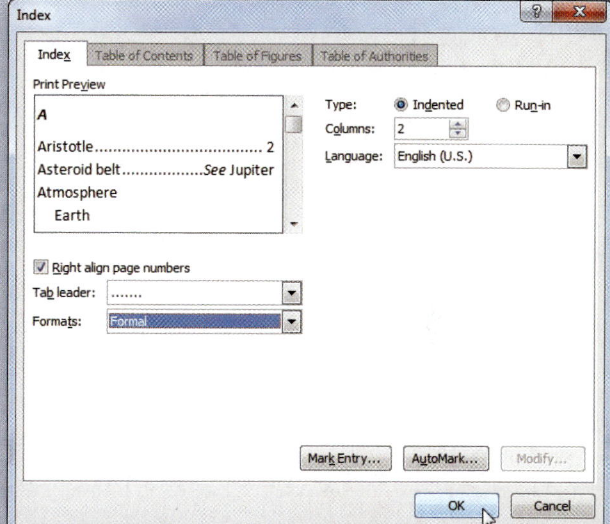

FIGURE WD 5.23

15. Scroll through the report and insert page breaks as necessary to keep information together.

16. Update the *Index.*

a. Click the *Index* at the end of the document.

b. On the *References* tab, in the *Index* group, click the **Update Index** button.

17. Go to the *Table of Contents* and update the entire table.

18. Save and close the document.

Skill Review 5.2

In this project you will be merging the *Expired Letter_05* document from Placer Hills Real Estate with the *Cavalli-PHRE* database.

1. Open the *Expired Letter_05* document.

2. Save this document as ***[your initials]*WD_SkillReview_5-2.**

3. Use the current document to create a mail merge.

a. Click the **Mailings** tab.

b. Click the **Start Mail Merge** button in the *Start Mail Merge* group and choose **Letters.**

4. Select the recipients to be merged into this letter.

a. Click the **Select Recipients** button in the *Start Mail Merge* group and choose **Use Existing List.** The *Select Data Source* dialog box will open.

b. Browse to your student data files, select the **Cavalli-PHRE** database file (an Access file), and click **Open.**

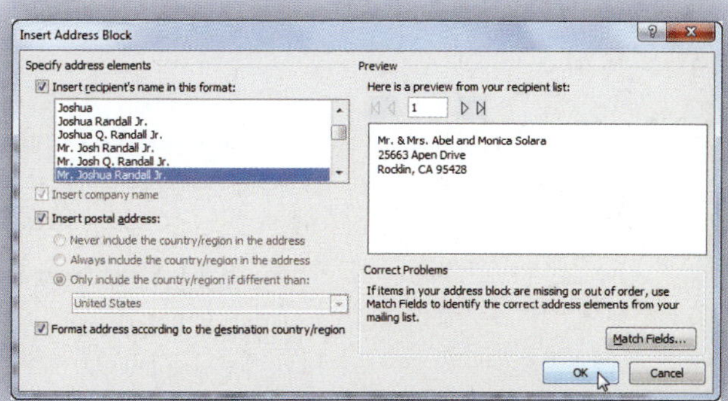

FIGURE WD 5.24

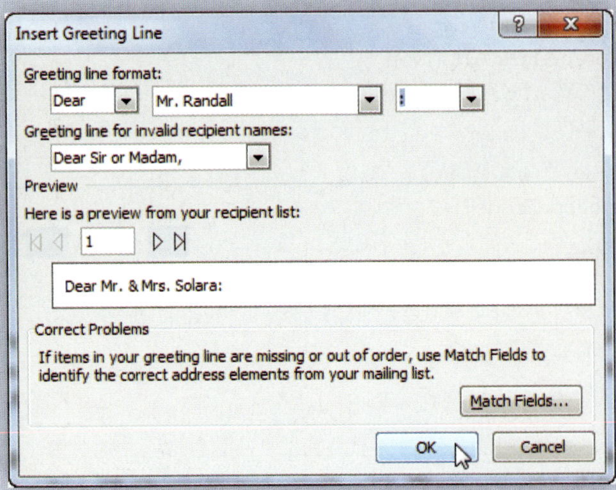

FIGURE WD 5.25

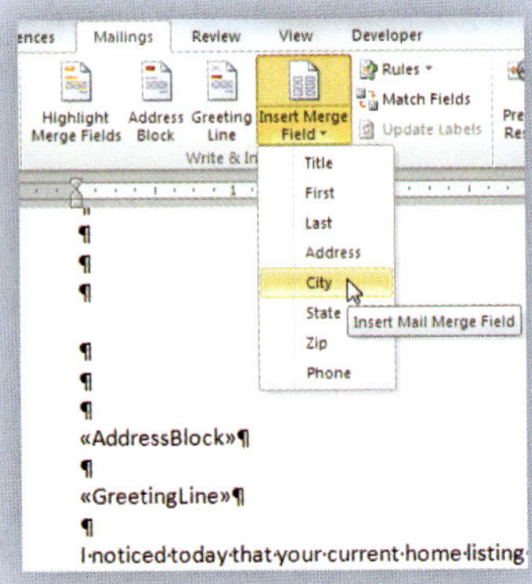

FIGURE WD 5.26

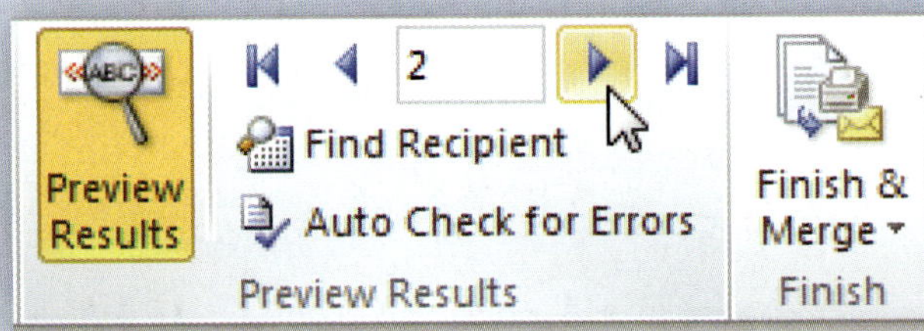

FIGURE WD 5.27

5. Insert the *Address Block* merge field into the business letter as the inside address.

   a. Click in front of the *[Inside Address]* placeholder text in the business letter.

   b. On the *Mailings* tab, in the *Write & Insert Fields* group, click the **Address Block** button. The *Insert Address Block* dialog box will open.

   c. In this dialog box, you can customize how the *Address Block* will be displayed. In the *Preview* area you can see how each record will be displayed in the letter.

   d. Click **OK** to accept the *Address Block* settings and insert the *Address Block* into the letter.

   e. The merge field code <<*AddressBlock*>> is inserted into the letter before the placeholder text *[Inside Address]*.

   f. Select and delete **[Inside Address]** after the *AddressBlock* merge code. Be sure not to delete any *Enters*.

6. Insert the *Greeting Line* merge field into the business letter as the salutation.

   a. Click in front of the *[Salutation]* placeholder text in the business letter.

   b. On the *Mailings* tab, in the *Write & Insert Fields* group, click the **Greeting Line** button. The *Insert Greeting Line* dialog box will open.

   c. In the *Greeting line format:* area, confirm that the greeting line consists of *Dear,* a courtesy title (*Mr., Mrs.,* etc.), and the last name, and change the ending punctuation to a **colon.**

   d. Click **OK** to accept the *Greeting Line* settings and insert the *Greeting Line* into the letter.

   e. The merge field code <<*GreetingLine* >> is inserted into the letter before the placeholder text *[Salutation]*.

   f. Select and delete **[Salutation]** after the *GreetingLine* merge code. Be sure not to delete any *Enters*.

7. Insert a merge field code into the body of the letter.

   a. Select and delete the **[City]** placeholder text in the first sentence in the first paragraph of the letter.

   b. In the *Write & Insert Fields* group, click the **Insert Merge Field** button and select **City.**

   c. The <<*City*>> merge code will be inserted into the letter.

   d. Make sure there is a space before and after this merge field.

8. Save the *[your initials]WD_SkillReview_5-2* document.

9. Preview the results of your merge.

   a. Click the **Preview Results** button in the *Preview Results* group. Data from the recipient list are displayed in the <<*AddressBlock*>>, <<*GreetingLine*>>, and <<*City*>> fields in the document.

   b. Click the **Next Record** button to display the contents of the next record in the letter.

   c. Click the **Preview Results** button to return to the letter with the merge field codes displayed.

10. Finish and review the results of your mail merge.

a. Click the **Finish & Merge** button in the *Finish* group and choose **Edit Individual Documents.** The *Merge to New Document* dialog box will open.

b. Click the **All** radio button and click **OK** to complete the merge. The letter will be merged with the recipient list into a new document.

c. Save this new document as **`[your initials]WD_merge_5-2`.**

d. Scroll through the document to verify that there are six letters and that the merged information from the recipient list is correctly placed in the document.

11. Add an envelope to the first letter.

a. On the *Mailings* tab, in the *Create* group, click the **Envelopes** button. The *Envelopes and Labels* dialog box will open. The inside address from the first letter is included in the *Delivery address:* area.

b. In the *Return address:* area type:

```
Emma Cavalli
Placer Hills Real Estate
7100 Madrone Road
Roseville, CA 95722
```

c. Click the **Add to Document** button.

d. A dialog box will open asking if you want to save the return address as the default address; click **No.** The envelope will be inserted on a separate page before the first letter.

12. Create a custom print to print only the merged letters and not the envelope.

a. Click the **File** tab to open the BackStage.

b. Click the **Print** button to display the print options.

c. In the *Pages:* area in the *Settings* section type: `2-7`

d. Click the **Print** button to print the six merged letters. The BackStage will close and you will be returned to the merged document.

13. Save and close both open documents.

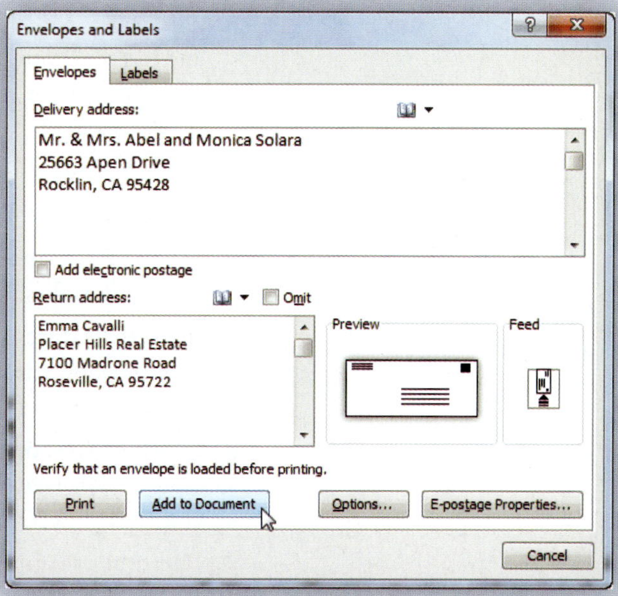

FIGURE WD 5.28

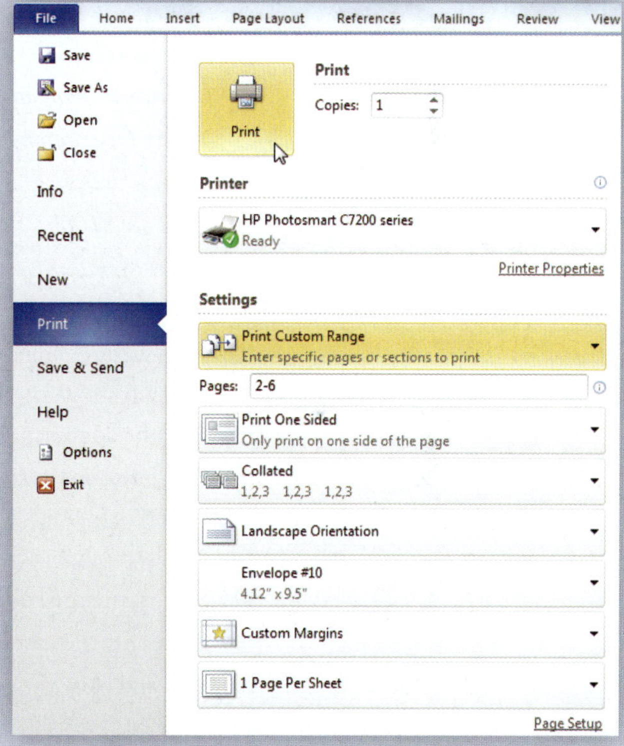

FIGURE WD 5.29

challenge yourself 1

In this project you will be merging the *Renewal Letter_05* document from Central Sierra Insurance with the *CSI_Souza_Renewals* database.

1. Open the *Renewal Letter_05* document.

2. Save this document as **`[your initials]WD_Challenge_5-3`.**

3. Click at the end of *Premium Basis* in the second column of the first row of the table and insert a footnote.
4. Type the following in the footnote: `Note: The actual premium will be determined by your actual sales following a final audit at policy year-end.`
5. Create a mail merge using this letter.
6. Use the **CSI_Souza_Renewals** database as your recipient list. This file is in your student data files.
7. Insert the **Address Block** merge field in the document where indicated by the bracketed placeholder text (e.g., *[Address Block]*). Make sure the company name is on the second line of the *Address Block*. Delete the bracketed placeholder text.
8. Insert the **Greeting Line** merge field in the document where indicated by the bracketed placeholder text. Edit the *Greeting Line* so there is no punctuation at the end of the line. Delete the bracketed placeholder text.
9. Insert the other merge fields as indicated by the bracketed placeholder text and delete the bracketed placeholder text. The merge fields you will be inserting are indicated by the bracketed placeholder text below:

   [Policy Number]

   [Company]

   [Insurance Company]

   [Policy Description]

   [Premium Basis]

   [Cost per $1000]

   [Total Premium]

   [First Name]
10. Preview the results of the mail merge. Make sure all the merge fields are in the correct location and there is proper spacing around them.
11. Save the document.
12. Finish the merge so you can edit the individual documents. There should be eight letters.
13. Scroll through the document to make sure the mail merge worked properly.
14. Save the merged document as ***[your initials]*WD_merge_5-3.**
15. Print only the first page of the merged document.
16. Save and close the open documents.

challenge yourself 2

In this project you will be editing the *Personal Training Program_05* document from American River Cycling Club.

1. Open the *Personal Training Program_05* document.
2. Save this document as ***[your initials]*WD_Challenge_5-4.**
3. Apply the **Austin** theme to the document.
4. Apply the **Heading 1** style to each of the bold section headings.
5. Apply the **Heading 2** style to each of the underlined section headings.

6. Use **MLA Sixth Edition** reference format.
7. At the end of the *Pace of Rides* section, add the following citation.

Type of Source	Book
Author	Burke, E. R.
Title	The Complete Book of Long-Distance Cycling
Year	2000
City	New York
Publisher	Rodale Books

8. At the end of the *Number of Rides per Week* section, add the following citation.

Type of Source	Book
Author	Chapple, T.
Title	Base Building for Cyclists
Year	2007
City	San Francisco
Publisher	VeloPress

9. At the end of the *Duration of Rides* section, add the following citation.

Type of Source	Web site
Corporate Author	USA Cycling
Name of Web Page	Training Guidelines
Year	2009
Month	April
Year Accessed	2011
Month Accessed	January
Day Accessed	12
URL	http://www.usacycling.com/training_guidelines

10. Insert a page break at the end of the document and insert a **Bibliography.**
11. Insert a blank page at the beginning of the document and insert a **Table of Contents** on this blank page. All headings marked as *Heading 1* and *Heading 2* should be displayed in the *Table of Contents.*
12. Find the first occurrence of each of the acronyms below and insert a footnote for each using the information below.

INSERT FOOTNOTE AFTER	TYPE TEXT IN FOOTNOTE
PTP	Personal training program
RPM	Revolutions per minute
VO2	The highest rate of oxygen consumption attainable during maximal or exhaustive exercise
BMI	Body mass index

13. Find and mark for index all occurrences of each of the words below. Use *Mark All* and don't mark an occurrence in the *Table of Contents* or in a heading.

PTP	Max VO2
heart rate	rest day
recovery	training log
BMI	muscles

14. On a separate page at the end of the document, type `Index` and apply the **Heading 1** style.
15. Insert a one-column *Index* of your choice.
16. Insert a footer of your choice into the document. Make sure the footer has a page number and that you set the footer to not appear on the first page (hint: different first page).
17. At the beginning of the document, insert a **Cover Page** of your choice. Add text as needed in the document property fields.
18. Turn off **Show/Hide** and scroll through your document inserting page breaks where necessary.
19. Update the *Table of Contents* and the *Index*.
20. Save and close the document.

on your own

In this project you will be creating mailing labels and return address mailing labels for Central Sierra Insurance.

1. Open a new Word document.
2. Save this document as ***[your initials]*WD_OnYourOwn_labels_5-5.**
3. Start a new mail merge job to create labels for all of the employees from Central Sierra Insurance. Use *Avery US Letter 5160* labels.
4. Use the *Central Sierra Insurance* database as the recipient list.
5. Insert an **Address Block** on the labels and do not include the company name.
6. Click on the **Update Labels** button so the *Address Block* is placed in each label.
7. Preview the labels to make sure they fit correctly on each label. You might have to adjust the before or after paragraph spacing.
8. Save the document.
9. Finish the merge to a new document and save as ***[your initials]*WD_OnYourOwn_merge_5-5.**
10. Open a new Word document.
11. Create **Labels** (don't start a new mail merge) to create return mailing labels for Central Sierra Insurance.
12. Type the address for Central Sierra Insurance:

    Central Sierra Insurance
    5502 Ridley Way
    Cameron Park, CA 94663
13. Use *Avery US Letter 5160* labels and use a full page of the same label.

14. Insert these return labels into a new document and save the document as ***[your initials]*WD_OnYourOwn_return_5-5.**

15. Close the open documents.

fix it

In this project you will be editing the *Society Training Guide_05* document from Courtyard Medical Plaza.

1. Open the *Society Training Guide_05* document.
2. Save this document as ***[your initials]*WD_FixIt_5-6.**
3. Apply a theme to this document to complement the colors of the Courtyard Medical Plaza logo.
4. Apply **Heading 1** and **Heading 2** styles to the main and subheadings in the document.
5. Apply the **Heading 3** style to each of the *Skiing Procedures* in the *Four-Track (4T) and Three-Track (3T)* and *Bi-Ski and Mono-Ski* sections.
6. Insert a **Table of Contents** before the first page. Make sure all three levels of headings are displayed.
7. Use text wrapping to appropriately position the picture next to the *Introduction to Equipment* subsection in the *Bi-Ski and Mono-Ski* section.
8. In each of the *Disabilities* sections, mark each disability as an entry for the *Index.*
9. Insert an **Index** of your choice after the last page of the document. Include a heading on the Index page and apply a style so it will appear in the *Table of Contents.*
10. Insert a footnote after each of the *Skiing Procedures* headings, and inform the reader that these procedures will vary based on the experience of both the participant and ski instructor.
11. Remove any extra lines in the document.
12. Insert a footer of your choice into the document. Include a page number and the title of the document.
13. Add a **Cover Page** to the document.
14. Turn off **Show/Hide** and insert any page breaks where necessary.
15. Update the *Table of Contents* and *Index.*
16. Print only the *Table of Contents* pages.
17. Save and close the document.

chapter 6

Exploring Advanced Document Features

In this chapter, you will learn the following skills:

- Work with the *Styles* task pane, and create and rename styles
- Apply columns in the middle of a document, and add horizontal lines and quote text boxes
- Apply appropriate section breaks, keep paragraphs together, and manage orphans and widows
- Use the Outline view
- Create a table of figures
- Navigate long documents, create bookmarks, and use *Go To*

skills

introduction

Styles in Microsoft Word are the cornerstone of every document you create. Styles provide you with consistency throughout your document and are essential when working with long documents. You will learn to use character and paragraph styles, as well as outlines and sections breaks, to create complex documents that mix and match different formatting.

6.1 Using Character Spacing

Character spacing gives you more control over the appearance of the text in your document. By expanding the spacing between characters, you can give your text a more open feel. By condensing the spacing between characters, you can fit text into a smaller space.

To change the spacing between characters:

1. Select the text you want to change.
2. On the *Home* tab, in the *Font* group, click the dialog launcher.
3. Click the **Advanced** tab.
4. From the *Spacing:* list, select **Expanded** or **Condensed.**
5. Enter a value for the spacing.
6. The *Preview* area displays an example of what your text will look like.
7. Click **OK** in the dialog box to apply the changes.

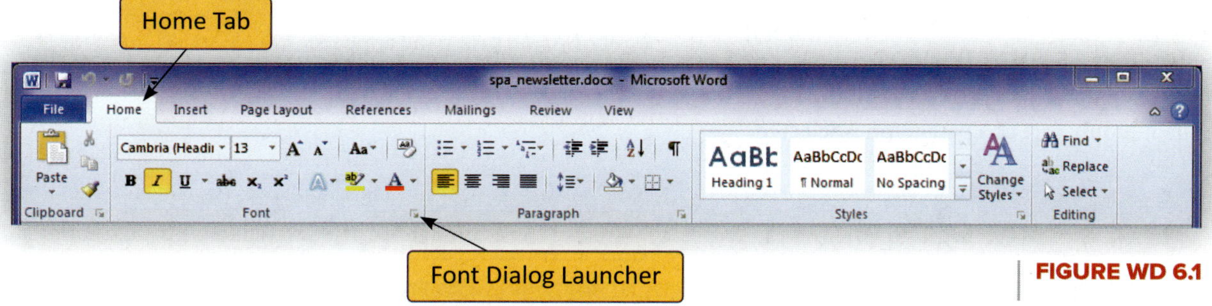

FIGURE WD 6.1

Clicking the **Advanced** tab in the *Font* dialog box gives you the following options:

Scaling allows you to resize the selected text, making it either larger or smaller.

Spacing alters the spacing between all selected letters by the same amount.

Positioning raises or lowers the selection in relation to the baseline.

Kerning is the amount of space between certain characters to create the appearance of even spacing.

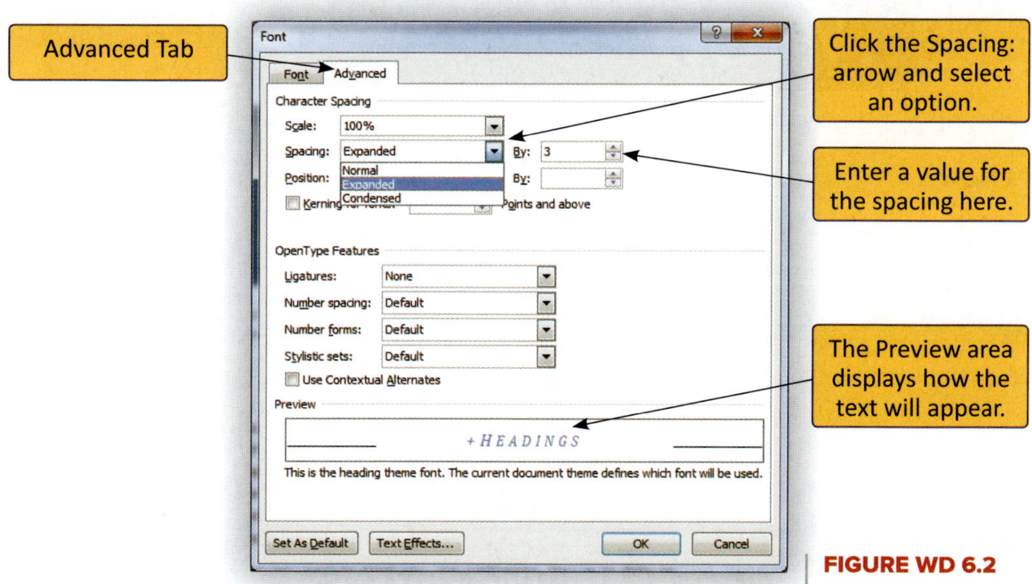

FIGURE WD 6.2

tips & tricks

Click the **Set as Default** button to change the default font style in the Normal template to the selected font formatting.

try this

To open the *Font* dialog box, you can also press Ctrl + D on the keyboard.

6.2 Working with the Styles Task Pane

The **Styles task pane** lists all the text styles available in a document. You can apply styles to text from the *Styles* task pane, as well as create new styles and modify existing styles.

There are five basic style types you can apply from the *Styles* task pane:

Paragraph—formatting applied to the entire paragraph (such as line spacing and alignment).

Character—formatting applied to the text characters only (such as font, font size, and font color).

Linked (paragraph and character)—formatting applied as paragraph or character styles (such as headings). If a paragraph is selected, the paragraph style of the linked style is applied. If only part of a paragraph is selected (such as a word or phrase), the character style is applied and the paragraph style is not affected.

Table—formatting applied to tables (such as borders and shading).

List—formatting applied to lists (such as bullet or numbering format).

To apply a style from the *Styles* task pane:

1. On the *Home* tab, in the *Styles* group, click the dialog launcher.
2. The *Styles* task pane appears.
3. Click a style in the task pane to apply that style to the selected text.

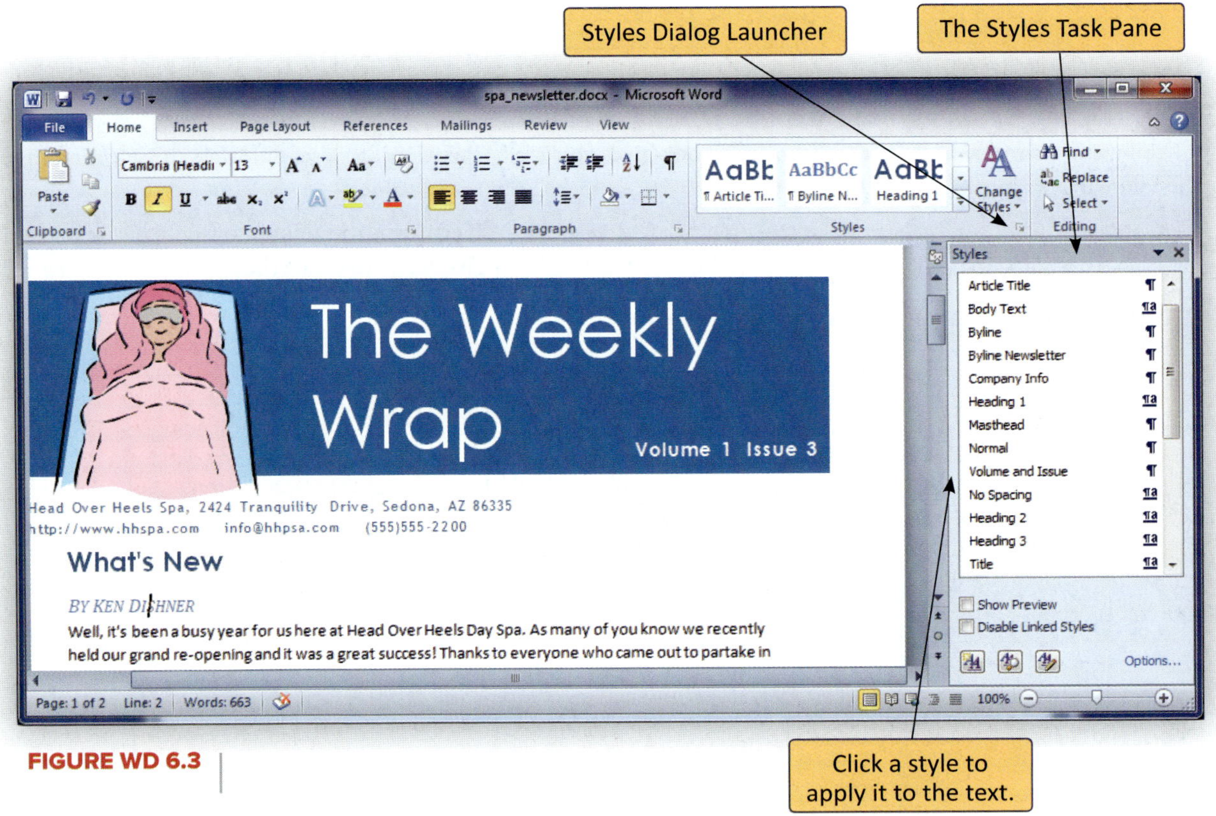

FIGURE WD 6.3

tips & tricks

Click the **Show Preview** check box, to change the style names in the list from plain text to formatted text that shows how text will appear when the style is applied to it.

tell me more

When you open the *Styles* task pane, each style is listed with an icon next to the name, indicating the type of style for each item in the task pane.

6.3 Creating a New Style

Text styles include all formatting applied to the text. This formatting includes paragraph styles, including alignment and line spacing, and character styles such as font and font color. Word comes with a number of built-in styles for you to use, but what if you want to save and reuse your own custom styles? You can save your own styles from the *Styles* task pane.

To create a new style:

1. Select the text you want to base the new style on.
2. On the *Home* tab, in the *Styles* group, click the *Styles* dialog launcher.
3. The *Styles* task pane displays.
4. Click the **New Style** button at the bottom of the task pane to open the *Create New Style from Formatting* dialog box.
5. Type the name of the new style in the *Name:* box.
6. Click the *Style type:* arrow and select **Character** or **Paragraph.**
7. If you want, change any options for the new style.
8. Click **OK.**

The new style appears in the task pane and in the *Styles* gallery. Click the style name to apply the new style to text.

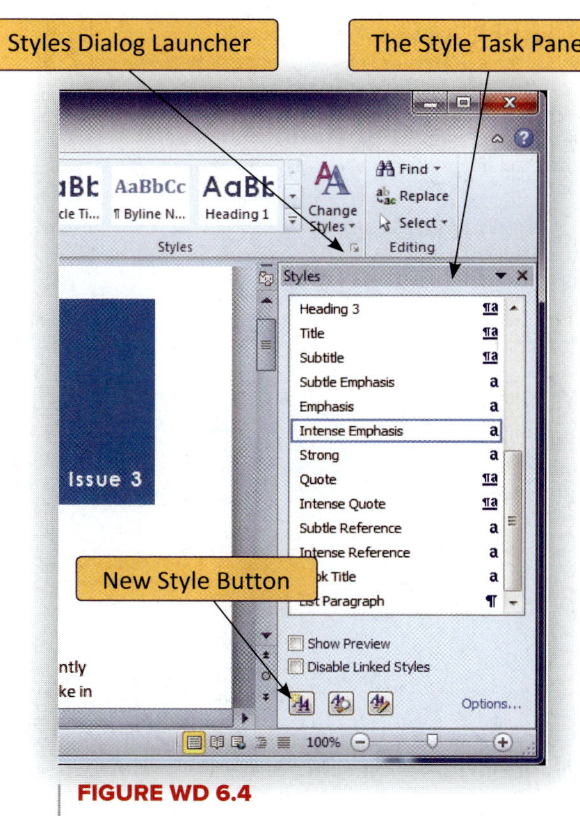

FIGURE WD 6.4

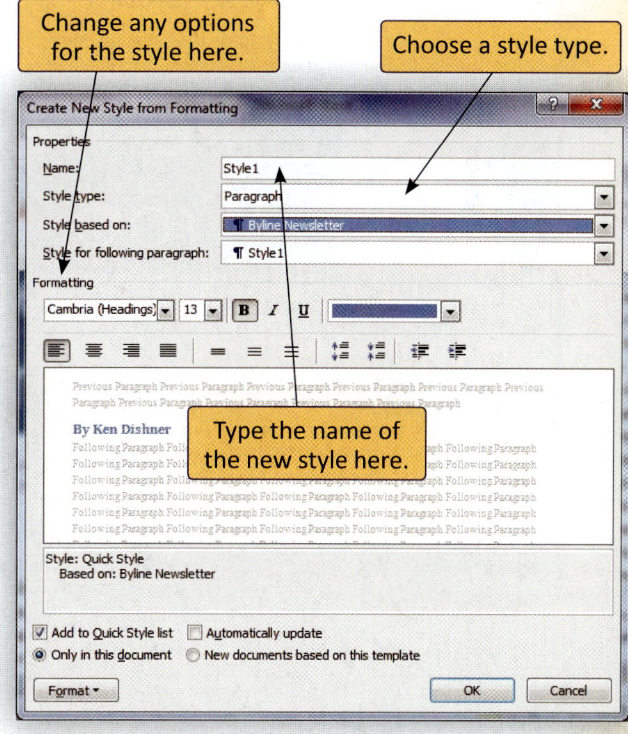

FIGURE WD 6.5

tips & tricks

In the *Create New Style from Formatting* dialog box, click the **Format** button to open additional dialog boxes to further modify the style. These include the *Font, Paragraph, Tabs, Borders and Shading, Language, Frame, Numbering and Bullets, Customize Keyboard,* and *Format Text Effects* dialog boxes.

tell me more

When you change the style type to *Character,* the paragraph options in the dialog box are disabled. The remaining available options only affect character formatting. These options include *Font, Font Size, Bold, Italic, Underline,* and *Font Color.* When you apply the character style to text in the document, only the character formatting will be applied to the new text. The paragraph formatting will remain the same.

6.4 Renaming Styles

The Word 2010 *Normal* template includes a standard set of styles with default style names. These style names are descriptive of the part of the document the style is applied to. For example, the *Normal* style is typically applied to paragraph text in a document, while the *Title* style is used for title text on a cover page. The *Heading 1, Heading 2,* and *Heading 3* styles are used for heading styles throughout the document. You can keep these default names, or you can rename a style to something more meaningful to you.

To rename a style:

1. On the *Home* tab, in the *Styles* group, click the **More** button.
2. Right-click the style in the *Styles* gallery, and select **Rename. . .** from the menu.
3. In the *Rename Style* dialog box, type the new name of the style and click **OK.**

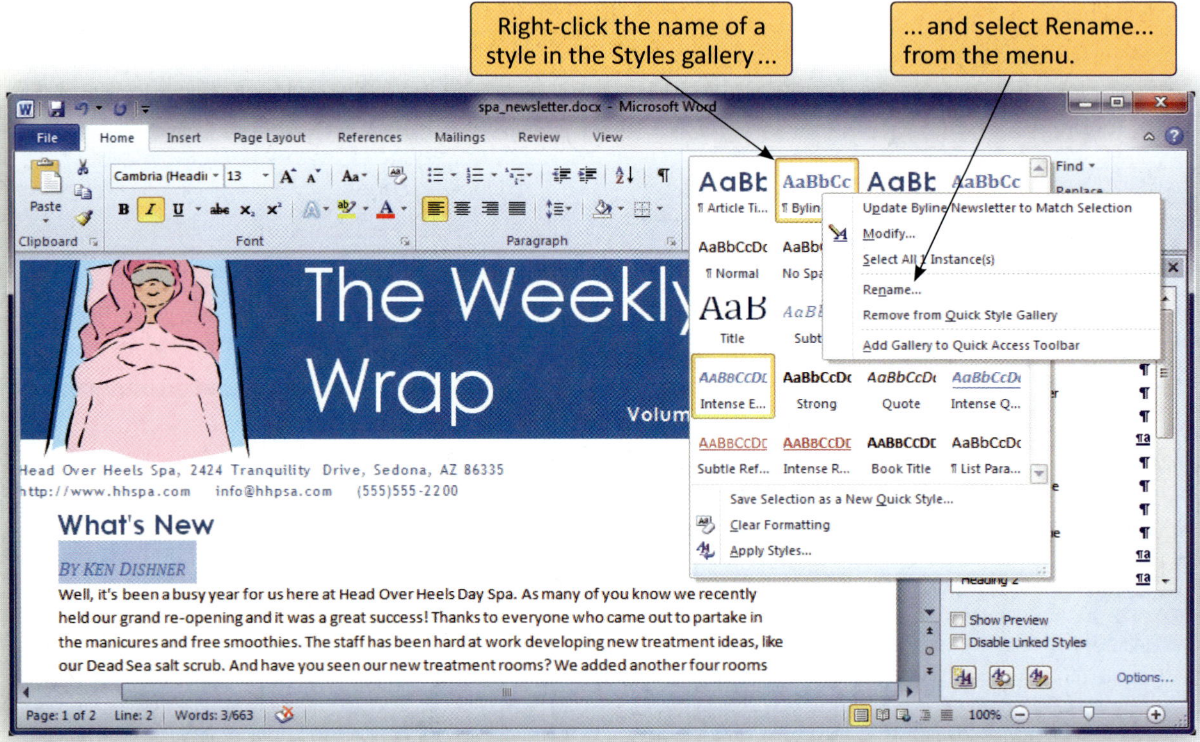

FIGURE WD 6.6

tell me **more**

When you change the name of a style, the new style name only appears in the document that was open when you changed the style. If you create a new document, it will not include the new style name.

try **this**

You can change the name of a style from the *Modify Style* dialog box. Type the new name in the *Name:* box, and click **OK**.

6.5 Inserting Symbols

A **symbol** is a special text character that is inserted into a document rather than typed on the keyboard. Symbols include special characters, such as copyright and trademark signs, mathematical operators, and foreign currency symbols.

Some of the more common symbols include:

©	Copyright sign
®	Registered sign
™	Trademark sign
€	Euro sign
£	Pound sign
¥	Yen sign

To insert a symbol:

1. Click the **Insert** tab.
2. In the *Symbols* group, click the **Symbol** button and select an option from the gallery.

The most recently used symbols appear in the *Symbols* gallery. To view addition symbols to insert, click **More Symbols...** at the bottom of the gallery. In the *Symbol* dialog box, you can choose to insert special characters or to insert symbols that are part of a font set.

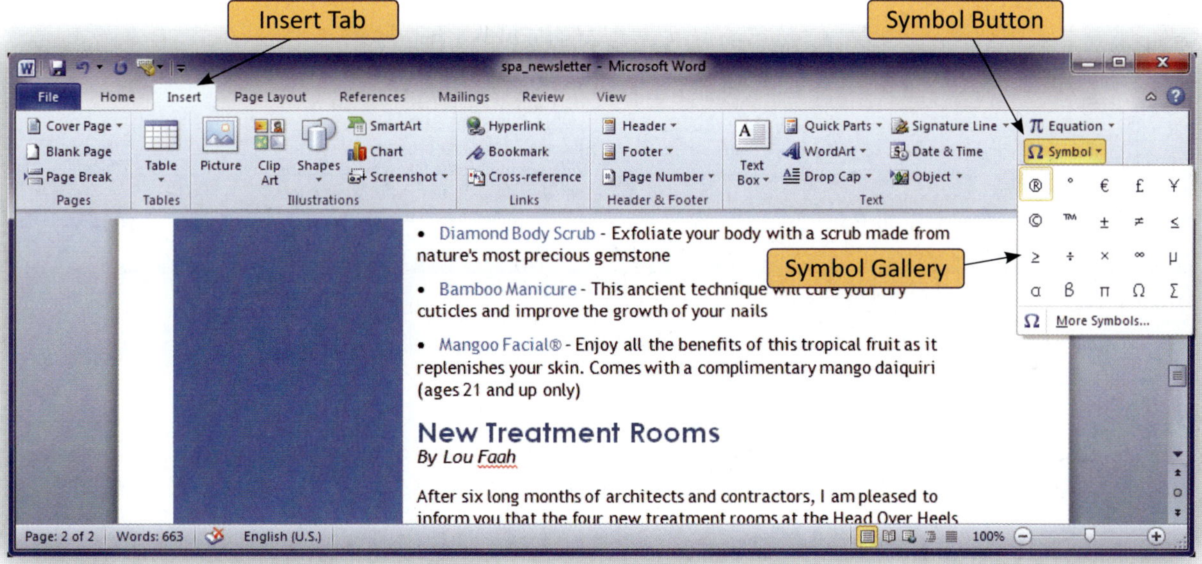

FIGURE WD 6.7

tips & tricks

The *Wingdings* font set includes a variety of pictographs for you to add to your documents.

tell me more

Word comes with a number of predefined mathematical equations you can add to documents. To add a mathematical equation to a document, click the **Insert** tab. In the *Symbols* group, click the **Equation** button and select an option.

try this

Some symbols can be inserted by typing a combination of keystrokes on the keyboard. For example, typing two equal signs followed by the greater than sign will automatically be changed to a right-pointing arrow (➔), and typing a colon, a hyphen, and a close parenthesis will be replaced by a smiley face (☺).

6.6 Applying Columns

Newsletter pages are often laid out in **columns.** The text of these pages continues from the bottom of one column to the top of the next column. Word makes it easy to arrange your document into columns.

To apply columns to text:

1. Click the **Page Layout** tab.
2. In the *Page Setup* group, click the **Columns** button and select an option.

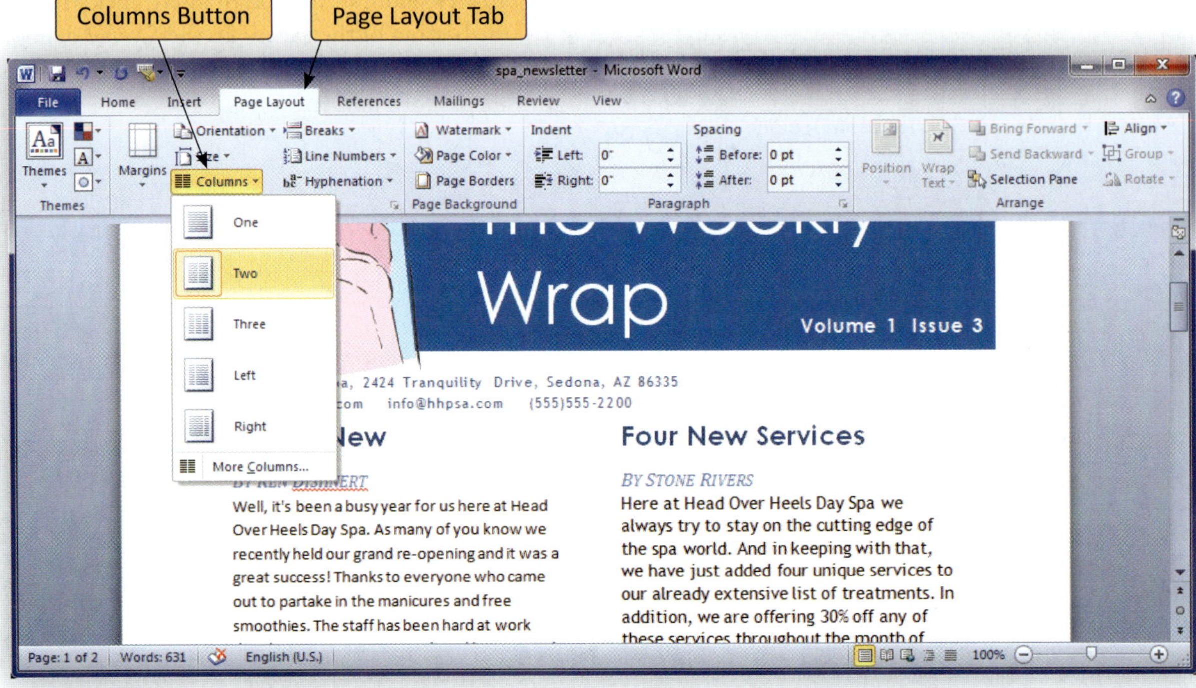

FIGURE WD 6.8

tips & tricks

- If you know you want your document to appear in column format, set the columns before you enter the document text.
- If you want text to appear at the top of a column, you can insert a column break before the text. To add a column break, in the *Page Setup* group, click the **Breaks** button select **Column.**

tell me more

Newspaper columns are often justified. To justify your text, click the **Justify** button on the *Home* tab of the Ribbon.

from the perspective of . . .

FREELANCE TECHNICAL WRITER

As a technical writer, I have to organize materials and complete a lot of writing assignments. With next-page and continuous section breaks I can now format a document to use a variety of columns, different margins, and different page orientations. It's like having multiple documents inside one file.

6.7 Using Automatic Hyphenation

When you come to the end of a line, word wrap automatically moves the cursor to the next line and places the next word you type at the beginning of the next line. This can leave the right side of a document looking ragged and uneven, or if a paragraph is justified, it can leave awkward space between words. One way to avoid this unsightly formatting is to allow Word to automatically hyphenate words for you. When **automatic hyphenation** is enabled, Word will add hyphens to words at the end of a line instead of placing the whole word on the following line.

To enable automatic hyphenation:

1. Click the **Page Layout** tab.
2. In the *Page Setup* group, click the **Hyphenation** button and select **Automatic.**
3. To turn automatic hyphenation off, click the **Hyphenation** button and select **None.**

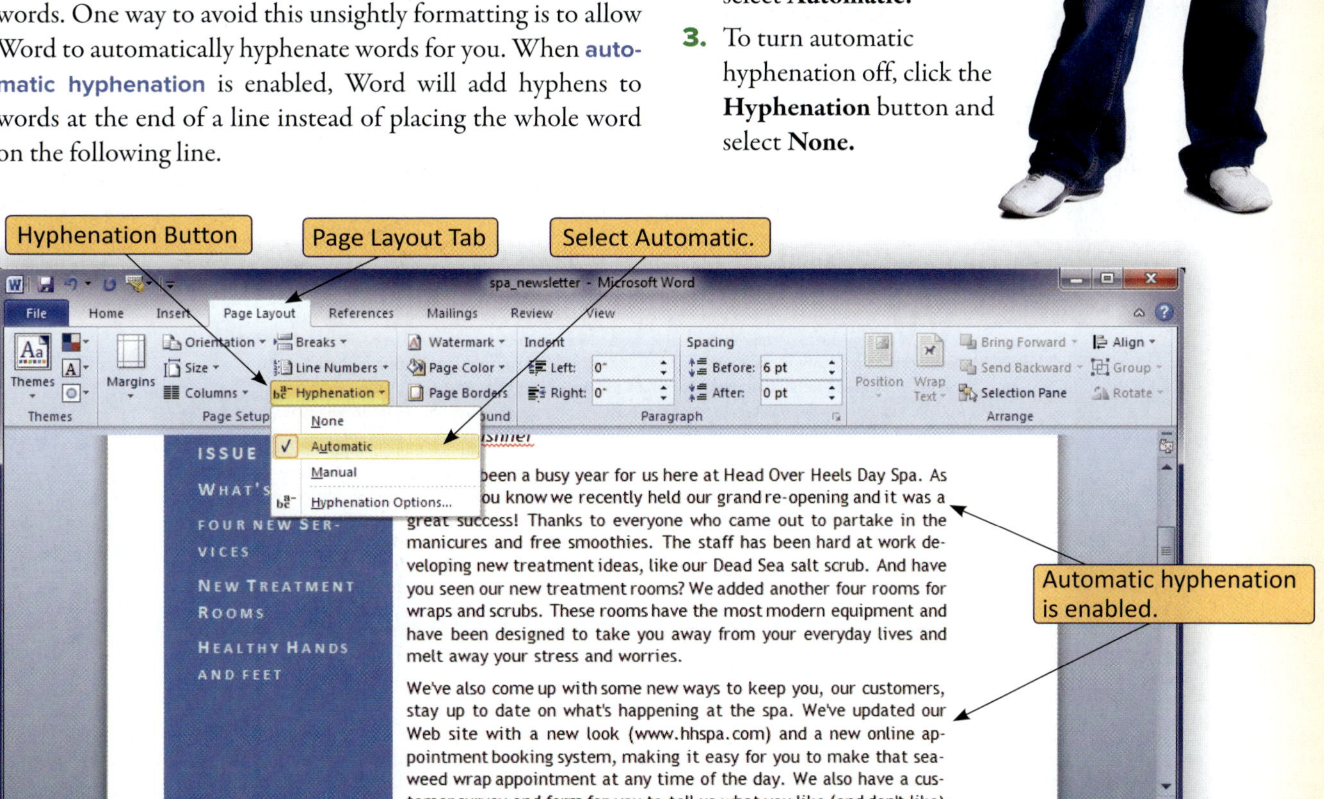

FIGURE WD 6.9

tips & tricks

With automatic hyphenation, Word chooses where to break the word across lines. If you want to choose where to hyphenate a word yourself, select **Manual** from the *Hyphenation* menu.

tell me more

The *Hyphenation* dialog box allows you to control the number of consecutive hyphens in a document as well as set a zone that will control the length of space allowed at the end of a line.

6.8 Adding a Drop Cap to a Paragraph

In some documents, you may notice that the first letter of a paragraph is larger and lower than the rest of the text. This is called a **drop cap.** Drop caps are often used in such layouts as brochures and newsletters to add visual interest and to draw the reader's attention to the text.

There are two basic styles of drop caps:

Dropped. The *Dropped* style places the drop cap in front of the number of specified lines of text (three by default). In the *Dropped* style, the remaining paragraph text wraps under the drop cap so the drop cap and the text of the paragraph are left-aligned.

In Margin. The *In Margin* style places the drop cap in the margin of the paragraph in front of the number of specified lines of text. With the *In Margin* style, the remaining paragraph text is left-aligned with the first lines of the paragraph, not the drop cap.

To add a drop cap to a paragraph:

1. Click in the paragraph where you want to add the drop cap.
2. Click the **Insert** tab.
3. In the *Text* group, click the **Drop Cap** button and select an option—**Dropped** or **In Margin.**

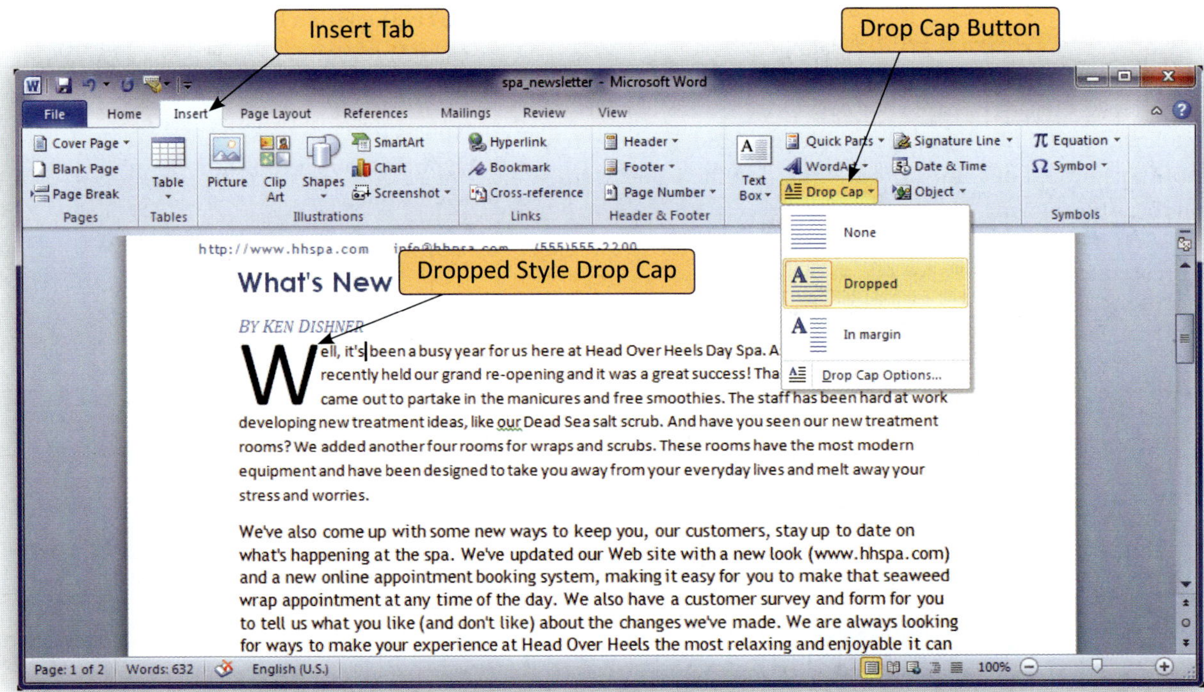

FIGURE WD 6.10

tips & tricks

- You can modify the look of your drop cap by clicking **Drop Cap Options. . .** on the menu. In the *Drop Cap* dialog box, you can change the type of drop cap, the font used, how tall the drop cap is, and how far the drop cap is from the paragraph text.
- To clear the drop cap, click **None** on the menu.

try this

You can also apply a drop cap from the *Drop Cap* dialog box. Click the **Drop Cap** button and select **Drop Cap Options. . .** to open the dialog box. Select a drop cap option and click **OK.**

6.9 Adding a Quote Text Box

A **pull quote** is a piece of text from your document that is "pulled" out and displayed as a graphic element on the page. Pull quotes can add visual interest to your document and give your readers a quick snapshot of its content.

A **sidebar** is a block of information separate from the main document. Sidebars are typically aligned along one side of the page or along the top or bottom of the page. They usually contain information related to the main document, but not found in the document. Unlike pull quotes, sidebars are usually anchored along one side of the page and extend for the length or width of the page.

To add a pull quote or a sidebar to your document:

1. Click the **Insert** tab.
2. In the *Text* group, click the **Text Box** button and select an option from the gallery.
3. Type your text in the box.

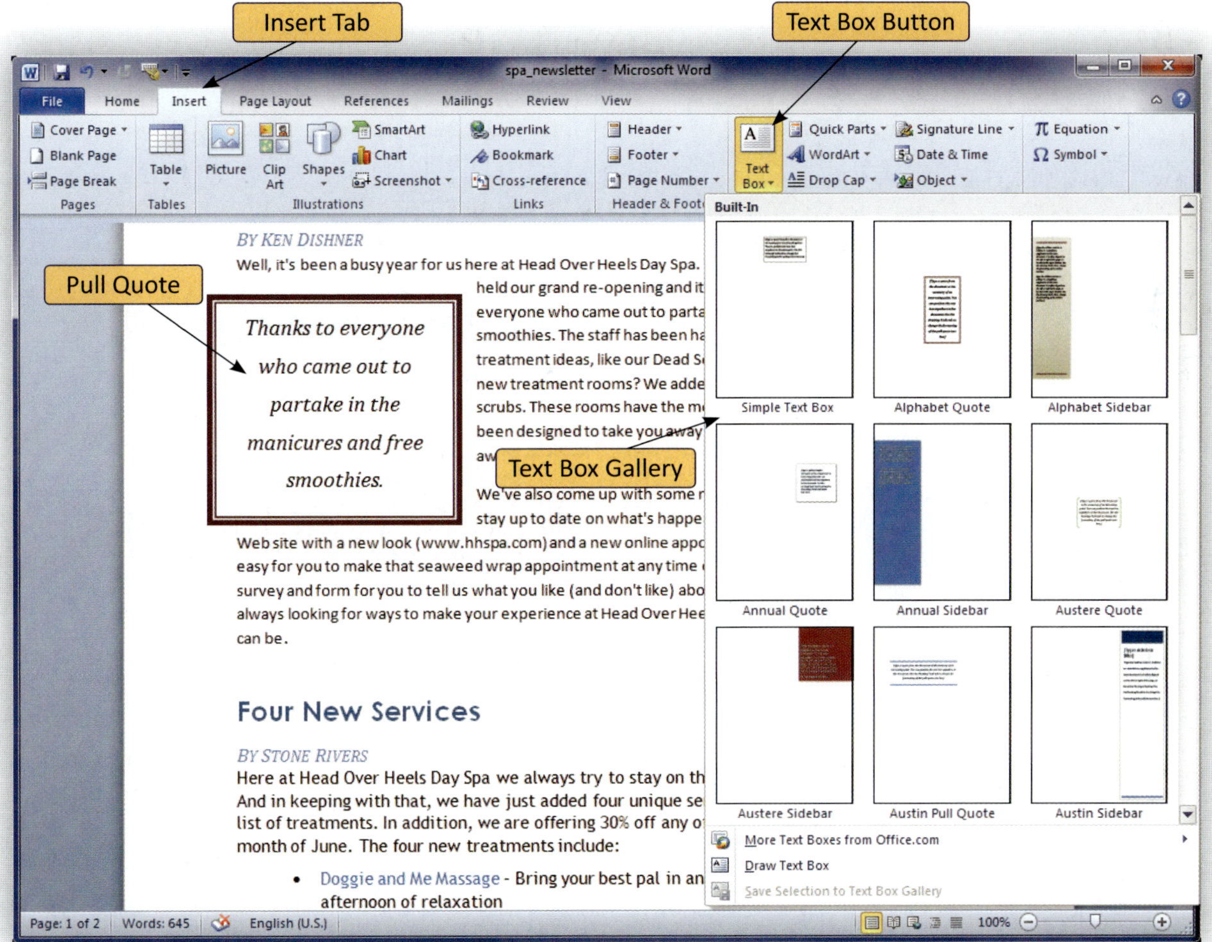

FIGURE WD 6.11

tips & tricks

To modify a pull quote or sidebar, click the *Format* tab under *Text Box Tools*. Here you can control text box styles, shadow effects, the size of the quote box, and the placement of the text box.

try this

You can also add a pull quote or sidebar through the *Building Blocks Organizer*.

6.10 Keeping Paragraphs Together

Sometimes you will want to be sure information in your document is displayed on the same page and not broken across two pages. You can adjust the settings of a paragraph so the text of the paragraph will never break across a page. You can also modify a paragraph so that it will always appear on the same page as the following paragraph.

To adjust how paragraph text breaks across a page:

1. Place the cursor anywhere in the paragraph you want to change.
2. On the *Home* tab, in the *Paragraph* group, click the dialog launcher.
3. In the *Paragraph* dialog box, click the **Line and Page Breaks** tab.
4. Under *Pagination,* select **Keep lines together** to prevent the paragraph from breaking across the page.
5. Select **Keep with next** to force the paragraph to print on the same page as the following paragraph.
6. Click **OK.**

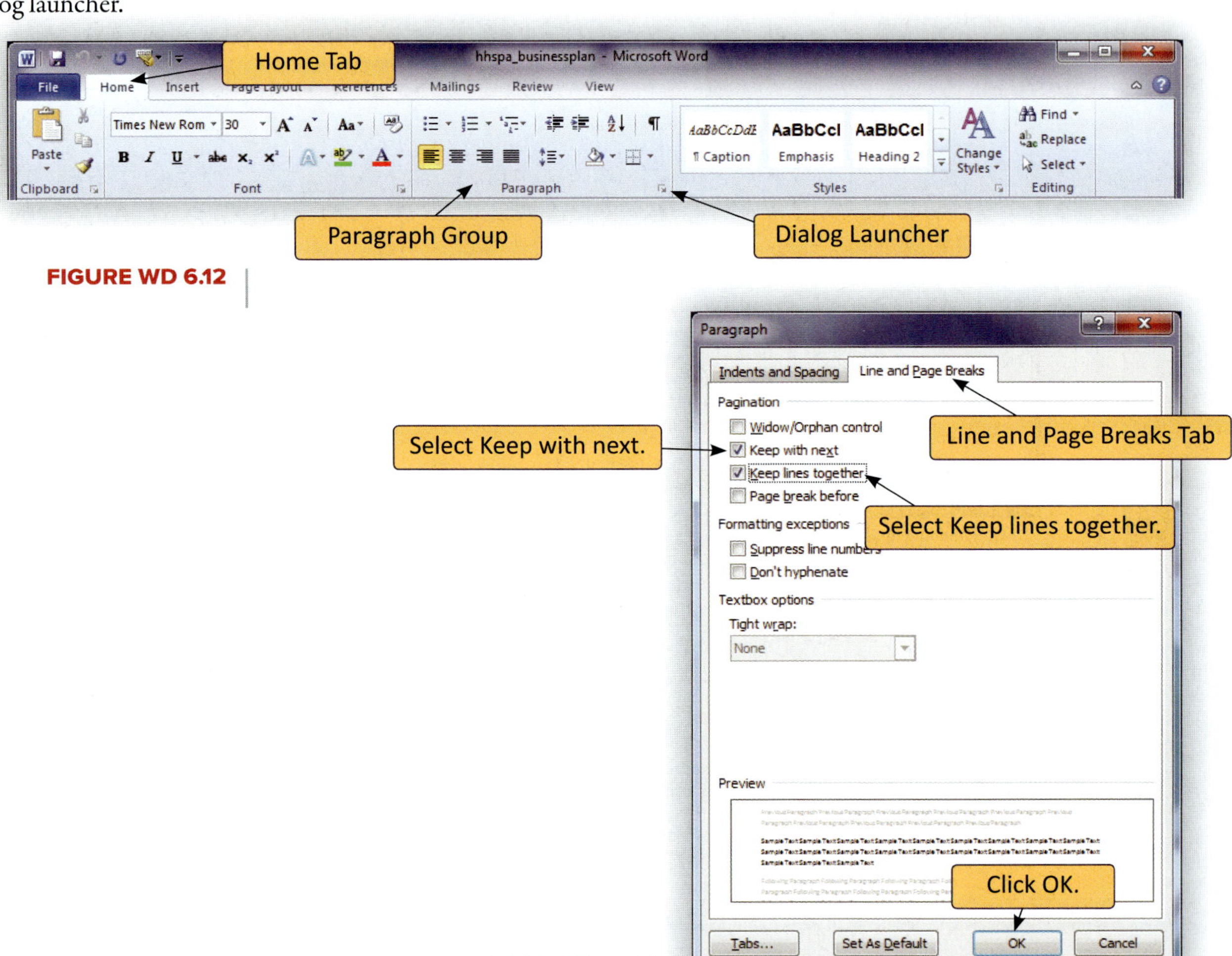

FIGURE WD 6.12

FIGURE WD 6.13

tips & tricks

To always force a paragraph to a new page regardless of where it appears on a page, on the *Line and Page Breaks* tab, click the **Page break before** check box.

tell me more

Many heading styles include the *Keep with next* setting as part of the default style.

try this

To open the *Paragraph* dialog box, you can also right-click the paragraph you want to change and select **Paragraph. . .** from the menu.

6.11 Managing Widows and Orphans

An **orphan** is the first line of a paragraph that prints at the bottom of a page by itself. A **widow** is the last line of a paragraph that prints at the top of a page by itself. Widows and orphans can be distracting and can make your document look unprofessional.

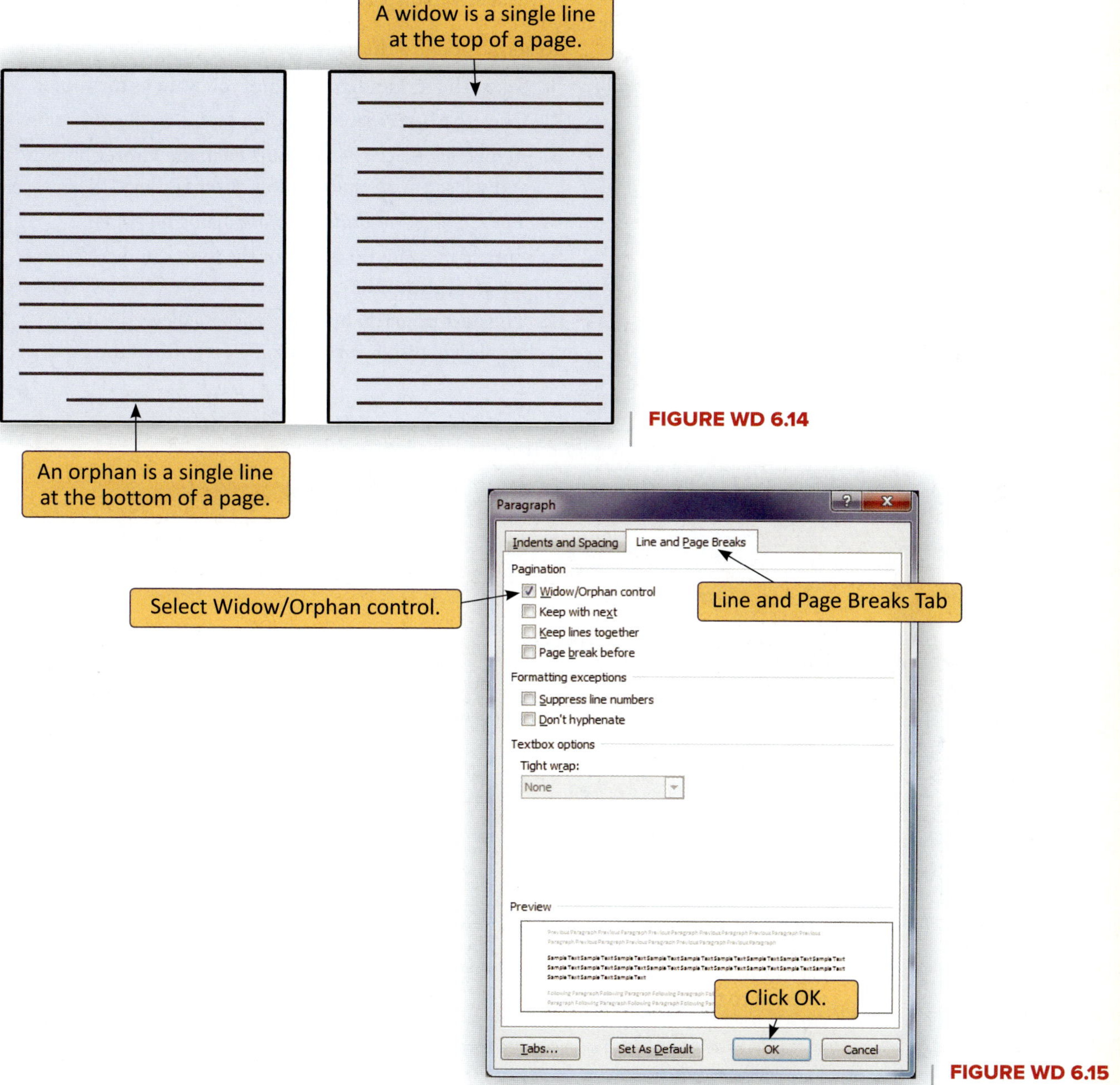

FIGURE WD 6.14

FIGURE WD 6.15

To prevent widows and orphans in a document:

1. Place the cursor anywhere in the paragraph you want to change.
2. On the *Home* tab, in the *Paragraph* group, click the dialog launcher.
3. In the *Paragraph* dialog box, click the **Line and Page Breaks** tab.
4. Under *Pagination,* select the **Widow/Orphan control** check box.
5. Click **OK.**

tell me more

When you first create a document, widow and orphan control is active by default.

6.12 Adding a Header or Footer to the Gallery

Word comes with a number of prebuilt headers and footers for you to add to your documents. But what if you have your own custom header, such as a company logo, or footer, such as a legal disclaimer? You can create headers and footers from parts of a document and add them to the *Header* gallery or the *Footer* gallery. After you add a new header or footer to the galleries, it will be available to all documents you create from that point forward.

To add a header to the gallery:

1. Select the text and/or graphics you want as the header.
2. Click the **Insert** tab.
3. In the *Header & Footer* group, click the **Header** button and select **Save Selection to Header Gallery**. . .
4. The *Create New Building Block* dialog box opens.
5. Enter a meaningful name for the header in the *Name:* box, and click **OK.**
6. The next time you open the *Header* gallery, the new header will display in the *General* section of the gallery.

To add a footer to the gallery:

1. Select the text and/or graphics you want as the footer.
2. Click the **Insert** tab.
3. In the *Header & Footer* group, click the **Footer** button and select **Save Selection to Footer Gallery**. . .
4. The *Create New Building Block* dialog box opens.
5. Enter a meaningful name for the footer in the *Name:* box, and click **OK.**
6. The next time you open the *Footer* gallery, the new footer will display in the *General* section of the gallery.

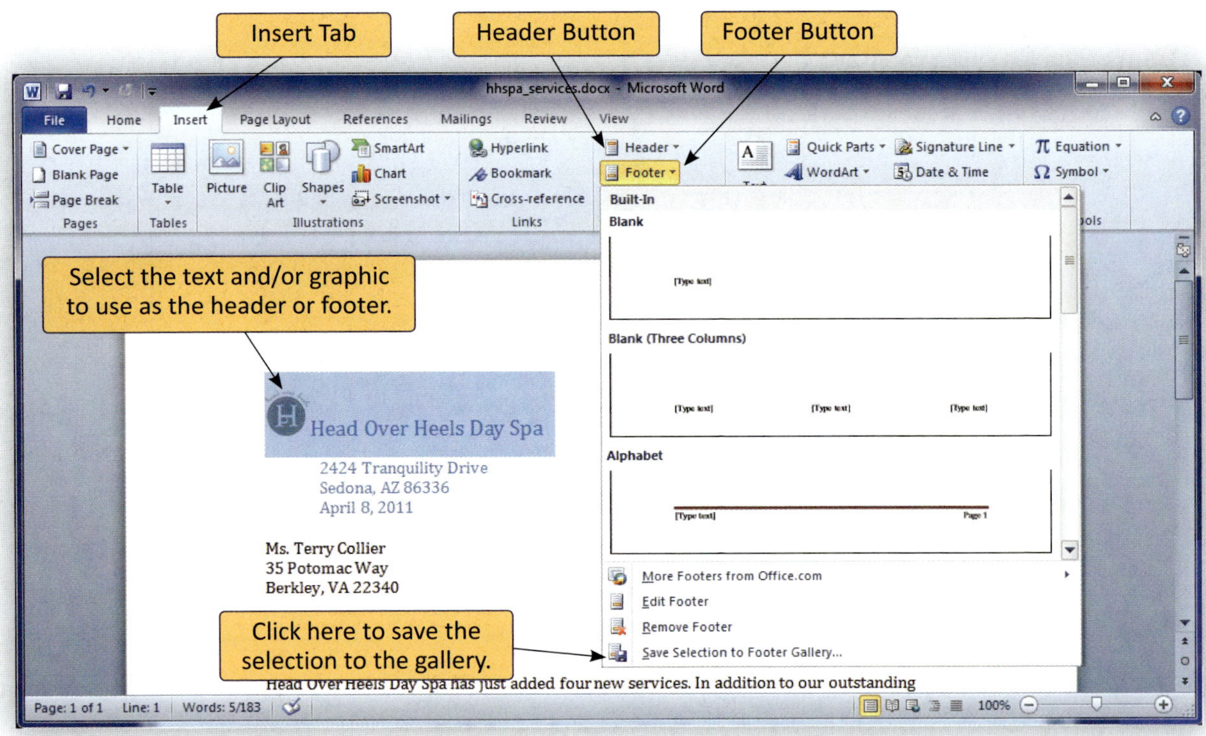

FIGURE WD 6.16

tips & tricks

To delete a custom header or footer you added, open the *Building Blocks Organizer.* Select the header or footer you created, and click the **Delete** button.

tell me more

When you add a custom header or footer to the gallery, the text is saved as a building block and can be accessed through the *Building Blocks Organizer.*

6.13 Navigating Long Documents

In past versions of Microsoft Word, if you wanted to view an outline of a document based on heading levels, you would use the *Document Map*. In Word 2010, the *Document Map* has been replaced by the **Navigation pane.**

The *Navigation* pane has three tabs. The first tab displays all the headings in your document, like an outline. The second tab displays a thumbnail of each page of a document. The third tab allows you to search for text in a document.

To use the *Navigation* pane:

1. Click the **View** tab.
2. In the *Show* group, click the **Navigation Pane** check box.
3. Click a heading on the first tab of the *Navigation* pane to jump to that part of the document.
4. Click the second tab to display thumbnails of each page in the document.
5. Scroll the pages and click a thumbnail to navigate to that page in the document.

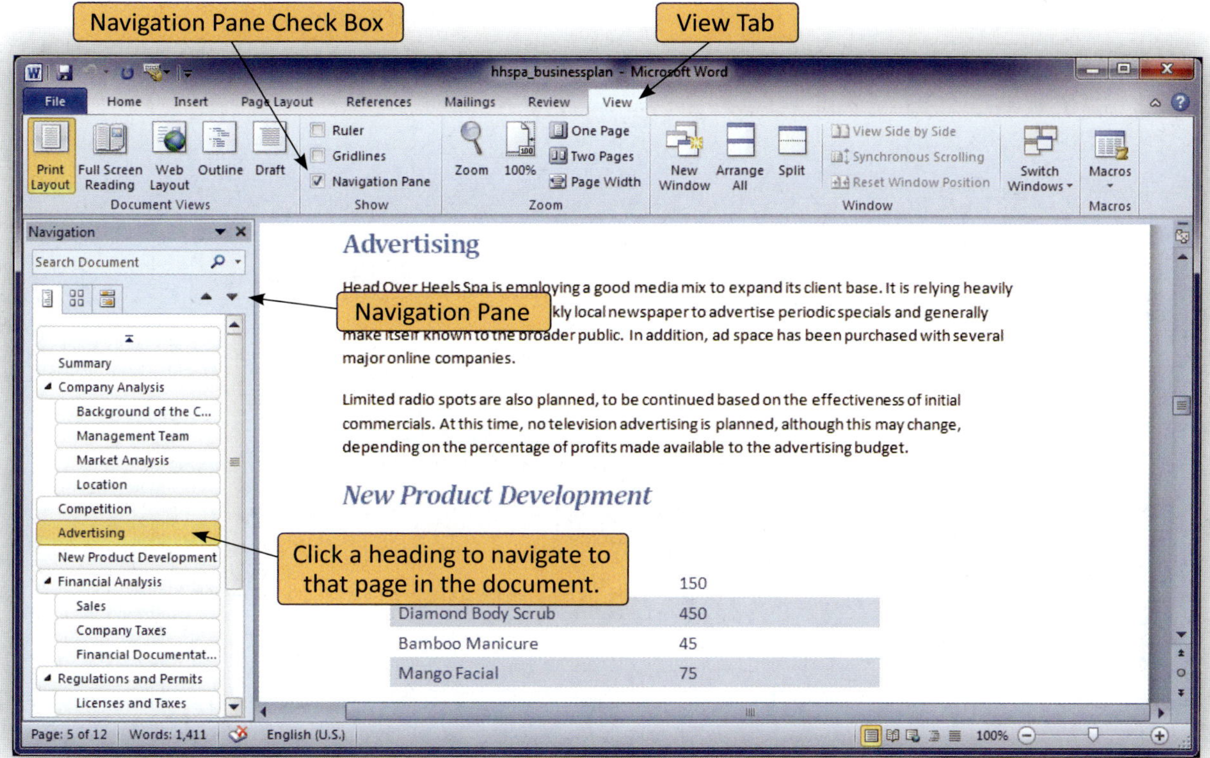

FIGURE WD 6.17

tips & tricks

- To close the *Navigation* pane, click the **X** in the upper-right corner of the pane.
- If a heading has subheadings associated with it, the heading will appear with a triangle to the left of the name. Click the triangle to hide or show any subheadings associated with the heading.

tell me more

The first tab of the *Navigation* pane, displays the hierarchy of headings, with *Heading 1* text being at the top and any associated subheadings listed below it. In order for headings to appear in this list, they must be formatted using a heading style.

try this

To display the *Navigation* pane, you can also press Ctrl + F on the keyboard. Using this method will open the *Navigation* pane with the third tab displayed.

6.14 Using Go To

The **Go To** command allows you to quickly "jump" to any part of a document. You can choose to navigate to a specific page, section, or line number. You can also navigate to a specific bookmark you inserted or comments made by a reviewer.

To use the *Go To* command to navigate to a page:

1. On the *Home* tab, in the *Editing* group, click the **Find** button arrow and select **Go To. . .**
2. The *Find and Replace* dialog box opens with the *Go To* tab selected.
3. In the *Go to what:* box, verify *Page* is selected.
4. In the *Enter page number:* box, enter the page number to navigate to and click **Go To.**

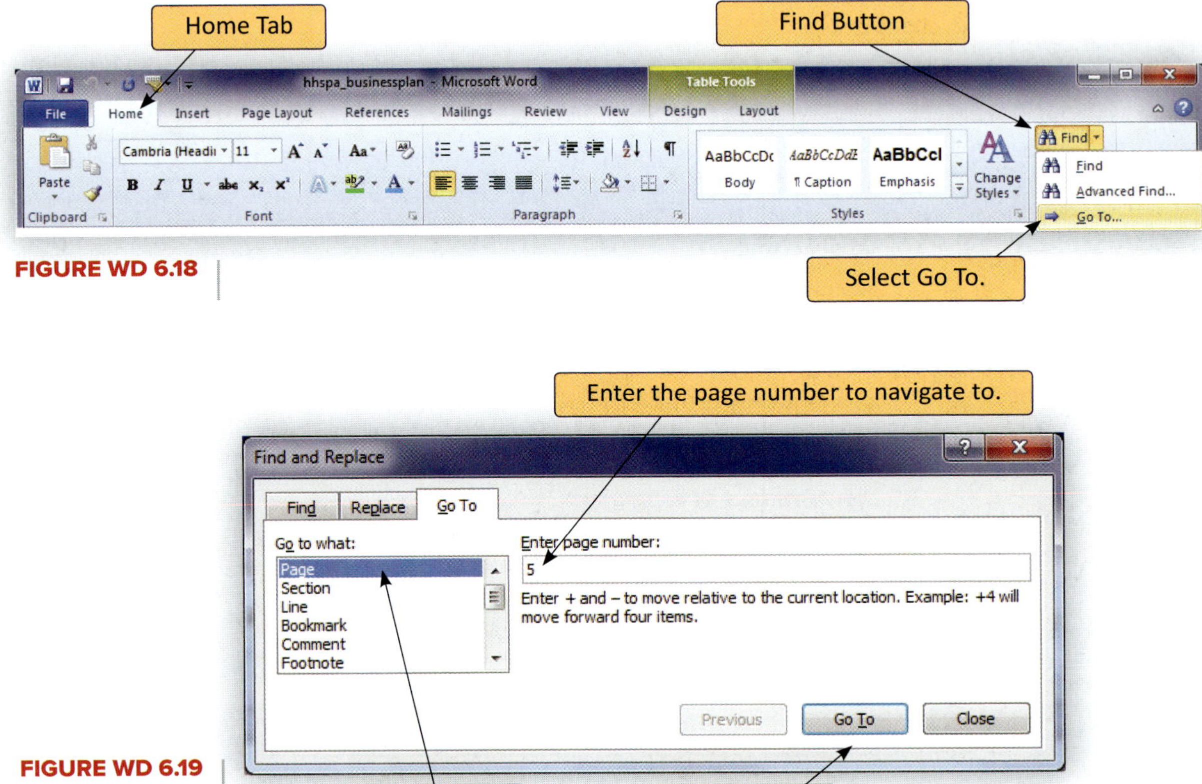

FIGURE WD 6.18

FIGURE WD 6.19

tips & tricks

If you do not know the exact details of where you want to navigate, you can type a + or - sign before a number to navigate that number of items forward or backward within a document. For example, instead of entering a specific line number, you can enter +25 to jump ahead 25 lines.

tell me more

You can use the *Go To* command to navigate to specific objects in a document, such as a table, graphic, or equation.

try this

To open the *Find and Replace* dialog box with *Go To* tab displayed, you can also press Ctrl + G on the keyboard.

6.15 Using Outline View

If you are creating a long document, more than likely, the document will be divided into multiple parts designated by heading styles. One way to organize the headings in your document is to use **Outline view.** In Outline view, you can add your main topics for a document and then insert subtopics as needed. Once you have created your outline, you can switch back to Print Layout view to type the main text of your document, or you can choose to continue working in Outline view.

To switch to Outline view, click the **Outline** button on the status bar of the window.

To change the level of a topic in Outline view:

1. Select the topic you want to change.
2. Click the **Promote** button to move the topic up one heading level.
3. Click the **Demote** button to move the topic down one heading level.
4. Use the **Move Up** and **Move Down** buttons to reorder topics in Outline view.
5. Use the **Expand** and **Collapse** buttons to display and hide subtopics in Outline view.
6. Click the **Close Outline View** button to return to Print Layout view.

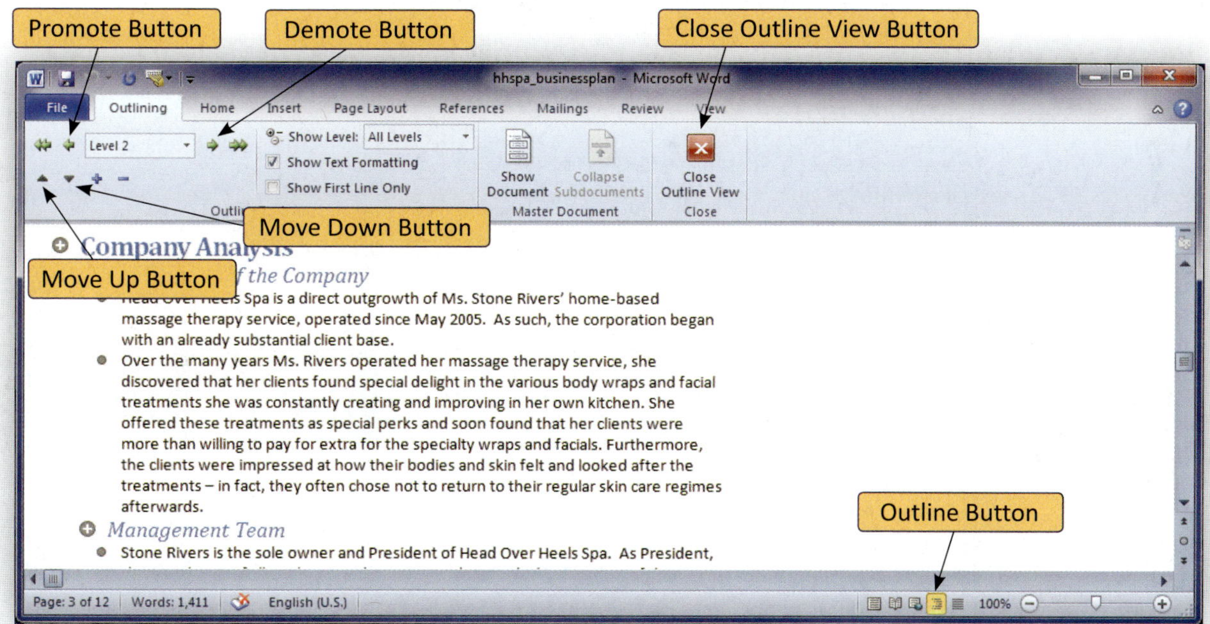

FIGURE WD 6.20

tell me **more**

- In Outline view, a minus sign next to a topic indicates there are no subtopics associated with that topic. A plus sign indicates that a topic includes the subtopics listed directly below it.
- Each level in Outline view will use the corresponding heading style from the style template. For example, *Level 1* topics will use the *Heading 1* style, *Level 2* topics will use the *Heading 2* style, and so on.

try **this**

- To switch to Outline view, you can also click the **View** tab. In the *Document Views* group, click the **Outline** button.
- To demote an item, you can also press Tab on the keyboard.

6.16 Adding Bookmarks

If you are working with a long document, you may want to mark certain places in the document to come back to at a later time. A **bookmark** is an invisible marker that allows you to quickly navigate back to a specific location in a document.

To add a bookmark to a document:

1. Place the cursor where you want to add the bookmark.
2. Click the **Insert** tab.
3. In the *Links* group, click the **Bookmark** button.
4. Type the name of the bookmark in the *Bookmark name:* box.
5. Click the **Add** button.

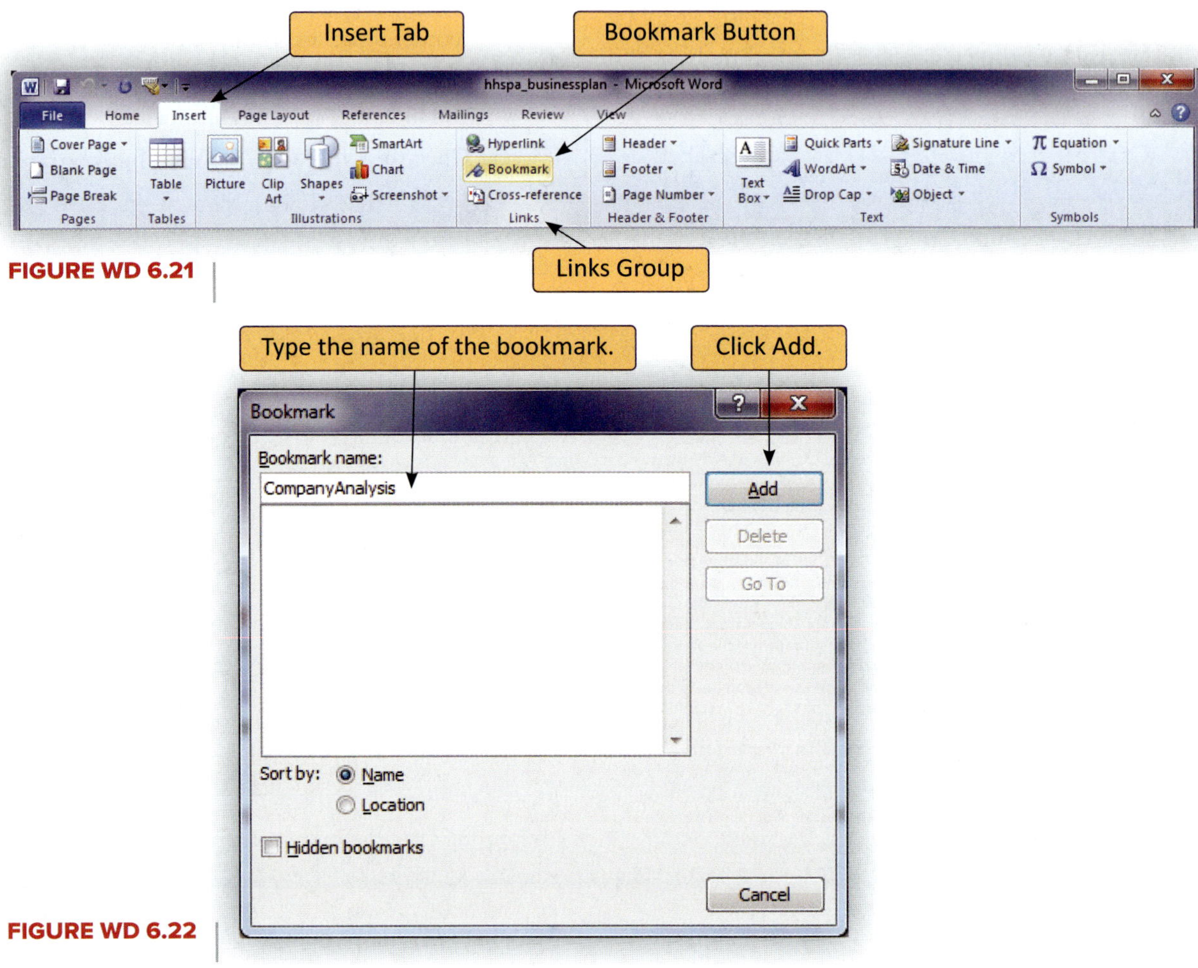

FIGURE WD 6.21

FIGURE WD 6.22

To navigate to a bookmark:

1. On the *Insert* tab, in the *Links* group, click the **Bookmark** button.
2. In the *Bookmark* dialog box, select the name of the bookmark you want to navigate to and click the **Go To** button.

tips & tricks

To delete a bookmark, select the name of the bookmark in the *Bookmark* dialog box, and click the **Delete** button.

try this

You can also navigate to a bookmark from the *Go To* tab in the *Find and Replace* dialog box.

tell me more

You cannot include spaces in bookmark names. If you want to include multiple words as the name of the bookmark, you should type the name without the spaces and capitalize each word in the name. For example, if you want to add a bookmark to the analysis section about a company, you could name the bookmark "CompanyAnalysis."

6.17 Adding Cross-References

If you are working with a long document, you may have content in one part of the document that relates to content in another part of the document. A **cross-reference** is a link you add to a document that directs the reader to another part of the document for more or related information. By default Word inserts cross-references as hyperlinks so your readers can use them to navigate to the related information.

To add a cross-reference:

1. Click the **Insert** tab.
2. In the *Links* group, click the **Cross-reference** button.
3. In the *Cross-reference* dialog box, click the *Reference type:* arrow and select the type of object you want to link to.
4. Click the *Insert reference to:* arrow, and select how the reference should appear.
5. In the *For which* box, select the object you want to link to, and click the **Insert** button.
6. The cross-reference is added to the document.

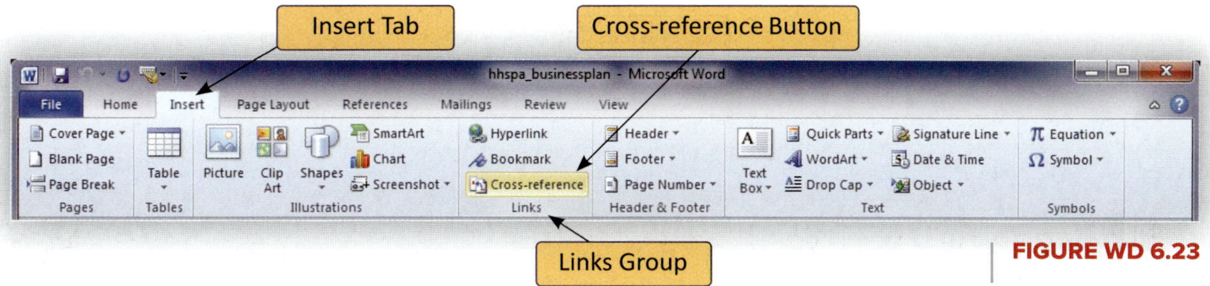

FIGURE WD 6.23

Cross-references often begin with directions to the reader, such as "See" or "Go to." When Word inserts the cross-reference, it will only insert the name of the cross-reference. You must type the directions to the reader for yourself. For example, if you want your cross-reference to read "See the Financial Statistics section" and the heading for the section is "Financial Statistics," you must type "See the" and then insert the cross-reference, and then type "section." Only the words *Financial Statistics* will be linked as the cross-reference.

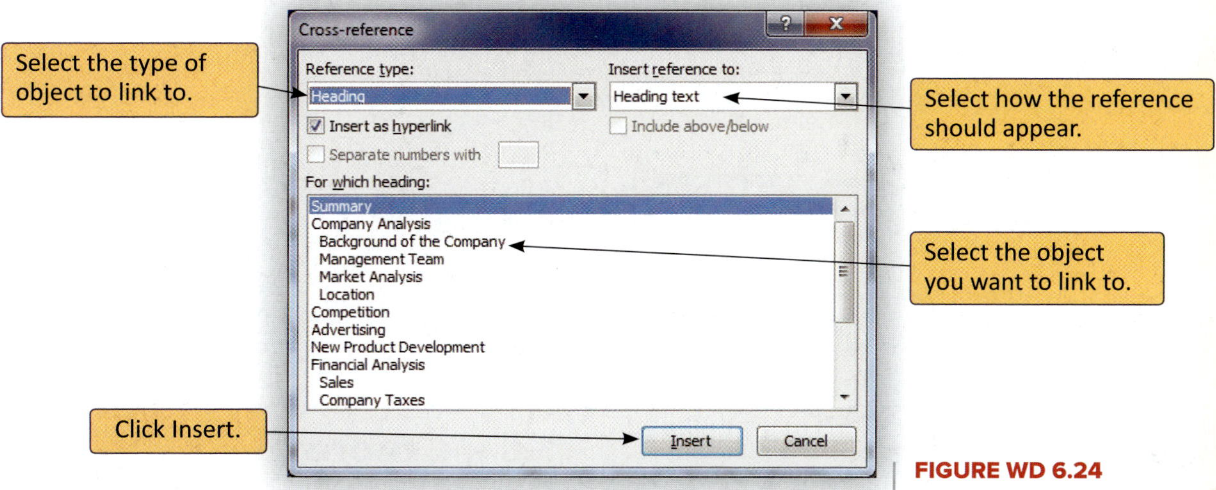

FIGURE WD 6.24

tips & tricks

Press Shift and click the cross-reference text to navigate to the linked location.

tell me more

You can choose to have the cross-reference display the exact text of what you are linking to, or a location in the document, such as a page number or the words "above" or "below."

6.18 Creating a Table of Figures

A **table of figures** lists all the illustrations, graphs, charts, equations, and pictures in a document, along with their associated page numbers. Adding a table of figures to your documents gives your readers a quick reference to find illustrations, tables, and equations that you considered important enough to warrant adding captions to.

To insert a table of figures:

1. Place your cursor where you want to insert the table of figures.
2. Click the **References** tab.
3. In the *Captions* group, click the **Insert Table of Figures** button.
4. In the *Table of Figures* dialog box, click the **Formats:** arrow and select a format.
5. Modify the other options until the preview looks the way you want.
6. Click **OK** to insert the table of figures into your document.

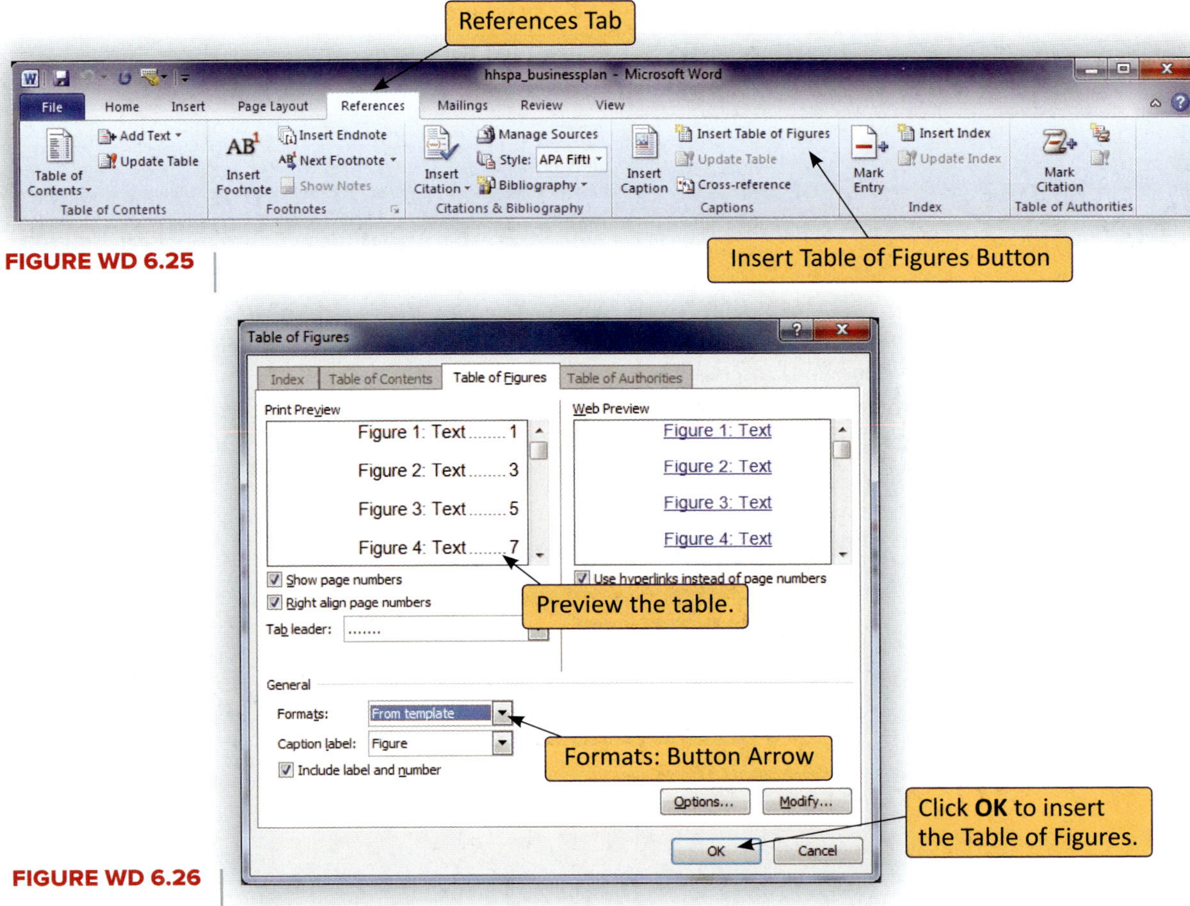

FIGURE WD 6.25

FIGURE WD 6.26

tips & tricks

- If you change any captions in your document, be sure to update the table of figures. To update the table of figures, click in the table of figures to select it, and click the **Update Table** button in the *Captions* group on the *References* tab.
- Adding a tab leader helps guide the reader's eye from the figure to its associated page number.

tell me **more**

A table of figures displays the page number of the caption associated with the figure; therefore, in order for a figure to be included in the table of figures, it must have a caption. To add a caption to a figure, click the **References** tab. In the *Captions* group, click the **Insert Caption** button. In the *Caption* dialog box, type the text for the caption in the *Caption:* box and select a type of label. Click **OK** to add the caption to the figure.

6.19 Changing Page Orientation

The default page orientation for Word documents is **portrait.** This means the height of the page is greater than the width (like a portrait hanging on a wall). Portrait works well if you are writing documents such as papers or letters. But what if you have a table that is wider than the standard page? **Landscape** orientation turns the page on its side so the width of the page is greater than the height.

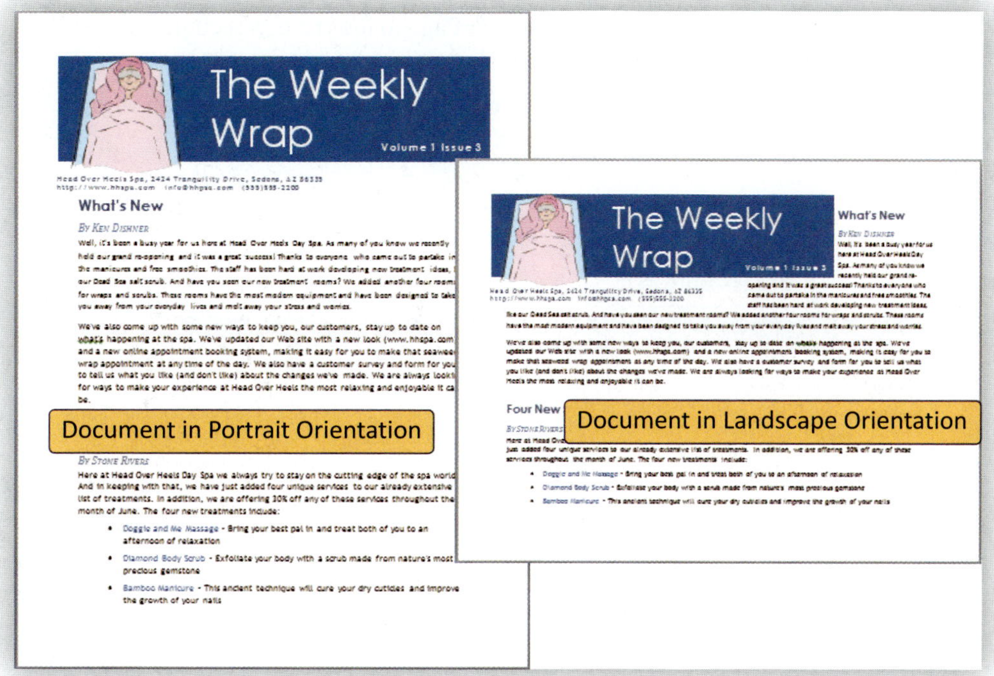

FIGURE WD 6.27

To change the orientation of a document:

1. Click the **Page Layout** tab.
2. In the *Page Setup* group, click the **Orientation** button and select an option—**Portrait** or **Landscape.**

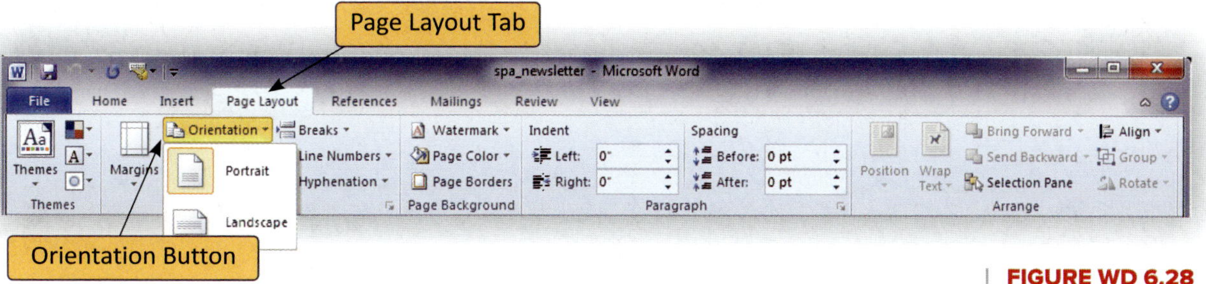

FIGURE WD 6.28

tips & tricks

If you have divided your document using section breaks, selecting an orientation will only affect the section you are in. To change the orientation for the entire document, click the dialog launcher in the *Page Setup* group to open the *Page Setup* dialog box. Click the orientation you want for the section, and then click the *Apply to:* arrow and select **Whole Document.**

try this

You can also change the orientation for a document in the *Page Setup* dialog box. To open the *Page Setup* dialog box, click the dialog launcher in the *Page Setup* group.

6.20 Adding Sections to Documents

If you have a part of a document that has a wide table or figure, it may not fit on the printed page in portrait orientation. You wouldn't want to change the entire document to landscape to fit one table, so what do you do? A **section** is a designated part of a document that can be formatted separately from the rest of the document. You can add the large table in its own section that is set to landscape orientation and keep the remaining document in portrait orientation.

To add a section to a document:

1. Click the **Page Layout** tab.
2. In the *Page Setup* group, click the **Breaks** button.
3. In the *Section Breaks* section:
   - Click **Next Page** to insert a new section and a hard page break.
   - Click **Continuous** to insert a new section without adding a page break.

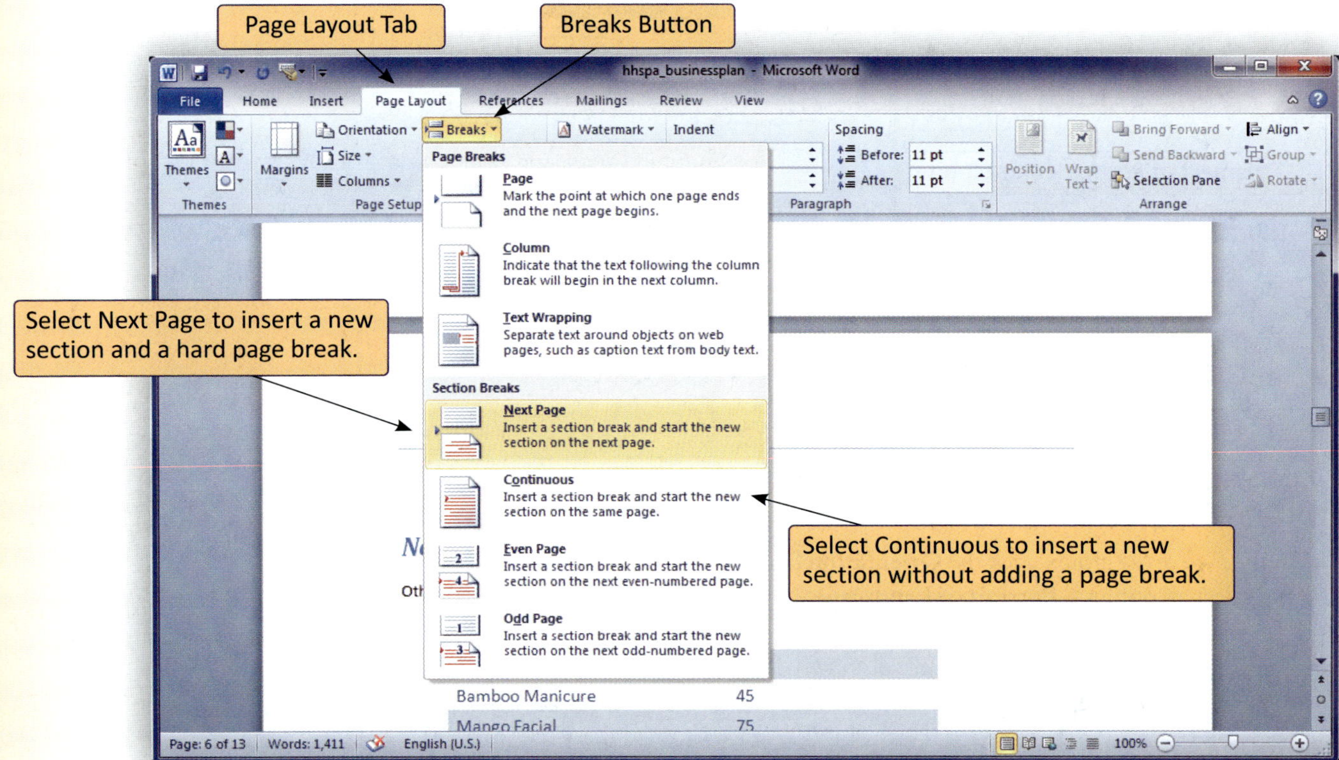

FIGURE WD 6.29

tips & tricks

To delete a section, switch to Draft view. Here all the section breaks are displayed. Select a section break and press the Del key on the keyboard to delete a section. When you delete a section, the content from the section takes on the formatting from the preceding section.

tell me more

There are two other section breaks you can add to documents:

Even Page—starts the new section on the next even-numbered page in the document.

Odd Page—starts the new section on the next odd-numbered page in the document.

6.21 Adding a Horizontal Line

As you work with long documents, you may find that you want to separate one piece of content from the surrounding text, but not create a new heading or section in the document. A **horizontal line** is a decorative element you can insert into a document. Use a horizontal line to add a visual divider to separate a part of a document without changing the underlying content structure.

To add a horizontal line to a document:

1. Place the cursor where you want the line to appear.
2. On the *Home* tab, in the *Paragraph* group, click the **Borders** button and select **Horizontal Line.**

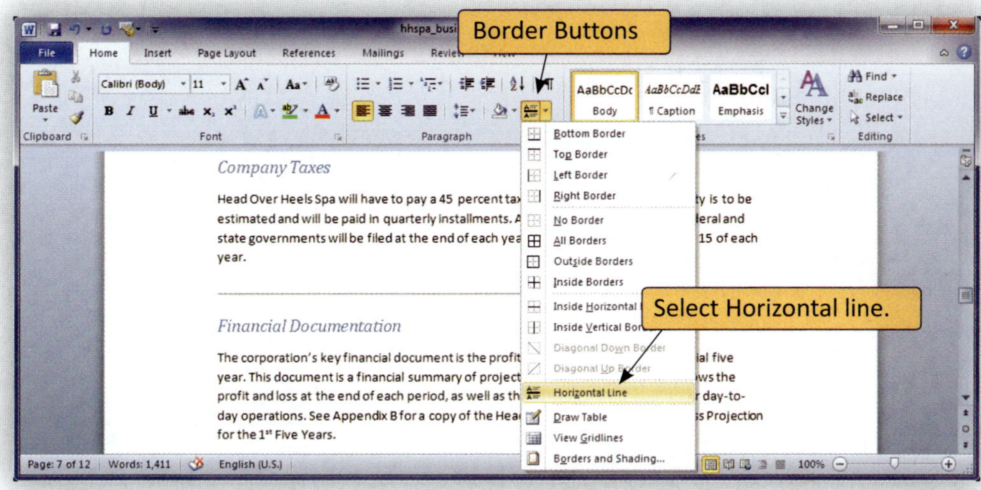

FIGURE WD 6.30

The default horizontal line is a simple gray line. If you want to add a more decorative horizontal line, the *Horizontal Line* dialog box includes a number of options for you to choose from.

FIGURE WD 6.31

To add a horizontal line from the *Horizontal Line* dialog box:

1. On the *Home* tab, in the *Paragraph* group, click the **Borders** button and select **Borders and Shading**. . .
2. In the *Borders and Shading* dialog box, click the **Horizontal Line**. . . button.
3. In the *Horizontal Line* dialog box, select an option and click **OK.**

tips & tricks

Once you have inserted a horizontal line from the *Horizontal Line* dialog box, you can insert the same line throughout the document by selecting **Horizontal Line** on the *Borders* menu.

tell me more

A horizontal line is not the same as a bottom border applied to a paragraph. Horizontal lines are more graphic in nature, typically incorporating illustration elements.

6.22 Using the Research Task Pane

When you are writing a document, you may find that you need to research information. You can search for information directly from Word 2010 by using the **Research task pane.** The *Research* task pane allows you to search for information using Internet search engines. The task pane also gives you access to reference tools, such as the Encarta Dictionary and Word's Thesaurus.

To display the *Research* task pane,

1. Place the cursor in the word you want to look up.
2. Click the **Review** tab.
3. In the *Proofing* group, click the **Research** button.
4. The *Research* task pane displays information from a variety of research sites.

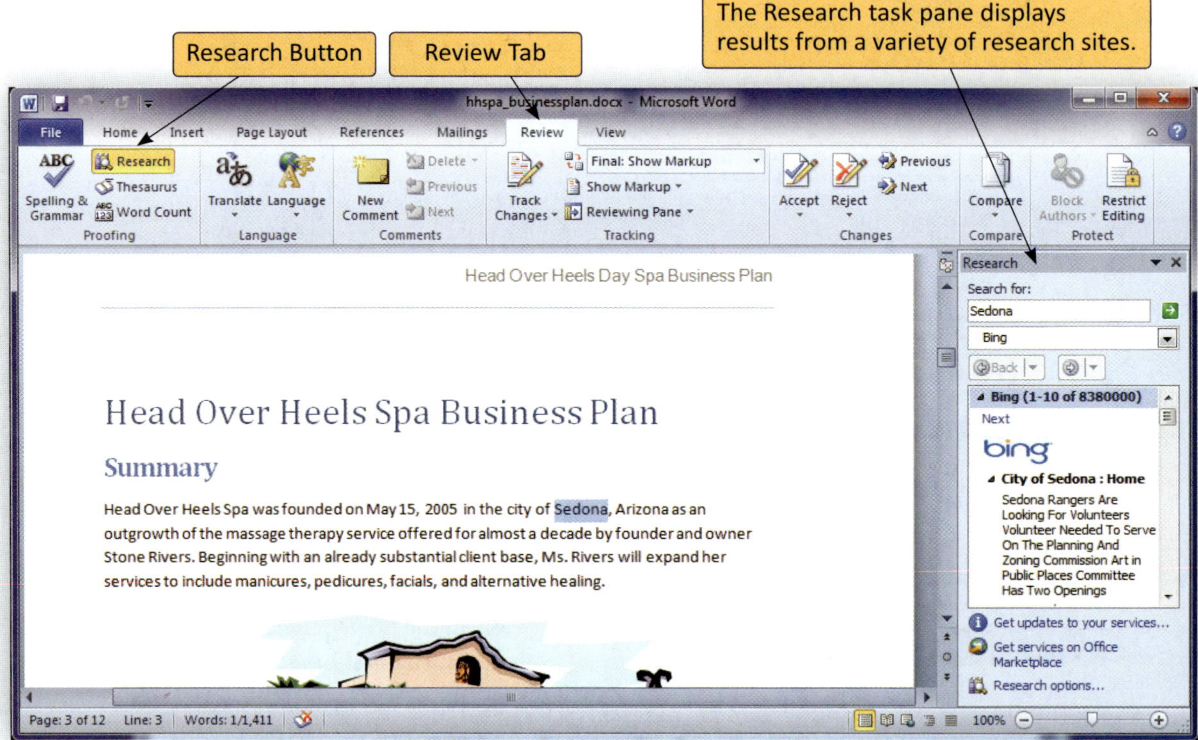

FIGURE WD 6.32

tips & tricks

When researching on the Internet, be aware of the sources you use. Some sources are more reliable than others. For example, while Wikipedia is a well-known research site, the information on the site is posted by the general public. Reliable entries on Wikipedia will list their own sources. When doing research, use Wikipedia as a "jumping off" point to find sources for research material.

tell me more

- The Encarta Dictionary is a built-in dictionary that you can use to look up the meanings and pronunciations of words.
- The *Research* task pane includes a translation tool that can translate words from English to any of 22 languages including Arabic, Spanish, Italian, French, Swedish, Russian, Chinese, and Japanese.

try this

To open the *Research* task pane, you can also press Alt and click the word you want to look up.

Data files for projects can be found on **www.mhhe.com/office2010skills**

projects

Skill Review **6.1**

In this project you will enhance a partially completed school calendar by adding columns and section breaks as well as such special features as symbols and drop caps.

1. Start Microsoft Word 2010.
2. Open *Pam Synovec School District.docx* and save it as **[your initials]WD_SkillReview_6-1.**
3. Create a new style to use for the title of the document.

   a. Select the title (all three lines), and click the dialog launcher in the *Styles* group.

   b. Click the **New Style** button at the bottom of the window.

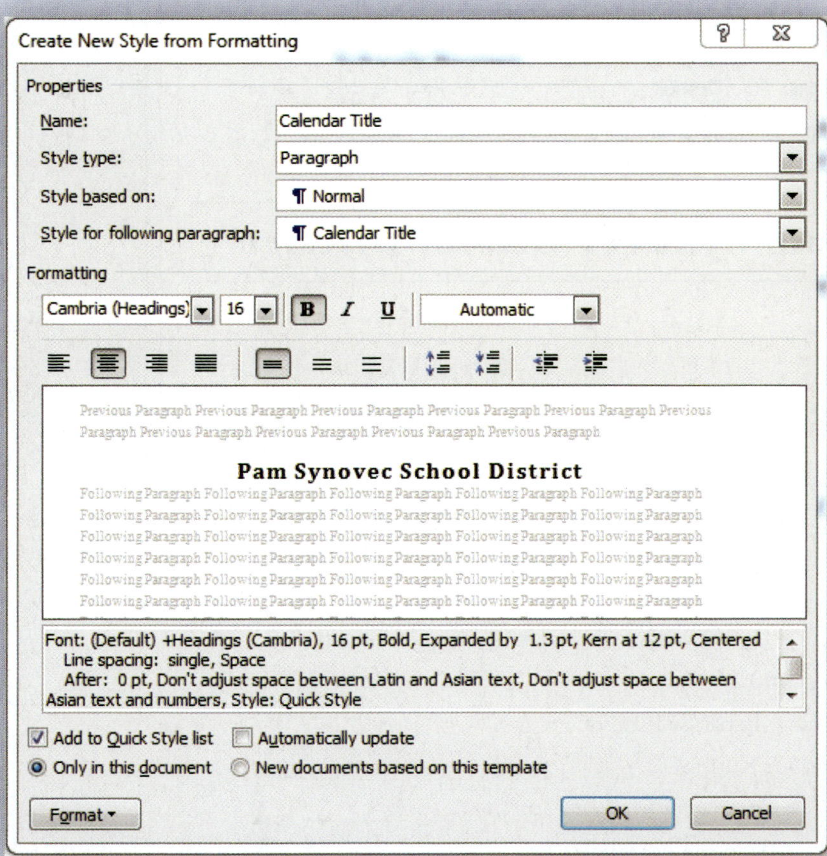

FIGURE WD 6.33

   c. In the *Create New Style from Formatting* dialog box, make the following edits:

      (1) *Name:* **Calendar Title**

      (2) *Style type:* Paragraph

      (3) *Formatting:* Cambria (Headings), 16 pt., bold

d. Click the **Format** button at the bottom of the window. Click **Font.**

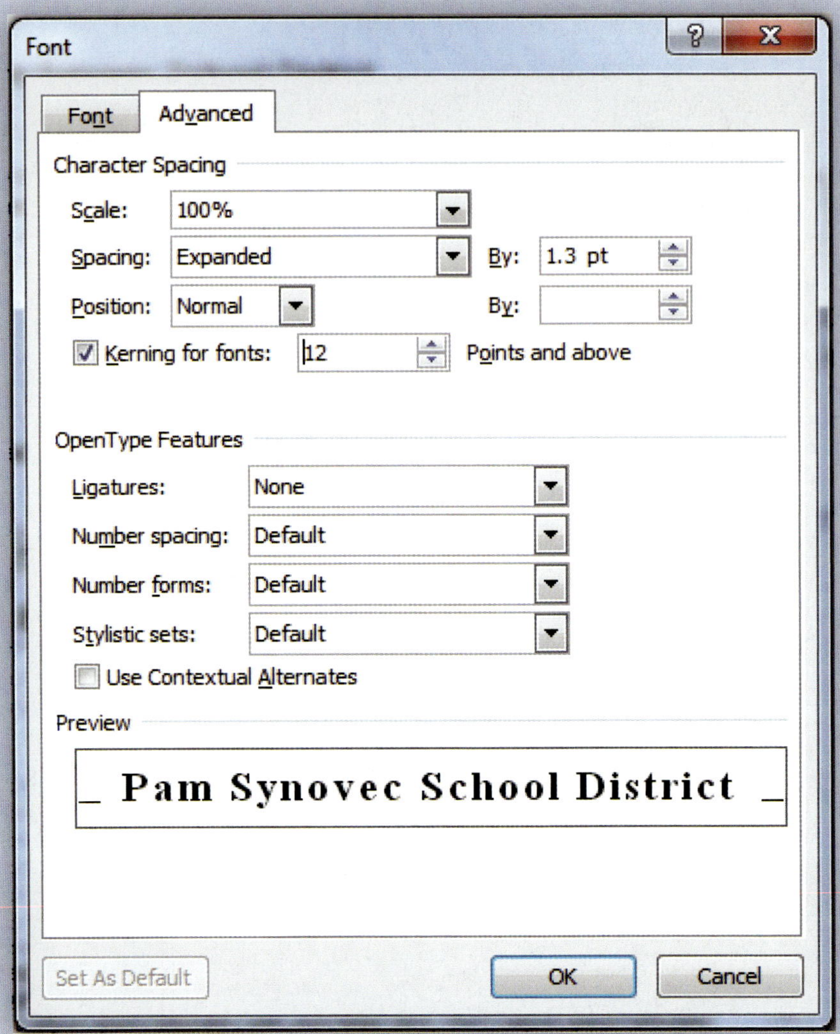

FIGURE WD 6.34

e. In the *Font* dialog box, click the **Advanced** tab.

f. Under *Character Spacing* make the following modifications:

(1) *Scale:* 100%.

(2) *Spacing:* Expanded, 1.3 pt.

(3) *Position:* Normal.

(4) Check *Kerning for fonts 12 Points and above.*

(5) Click **OK** in the *Font* dialog box.

(6) Click **OK** in the *Create New Style from Formatting* dialog box.

4. Clear the style and reapply the style you created.

a. Make sure the title lines are selected.

b. At the bottom of the *Styles* task pane, click the **Style Inspector** button.

c. Click the **Clear All** button to remove the current formatting.

d. On the *Home* tab, in the *Styles* group, click the **Calendar Title** style (the one you created), and your formatting will be restored.

e. Close the *Style Inspector* dialog box. Close the *Styles* task pane.

5. Below the spring schedule add a sidebar that describes the dismissal policy on abbreviated days.

a. On the *Insert* tab, in the *Text* group, click the **Text Box** button, scroll through the gallery and select the **Stacks Sidebar.**

b. Move the sidebar so it appears below the table, and resize the sidebar to be approximately the width of the text above it and one line of text tall.

c. Insert the following text: **`On all abbreviated days, dismissal will be 2 hours and 15 minutes early. The cafeteria will be open on all abbreviated days.`**

d. Your sidebar should look similar to Figure WD 6.35.

May 30 (Mon.)	Memorial Day/Schools Closed
June 8 (Wed.)	Elem./Middle/Synovec Abbrev. Day
June 9 (Thurs.)	Elem./Middle/Synovec Abbrev. Day
June 10 (Fri.)	Elem./Middle/Synovec Abbrev. Day - Last Student Day
June 13 (Mon.)	Teacher In-Service

On all abbreviated days, dismissal will be 2 hours and 15 minutes early. The cafeteria will be open on all abbreviated days.

FIGURE WD 6.35

6. Insert a line across the page to provide a visual separation for the second half of the calendar.

a. Place the cursor below the sidebar.

b. On the *Home* tab, in the *Paragraph* group, click the **Borders** button and select **Horizontal Line.**

7. Add a section break.

a. Place the cursor just below the horizontal line, and click the **Page Layout** tab.

b. In the *Page Setup* group, click the **Breaks** button.

c. Under *Section Breaks* choose **Continuous.**

8. Format the section with a two-column layout, and add the exam schedule information.

a. In the *Page Setup* group, click the **Columns** button.

b. Choose **Two** columns.

c. Insert the following text into the left column:

```
Exam Schedule & Senior End-of-Year Information
Underclassmen Semester Exams
June 8-9-10, 2011
Senior Last Day of Regular Classes
May 25, 2011
Senior Examinations
May 26 & 27, 2011
Senior Awards Program
June 2, 2011
Commencement
June 4, 2011
```

d. Select the text and format as Cambria, 11 pt.

e. Double-space the text.

f. Bold all the lines except the dates.

9. Add a symbol and format it as a drop cap.

a. Place the cursor at the beginning of the first column next to *Exam.*

b. On the *Insert* tab, in the *Symbols* group, click the **Symbol** button.

c. Select **More Symbols.**

d. If necessary, select the Wingdings font and select ♎. Click the **Insert** button.

e. Close the *Symbol* dialog box.

f. On the *Insert* tab, in the *Text* group, click the **Drop Cap** button and select **Dropped.**

g. Click the **Drop Cap** button again and select **Drop Cap Options.**

h. Enter **2** in the *Lines to drop:* box and click **OK.**

Exam Schedule & Senior End-of-Year Information

Underclassmen Semester Exams

June 8-9-10, 2011

Senior Last Day of Regular Classes

May 25, 2011

Senior Examinations

May 26 & 27, 2011

FIGURE WD 6.36

10. Add a column break.

a. Go to the end of the column. On the *Page Layout* tab, in the *Page Setup* group, click the **Breaks** button.

b. Under *Page Breaks* select **Column.** This will end this column and allow you to go to the second column without filling up the first with text.

11. With your cursor in the second column, insert a text box.

a. On the *Insert* tab, in the *Text* group, click the **Text Box** button.

b. Select the first choice, **Simple Text Box.**

c. If necessary, move the text box so it appears in the second column to the right of the exam schedule information you just typed.

d. Insert the following quote:

`"Where Educational Excellence Is a Tradition"`

e. Select the text, and change the font to Cambria, 16 pt.

f. Italicize and center the text.

12. Save and close the document.

Skill Review **6.2**

In this project you will use and modify styles to help manage the formatting and appearance of long documents.

1. Start Microsoft Word 2010.

2. Open *Strategic Initiative - Collaboration.docx* and save it as ***[your initials]*WD_SkillReview_6-2.**

3. Create and save a custom header.

a. On the *Insert* tab, in the *Header & Footer* group, click the **Header** button.

b. Click the **Blank** style and type **Student Success Initiative**

c. Tab to right margin.

d. On the *Header & Footer Tools* contextual tab, in the *Insert* group, select **Date & Time.**

e. Choose the option that spells out the month, day, and year as highlighted in Figure WD 6.37.

f. Select the **Update automatically** check box.

g. Click **OK** in the *Date and Time* dialog box.

h. Press **Ctrl + A** on the keyboard to select all the text in the header.

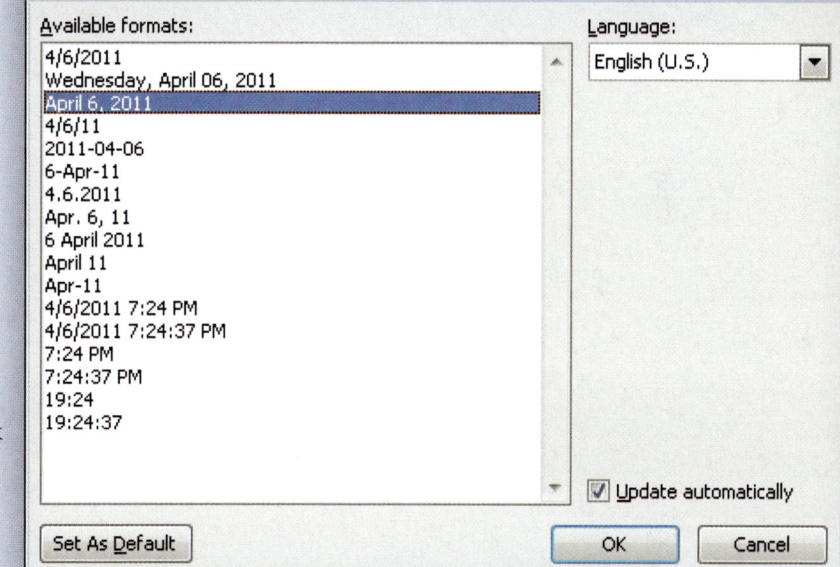

FIGURE WD 6.37

i. On the same tab, in the *Header & Footer* group, click the **Header** button, and select **Save Selection to Header Gallery.**

j. Type **Student Initiative Header** in the *Name* box.

k. Click **OK** in the *Create New Building Block* dialog box.

4. Add page numbers to the footer area of the document.

a. In the *Header & Footer* group, click **Page Number,** point to **Bottom of Page,** and select **Plain Number 3.**

b. On the *Header & Footer Tools* contextual tab, in the *Close* group, click the **Close Header and Footer** button.

5. Change the style set for the document, and apply a heading style to text.

a. On the *Home* tab, in the *Styles* group, click the **Change Styles** button.

b. Point to **Style Set** and choose **Perspective.**

c. Select the text *Strategic Goal: Student Success.*

d. Select **Heading 1** in the *Styles* gallery.

6. Create a new paragraph style for the body text of the document.

a. Click in the body of the document.

b. On the *Home* tab, in the *Styles* group, click the dialog launcher.

c. At the bottom of the task pane, click the **New Style** button.

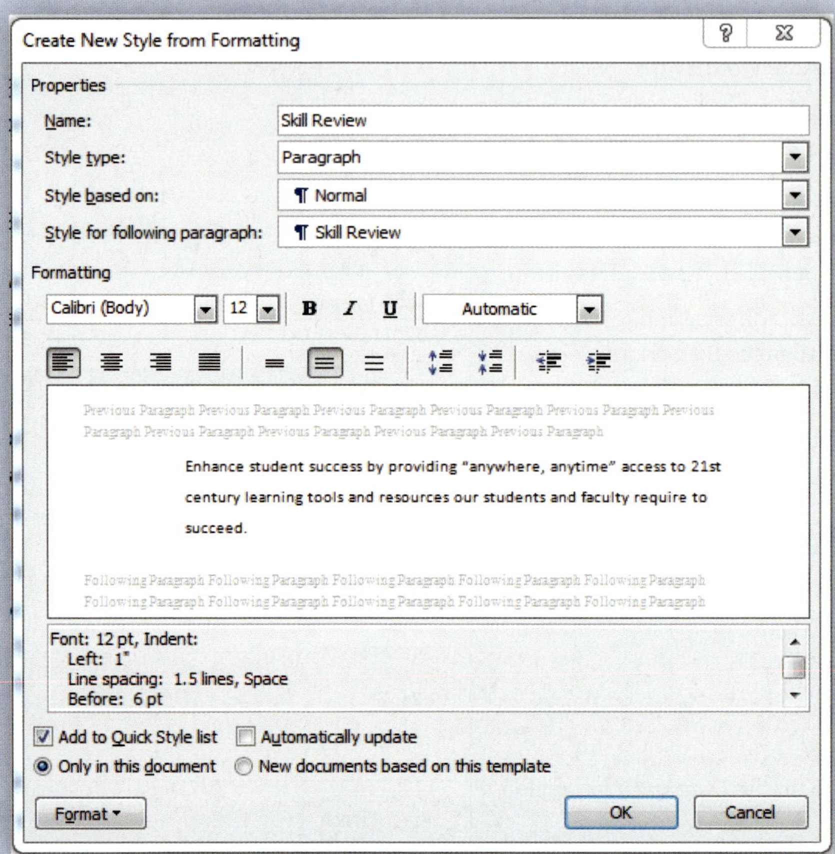

FIGURE WD 6.38

d. Type **`Skill Review`** as the name of the style.

e. Change the font size to 12 points.

f. Change the spacing to 1.5, the middle icon.

g. Increase the left indent by one increment by clicking the **Increase Indent** button (the button on the far right of the toolbar in the dialog box).

h. Click the **Format** button and select **Paragraph.**

(1) On the *Indents and Spacing* tab, set the paragraph spacing to 6 points before and 15 points after.

(2) Click the **Line and Page Breaks** tab.

(3) Ensure that *Widow/Orphan control* is checked.

(4) Click the **Keep with next** check box to select it.

(5) Click the **Keep lines together** check box to select it.

(6) Click **OK** in the *Paragraph* dialog box.

i. Click **OK** in the *Create New Style from Formatting* dialog box.

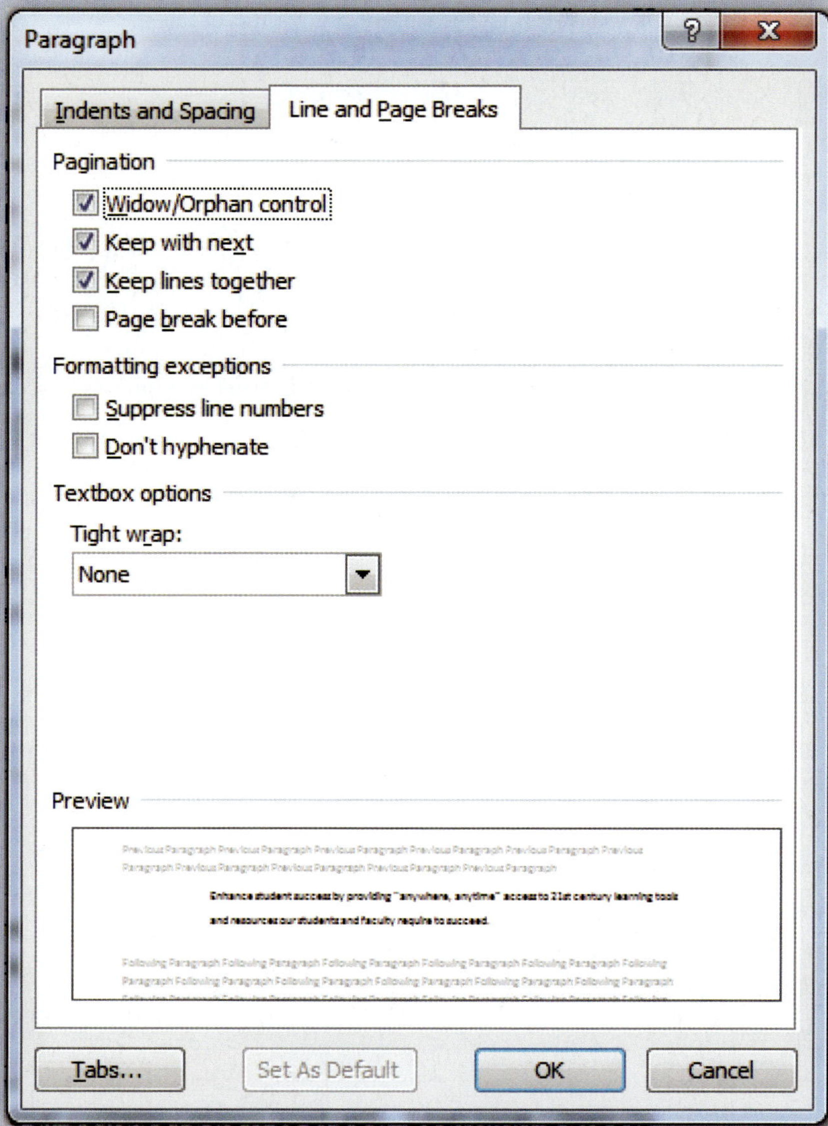

FIGURE WD 6.39

7. Apply the new style to all the text in the document.
   a. Select all the text in the document (**Ctrl + A**).
   b. In the *Styles* gallery select the style **Skill Review.** You should see your setting applied to the document.
8. Use outlining to promote text in the document.
   a. On the *View* tab, in the *Document Views* group, select **Outline.**

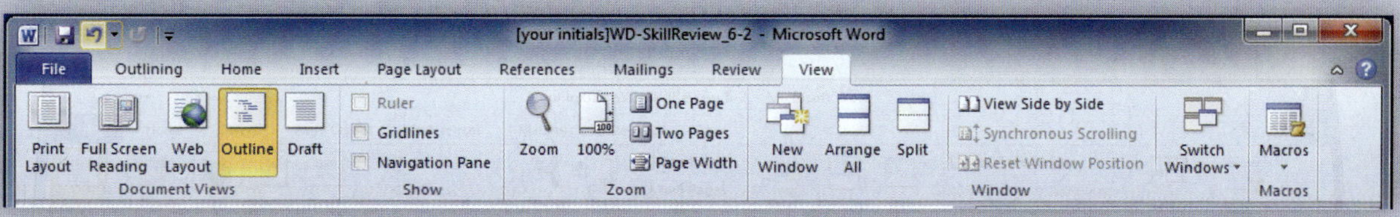

FIGURE WD 6.40

   b. The *Outlining* tab displays.

c. If the *Show Text Formatting* box is not checked, ensure that it is checked.

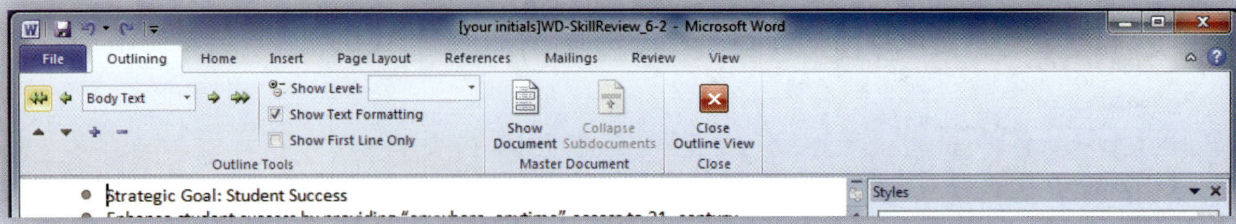

FIGURE WD 6.41

d. Select *Strategic Goal: Student Success,* and click the double arrow to promote it to *Heading 1.*

e. Select *Initiative: Collaboration using Social Software,* and click the **Promote to Heading 1** button (the double arrow pointing to the left).

f. Select *Background* and click the **Promote to Heading 1** button. Click the **Demote** button (the single arrow pointing to the right) to make the text a *Heading 2.*

g. Use these steps to apply the *Heading 2* style to the following: *Scope:, Deliverables:, Benefits:, Risks:, Costs:, Resources:,* and *Timeline:.*

h. Click the **Close Outline View** button.

9. Use the *Navigation* pane to review the heading levels.

a. Click the **View** tab.

b. In the *Show* group, click the **Navigation Pane** check box.

c. Review the headings in the document, and close the *Navigation* pane.

10. Add bookmarks to the document.

a. Navigate to the *Costs:* section, and place the cursor before the heading.

b. Click the **Insert** tab. In the *Links* group, click the **Bookmark** button.

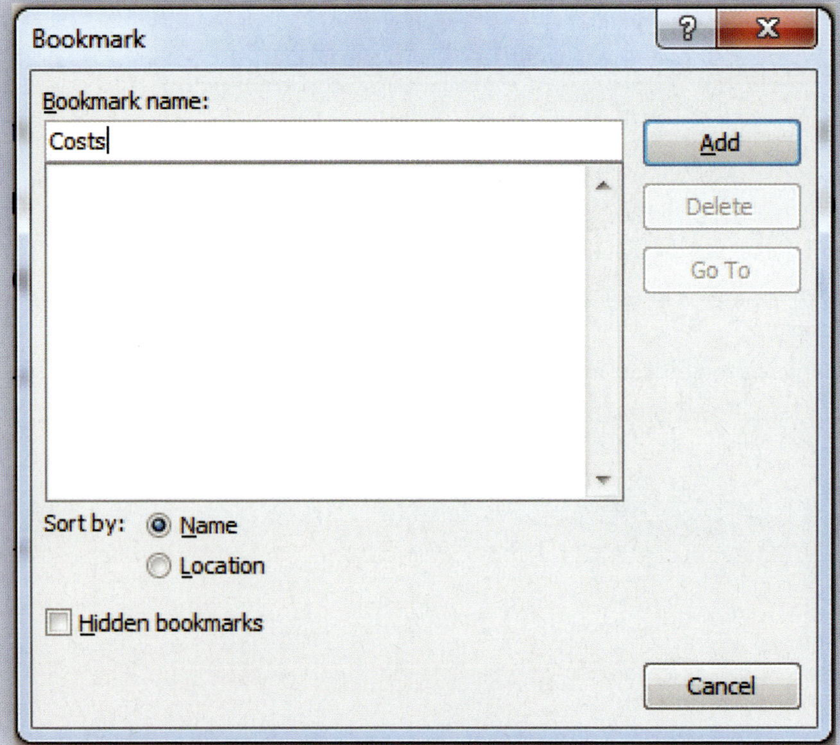

FIGURE WD 6.42

c. In the *Bookmark* dialog box, enter the name **`Costs`** for the bookmark. Click the **Add** button.

d. Navigate to the *Resources:* section, and place the cursor before the heading.

e. In the *Links* group, click the **Bookmark** button.

f. In the *Bookmark* dialog box, enter the name **`Resources`** for the bookmark, Click the **Add** button.

11. Use the *Go To* command to navigate to the bookmarks you added.

a. Press **Ctrl + Home** to navigate to the beginning of the document.

b. Click the **Home** tab. In the *Editing* group, click the **Find** button arrow and select **Go To.**

c. On the *Go To* tab of the *Find and Replace* dialog box, click **Bookmark.**

d. Verify *Costs* is selected under *Enter bookmark name:*. Click the **Go To** button.

e. Select the table in the *Costs:* section. On the *Home* tab, in the *Styles* group, click the **No Spacing** style.

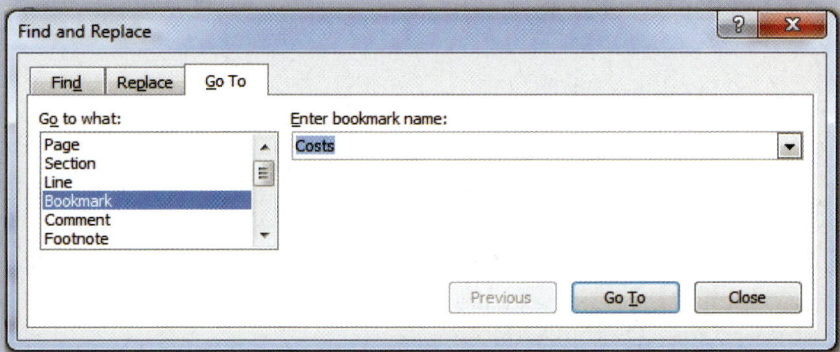

FIGURE WD 6.43

f. In the *Find and Replace* dialog box, click the *Enter bookmark name:* arrow and select **Resources.** Click the **Go To** button.

g. Select the table in the *Resources:* section. On the *Home* tab, in the *Styles* group, click the **No Spacing** style.

h. Close the *Find and Replace* dialog box.

12. Apply automatic hyphenation to the document.

a. Click the **Page Layout** tab.

b. In the *Page Setup* group, select **Hyphenation.**

c. Select **Automatic** to enable automatic hyphenation.

13. Save and close the document.

challenge yourself 1

In this project you will set the styles and formatting for a business case template document. You will be adding captions to figures and then creating a table of figures. You will also be adding bookmarks, a hyperlink, and a table of contents to the document.

1. Start Microsoft Word 2010.

2. Open the *Business Case Template.docx* and save it as **`[your initials]WD_Challenge_6-3.`**

3. Insert a page number at bottom of the page using *page "x of y" Bold Numbers 3* option.

4. Find *Project Request,* and select both words. Go to *Heading 1* in the *Styles* gallery.
   a. Modify the *Heading 1* style as follows:
      (1) *Font:* Arial, 16 pt., bold, kerning 16 points and above.
      (2) *Line spacing:* single.
      (3) *Paragraph:* Space After: 12 pt.; Keep with next.
5. Apply the *Heading 1* style to all the headings.
6. Use the *Outlining* tab to demote the following to Level 2.
   a. *Option A:*
   b. *Description*
   c. *Assumptions* (under *Solution Options*)
   d. *Benefits*
   e. *Risks*
   f. *Costs*
7. Use the *Outlining* tab to demote the following to Level 3.
   a. *Resources*
   b. *Timeline*
8. Close Outline view.
9. Display the *Navigation* pane to review the headings. When you are finished, close the *Navigation* pane.
10. Add a horizontal line directly below the first table in the *Cost* section. Add another horizontal line directly below the first table in the *Resources* section.
11. Add the following captions below each table by clicking the **References** tab and clicking the **Insert Caption** button in the *Captions* group:
    a. Project Team Table:
       (1) **`Table 1: Project Team`**
    b. Cost Tables (two tables):
       (1) **`Table 2: One Time Funding`**
       (2) **`Table 3: Recurring Funding`**
    c. Resources Tables (two tables):
       (1) **`Table 4: Resource Manpower Estimates for Implementation`**
       (2) **`Table 5: Resource Manpower Estimates for Maintenance`**
12. Below Appendix A, type **`Table of Figures`** and press **Enter.**
13. At this insertion point, from the *References* tab, insert a table of figures using the default settings.
14. Select the table of figures, and bookmark with the name **`Figures`**.
15. Place the insertion point at the top of the blank (second) page. From the *References* tab, insert a table of contents using the built-in *Automatic Table 1* option.
16. Navigate to the table of figures using the bookmark you created.
17. Save and close the document.

challenge yourself 2

In this project you will take an existing document and make some quick edits using paragraph and character styles. You will add a drop cap to a paragraph, insert a symbol, and change the orientation of the document.

1. Start Microsoft Word 2010.
2. Open the document *PECO Request.docx* and save it as `[your initials]WD_Challenge_6-4.`
3. Create a new style named `Sections` based on the *Heading 1* style.
   a. *Font:* Arial, 16 pt.
   b. *Alignment:* Left.
   c. *Paragraph:* Space Before: 6 pt.; Space After: 12 pt.; Keep with next.
4. Apply the *Sections* style to the following headers.
   a. *4a. Scope*
   b. *4b. How does this project affect any academic programs?*
   c. *Breakdown of cost estimates:*
5. Select the title: *PECO Request: Open-Use Computer Lab.*
   a. Choose the character style *Book Title.*
   b. Modify the *Book Title* style as follows:
      (1) Font size: 16 pt.
      (2) Character spacing: Expanded by 2 pt.
6. Add a drop cap in the dropped style to the first paragraph.
7. At the end of the first numbered item, replace the word *degrees* with the degree symbol (°).
8. From the *Page Layout* tab, change the orientation to landscape.
9. Save and close the document.

on your own

In this project you will take a fourth-grade lesson plan and spruce it up by selecting a style set and modifying styles in the *Styles* gallery using shading to distinguish the different levels instead of using indentation. You will then use Outline view to demote items in the lesson plan, and then use the *Research* task pane to look up information about the subject of the lesson plan.

1. Start Microsoft Word 2010.
2. Open the *Poetry Lesson Plan.docx* and save it as `[your initials]WD_OnYourOwn_6-5.`
3. Change the style set to *Modern.*
4. Modify style headings 1, 2, and 3 as follows:
   a. *Heading 1:*
      (1) Font size: 16.
      (2) Format border: *Box, 3 pt., Blue Accent 1, Darker 25%.*
      (3) Format shading: *Blue, Accent 1, Darker 25%.*

b. *Heading 2:*

(1) Font size: 14.

(2) Format border: *Box, 3 pt., Blue Accent 1, Lighter 40%.*

(3) Format shading, *Blue Accent 1, Lighter 40%.*

c. *Heading 3:*

(1) Font size: 12.

(2) Format border: *Box, ¾ pt., Blue Accent 1, Lighter 80%.*

(3) Format shading: *Blue Accent 1, Lighter 80%.*

5. Change any *Heading 1* text so it always appears on the same page with the following *Heading 2* text.

6. Display the *Navigation* pane to review the headings in the document.

7. Switch to Outline view, and demote all the headings under the *Objective:* section and the *Targeted Bloom's Taxonomy Levels:* section to *Level 3* headings.

8. Use the *Research* task pane to look up information about *Shel Silverstein.*

9. Save and close the document.

fix it

In this project you will fix a sample nomination document sent to you in a column format with a title that is a bit overboard with its text effects. You will remove the formatting and columns and modify the document as a single-column document using alternative paragraph and character styles.

1. Start Microsoft Word 2010.

2. Open *Sample Nomination.docx* and save it as **`[your initials]WD_FixIt_6-6.`**

3. Clear the current formatting of the title.

4. Remove the continuous section break, and return the document to one column.

5. Select and center the title.

6. Apply the character style *Strong,* and modify it as follows:

a. *Font size:* Calibri, 18 pt.

b. *Font color:* Dark Blue, Text 2.

c. *Character spacing:* Expanded, 1.5 pt.

7. Modify the *Heading 1* style as follows:

a. *Font size:* Calibri, 14 pt.

b. *Font color:* Blue, Accent 1.

c. *Paragraph:* Spacing, 6 pt. before and 6 pt. after.

8. Insert the text **`Introduction`** a line above the first paragraph.

a. Apply the *Heading 1* style to *Introduction.*

9. Insert the text **`Justification`** a line above the second paragraph.

a. Apply the *Heading 1* style to *Justification.*

10. Insert the text **`Summary`** a line above the last paragraph.

a. Apply the *Heading 1* style to *Summary.*

11. Apply automatic hyphenation to the document.
12. Add a pull quote using the *Austin Pull Quote* style with the following text: **`His strong leadership enables our students, teachers, staff, and parents to know our school is a welcoming, vibrant, responsive, engaging, and safe environment.`**
13. Resize the pull quote box so none of the words is hyphenated. Move the pull quote to the beginning of the document so it appears to the right of the *Introduction* and *Justification* paragraphs.
14. Save and close the document.

chapter 7

Exploring Advanced Tables, Charts, and Graphics

In this chapter, you will learn the following skills:

- Add formulas to tables
- Convert text to a table
- Create a chart
- Apply artistic effects, and crop and correct pictures
- Remove the background from pictures
- Use table styles

Skill **7.1** Defining a Header Row in a Table
Skill **7.2** Adding Formulas to Tables
Skill **7.3** Converting Text to a Table
Skill **7.4** Creating a New Table Style
Skill **7.5** Creating a Chart
Skill **7.6** Applying Artistic Effects to Pictures
Skill **7.7** Removing the Background from Pictures
Skill **7.8** Correcting Pictures
Skill **7.9** Changing the Color of Pictures
Skill **7.10** Cropping Graphics
Skill **7.11** Compressing Pictures
Skill **7.12** Aligning, Grouping, and Rotating Images
Skill **7.13** Resetting Pictures

skills

introduction

In Chapter 4, you were introduced to tables and graphics and how they can enhance the appearance and readability of a document. We carry this a bit further in this chapter, in which you will learn more advanced skills for working with tables, including converting text into tables, using formulas in tables, and creating new table styles. Additionally, you will learn how to add a chart to a document. You will learn how to use the new picture tools in Word 2010, including applying artistic effects and removing the background from pictures. Other advanced graphic skills, such as cropping images and grouping images, are covered in this chapter giving you the foundation to create graphic-rich, professional-looking documents.

7.1 Defining a Header Row in a Table

When you apply a table Quick Style, you can choose from formats that include banded rows, first columns, or a header row. A **header row** is the first row in a table and contains headings for each column in the table. Think of the header row as the top anchor for a table. If you have a long table that breaks across a page, you will want the header row to repeat on the top of the next page.

To set header rows to repeat across pages:

1. Place your cursor in the first row of the table.
2. Click the **Layout** tab, under *Table Tools.*
3. In the *Data* group, click the **Repeat Header Rows** button.

To turn off the *Repeat Header Rows* feature, click the **Repeat Header Rows** button again.

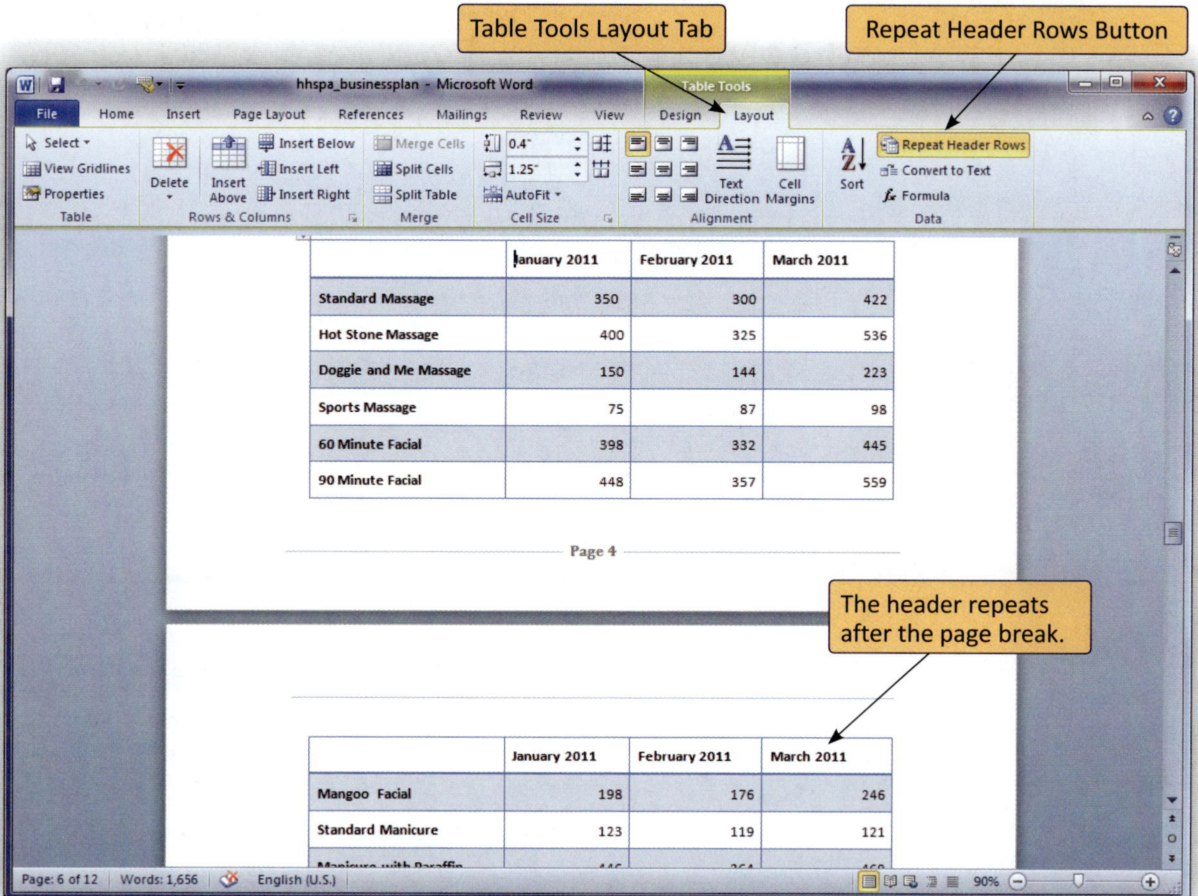

FIGURE WD 7.1

tips & tricks

You can assign more than one row to repeat at the top of the page. Select all the rows you want to repeat at the top of each page, and click the **Repeat Header Rows** button. Now when the table breaks across a page, all the rows you selected will appear at the top of the table.

tell me more

You must begin your selection with the first row of the table. If your cursor is in a later row in the table, the *Repeat Header Rows* button will not be active.

7.2 Adding Formulas to Tables

Spreadsheet programs like Microsoft Excel use **formulas** to perform calculations. You can add formulas to a table in Word to perform similar calculations, such as adding a column of numbers or calculating the average of a set of numbers. A formula begins with an equal sign and contains arguments, operators, and functions.

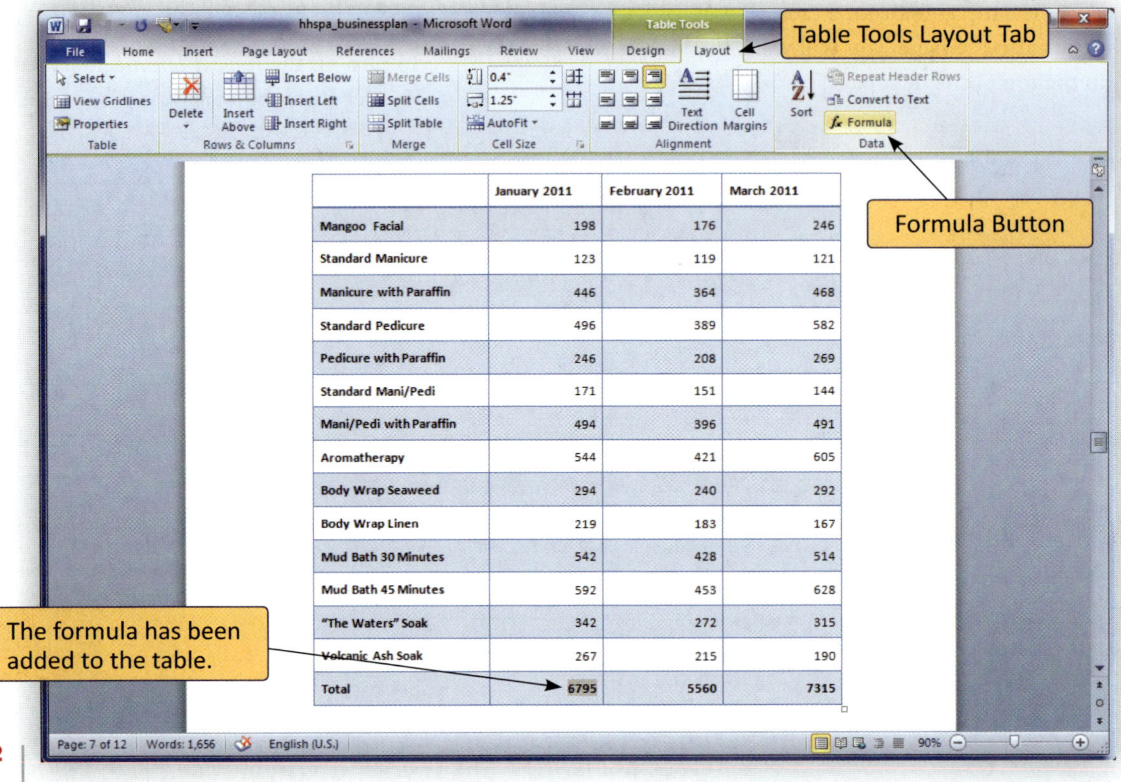

	January 2011	February 2011	March 2011
Mangoo Facial	198	176	246
Standard Manicure	123	119	121
Manicure with Paraffin	446	364	468
Standard Pedicure	496	389	582
Pedicure with Paraffin	246	208	269
Standard Mani/Pedi	171	151	144
Mani/Pedi with Paraffin	494	396	491
Aromatherapy	544	421	605
Body Wrap Seaweed	294	240	292
Body Wrap Linen	219	183	167
Mud Bath 30 Minutes	542	428	514
Mud Bath 45 Minutes	592	453	628
"The Waters" Soak	342	272	315
Volcanic Ash Soak	267	215	190
Total	6795	5560	7315

FIGURE WD 7.2

To add a formula to a table:

1. Place your cursor in the cell where you want to insert the formula.
2. Click the **Layout** tab under *Table Tools.*
3. In the *Data* group, click the **Formula** button.
4. Word displays a default formula based on the data in the table in the *Formula:* box.
5. Click **OK** to add the formula to the table.

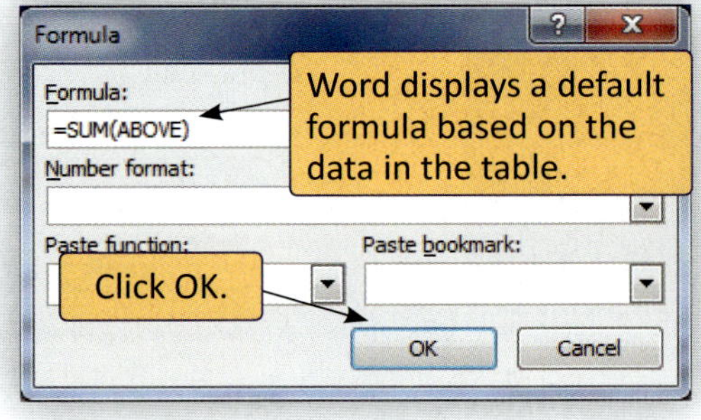

FIGURE WD 7.3

tips & tricks

Word creates a default formula based on the data in your table. You can enter your own formula in the *Formula:* box:

1. In the *Formula:* box, delete the formula, leaving the equal sign.
2. Click the **Paste function:** arrow.
3. Select a function.
4. Enter the arguments (cells you want to calculate) between the parentheses.

tell me more

Formulas may include functions. Functions are preprogrammed shortcuts for calculating complex equations (like the average of a group of numbers). Word includes 18 predefined functions you can use to perform calculations. Some common functions include:

Sum	Totals the values in the column or row
Average	Calculates the average of the values in the column or row
Max	Displays the largest value in the column or row
Min	Displays the smallest value in the column or row

7.3 Converting Text to a Table

Sometimes information displayed in a table can be more easily understood. If you have a list of names, addresses, and phone numbers, it makes sense to create a table with three columns to present your information. But what if you have already entered information in paragraph format? Microsoft Word allows you to convert text from paragraphs into a table.

To convert text to a table:

1. Select the text you want to convert to a table.
2. Click the **Insert** tab.
3. Click the **Table** button and select **Convert Text to Table . . .**
4. In the *Convert Text to Table* dialog box, click an option in the *Separate text at* section.
5. Click **OK** to convert the text to a table.

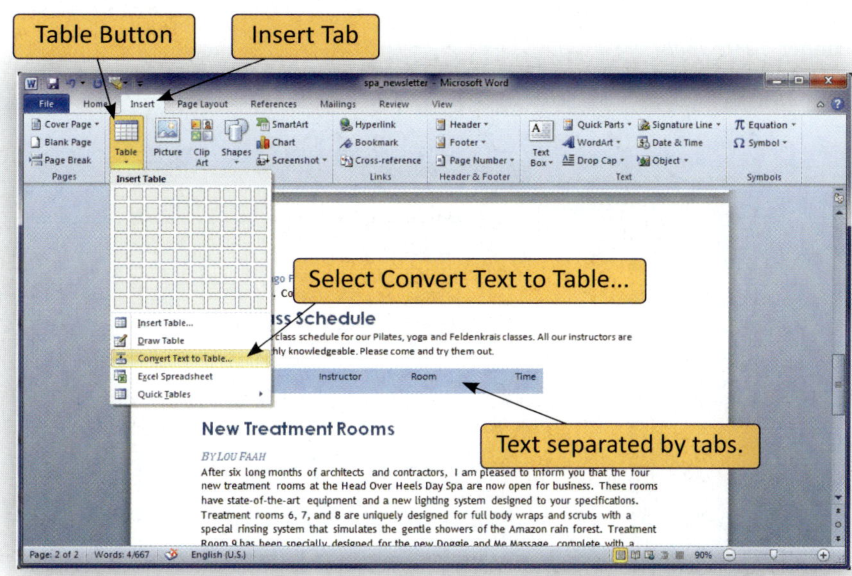

FIGURE WD 7.4

When you convert text to a table, Word looks for specific characters that serve as column separators. Characters that commonly serve as column separators include paragraphs, tabs, and commas.

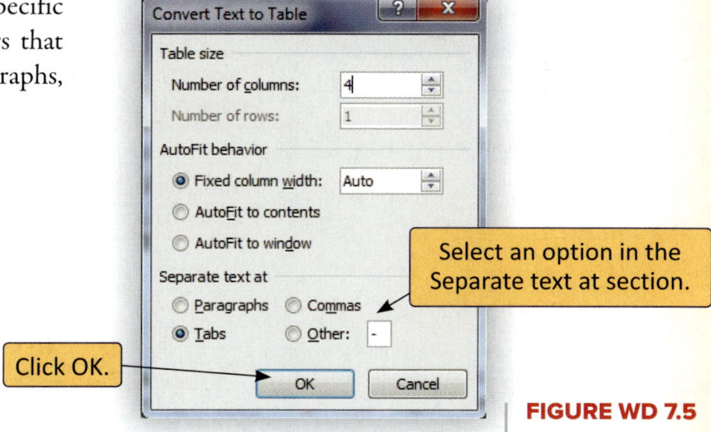

FIGURE WD 7.5

tips & tricks

Just as you can convert text into a table, you can also convert a table back into text:

1. Select the table you want to convert.
2. Click the **Layout** tab under *Table Tools*. In the *Data* group, click the **Convert to Text** button.

tell me more

You can use almost any character to mark where you want to separate your columns of text. Type the character in the *Other:* box. The number of columns will change to display the number of columns created based on the character you entered. If the number of columns appears to be correct, click **OK** to create the table.

7.4 Creating a New Table Style

Word comes with a number of built-in Quick Styles for you to apply to tables in your documents. These Quick Styles include shading, borders, and other design elements that you can apply to a table with one command. But what if you have your own table style that you want to use throughout a document? You can create and save your own table styles in Word and then apply that style just as you would apply any other table Quick Style.

To create a new table style:

1. Select the table with the formatting you want to save.
2. Click the **Design** tab under *Table Tools.*
3. In the *Table Styles* group, click the **More** button.
4. Click **New Table Style. . .**
5. In the *Create New Style from Formatting* dialog box, type the name of the table style in the *Name:* box.
6. Make changes to the table formatting, such as border width, border color, or fill color.
7. Click **OK.**

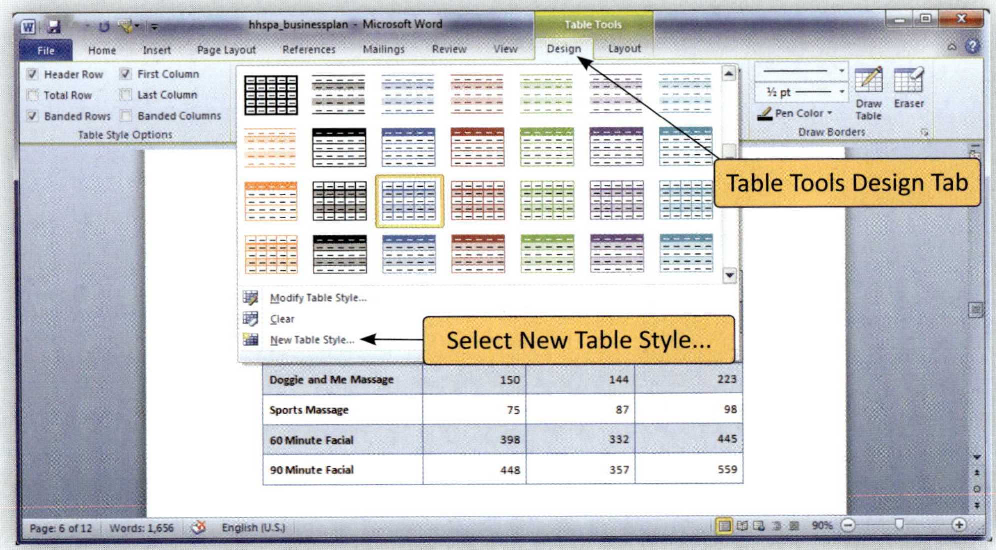

FIGURE WD 7.6

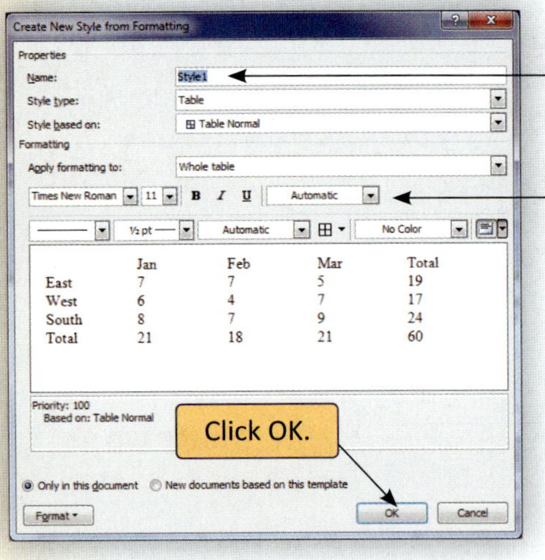

FIGURE WD 7.7

To apply the saved style to a table:

1. Click the **Design** tab under *Table Tools.*
2. In the *Table Styles* group, click the **More** button.
3. Click the name of the table style you created.

tips & tricks

When you save a table style, you can choose to have the formatting apply to the whole table or specific parts of the table, such as a header row. The *Preview* area will show you how the formatted table will appear.

tell me more

When you create a new table style, it is added under the *Custom* section of the *Table Styles* gallery.

7.5 Creating a Chart

Charts allow you to take raw data and display them in a visual way. A **chart** takes the values you have entered in a spreadsheet and converts them to graphic representation. In Word, you can create a wide variety of charts, including bar charts (both stack and 3-D), pie charts, column charts, scatter charts, and line charts.

To add a chart to a document:

1. Click the **Insert** tab.
2. In the *Illustrations* group, click the **Chart** button.
3. In the *Insert Chart* dialog box, click a chart type category to display that category in the right pane.
4. Click a chart type in the right pane to select it.
5. Click **OK** to add the chart to the document.

Word automatically launches Microsoft Excel, with sample data for the chart entered for you.

1. Replace the sample data with your own data.
2. Close Excel and return to Word to see your finished chart.

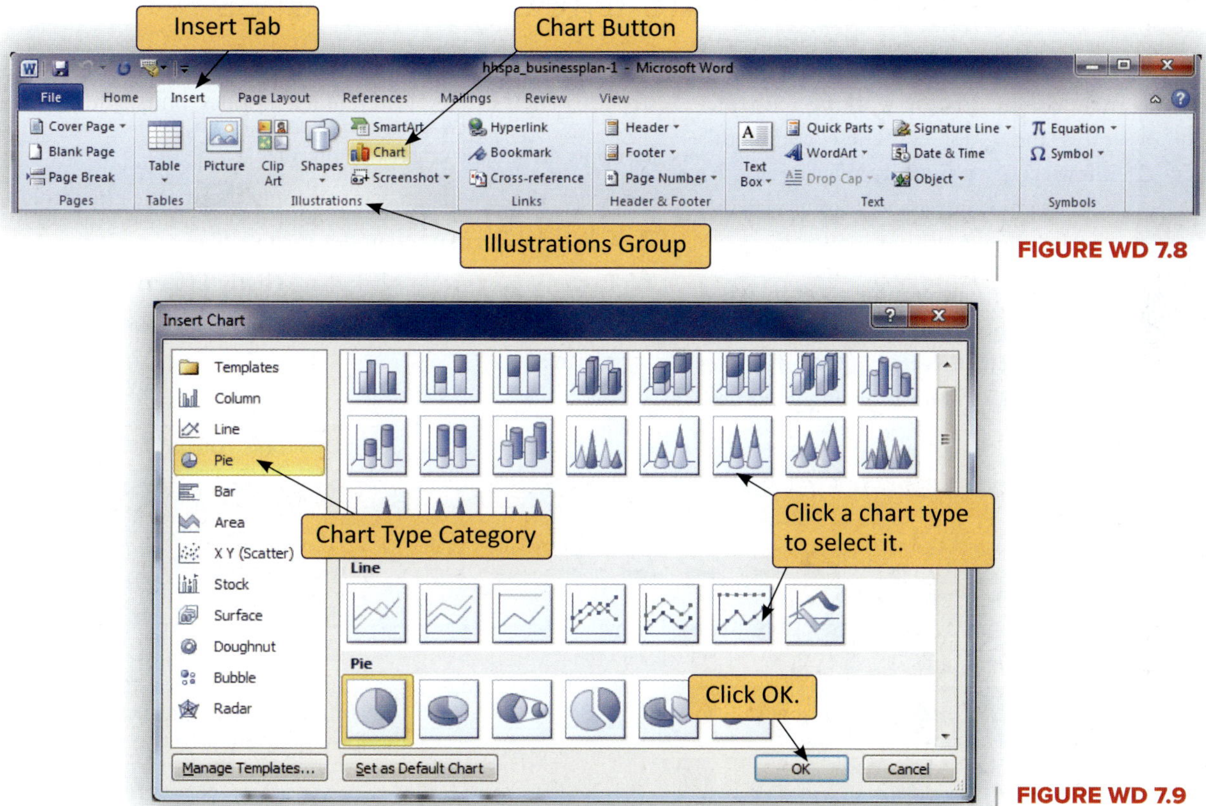

FIGURE WD 7.8

FIGURE WD 7.9

tips & tricks

If you typically use one type of chart for your documents, you can set that chart type as the default chart type. In the *Insert Chart* dialog box, select the chart type you want to set as the default. Next, click the **Set as Default Chart** button. When you open the *Insert Chart* dialog box, that chart type will automatically be selected.

tell me more

When the chart is selected, the *Chart Tools* contextual tabs are available. These tabs provide design, layout, and formatting options for customizing the chart.

Design tab—allows you to change the chart type, layout, and chart style. You can also modify the chart data from the *Design* tab.

Layout tab—allows you to change the individual elements of the chart layout, such as the appearance of the legend or chart title.

Format tab—allows you to change the individual formatting elements of the chart, such as fill, outline, and effects.

from the perspective of . . .

LIBRARIAN

We use charts and graphics when planning client-centered programs, such as special services for corporate clients, storytelling for children, newsletters, or programs for special groups. Our services are more appreciated now that they are illustrated.

7.6 Applying Artistic Effects to Pictures

Word 2010 comes with a number of new commands for working with pictures and graphics. These commands allow you to modify pictures using tools that in the past were only available through image editing applications.

One of the new graphic tools in Word 2010 is the *Artistic Effects* command. The **Artistic Effects** command applies a graphic filter to an image. These filters mimic a wide variety of artistic tools, including paint strokes, pencil strokes, watercolors, mosaics, blurs, and glows.

To apply an artistic effect to a picture:

1. Select the image you want to apply the artistic effect to.
2. Click the **Format** tab under *Picture Tools.*
3. In the *Adjust* group, click the **Artistic Effects** button.
4. Select an option from the gallery to apply it to the picture.

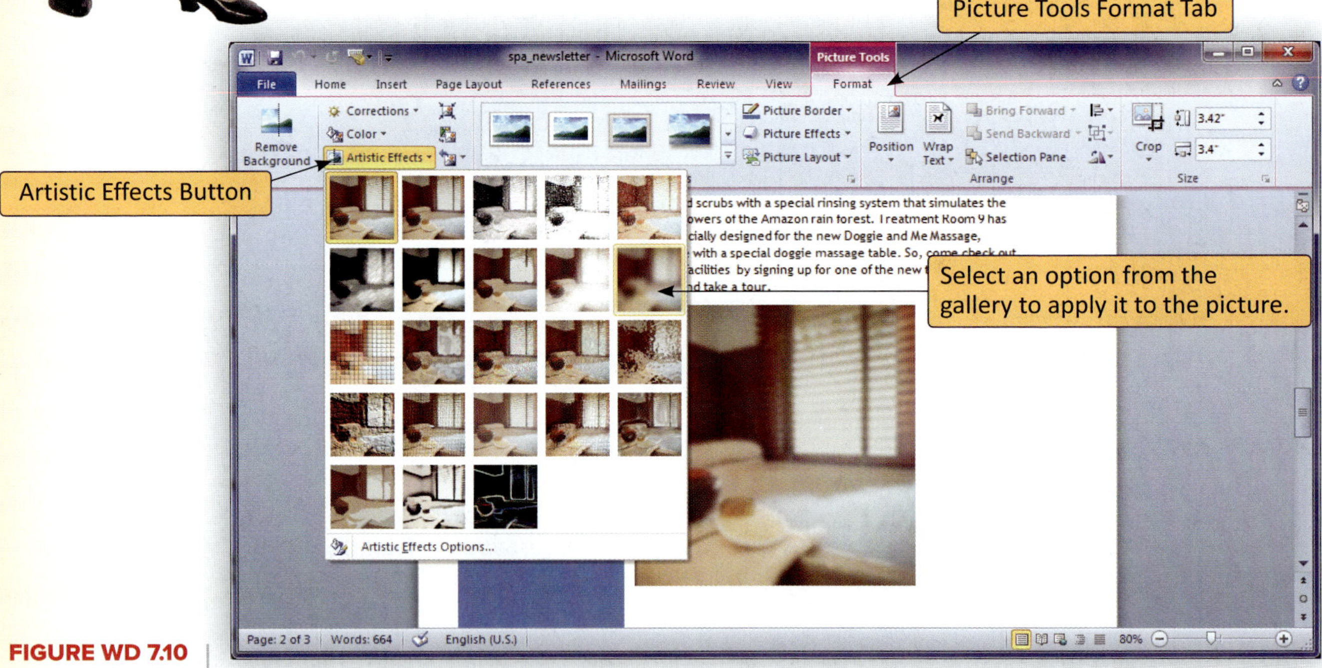

FIGURE WD 7.10

tips & tricks

If you have Live Preview enabled, when you roll your mouse over an option in the gallery, the effect is previewed on the selected image.

tell me more

The *Artistic Effects* command can only be used on photographs, not on illustrations.

7.7 Removing the Background from Pictures

One way to modify a picture is to remove its background. When you remove the background from a picture, Word analyzes the picture and calculates which areas are the background. Word then marks the background areas for removal. The resulting effect is as if you had traced the main part of the picture and then erased the background, leaving you with an outline of the picture.

To remove the background from a picture:

1. Select the image you want to remove the background from.
2. Click the **Format** tab under *Picture Tools.*
3. In the *Adjust* group, click the **Remove Background** button.
4. The *Background Removal* tab displays.
5. Adjust the marked area until the image appears as you want it.
6. Click the **Keep Changes** button to remove the background from the image.

FIGURE WD 7.11

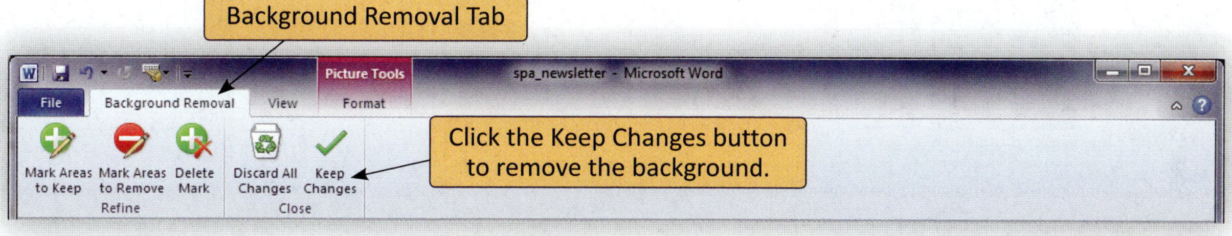

FIGURE WD 7.12

tips & tricks

Click the **Discard All Changes** button to close the *Background Removal* tab and not change the picture.

try this

To accept the changes, you can also:

- Click outside the picture.
- Press Enter on the keyboard.

tell me more

You can modify the area marked for removal from the *Refine* group on the *Background Removal* tab:

Mark Areas to Keep—allows you to draw lines indicating areas not to delete when the background is removed.

Mark Areas to Remove—allows you to draw lines indicating areas to delete when the background is removed.

Delete Mark—removes lines you have added marking areas to keep or remove.

7.8 Correcting Pictures

After you have added a picture to a document, you may find that it does not appear quite the way you want. It may appear too dark or too light, or it could appear slightly blurry. You can correct problems in pictures from the *Picture Tools Format* tab.

To adjust a picture:

1. Select the image you want to modify.
2. Click the **Format** tab under *Picture Tools.*
3. In the *Adjust* group, click the **Corrections** button.
4. The gallery displays how the selected image will appear with the correction applied.
5. Select an option from the gallery to make the change.

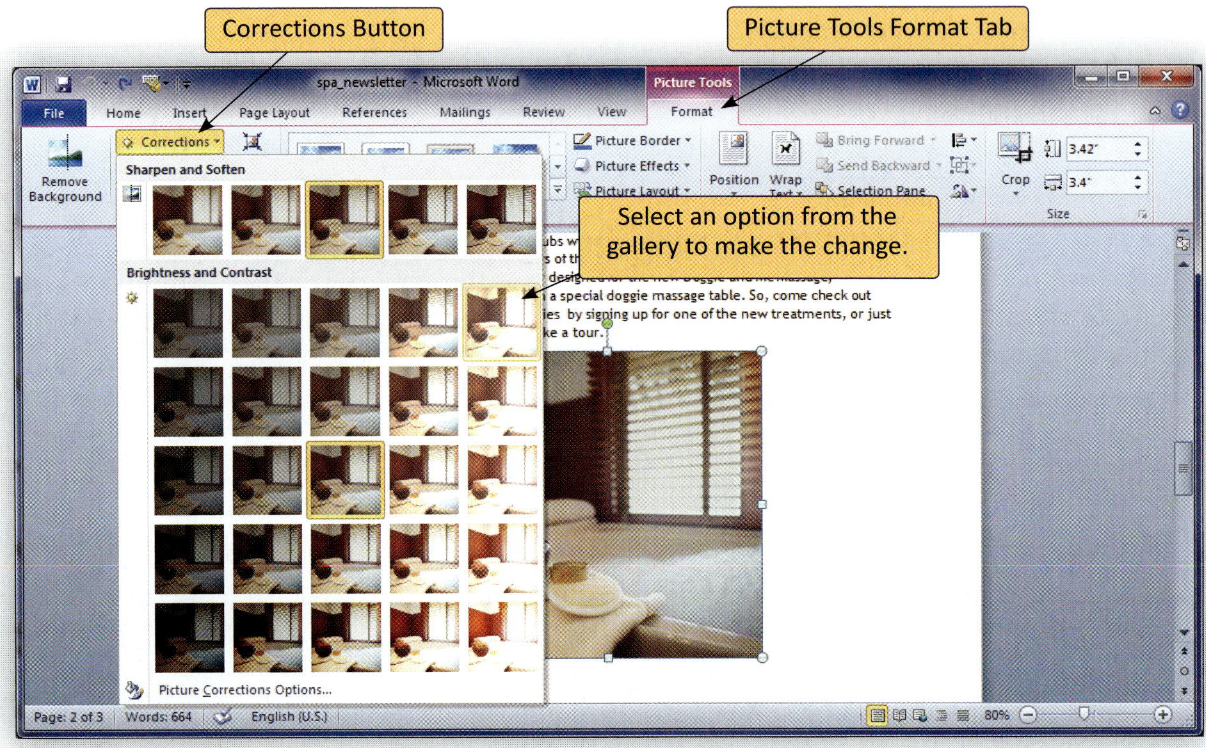

FIGURE WD 7.13

When you make corrections, you are changing the following properties for a picture:

Brightness—makes the overall picture darker or lighter.

Contrast—changes the range of color intensity within the picture. A picture with high contrast will have bolder colors, while a picture with lower contrast will have more muted colors.

Softness—removes hard edges, giving the picture a smoother feel.

Sharpness—removes any blurriness, giving the picture a crisper feel.

tips & tricks

The *Corrections* gallery displays the preset options for correcting images. If you want to adjust the picture manually, you should use the *Format Picture* dialog box. To open the *Format Picture* dialog box, click **Picture Corrections Options . . .** at the bottom of the *Corrections* gallery.

tell me more

If the picture you want to change is a drawing, you can adjust the brightness and contrast. If the picture you want to change is a photograph, you can adjust the sharpness of the image in addition to the brightness and contrast.

7.9 Changing the Color of Pictures

Another graphic effect you can apply to a picture in Word is to recolor the image. When you **recolor** an image, Word takes the image and applies a color overlay. All colors are removed from the image and replaced with shades of one color. The resulting effect is as if you were looking at the image through colored glass.

To color a picture:

1. Select the image you want to color.
2. Click the **Format** tab under *Picture Tools.*
3. In the *Adjust* group, click the **Color** button.
4. The gallery displays how the selected image will appear with the color applied.
5. Select an option from the gallery to apply it to the picture.

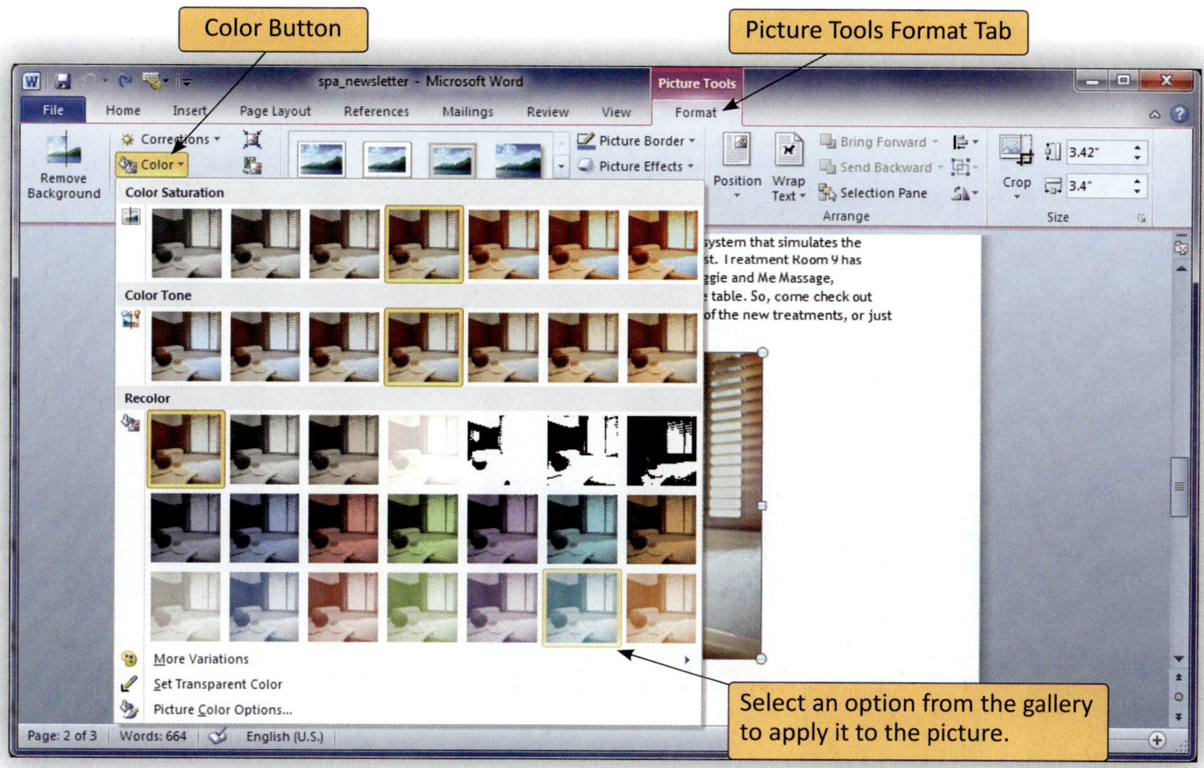

FIGURE WD 7.14

tips & tricks

- You can choose to make any color in the picture transparent. Click **Set Transparent Color** at the bottom of the gallery. Click any part of the image that has the color you want to make transparent. Word makes all matching areas of the image transparent.
- Point to *More Variations* at the bottom of the gallery to choose from other colors in the document's color theme.

tell me more

In addition to recoloring a picture, you can change the saturation and color tone of the picture. Adjusting the saturation will change the color intensity of the picture. Adjusting the color tone will give the picture a warmer or cooler appearance by adjusting the picture's temperature.

7.10 Cropping Graphics

When you add an image to a document, you may only want to show part of the image. You could edit the picture in an image editing application, or you could use the **Crop** tool in Word to trim the picture.

To crop a picture:

1. Select the image you want to crop.
2. Click the **Format** tab under *Picture Tools.*
3. In the *Size* group, click the **Crop** button.
4. Word displays black lines around the edges of the image. These are cropping handles.
5. Point to a cropping handle. When the cursor changes to one of the crop cursors, click and drag toward the center of the image.
6. Press Enter to accept the changes.

Notice that the size of the objects in the image does not change. When you crop an image, you are removing part of the image, hiding it from sight.

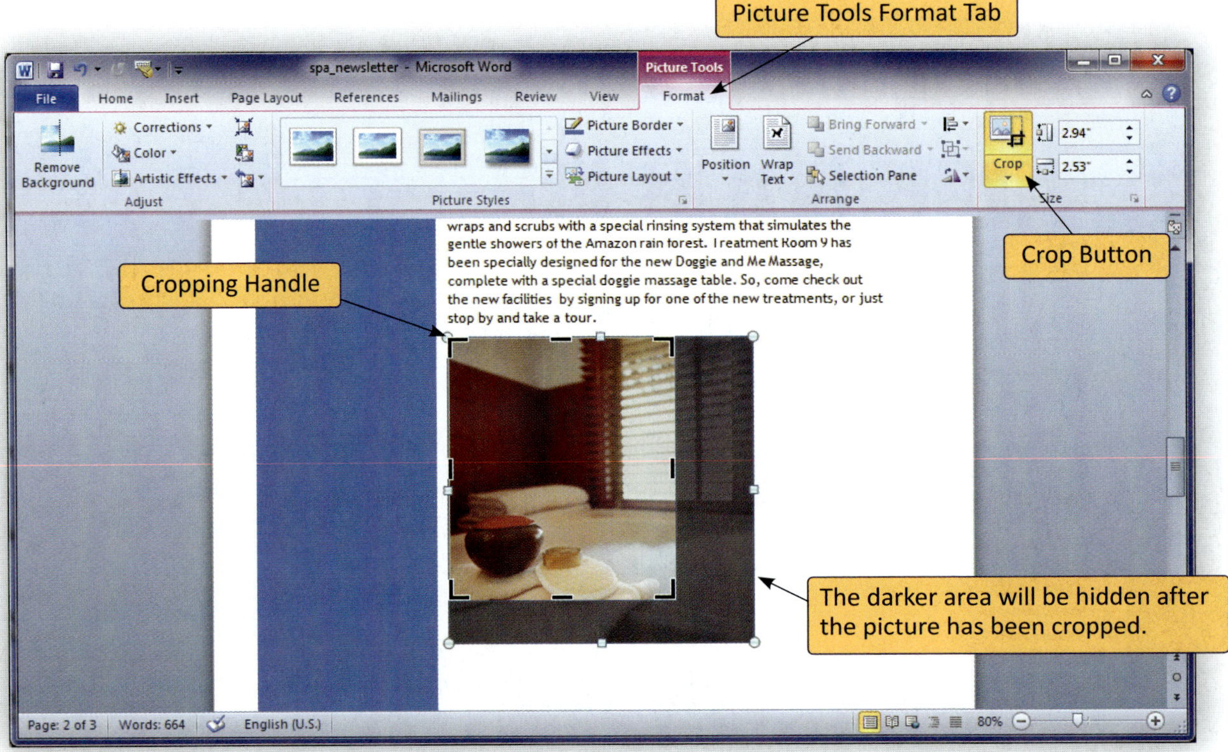

FIGURE WD 7.15

tips & tricks

- When you crop an image, the entire image remains as part of the document. The cropped areas are simply hidden from sight. If you want to restore part of an image, use the *Crop* tool to expand the cropped area, and the previously hidden area will be visible.
- If you know you will not need to restore the image in the future, you can remove the cropped areas of pictures by compressing the images in your document.

tell me more

Other cropping options include:

- **Crop to Shape**—allows you to crop an image using the any of Word's built-in shapes as an outline.
- **Aspect Ratio**—crops the image to a rectangular shape with a ratio of a specific width by height.

7.11 Compressing Pictures

The more images you add to a document, the larger the document's file size will become. Before sending a document to others, a good practice is to reduce the file size as much as possible. One way to reduce the file size of documents is to compress large pictures in the document.

To compress pictures:

1. Select a picture in the document.
2. Click the **Format** tab under *Picture Tools.*
3. In the *Adjust* group, click the **Compress Pictures** button.
4. Notice the *Apply only to this picture* and the *Delete cropped areas of pictures* check boxes are selected by default.
5. Click **OK** in the *Compress Pictures* dialog box.

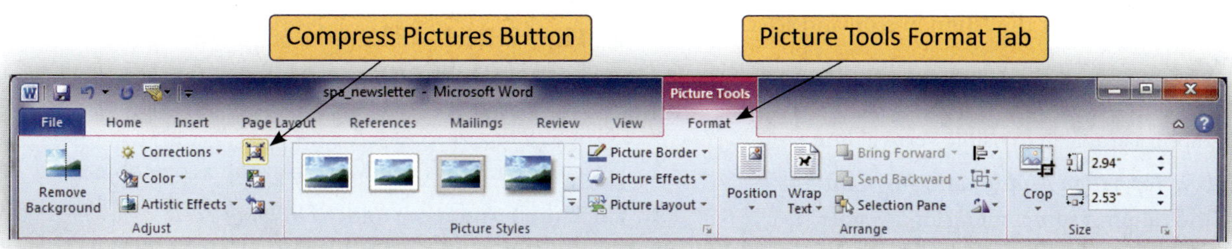

FIGURE WD 7.16

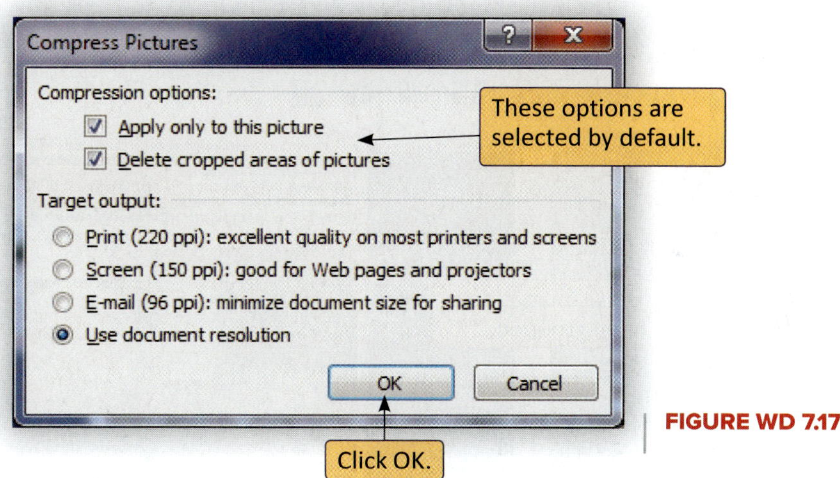

FIGURE WD 7.17

tips & tricks

- To compress all the pictures in the document, deselect the *Apply only to this picture* check box.
- If the *Delete cropped areas of pictures* check box is selected, all cropped areas of the picture will be removed when you compress the picture. Only check this option if you have cropped images and know you will not need to restore the images in the future.

tell me more

The *Target Output:* allows you to control how much the picture is compressed—the higher the resolution, the less compression of the image. The lower the resolution, the more the image will be compressed, resulting in a smaller file size, but potentially lesser quality images.

7.12 Aligning, Grouping, and Rotating Images

When adding images to a document, it is important to place the images so they will have the most impact on the reader. Any graphics that appear in a straight line should be aligned, to ensure that they are precisely placed. On the other hand, you may want to rotate one graphic to make it stand out on the page. You can also select multiple images and **group** them together, thus turning multiple objects into one object that you can easily modify.

To align graphics:

1. Click the **Format** tab under *Drawing Tools.*
2. In the *Arrange* group, click the **Align** button and select an option:
   - The *Align Left, Align Center,* and *Align Right* commands align graphics along an invisible vertical line.
   - The *Align Top, Align Middle,* and *Align Bottom* commands align graphics along an invisible horizontal line.
   - The *Distribute Horizontally* and *Distribute Vertically* options evenly space the graphics on the page.

To rotate graphics:

1. Click the **Format** tab under *Drawing Tools.*
2. In the *Arrange* group, click the **Rotate** button and select an option:
   - **Rotate Left 90°**—rotates the graphic 90 degrees counterclockwise.
   - **Rotate Right 90°**—rotates the graphic 90 degrees clockwise.
   - **Flip Horizontal**—reflects the graphic along the vertical axis.
   - **Flip Vertical**—reflects the graphic along the horizontal axis.

To group graphics:

1. Select the graphics you want to group as one object.
2. Click the **Format** tab under *Drawing Tools.*
3. In the *Arrange* group, click the **Group** button and select an option.

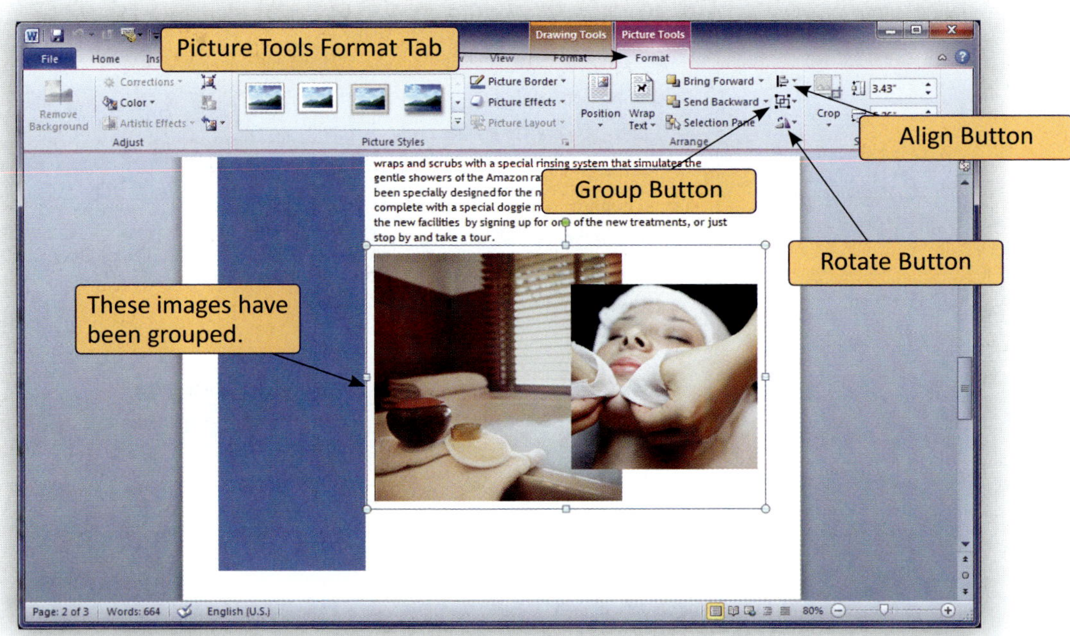

FIGURE WD 7.18

tips & tricks

From the *View* tab you can display gridlines on the page, which are helpful when you have many graphics you want to align.

try this

To group graphics, you can also right-click a graphic, point to **Group,** and select an option.

tell me more

These steps cover aligning, rotating, and grouping images, such as shapes. These steps also apply to formatting clip art and pictures, and the same commands can be accessed from the *Picture Tools Format* tab.

7.13 Resetting Pictures

If you have made several changes to an image and decide to undo the changes you made, you could use the *Undo* command to revert the picture to its original state, or you could use the **Reset Picture** command. The *Reset Picture* command removes all Word formatting applied to the picture, reverting the picture to its state before any formatting was applied.

To reset a picture:

1. Click the **Format** tab under *Picture Tools.*
2. In the *Adjust* group, click the **Reset Picture** button.
3. Any Word formatting you added to the picture is removed.

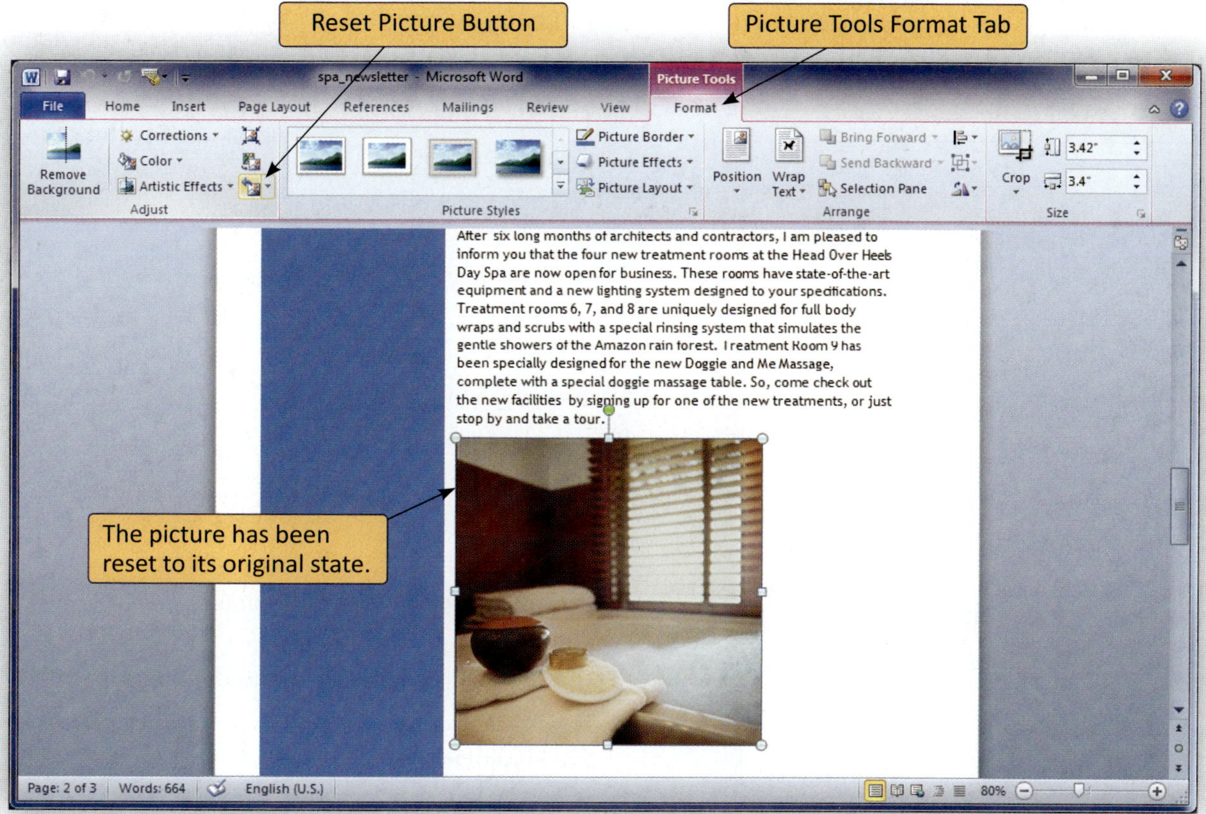

FIGURE WD 7.19

tips & tricks

Clicking the *Reset Picture* button does not revert the image to the original size. If you want to remove the formatting and change the picture back to the size it was when you first added it to the document, click the arrow next to *Reset Picture* and select **Reset Picture & Size.**

try this

To reset a picture, removing any formatting you added in Word, you can also click the **Reset Picture** button arrow and select **Reset Picture.**

projects

Data files for projects can be found on
www.mhhe.com/office2010skills

Skill Review 7.1

In this project you will edit a mass-mailing letter *GreenScapes_01,* for which you will convert the text to a table, modify the table style, and create a chart.

1. Open Microsoft Word 2010.
2. Open the *GreenScapes_01.docx* document and save it as **[your initials]WD_SkillReview_7-1.**

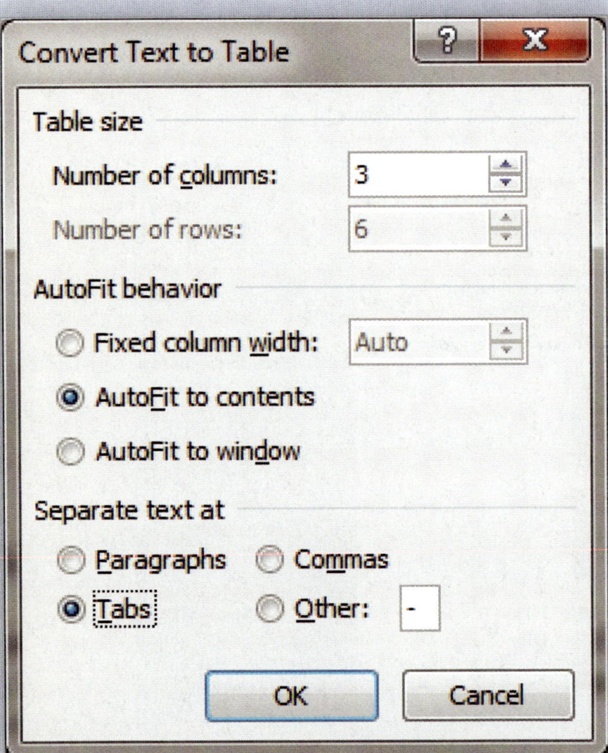

FIGURE WD 7.20

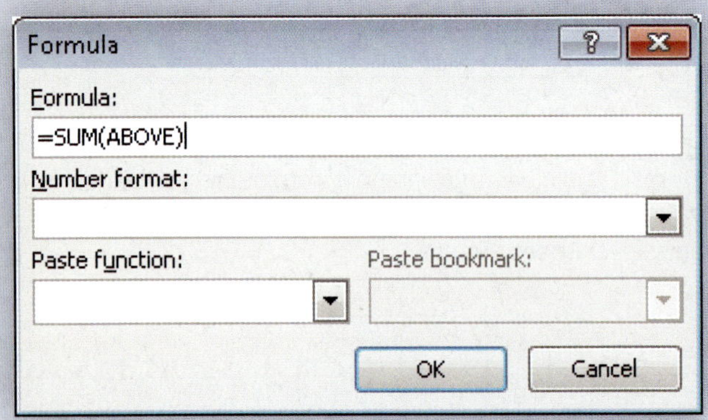

FIGURE WD 7.21

3. Convert text to a table.
   a. Select the text from *Lawn Care* to *TBD.*
   b. Click the **Insert** tab.
   c. In the *Tables* group, click the **Table** button and select **Convert Text to Table.**
   d. The *Convert Text to Table* dialog box opens.
   e. Select *AutoFit to contents* and *Tabs* under *Separate text at.* Click **OK.**
4. Add a formula to the table.
   a. Place the insertion point in the third column of the fifth row.
   b. Under *Table Tools,* click the **Layout** tab.
   c. In the *Data* group, click the **Formula** button.
   d. In the *Formula* box multiply the formula *=SUM(Above)* by *.85.*
      (1) Enter **=SUM(ABOVE)*.85** in the *Formula* box.
      (2) Click the *Number format* arrow and select **$#.##0.00;($#.##0.00).**
      (3) Click **OK.**
      (4) You should see *$121.13 per month* as the sum.
5. Apply a table style and then modify the table style.
   a. Place the insertion point within the table, and click the **Design** tab under *Table Tools.*
   b. In the *Table Styles* group, click the **More** button to open the gallery and view the options.
      (1) Select the *Light List Accent 3* option in the gallery (*Hint:* It has green shading)
      (2) Move the table to align under the *GreenScapes* paragraph.
   c. Click the **More** button again to expand the *Tables Styles* gallery, and choose **Modify Table Style.**
      (1) Under *Formatting,* click the *Apply formatting to:* arrow and select **Header row.**
      (2) Click the arrow for *Fill Color* and select green.
      (3) Click **OK** in the *Modify Style* dialog box.

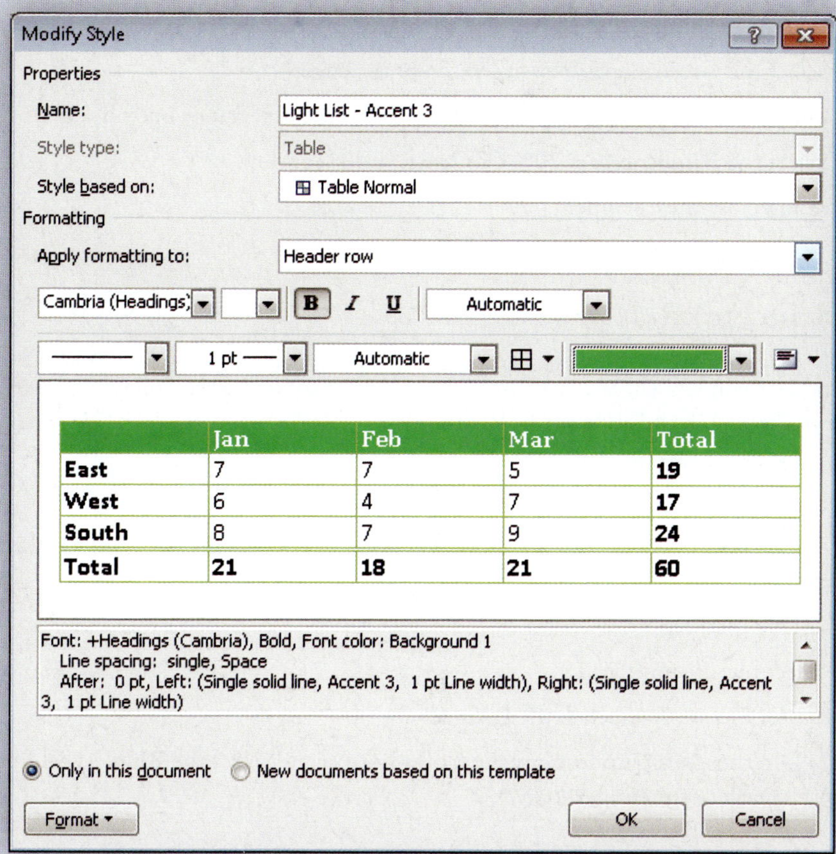

FIGURE WD 7.22

6. Press **Enter** after the table, and type the following: **`The graph below depicts your annual savings when you use all of our regular services.`**

7. Insert a graph below the inserted sentence.
   a. Press **Enter** after the sentence you typed.
   b. Click the **Insert** tab, and in the *Illustrations* group, click the **Insert Chart** button.
   c. Select **Clustered Column Chart** and click **OK.**

8. Edit the chart values in the Excel spreadsheet by:
   a. Deleting column D.
   b. Deleting rows 3, 4, and 5.
   c. Replace *Category 1* in A2 with **`Full Service.`**
   d. Change the value in B2 to **`$1710`**
   e. Change the value in C2 to **`$1453`**
   f. Replace *Series 1* in B1 with **`Annual Cost`**
   g. Replace *Series 2* in C1 with **`Annual Cost w/ Discount`**
   h. Close Excel.

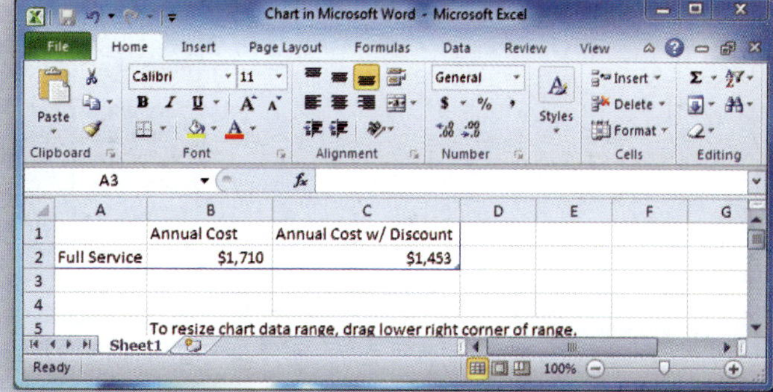

FIGURE WD 7.23

9. Click the **Format** tab under *Chart Tools*. In the *Size* group, resize the chart to 1.5" high and 4" wide.

10. Adjust the brightness and contrast of an image.
    a. Select the GreenScapes logo at the top of the page.
    b. On the *Format* tab under *Picture Tools,* click the **Corrections** button.
    c. Select the **Brightness: +20% Contrast: +40%** option.
11. Save and close the document.

Skill Review **7.2**

In this project you will enhance pictures to set up an exam question. You will have to adjust the pictures to match the question.

1. Open Microsoft Word 2010.
2. Open the *Question 8.docx* document and save it as ***[your initials]*WD_SkillReview_7-2.** The file has a photo taken at the Lincoln Memorial, which was being restored.
3. Recolor a picture.
    a. Select picture number 1.
    b. Under *Picture Tools,* click the **Format** tab.
        (1) In the *Adjust* group, click the **Color** button and select the **Blue, Accent color 1 Dark** option under *Recolor.*

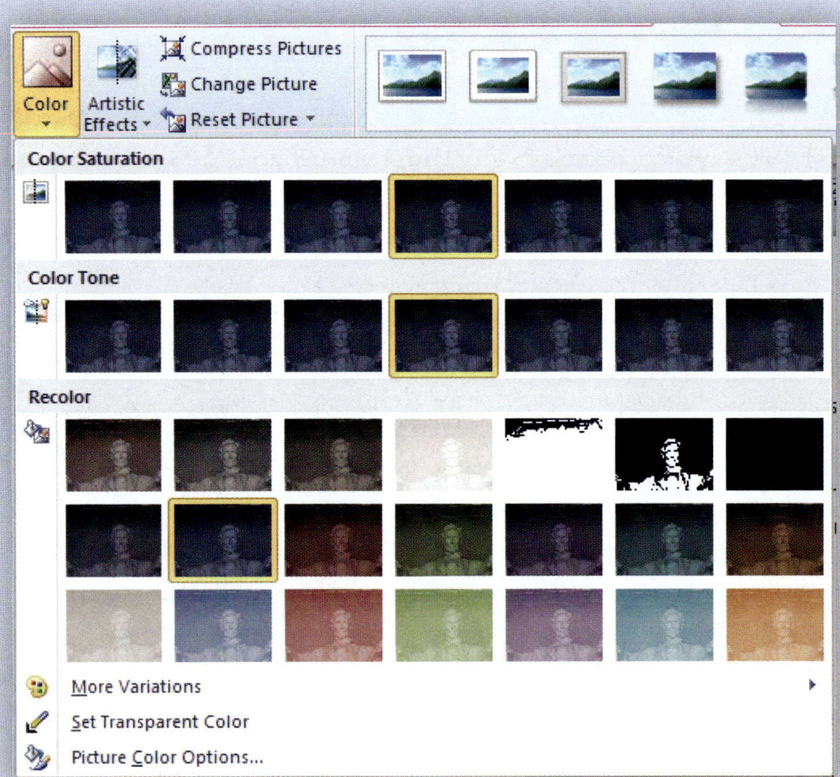

FIGURE WD 7.24

4. Apply artistic effects to a picture.
    a. Select picture number 2.
    b. In the *Adjust* group, click the **Artistic Effects** button.

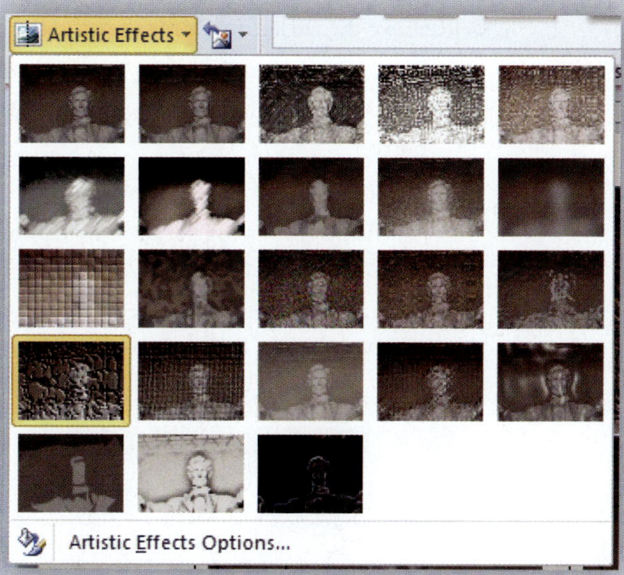

FIGURE WD 7.25

(1) Choose **Cement,** first column, fourth row.

5. Adjust the brightness and contrast of a picture.

a. Select picture number 3.

b. In the *Adjust* group, click the **Corrections** button.

c. Select the option to increase the brightness by 20% and increase the contrast by 40%.

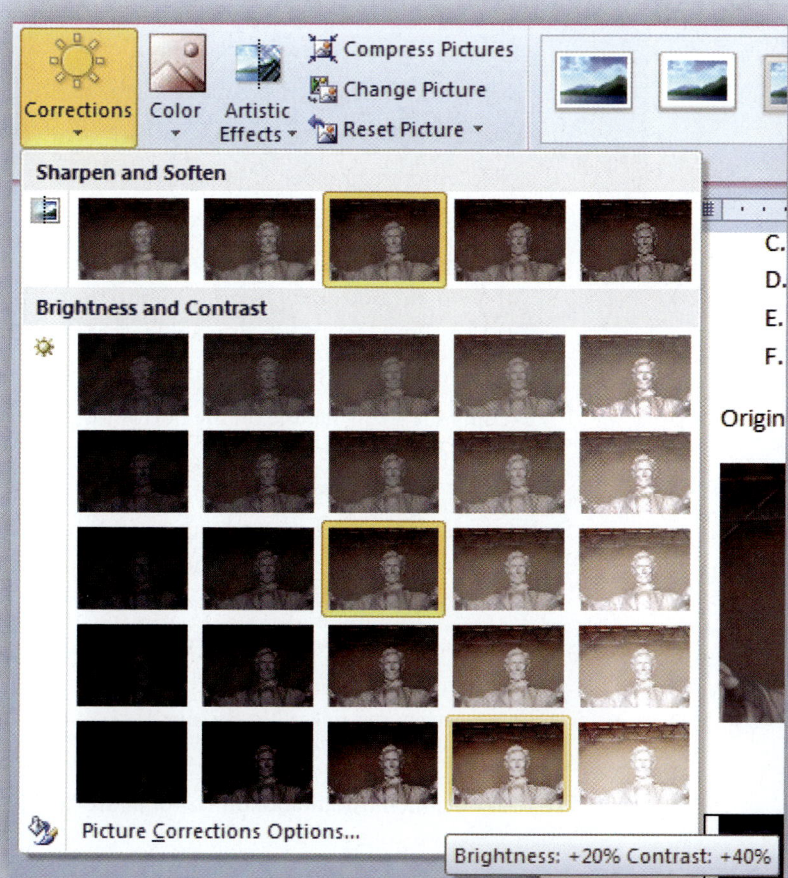

FIGURE WD 7.26

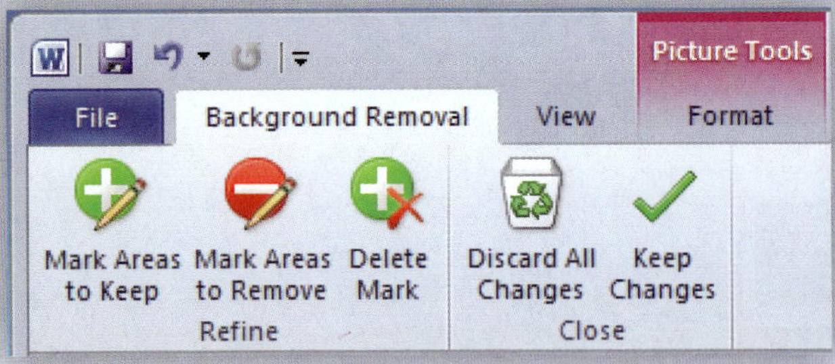

FIGURE WD 7.27

6. Remove the background from a picture.
   a. Select picture number 4.
   b. In the *Adjust* group, click the **Remove Background** button.
   c. The *Background Removal* tab displays.
      (1) Adjust the sizing handles so that only President Lincoln's head appears.
      (2) Click the **Keep Changes** button to remove the background and close the *Background Removal* tab.

FIGURE WD 7.28

FIGURE WD 7.29

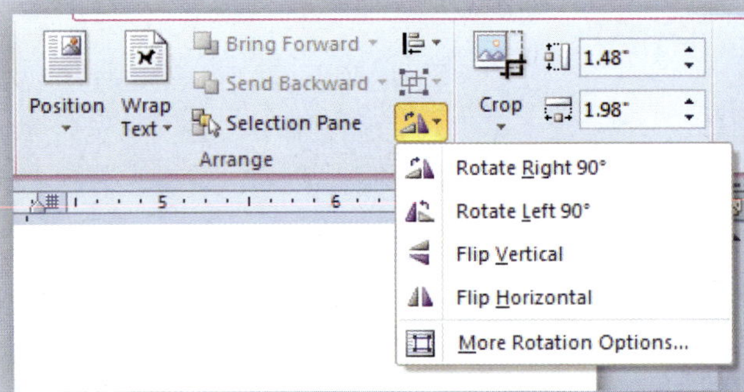

FIGURE WD 7.30

FIGURE WD 7.31

7. Rotate a picture.
   a. Select picture number 5.
   b. On the *Picture Tools Format* tab, in the *Arrange* group, click the **Rotate** button.
   c. Rotate the image 90 degrees to the left.
8. Crop a picture.
   a. Select picture number 6.
   b. In the *Size* group, click the **Crop** button.
   c. Use the cropping handles to remove the scaffolding at the top, the bottom of his jacket up to the opening of the vest, and his arms to the shoulders at the sides.
   d. Click outside the picture.
   e. Using the sizing handle on the bottom-right corner, expand the cropped image to approximately the same height as picture number 3.
9. Select all pictures in the two-by-three table by placing the cursor on the left-hand side of the page outside the table and dragging until all six pictures are selected.
   a. Under *Table Tools,* click the **Design** tab.
      (1) In the *Table Styles* group, click the **Borders** button arrow, and select **No Border.**
10. Save the document.
11. Your document should be similar to Figure WD 7.32.

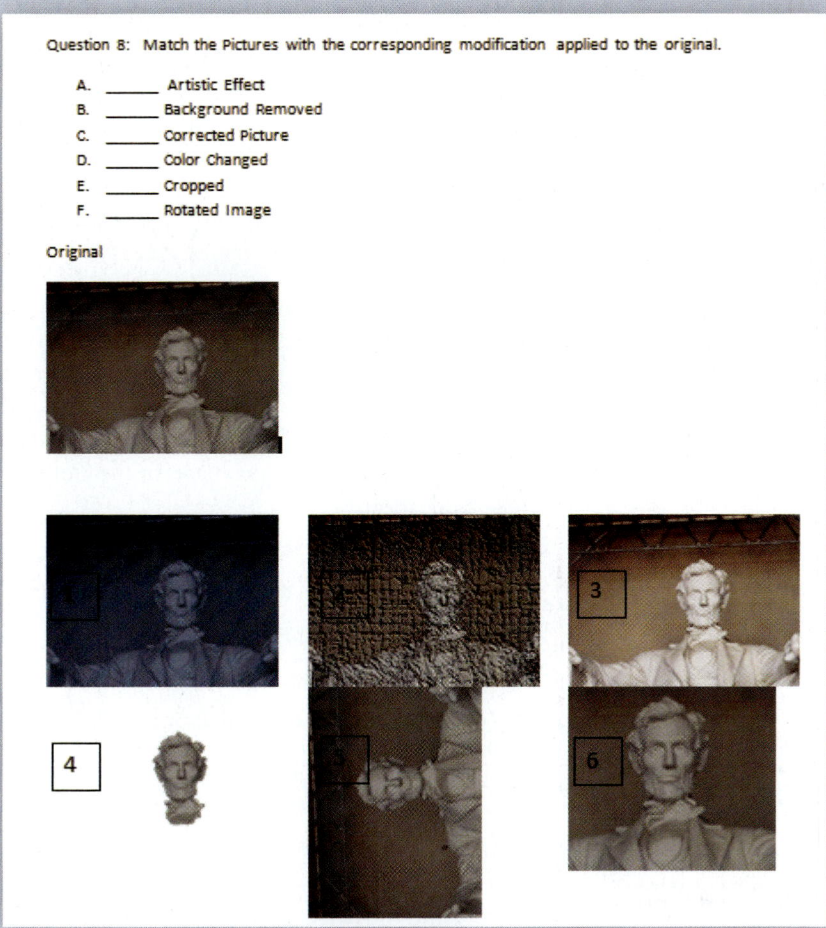

FIGURE WD 7.32

challenge yourself 1

Student Head Count by Gender Project: In this project you will apply your table and charting skills by creating a table from text, determining the percentage of undergraduate female students at HSU, and charting that information.

1. Open Microsoft Word 2010.
2. Open the *Admissions Memo.docx* document and save it as **`[your initials]WD_Challenge_7-3.`**
3. Modify the picture at the top of the page.
   a. Color the image using the *Red, Accent color 2 Dark* option.
   b. Adjust the image to be 20% brighter and with 40% less contrast.
   c. Remove the sky from the image using the *Remove Background* command.
4. Convert the text starting with *Undergraduate Head Count* and ending with *15,772* to a table.
   a. Choose *Fixed column width: Auto.*
   b. Choose *Separate text at: Tabs.*
5. Merge the first row cells.
6. Add a row to the bottom of the table.
   a. In the first column of the last row, add **`Percent Female`**
   b. In the second column of the last row, use a formula to determine the percentage of

female student enrolled in the College of Education. *Hint:* You need to divide the 1,678 female students into the =*Sum(Above)* and then multiply by 100. Do not forget to set the number format to 0%.

c. Repeat step 5.b for the third column for the university.

d. Select the table and change the font size to 10 pt.

7. Create a new table style based on the current table style named *Head Count.*

a. Apply the formatting to the whole table.

b. Fill the table using the *Blue, Accent 1, Lighter–80%* color.

c. Change the border color for the table to *Dark Blue, Text 2.*

8. Insert a pie chart below the table.

9. Modify the spreadsheet to display the male and female student graduates in the College of Education.

a. In B1 change *Sales* to **`EDU`**

b. Change A2 to **`Male`**

c. Change A3 to **`Female`**

d. Delete rows 4 and 5.

e. Insert appropriate values into cells B2 and B3.

f. Close Excel.

10. Modify the chart.

a. Select the chart, and choose **Layout 1** in the *Chart Layouts* group to display a centered title, and the percentage of males and females inside the chart.

b. Using the proportional sizing handle, adjust the chart size to where the right side is approximately at the 4-inch mark on the horizontal ruler and the bottom is approximately at the 8-inch mark on the vertical ruler.

11. Adjust to provide space after the chart and still keep entire memo on one page.

12. Your document should look similar to Figure WD 7.33.

13. Save and close the document.

Memorandum from the Office of Admissions

To: Dr. John Smith

From: Sandra Russell

Date: 6/28/2011

Re: Undergraduate Headcount by Gender

John,

There are approximately 3000 more undergraduate female students than male students at Hillsborough State University. As requested I have provided a breakdown of the impact of the College of Education on our gender ratio. HSU gender ratio is consistent the rest of the US colleges and universities. The American Council on Education reported the current enrollment in higher education is 57% women and 43% men.

Without going into great detail the College of Education undergraduate head count is 7.4% of the total student body. It makes up 10.6% of the female undergraduate student population. The female-to-male ratio at the College of Education is similar to our state ratio of 74% of the classrooms being taught by female K-12 teachers.

Undergraduate Head Count		
	College of Education	University Total
Male	454	12,911
Female	1678	15,772
Percent Female	79%	55%

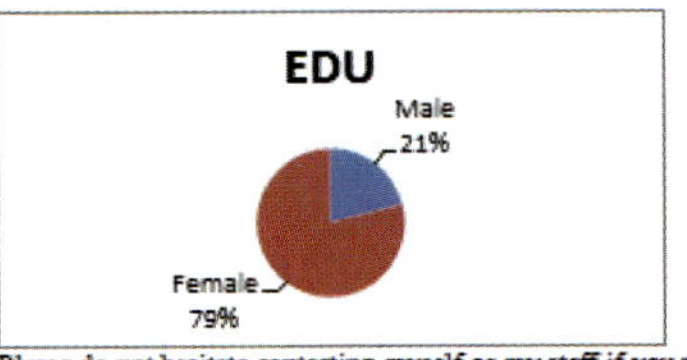

Please do not hesitate contacting myself or my staff if you need additional information.

Regards,

Sandra Russell
Assistant Director, HSU Admissions Office

FIGURE WD 7.33

challenge yourself 2

Employee Handbook Cover Page Project: In this project you insert graphic files, group them, and modify the files for the GreenScapes landscaping company.

1. Open Microsoft Word 2010.

2. Open *Orientation_Cover_Page.docx* and save it as *`[your initials]`*`WD_Challenge_7-4`.

3. Add a drawing canvas to the document.
    a. Place the insertion point to the right of the text in the upper half of the page. If necessary, show the formatting marks in the document. When you are done, hide the formatting marks again.
    b. On the *Insert* tab, in the *Illustrations* group, click the **Shapes** button.
    c. At the bottom of the gallery, select **New Drawing Canvas.**
    d. Adjust the canvas to fit on the screen, and drag from the bottom to about 9 inches on the vertical ruler so the drawing canvas is almost the height of the page.
4. Insert the GreenScapes logo in the canvas.
    a. Move the logo to align with the line at the top of the page.
    b. Enlarge the image by using proportional sizing handles so that the right side is at the 6-inch mark on the horizontal ruler.
5. In the bottom half of the canvas, insert the *Services 1, Services 2,* and *Services 3* images.
    a. Align the three images in order diagonally down and across starting at about the 4-inch mark of the vertical ruler.
6. Select the last image in the set of bottom three images.
    a. Apply the *Chalk Sketch* artistic effect to the image.
    b. Remove the background from the image using the default selection.
    c. Use the *Reset Picture* command to restore the image to its original state.
7. Select the middle image in the set of bottom three images.
    a. Increase the brightness by 40% and decrease the contrast by 20%.
8. Group the three service pictures in the canvas.
    a. Select the group and the GreenScapes logo in order to change the color.
        (1) Recolor all four images using the *Olive Green, Accent color 3 Dark* option.
    b. Select only the grouped images.
        (1) Apply the *Reflective Perspective Right* picture style to the grouped images.
9. Your document should look similar to Figure WD 7.34.
10. Save and close the document.

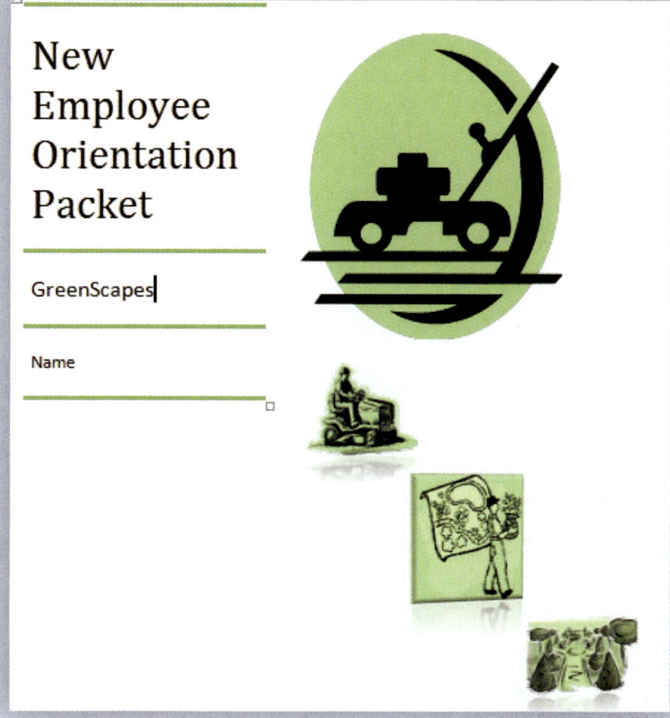

FIGURE WD 7.34

on your own

In this project you will create a table from existing text, add more information, and chart the information in a line chart.

1. Open Microsoft Word 2010.
2. Open *Tradewinds_03.docx* and save it as
   `[your initials]WD_OnYourOwn_7-5.`
3. Remove the aqua background from the image at the top of the document.
4. Apply an artistic effect that gives the image the appearance of having been painted or drawn.
5. Convert text into a table starting with *Price* to *$101.50.*
   a. Autofit the contents using tabs.
   b. Adjust spacing on the paragraph after the table so it appears spaced 6 pt. below the table.
6. Save the document.
7. Create a line chart comparing the cost of a $100 grocery basket and the fuel cost for a round-trip to both stores.
   a. Insert the chart after the paragraph starting with *Customer savings.*
   b. Choose **Line Chart.**
   c. The chart should look similar to the one below.

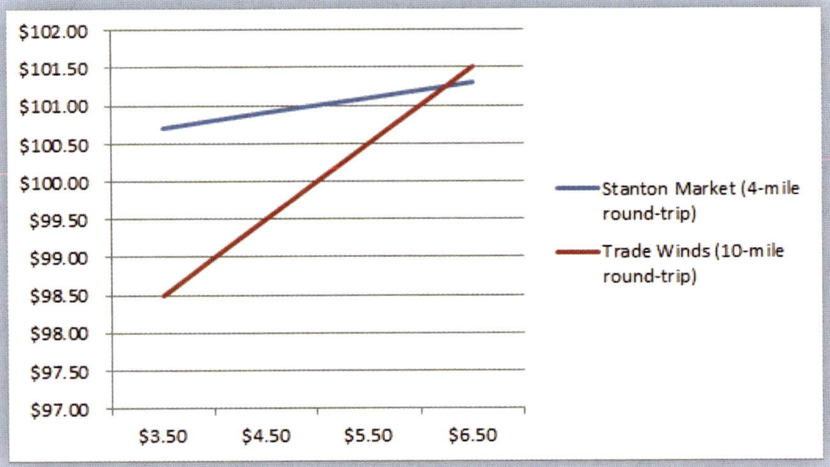

FIGURE WD 7.35

8. Save and close the document.

fix it

In this project you will fix a cover page for a tourist brochure.

1. Start Microsoft Word 2010.
2. Open *Carolina Travel Cover Page.docx* and save it as
   `[your initials]WD_FixIt_7-6.`
3. Crop the vista view to remove the cable that appears in the upper-right-hand portion of the picture.
   a. Drag the right edge of the picture until it is even with the header margin.
   b. Click away from the picture, and then drag the top edge up. The picture will be approximately 9.5" high.

4. Delete the "Carolina Travel" heading text box, and move the address text box to the top blue banner area. Center-align the text.
5. Reposition the text box starting with *Let Carolina Travel . . .* to the lower right of the cover page.
   a. Change the paragraph to read **`Let Carolina Travel elevate your trip to new heights in beautiful Blowing Rock and surrounding areas.`**
6. Insert the *Majestic* picture.
   a. Remove the background so only the tourists remain in the picture, and set the text wrapping to tight.
   b. Resize the tourists to approximately 4.6" high and 3.5" wide. Adjust the two tourists to the lower-right position on the page, as shown below.
   c. Adjust the picture so it is 20% brighter and has 20% more contrast.
   d. Change the picture so it appears behind the text.

FIGURE WD 7.36

7. Change the font color in *Blowing Rock* to *Dark Blue, Text 2, Lighter 40%* using a gradient fill of linear left.
8. Save and close the document.

chapter 8

Collaborating with Others

In this chapter, you will learn the following skills:

- Add, hide, and show comments
- Track, accept, and reject changes
- Combine and compare documents
- Prepare document for sharing, and encrypt a document with a password
- Save documents as PDF, publish to a blog, and send documents through e-mail
- Create a template

Skill **8.1** Adding Comments
Skill **8.2** Using Track Changes
Skill **8.3** Accepting and Rejecting Changes in a Document
Skill **8.4** Hiding and Showing Changes in a Document
Skill **8.5** Combining Documents
Skill **8.6** Comparing Documents
Skill **8.7** Adding a Digital Signature to a Document
Skill **8.8** Saving a Document as a PDF
Skill **8.9** Publishing a Document as a Blog Post
Skill **8.10** Sending Documents through E-mail
Skill **8.11** Creating a Template
Skill **8.12** Encrypting a Document with a Password
Skill **8.13** Checking for Compatibility with Previous Versions of Word
Skill **8.14** Inspecting Your Document

skills

introduction

In this chapter you will learn to use the tools available in Word to collaborate with others. You will learn that others can review, comment, and make changes to a document and that you can then accept or reject changes made by reviewers. You will learn to save documents in a variety of formats. You will learn to ensure that your document is compatible with other versions of Word, and how to protect a document by adding a password.

8.1 Adding Comments

A **comment** is a note you add to a document that is not meant to be a part of the document. When you add a comment, it appears in the margin of the document. Comments are useful when you are reviewing a document and want to add messages about changes or errors.

To insert a comment:

1. Click the **Review** tab.
2. In the *Comments* group, click the **New Comment** button.
3. The comment balloon appears in the margin of the document.
4. Click in the balloon and type your comment.
5. Click outside the balloon to deselect the comment and continue working.

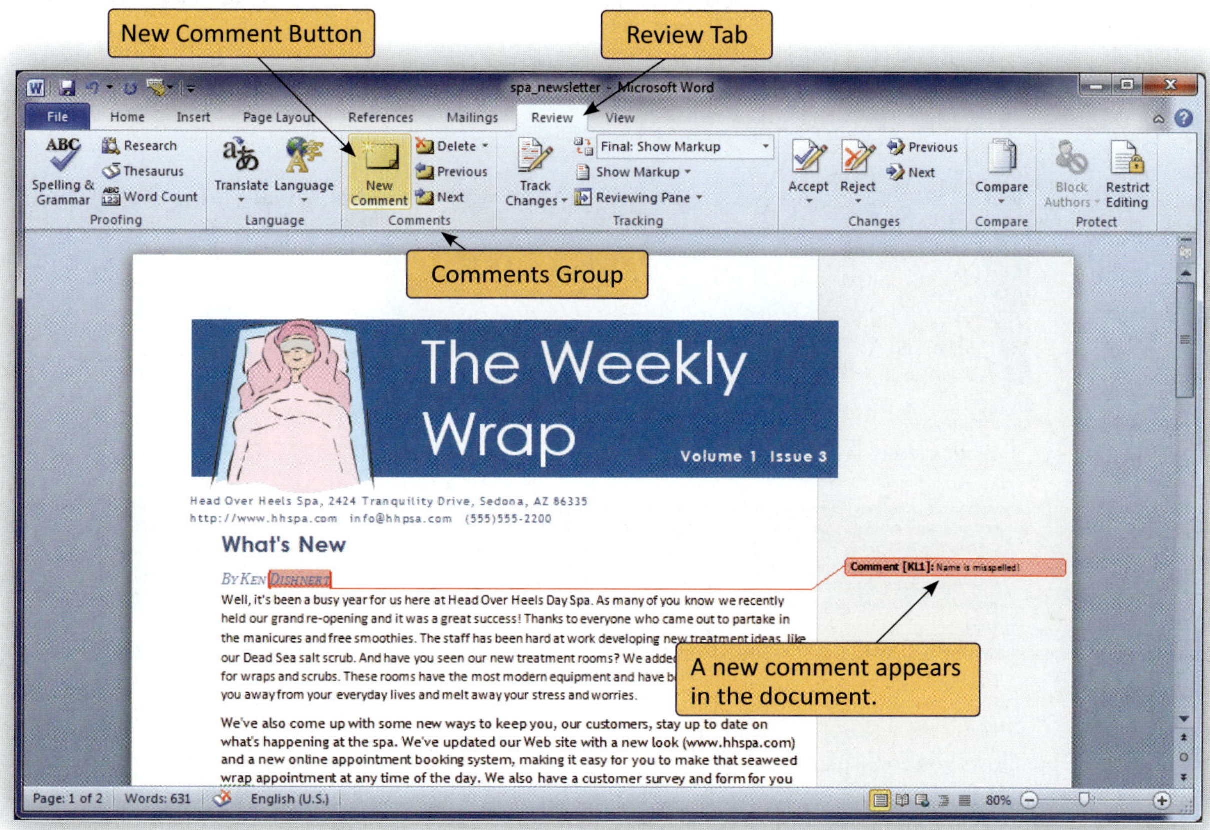

FIGURE WD 8.1

If your document contains multiple comments, click the **Previous Comment** and **Next Comment** buttons to navigate between comments.

To delete a comment, select the comment you want to delete. In the *Comments* group on the *Review* tab, click the **Delete Comment** button.

tips & tricks

You can comment on a comment. Click inside the comment balloon; then click the **New Comment** button. A new balloon opens just below the first balloon. Type your new comment.

tell me more

When you click outside the comment balloon, the comment appears lighter in color, indicating the comment is inactive and what you type now will be part of the document.

8.2 Using Track Changes

The **Track Changes** feature in Word marks any changes made to a document by reviewers. Such changes include any deletions, insertions, or formatting. Word displays some changes directly in the document and other changes in balloons displayed in the margin. When the *Track Changes* feature is active, the *Track Changes* button appears in its active state.

To track changes to a document:

1. Click the **Review** tab.
2. In the *Tracking* group, click the **Track Changes** button.
3. When changes are made to the document, they display either in-line (for insertions and deletions) or in the margin (for comments and formatting changes).
4. Click the **Track Changes** button again to turn the feature off.

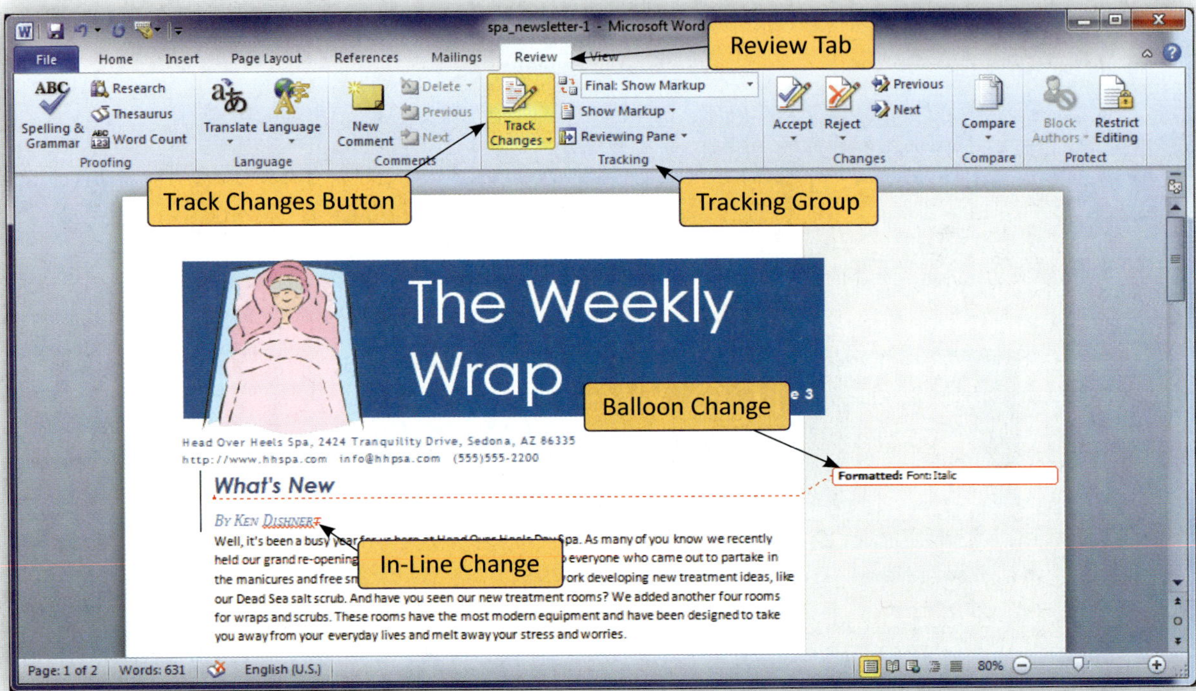

FIGURE WD 8.2

The *Display for Review* menu allows you to display the document in a number of states, including the final version with the markup for changes, the final version without the markup for changes, the original document with the markup for changes, and the original document without any markup.

tips & tricks

- You can choose to have all revisions display in balloons or all revisions display in-line. By default revisions are displayed in-line and comments and formatting changes are displayed in balloons.
- You can choose to review changes by all reviewers or specific reviewers. You can also specify the type of changes you want to display.

tell me more

The **Reviewing pane** displays all the changes in a document. It shows a summary of the revisions in a document, including the number of insertions, deletions, moves, formatting changes, and comments. To display the *Reviewing* pane, click the **Reviewing Pane** button in the *Tracking* group on the *Review* tab.

try this

To turn on the *Tracked Changes* feature, you can also click the bottom half of the **Track Changes** button and select **Track Changes** from the menu.

8.3 Accepting and Rejecting Changes in a Document

When you send a document for review with *Tracked Changes* on, the document you receive will show all the changes made by reviewers. To finalize the document, you need to accept or reject each change suggested.

There are a number of ways you can accept and reject changes:

Accept or Reject Change and Move to Next—accepts or rejects the change and automatically moves to the next change in the document.

Accept or Reject Change—accepts or rejects the change and does not move to the next change in the document.

Accept or Reject All Changes Shown—accepts or rejects only the currently displayed changes.

Accept or Reject All Changes in Document—accepts or rejects both visible and hidden changes in the document.

To accept or reject changes in a document:

1. Click the **Review** tab.
2. In the *Changes* group, click the **Next Change** button to navigate to the first change in the document.
3. To accept the selected change and move to the next change, click the **Accept and Move to Next** button.
4. To reject the selected change and move on to the next change, click the **Reject and Move to Next** button.

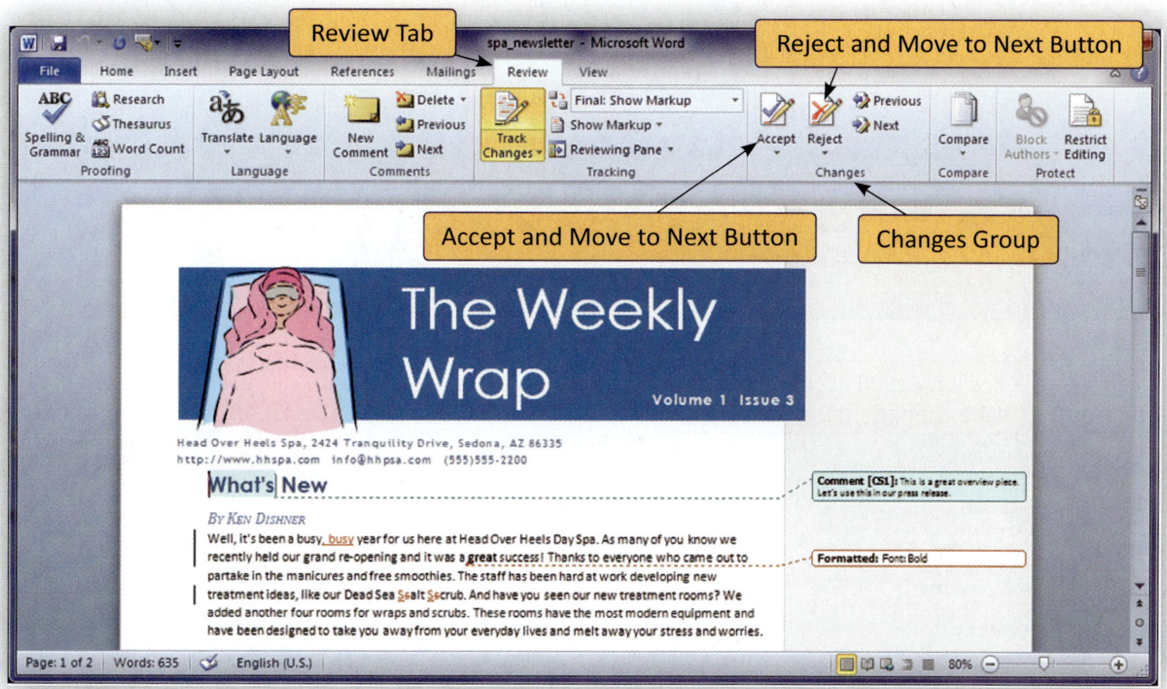

FIGURE WD 8.3

tips & tricks

To navigate between changes in a document, click the **Previous Change** and **Next Change** buttons.

try this

- To accept a change and automatically move to the next change, you can click the **Accept and Move to Next** button arrow and select the **Accept and Move to Next** command from the menu.
- To reject a change and automatically move to the next change, you can click the **Reject and Move to Next** button arrow and select the **Reject and Move to Next** command from the menu.

tell me more

If you have sent the document to multiple reviewers, each reviewer's comments and changes will be displayed in a specific color. To see which reviewer is represented by which color, in the *Tracking* group, click the **Show Markup** button and point to **Reviewers.** Each reviewer is listed in the menu by color. If a check mark appears next to the reviewer's name, that reviewer's comments and changes are visible. If there is no check mark next to the reviewer's name, that reviewer's comments and changes have been hidden. Click a reviewer's name on the menu to hide or show comments and changes from that reviewer.

8.4 Hiding and Showing Changes in a Document

When you activate the *Track Changes* feature in Word, all changes are displayed by default. This includes any comments, deletions, insertions, or formatting changes. Word displays some changes directly in the document and other changes in balloons displayed in the margin. If your document has gone through some major revisions, it may be difficult to differentiate between all the tracked changes. You can show and hide the various changes from the *Tracking* group on the *Review* tab of the Ribbon.

To show and hide the different types of tracked changes in a document:

1. Click the **Review** tab.
2. Click the **Show Markup** button.
3. If a change type appears with a check mark next to it, then it is currently displayed in the document. If a change type appears without a check mark next to it, then it is currently hidden in the document.
4. Click an option on the menu to hide that type of change in the document.
5. Click the same option again to display the hidden changes.

From the *Show Markup* button, you can show or hide comments, ink notations, insertions and deletions, and formatting changes.

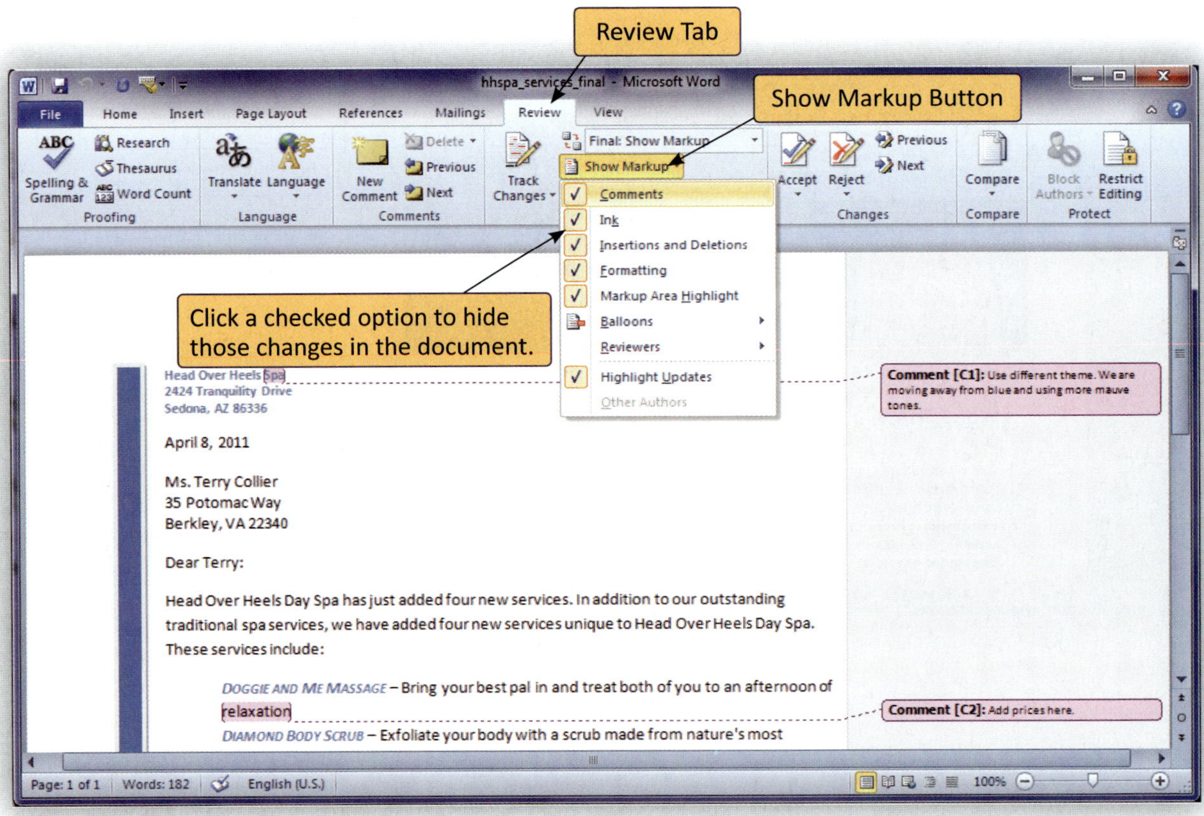

FIGURE WD 8.4

tips & tricks

You can choose to review all changes by all reviewers or specify the type of changes you want to review and by which reviewer. To modify which reviewer's comments are displayed, click the **Show Markup** button in the *Tracking* group, point to **Reviewers,** and select the reviewer(s) you want.

tell me more

From the *Tracking* group, you can also change how the document is displayed—in its final form, in its final form including changes, in its original form, or in its original form including changes.

8.5 Combining Documents

If you send your document out to multiple reviewers, you will want to take the changes and combine them into a single document. Word's **Combine** feature allows you to combine two documents into a single document. When you combine two documents, the differences between the two documents are displayed as tracked changes. You can continue combining versions of the same document by different reviewers into the original document. When you are finished, you will have one document with changes from multiple reviewers.

To combine documents into a single document:

1. Click the **Review** tab.
2. In the *Compare* group, click the **Compare** button and select **Combine. . .** from the menu.
3. Click the **Original document** drop-down arrow, and select a document.
4. Click the **Revised document** drop-down arrow, and select another version of the document.
5. Click **OK.**
6. Word creates a third document with the differences marked as tracked changes.
7. Repeat these steps to continue combining versions of the same document.

Click the **Show Source Documents** button on the *Compare* menu to select which documents to display along with the new document—the original, the revised, both versions, or none of the documents.

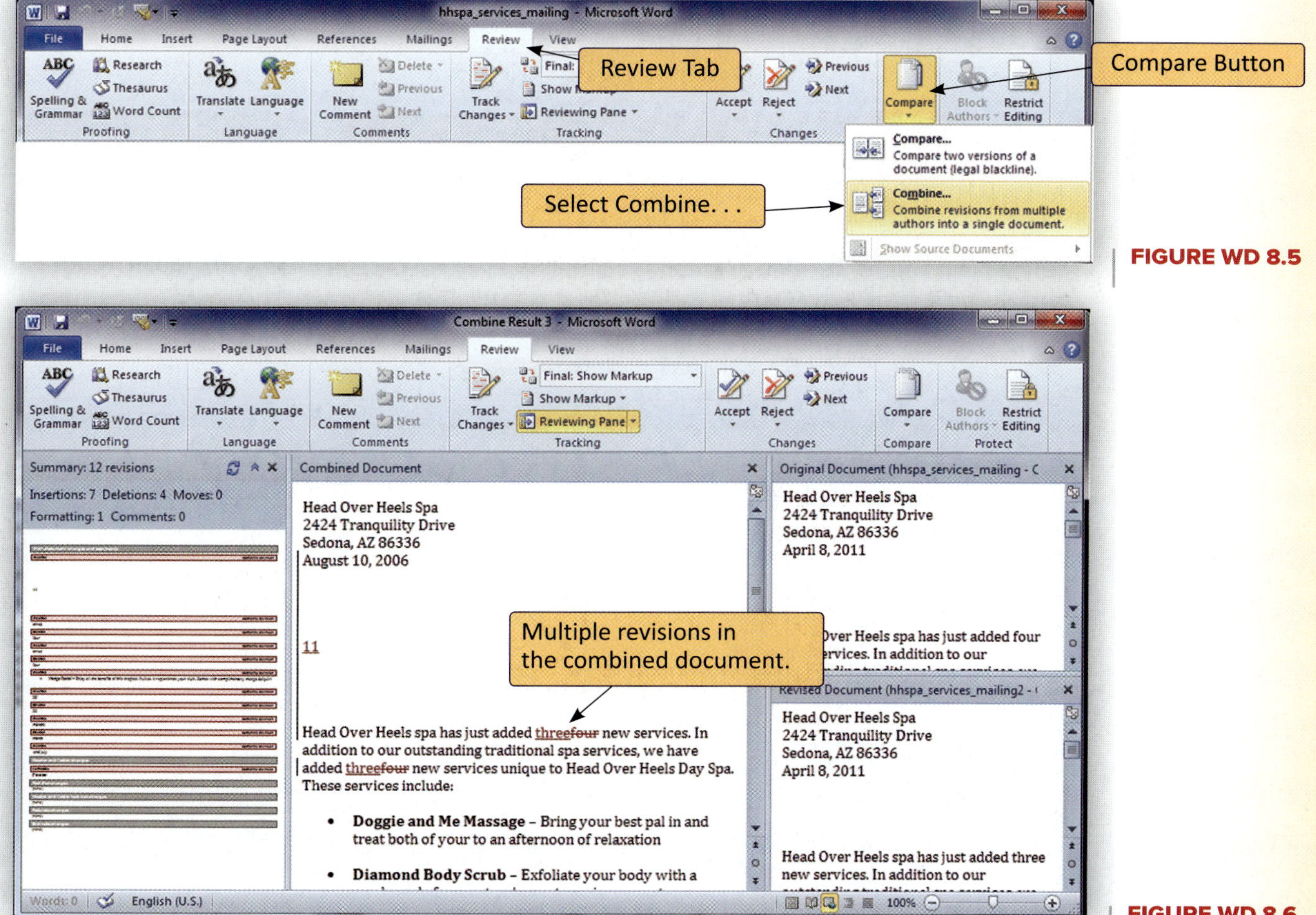

FIGURE WD 8.5

FIGURE WD 8.6

tips & tricks

If the documents you are looking for do not appear in the drop-down list, click the **Open** button next to the drop-down arrow. In the *Open* dialog box, navigate to the file you want to use and click **Open**.

tell me more

The *Combine* feature is used to combine revisions from multiple people into a single document. The *Compare* feature is used to display the differences between two different documents in a single document.

8.6 Comparing Documents

When you are working on multiple versions of the same document, you may not be able to easily find subtle differences between two versions. Word 2010 includes a **Compare** feature that allows you to take two documents and create a single document displaying the differences between the two. Word displays the differences as tracked changes which you can then accept or reject to create a final version of the compared documents.

To create a new document that displays the changes between two documents:

1. Click the **Review** tab.
2. In the *Compare* group, click the **Compare** button and select **Compare. . .** from the menu.
3. Click the **Original document** drop-down arrow, and select a document.
4. Click the **Revised document** drop-down arrow, and select another version of the document.
5. Click **OK.**
6. Word creates a third document with the differences marked as tracked changes.
7. Accept or reject any changes and save the document.

Click the **Show Source Documents** button on the *Compare* menu to select which documents to display along with the new document—the original, the revised, both versions, or none of the documents.

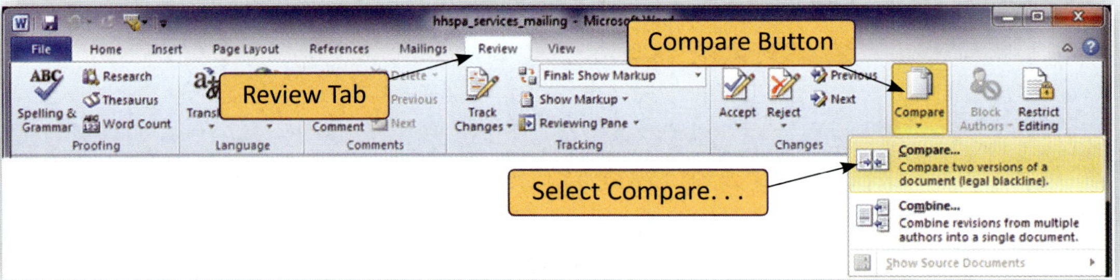

FIGURE WD 8.7

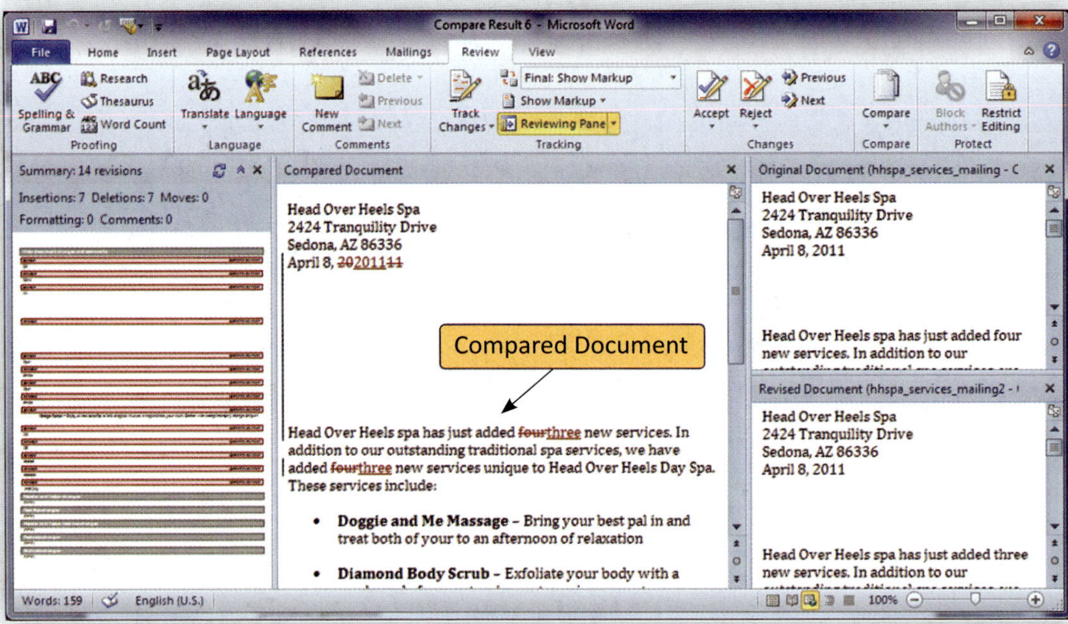

FIGURE WD 8.8

tips & tricks

If the documents you are looking for do not appear in the drop-down list, click the **Open** button next to the drop-down arrow. In the *Open* dialog box, navigate to the file you want to use and click **Open.**

tell me more

The *Compare* feature is also referred to as *legal blackline.* Use this feature if you want to compare two documents and display the changes between them in a third document. When you compare documents, you are doing just that, comparing the documents. You are not changing the documents themselves.

8.7 Adding a Digital Signature to a Document

A digital signature is a way to electronically sign documents, verifying that the document came from the person who signed it and has not been altered. **Digital certificates** verify that the file came from the signer. **Digital signatures** verify that the file has not been altered. Digital signatures can be hidden in a document, or they can be displayed on a signature line.

To add a signature line to a document:

1. Place your cursor where you want to add the signature line.
2. Click the **Insert** tab.
3. In the *Text* group, click the **Signature Line** button.

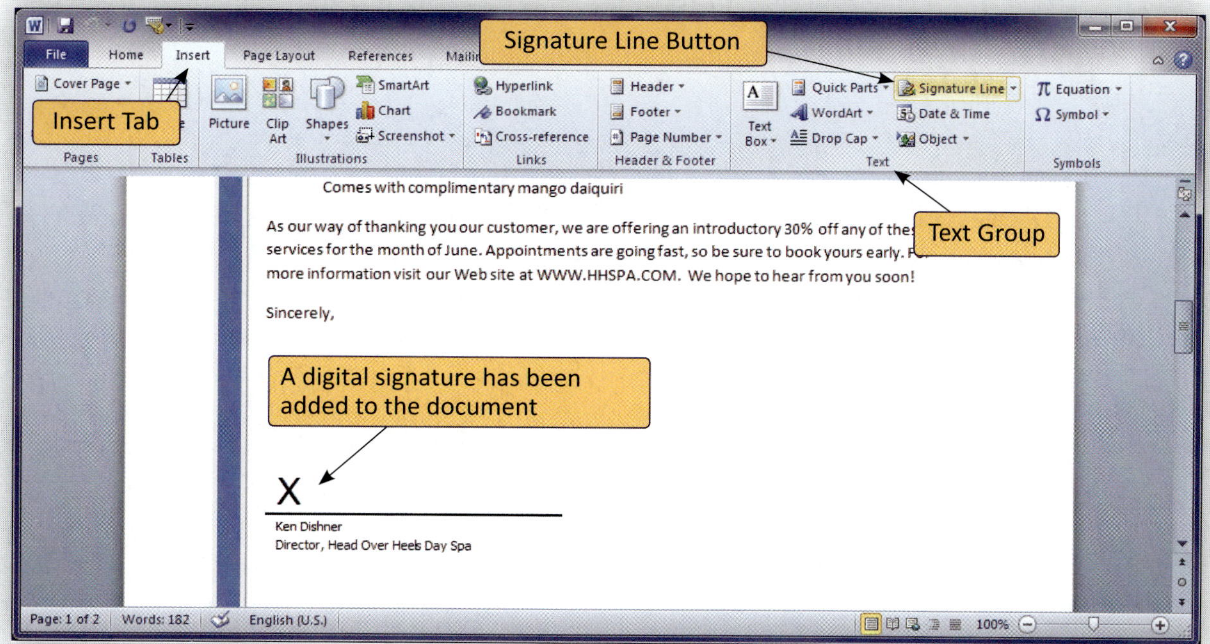

FIGURE WD 8.9

4. The *Signature Setup* dialog box opens.
5. Type the signer's name in the *Suggested signer* box.
6. Type the signer's title in the *Suggested signer's title* box.
7. Type the signer's e-mail address in the *Suggested signer's e-mail address* box.
8. Type any instructions for the signer in the *Instructions to the signer* box.
9. Click **OK** to add the digital signature line to the document.

FIGURE WD 8.10

from the perspective of . . .

MEDIA ASSISTANT

In my job, I have to "proofread" with several other employees. Thanks to track changes, I can share a file with several colleagues, review their input, and decide which changes I want to accept or reject. The result is a document worth reading!

To sign a document:

1. Double-click the signature line.
2. In the *Sign* dialog box, type your signature in the box, or click the **Select image. . .** link to insert an image of your signature.
3. Click the **Sign** button.
4. The signature appears next to the *X* on the signature line.

tips & tricks

When a document contains a digital signature, the **Signatures** icon appears on the status bar of the document window, . Click the **Signatures** icon to display the *Signatures* pane and view the signatures for the document.

try this

To open the *Signature Setup* dialog box, you can also click the **Signature Line** button arrow and select **Microsoft Office Signature Line. . .**

8.8 Saving a Document as a PDF

If you want to send a document out for others to read and print, but are not sure if your readers are able to open Word documents, you should send it as a PDF file. **PDF** stands for *portable document file,* which is Adobe's custom format for displaying forms and documents in a Web browser. When you save a file in PDF format, all your formatting (including fonts, images, and styles) is preserved. PDF files can be read by any computer with Adobe's Acrobat Reader installed, but they cannot be changed by those reading the file. So only use a PDF when you need to send a copy of the file to someone for reading purposes, not editing purposes.

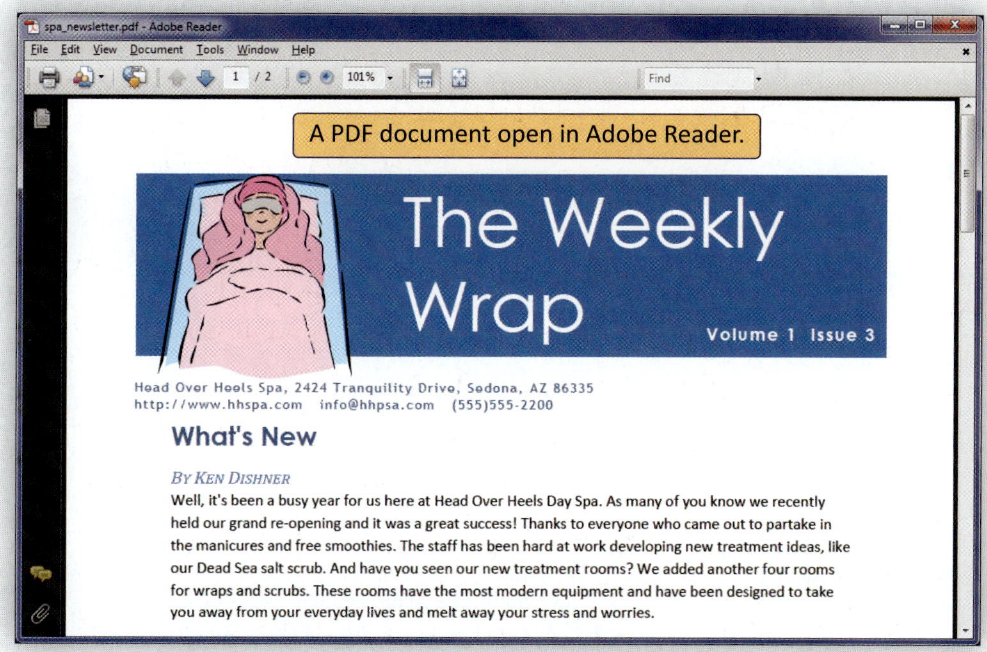

FIGURE WD 8.11

To save a document as a PDF:

1. Click the **File** tab.
2. Click the **Save & Send** tab.
3. Under *File Types,* click the **Create PDF/XPS Document** button.
4. Under *Create a PDF/XPS Document,* click the **Create PDF/XPS** button.
5. In the *Publish as PDF or XPS* dialog box, navigate to where you want to save the file.
6. Click in the *File name:* box and type a file name.
7. Click the **Publish** button.
8. Word saves the file and opens it in Adobe Reader.

An **XPS (XML Paper Specification)** file is another file format that preserves the formatting of the document and is easily readable, but not easily editable. XPS files can be opened with Microsoft's XPS Viewer, which comes installed with Windows Vista and Windows 7.

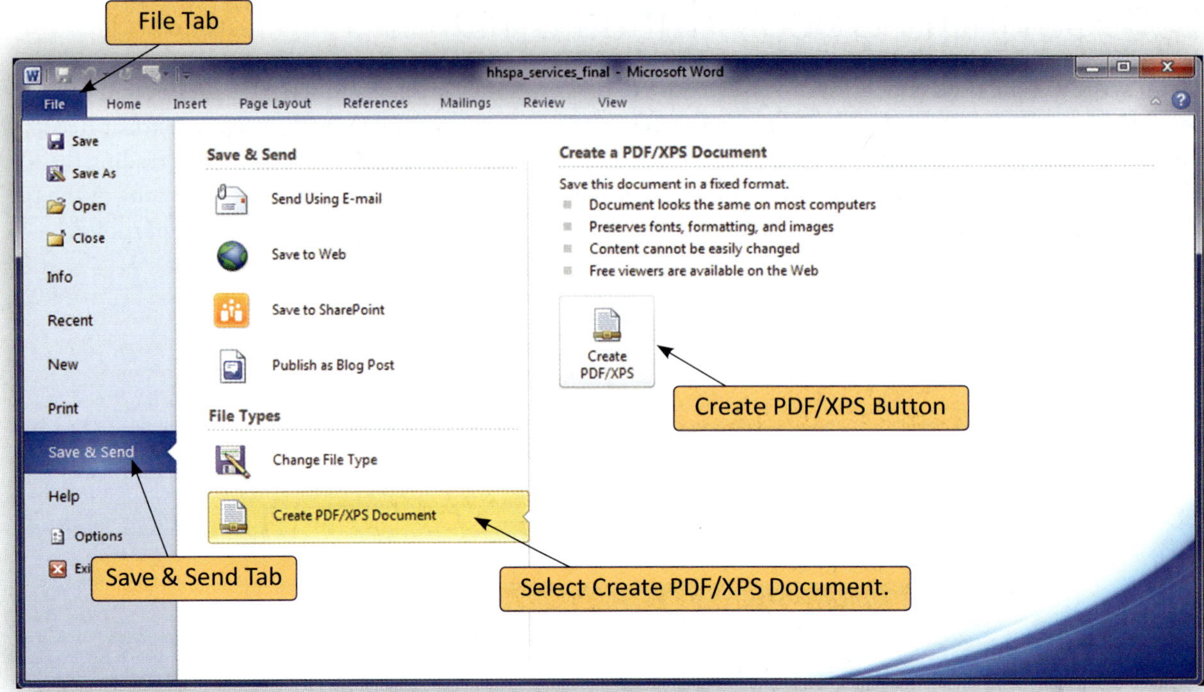

FIGURE WD 8.12

tips & tricks

You can also send a document through e-mail as a PDF file:

1. On the *Save & Send* tab, verify the **Send Using E-mail** option is selected.
2. Click the **Send as PDF** button.
3. Your default e-mail program opens with the subject line filled in and the document in PDF format attached.

tell me more

In order to read PDF files, your readers must have the Adobe Reader program installed. This program can be downloaded for free from Adobe's site:

1. Open your browser and navigate to http://get.adobe.com/reader/.
2. Click the **Download** button.
3. In the *Security Warning* dialog box, click **Install.**
4. The install program launches. When the program has finished installing, click **OK.**

8.9 Publishing a Document as a Blog Post

A **blog**, or "Web-log," is a personal online journal available for anyone to visit and read. Blogs are typically updated every day and can include everything from the author's personal musings to reporting of local, national, and international events. You can publish documents as blog posts from Word.

To publish a document as a blog post:

1. Click the **File** tab.
2. Click the **Save & Send** tab.
3. Under *Save & Send*, click **Publish as Blog Post.**
4. Under *Publish as Blog Post,* click the **Publish as Blog Post** button.
5. Word creates the blog post as a new document incorporating all the elements of a blog entry.

Word supports the following blog sites: SharePoint Blog, WordPress, Blogger, Windows Live Spaces, Community Server, and TypePad.

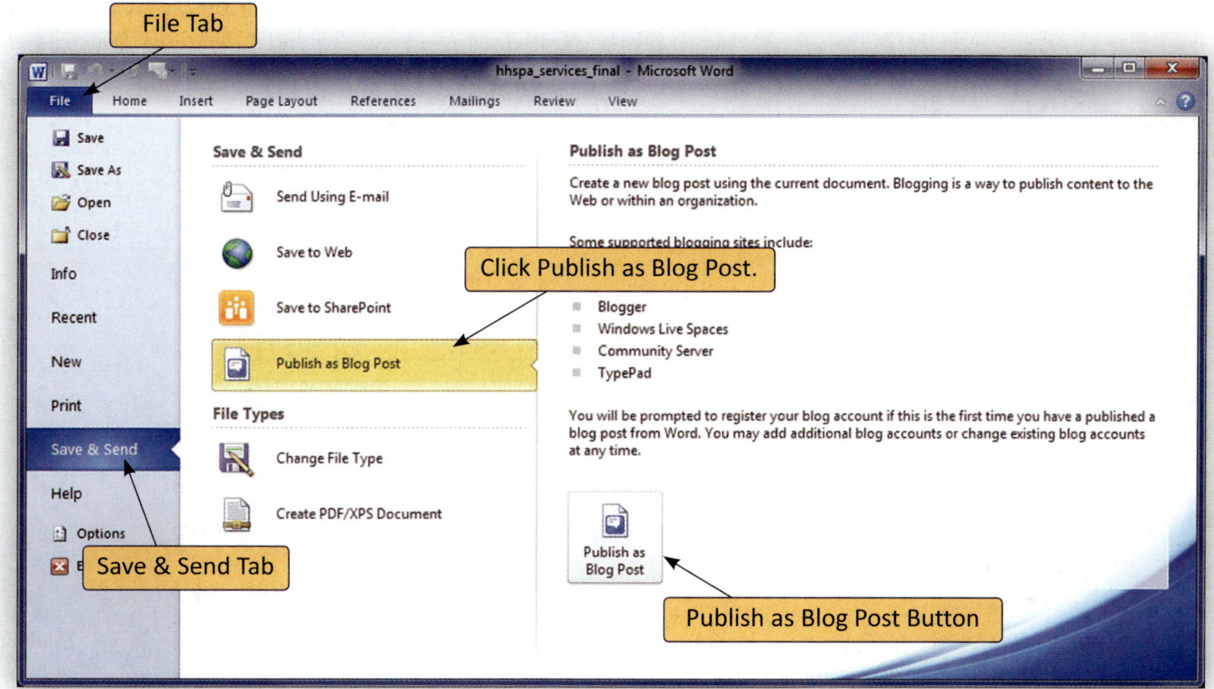

FIGURE WD 8.13

tips & tricks

Before you first publish a blog, you must register the blog with a blog site.

tell me more

Typically bloggers use an informal style of writing, and people who read the blog have the ability to reply to the posted items. Some blogs are visited by thousands of people every day, while others have a few visitors a week. When you visit a blog site, you will notice that the postings are listed with the most recent posting at the top of the page.

8.10 Sending Documents through E-mail

You can send your document to colleagues for review—allowing them to enter comments and make changes. The easiest way to send a review copy is via e-mail. After reviewing the document, the person can then send the document back the same way.

The *Save & Send* tab in Backstage view gives you a number of options for sending documents to others. When you send a document via e-mail, Word will automatically launch your default e-mail program and create a new message with the document as an attachment.

To send a document via e-mail:

1. Click the **File** tab.
2. Click the **Save & Send** tab.
3. The *Send Using E-mail* option is selected by default.
4. Click the **Send as Attachment** button.
5. Your default e-mail program opens with the subject line filled in and the document attached.
6. Enter the recipients for the message.
7. Type and send the message.

When you send a document to others via e-mail, each person works on an individual copy of the document. Any changes must be incorporated back into the original manually. To learn how to combine multiple documents from reviewers into a single document, see the skill *Combining Documents* earlier in this chapter.

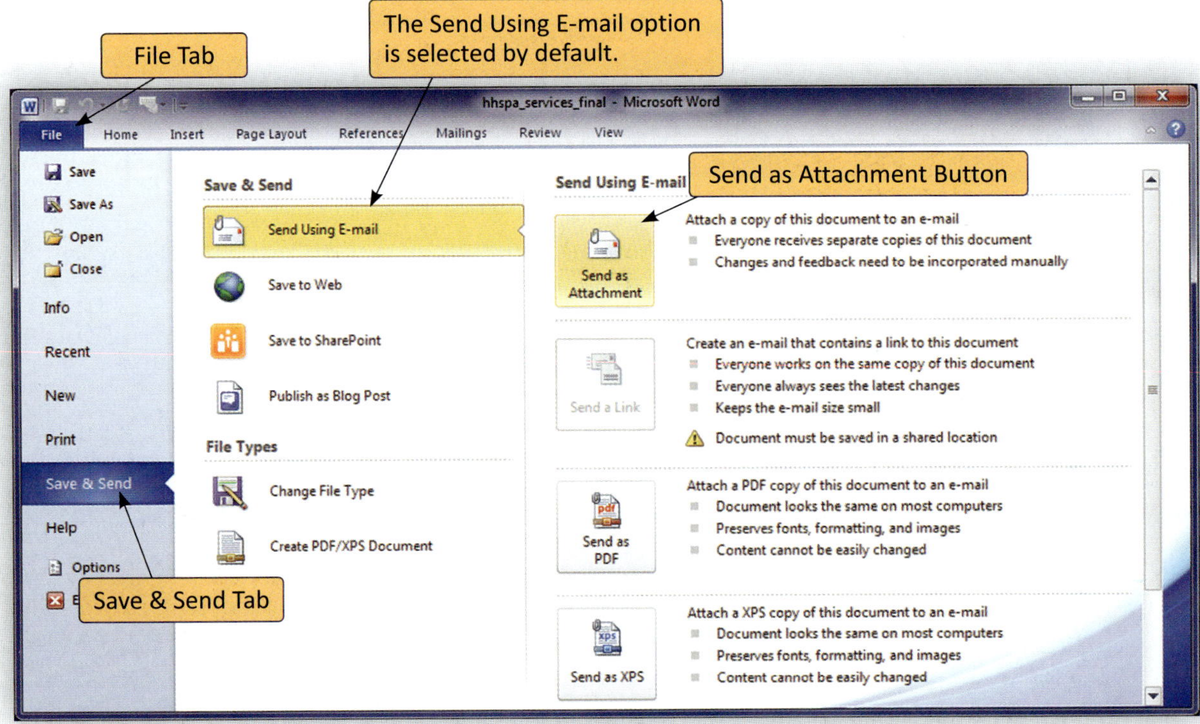

FIGURE WD 8.14

tips & tricks

Before you send a document to others for review, be sure to restrict the formatting and editing permissions on the document, so only certain types of changes can be made. To restrict formatting and editing on a document, click the **File** tab. On the *Info* tab, click the **Protect Document** button and select **Restrict Editing.** Use the *Formatting and Editing* task pane to limit formatting and editing on the document.

tell me more

If your document is saved to a shared location, you can use the *Send a Link* command to distribute your document. When you use the *Send a Link* command, the file is not included as an attachment, but a link to the file is included in the message. The *Send a Link* command allows multiple people to work on the same document. Each person sees the latest changes, and thus there is no need to update the document manually.

8.11 Creating a Template

A **template** is a document with predefined settings that you can use as a pattern to create a new file of your own. Word comes with a number of built-in templates that you can use to create documents, or you can create your own templates and save them to use to create other documents.

To create a new document as a template:

1. Click the **File** tab.
2. Click the **New** tab.
3. Under *Available Templates,* click **My Templates.**
4. In the *New* dialog box, select **Blank Document.**
5. Click the **Template** radio button.
6. Click **OK.**
7. A blank template file is created.

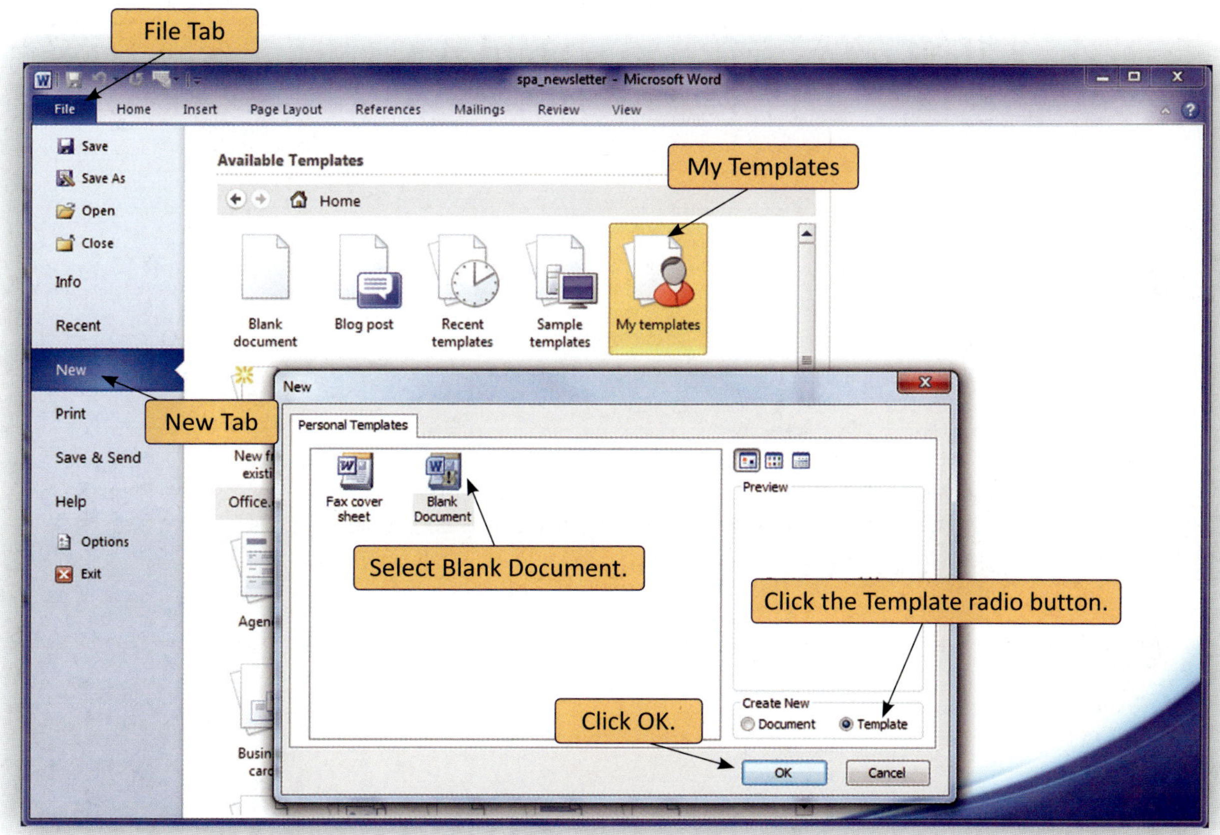

FIGURE WD 8.15

After you have created a new template, enter the information for the framework of the template. Your template file should include sample content, as well as named styles for formatting parts of the document. Once you have created the template, you will need to save it for future use.

To save a template:

1. Click the **File** tab.
2. Click **Save As.**
3. The *Save As* dialog box opens to the *Templates* location.
4. Click in the *File name:* box and type a file name.
5. Notice that *Word Template* is automatically selected as the file type.
6. Click the **Save** button.

Now, when you click the **My Templates** button, the template you saved will be available from the *New* dialog box.

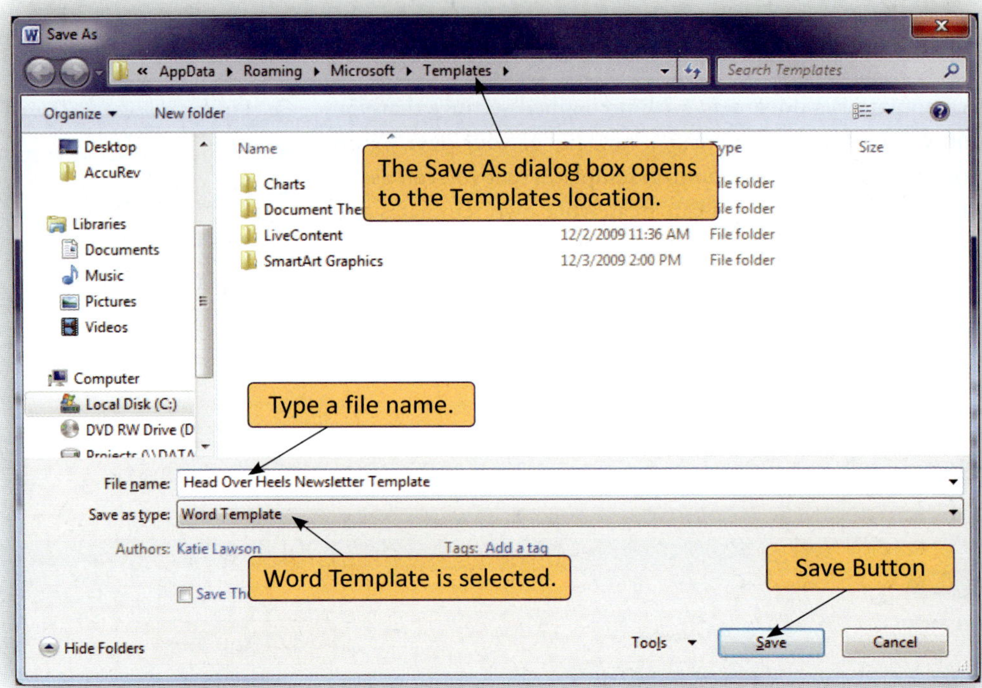

FIGURE WD 8.16

tips & tricks

When you save a template to the default template location, the template will only be available locally on your machine. If you want other people to be able to use the template, you should save the template in a location that is accessible to others, such as a shared network drive.

8.12 Encrypting a Document with a Password

When you post a document on a network, you make it available to everyone who has access to that network. You may find that you want to distribute a document to a limited group of people. One way to control who can and cannot view your document is to assign a **password** to the document and then share the password with only those people you want to have access to the document.

To add a password to a document:

1. Click the **File** tab.
2. On the *File* tab, click the **Protect Document** button and select **Encrypt with Password.**
3. In the *Encrypt Document* dialog box, type a password in the **Password:** box.
4. Click **OK.**
5. Type the password again in the **Reenter password:** box.
6. Click **OK.**

Passwords can contain numbers, symbols, and spaces, as well as letters. Passwords are case-sensitive, so remember to write down the password exactly as you entered it.

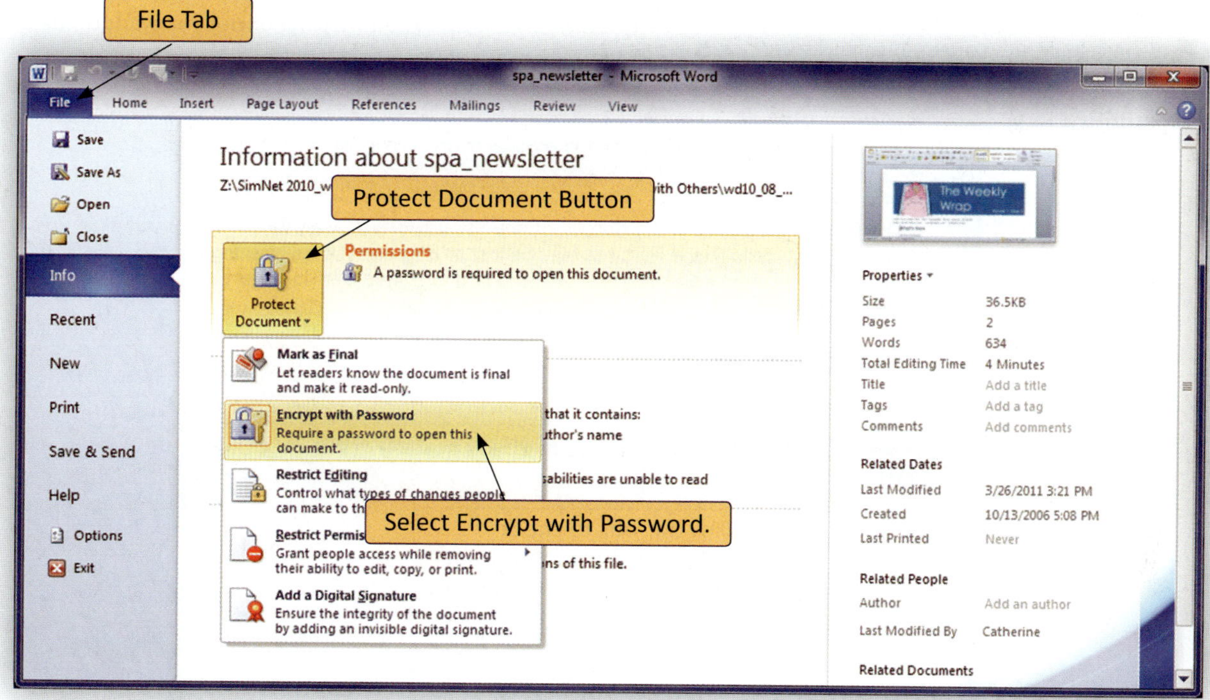

FIGURE WD 8.17

tips & tricks

- When you create a password, be sure to write it down. If you encrypt your document, you will not be able to open it without first typing in the password.
- To remove a password, open the *Encrypt Document* dialog box, delete the password, and click **OK**.

tell me more

When a password has been assigned to a document, a message appears next to the *Protect Document* button, indicating that a password is required to open the document.

8.13 Checking for Compatibility with Previous Versions of Word

Some features in Word 2010 are not available in previous versions of the application. If a document uses one of the new features, opening it in a previous version of Word may have unintended consequences. For example, if you apply Quick Styles to images in a document, the styles will be converted to static images in Word 2003. If you are sharing a document created in Word 2010 with someone who may be using an earlier version of Word, you should check the document for compatibility issues.

To check your document to see if it contains elements that are not compatible with earlier versions of Word:

1. Click the **File** tab.
2. The *Info* tab in Backstage view opens automatically. Click the **Check for Issues** button, and then click **Check Compatibility.**
3. The *Compatibility Checker* dialog opens. The Compatibility Checker lists the items in your document that may be lost or downgraded if you save the document in an earlier Microsoft Word format. For each item, the dialog lists the number of times the issue occurs in the document (*occurrences*).
4. Review the compatibility issues, and then click **OK** to close the Compatibility Checker.

Note: Running the Compatibility Checker does not change your document. It only lists the items that will lose functionality when the document is saved in an earlier Microsoft Word format. It is up to you whether or not you want to make any changes to the document.

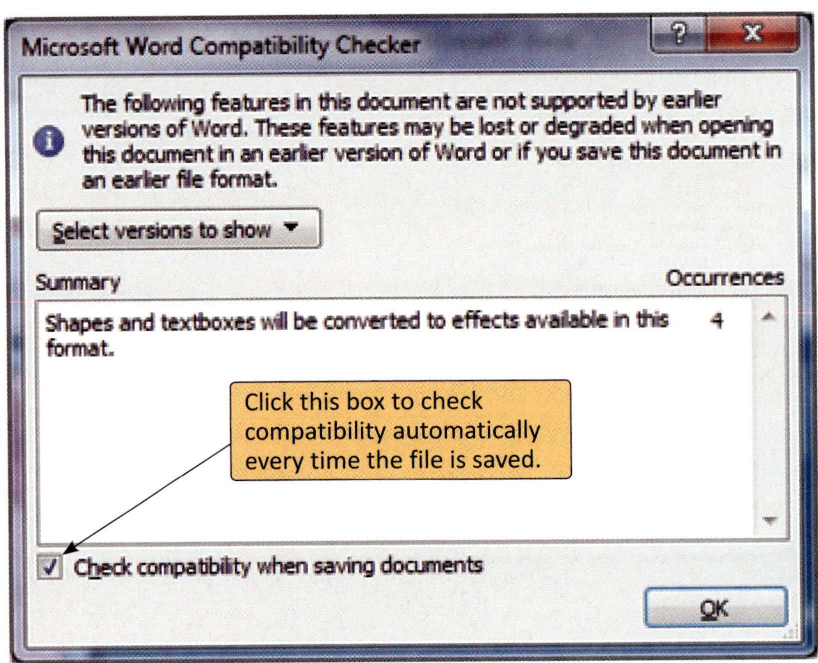

FIGURE WD 8.18

tips & tricks

If you often share documents with people using an older version of Microsoft Word, you can set the Compatibility Checker to run every time you save the document. Open the *Compatibility Checker* dialog, and then click the **Check compatibility when saving** check box to add a check mark. Click **OK.**

tell me more

In the Compatibility Checker, you can check for compatibility with Word 2007 or Word 97-2003. Click the **Select versions to show** button, and click the option you want. There are few compatibility issues between Word 2010 and Word 2007, but there may be quite a few between Word 2010 and Word 97-2003.

try this

To close the *Compatibility Checker* dialog box, you can also click the red **X** in the upper-right corner of the dialog box.

8.14 Inspecting Your Document

When you send a document to business clients or colleagues, you most likely do not want to include any personal information in the document. Other data you may want to remove before sharing a document include comments, revisions, hidden text, and custom XML. The *Inspect Document* command in Word allows you to check your document for hidden data and other personal information before you finish the document and send it to others.

To inspect your document for hidden data or personal information:

1. Click the **File** tab to open Backstage view.
2. Click **Info.**
3. Click the **Check for Issues** button, and select **Inspect Document.**
4. In the *Document Inspector* dialog box, select the items you want to check.
5. Click the **Inspect** button.
6. Click the **Remove All** button next to the items you want to remove from your document.

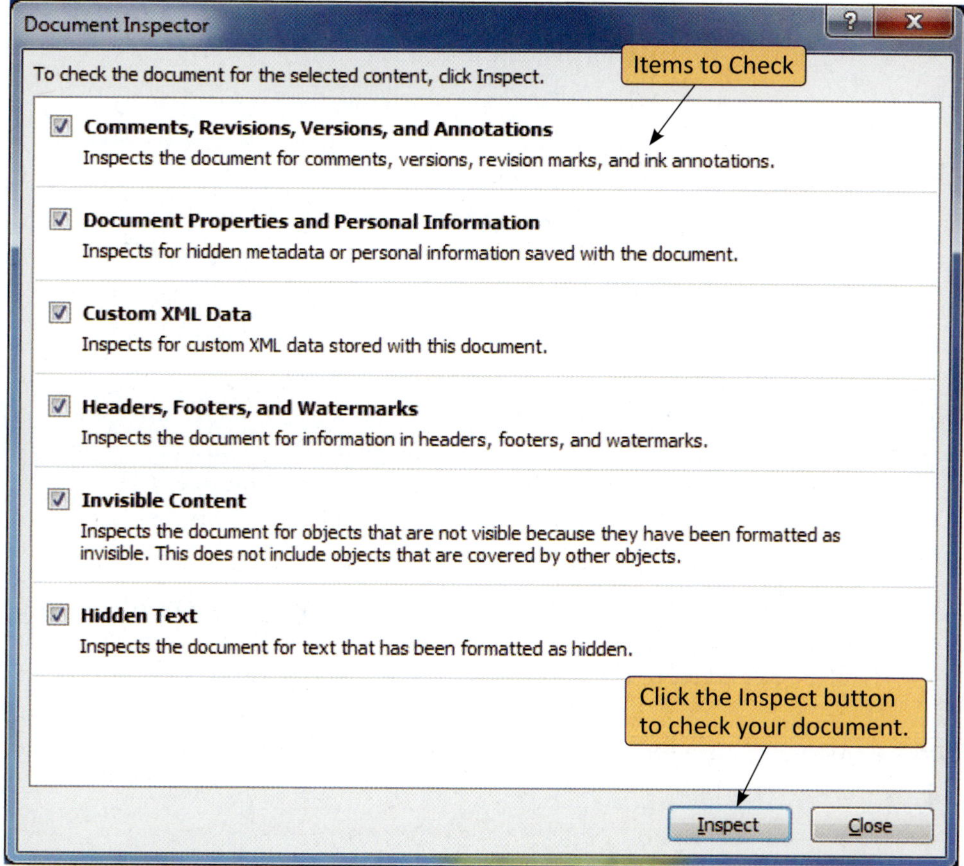

FIGURE WD 8.19

tips & tricks

If you did not choose to inspect all the options in the *Document Inspector* dialog box, you can click the **Reinspect** button to return to the list and select additional options.

projects

Data files for projects can be found on **www.mhhe.com/office2010skills**

Skill Review 8.1

In this project, you will be editing a communication plan with the *Track Changes* feature enabled. You will also add a comment to the document. You will practice sending the document as an attachment to an e-mail, and then saving the document in PDF format.

1. Start Microsoft Word 2010.
2. Open *Communication Plan.docx* and save it as **`[your initials]WD_SkillReview_8-1`**.

FIGURE WD 8.20

3. Turn on track changes.
   a. Click the *Review* tab, and in the *Tracking* group, select **Track Changes.**
4. Insert a comment under the *Stakeholder* column in the *Users* cell.
   a. Click in the table cell with the word *Users* in it.
   b. On the *Review* tab, in the *Comments* group, select **New Comment.**
   c. Enter this text as the comment: **`The users are critical to any implementation project. Please look for more communication vehicles for us to use.`**
   d. In the *Tracking* group, click the **Show Markup** button, and ensure that *Comments* has a check mark.
5. Delete text and then enter new text with track changes on.
   a. Select the text in the cell where the *Communication Needs* column and the *Business Leads* row intersect. Press **Delete** on the keyboard to remove the text.
      (1) You should see a line through the text. If not, go back to step 3 and ensure you have track changes turned on.
      (2) Replace the text with the following: **`Need to provide input into project business decisions and need to understand the critical success factors for the project`**

Business Leads	Responsible for developing overall strategic and operational processes and signing off on requirements and documents and project milestones	~~Need to understand the critical stages of the projects and be able to express ideas to a wide audience~~Need to provide input into project business decisions and need to understand the critical success factors for the project	• Monthly update meeting

FIGURE WD 8.21

   b. Select the text in the cell where the *Communication Needs* column and the *Users* row intersect. Press **Delete** on the keyboard to remove the text.
      (1) You should see a line through the text. If not, go back to step 3 and ensure you have track changes turned on.

(2) Replace the text with the following: **`Need an in-depth knowledge of the solution and how to support: password, browser, and log-in issues`**

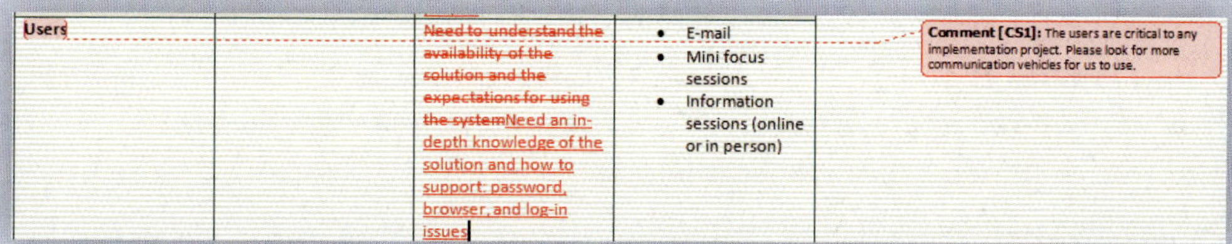

FIGURE WD 8.22

6. Save the document.
7. Send the document to John Smith via e-mail for review.
   a. Click the **File** tab.
   b. Click the **Save & Send** tab.
   c. *Send Using E-mail* is selected by default.
   d. Click the **Send as Attachment** button.

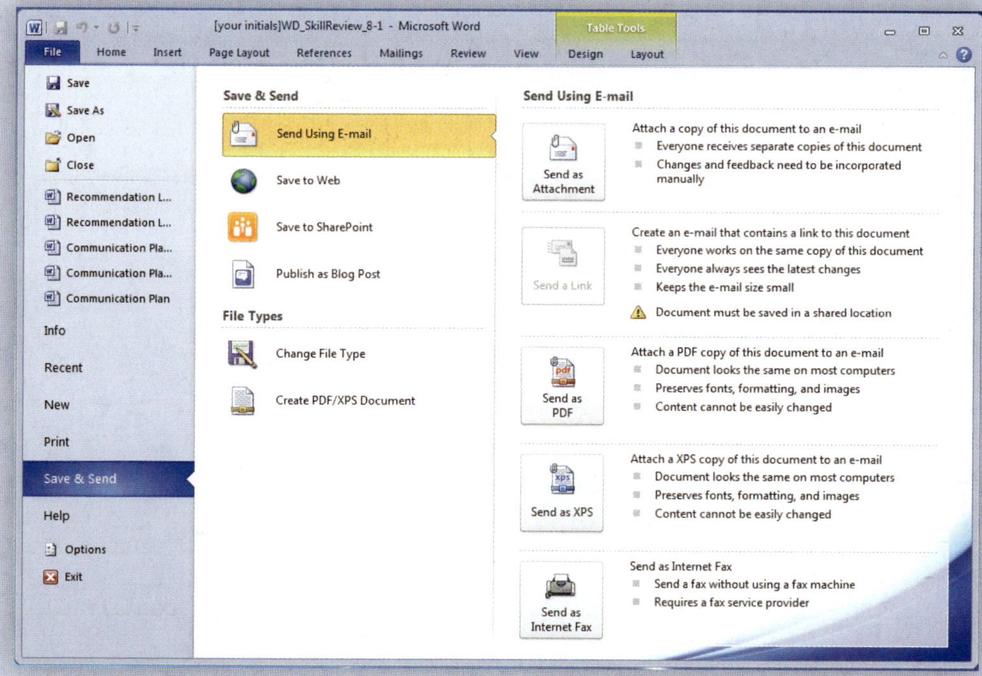

FIGURE WD 8.23

   e. As an exercise you can send it to yourself, if your school settings permit. For this project we are simulating that an e-mail is being sent to John Smith.
   f. Save and close the document.
8. John Smith has sent you a revised version of the document. However, you have made some changes to your version after you sent the document to John Smith. Combine the two documents into a single document for review.
   a. On the *Review* tab, in the *Compare* group, click the **Compare** button, and select **Combine.**
   b. Click the **Open** button next to the *Original document* box. Navigate to your student data files, and select the *Communication Plan_CS.docx* file.

c. Click the **Open** button next to the *Revised document* box. Select the *Communication Plan_JS.docx* file.

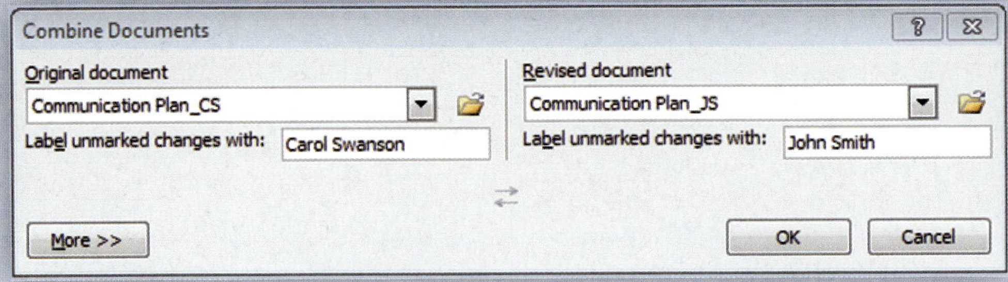

FIGURE WD 8.24

d. Click **OK** in the *Combine Documents* dialog box.

e. A new document is created showing the differences between the two files.

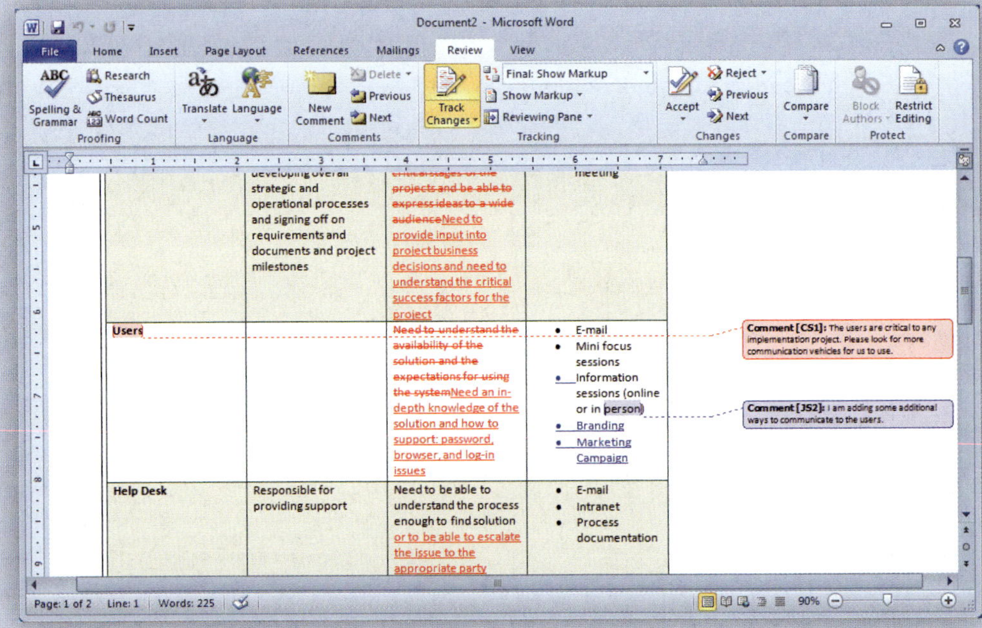

FIGURE WD 8.25

f. Your document should be similar to the one above.

g. Save the file as **`[your initials]WD_SkillReview_8-1_combined`**.

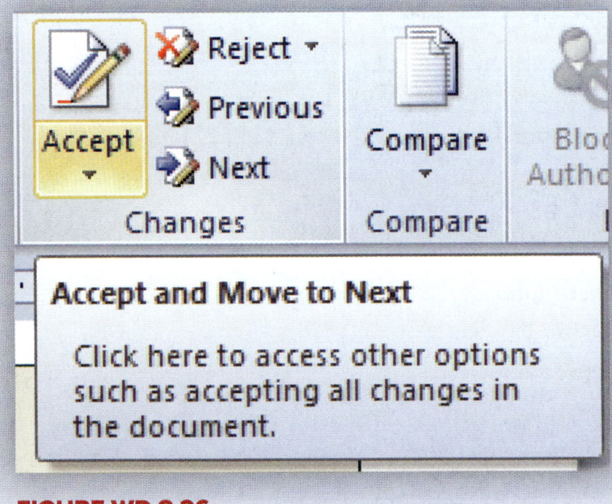

FIGURE WD 8.26

9. Hide and show comments.

a. On the *Review* tab, in the *Tracking* group, click the **Show Markup** button and select **Comments** to hide the comments in the document.

b. Click the **Show Markup** button again, and select **Comments** to redisplay the comments.

10. Review each change in the document and accept the changes.

a. Press **Ctrl** + **Home** on the keyboard to navigate to the beginning of the document.

b. Click the **Review** tab.

c. In the *Changes* group, click the **Next Change** button.

d. Click the **Accept and Move to Next** button.

11. Continue reviewing and accepting every change in the document. Perform a spell check.
12. Save the document.
13. This is your working document. You want to create a PDF document for others to read but not edit.
    a. Click the **File** tab.
    b. Click the **Save & Send** tab.
    c. Under *File Types,* click the **Create PDF/XPS Document** option.
    d. On the right side of the window, click the **Create PDF/XPS** button.
    e. In the *Publish as PDF or XPS* dialog box, click the **Publish** button.

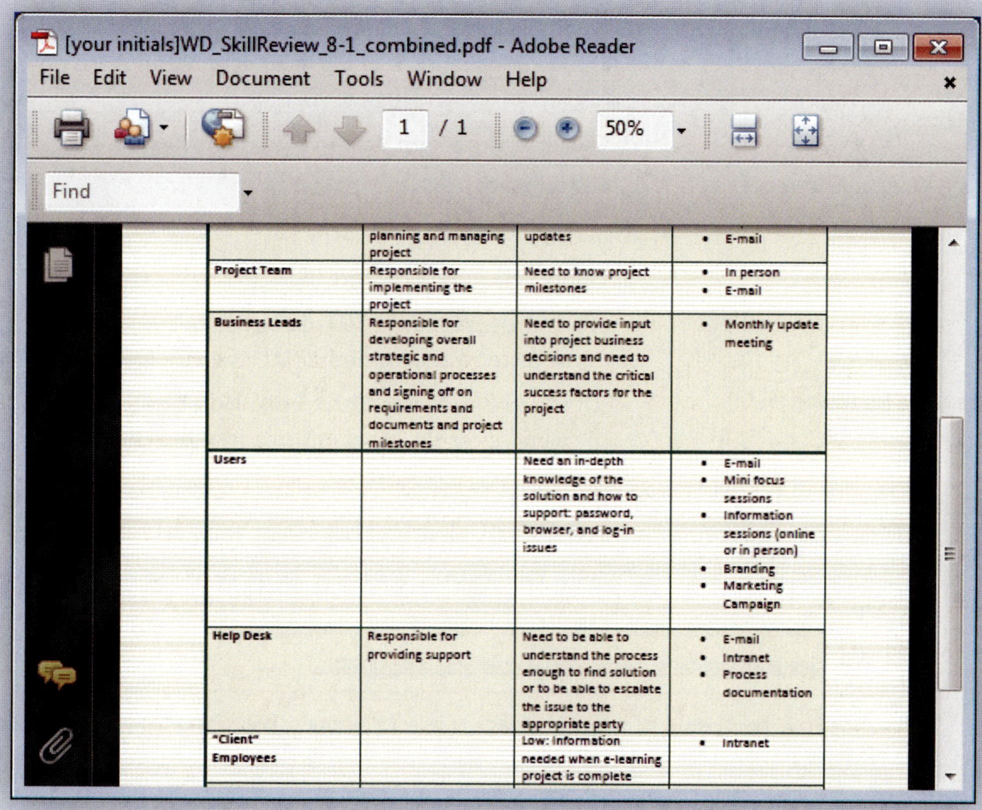

	planning and managing project	updates	• E-mail
Project Team	Responsible for implementing the project	Need to know project milestones	• In person • E-mail
Business Leads	Responsible for developing overall strategic and operational processes and signing off on requirements and documents and project milestones	Need to provide input into project business decisions and need to understand the critical success factors for the project	• Monthly update meeting
Users		Need an in-depth knowledge of the solution and how to support: password, browser, and log-in issues	• E-mail • Mini focus sessions • Information sessions (online or in person) • Branding • Marketing Campaign
Help Desk	Responsible for providing support	Need to be able to understand the process enough to find solution or to be able to escalate the issue to the appropriate party	• E-mail • Intranet • Process documentation
"Client" Employees		Low: Information needed when e-learning project is complete	• Intranet

FIGURE WD 8.27

    f. You can now send the PDF file for placement on the company's Web site.

Skill Review 8.2

In this project, you will be working with a recommendation letter. You will add a digital signature to the document and check the document for compatibility with previous versions of Microsoft Word. You will also protect the document by adding a password.

1. Open Microsoft Word 2010.
2. Open the *Recommendation Letter.docx* and save it as
   `[your initials]WD_SkillReview_8-2_Letter.`
3. Add a digital signature to the document.
   a. Place the cursor three lines below *Respectfully.*

b. One the *Insert* tab, in the *Text* group, click the **Signature Line** button.

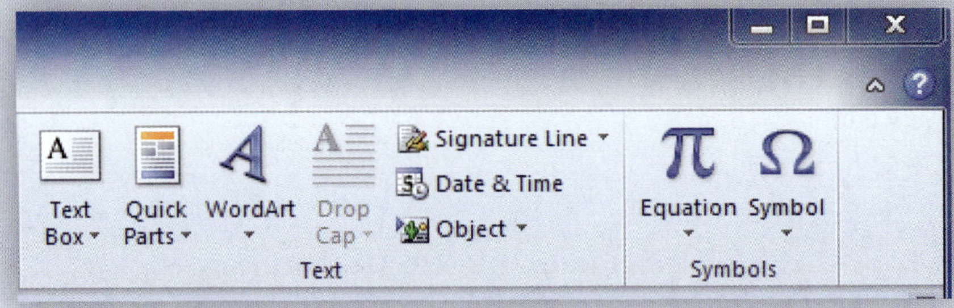

FIGURE WD 8.28

FIGURE WD 8.29

c. Fill in the suggested signer and suggested signer's title as shown in Figure WD 8.29, and remove the instructions to the signer.

d. Uncheck **Show sign date in signature line.**

e. Click **OK.**

4. Sign the document.

a. Double-click the signature block.

(1) If the *Get a Digital ID* dialog box opens, select **Create your own digital ID** and click **OK.**

(2) If necessary, enter **`Charles Matthews`** as the name, clear any other information, and click **OK.**

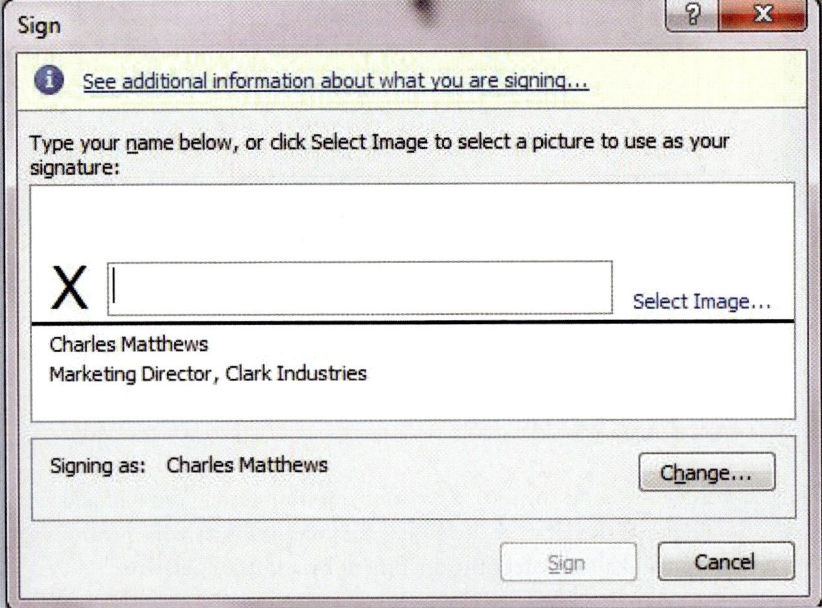

FIGURE WD 8.30

b. In the *Sign* dialog box, click the **Select Image. . .** link. Navigate to the *Signature.jpg* file and insert it.

c. Click the **Sign** button.

FIGURE WD 8.31

(1) You may see a message that your signature was successful. Click **OK.**

(2) If you are not able to certify the signature via the network, you will see a *Certificate not trusted* message in the *Signature Details* dialog box, similar to the one below. You will manually verify the signature is valid.

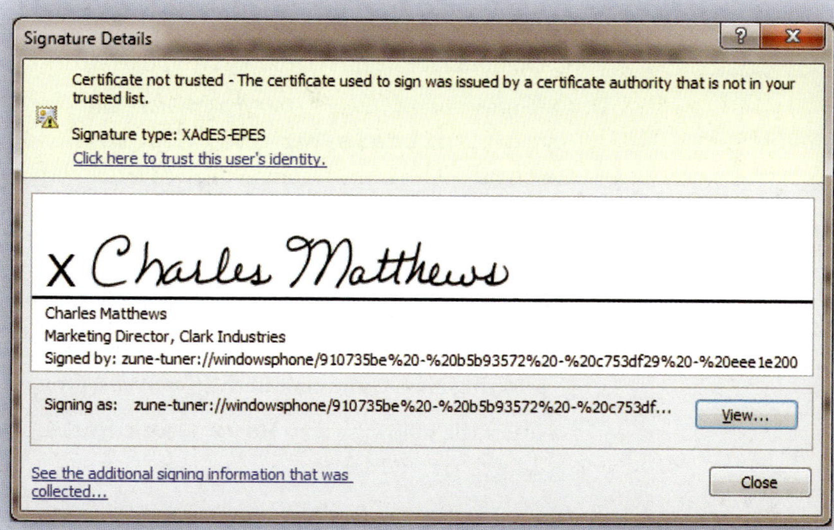

FIGURE WD 8.32

(3) Above the signature, click the **Click here to trust this user's identity** link.

(4) The invalid indicator will disappear, and you will lose the signature if you edit the document after this point.

5. At this point send the recommendation letter to the committee via e-mail. This is a signed document and is marked as final. Let's see what happens when the committee sends it back with a comment.

a. Click the **File** tab.

b. On the *Info* tab, click **Check for Issues,** and select **Check Compatibility.**

c. You should see zero issues.

d. Click **OK** in the *Microsoft Word Compatibility Checker* dialog box.

e. Click the **File** tab and click **Save & Send.**

f. Select **Send as Attachment.**

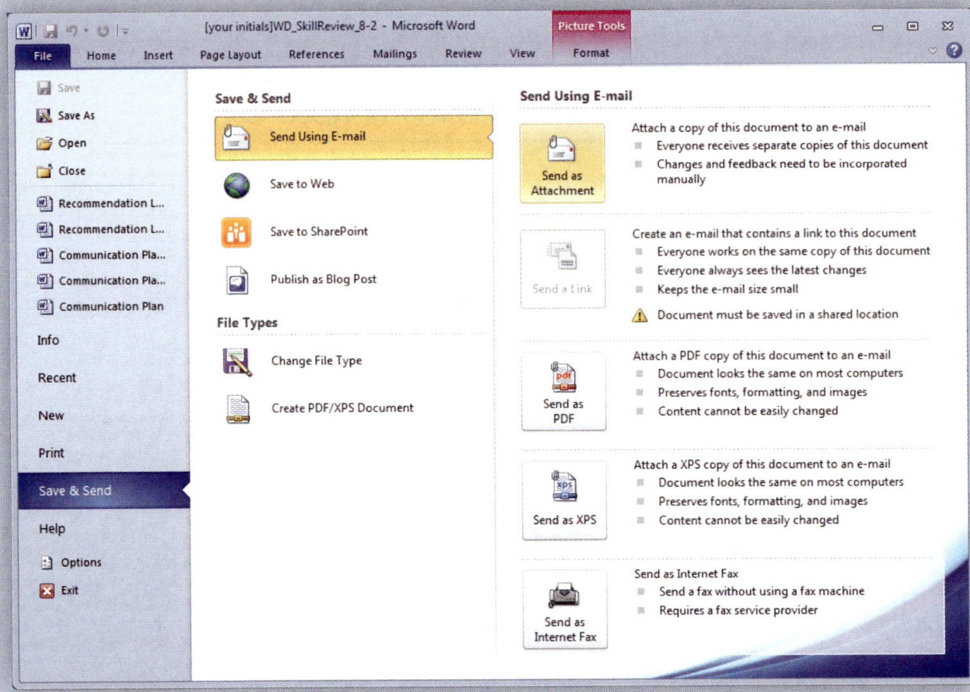

FIGURE WD 8.33

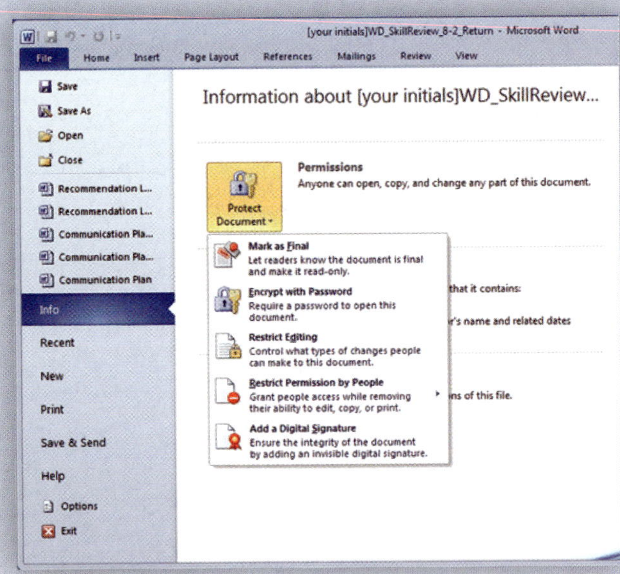

FIGURE WD 8.34

g. Do not send the message, but save and close the file.

6. Open *Recommendation Letter Return.docx* and save it as **`[your initials]WD_SkillReview_8-2_Return.`** This is the recommendation letter with a comment returned to you.

7. Add a comment to the returned letter.

a. Select *local accounts* on line 3 of paragraph 1.

b. Insert a comment by selecting the **Review** tab and selecting **New Comment** in the *Comments* group.

c. Insert the following text: **`Have Jack pull her list of clients.`**

8. On the *Review* tab, in the *Changes* group, click the **Accept and Move to Next** button. Click the **Accept and Move to Next** button again to accept the inserted text change.

9. You are going to save the file until you gather the information the Awards Committee requested. You do not want anyone to have access to the file, so you need to protect the document.

a. Click the **File** tab.

b. On the *Info* tab, click the **Protect Document** button, and select **Encrypt with Password.**

c. Type **CM357CI** in the *Password* box. Click **OK.**

d. Retype the password in the *Reenter password* box, and click **OK.**

10. Save and close the document, and write down the password so you do not forget it.

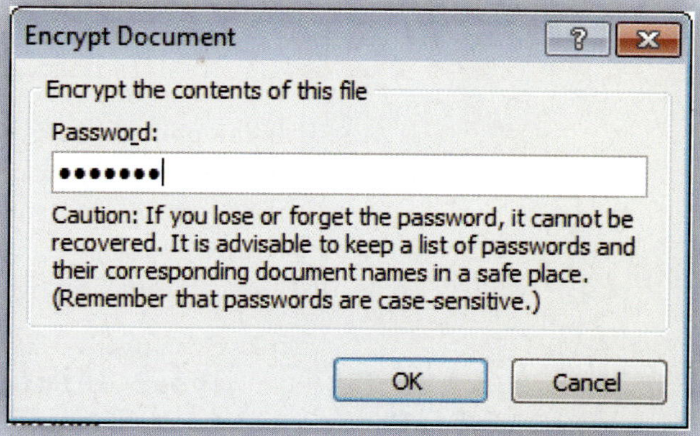

FIGURE WD 8.35

challenge yourself 1

In this project you will make, reject, and track changes in a how to guide. You will inspect your document and then save it. You will then create a template from the edited how to guide and create a generic template that can be used with any mail server. Once you have created the template, you will simulate posting it to a blog.

1. Start Microsoft Word 2010.

2. Open *iTouch Exchange Setup.docx* and save it as ***[your initials]*WD_Challenge_8-3_Setup.**

3. Turn on track changes.

a. Delete the last sentence in the first paragraph that begins with, *Generally speaking.*

b. Delete the paragraph that starts, **This is.*

4. Add the comment **Describe what the Settings icon looks like** at the end of the step that begins with *At the main window.*

5. Hide comments in the document.

6. Select the first two sentences of the deleted paragraph that began, **This is.* Reject the change.

7. Select the last sentence of the same paragraph, and reject the change.

8. Turn off track changes.

9. Inspect your document.

10. Edit the document as follows:

a. Delete the first paragraph starting with, *If you are setting.*

b. Show comments again. Delete the comment you added earlier.

c. Change *galaxy.hsu.edu* to **enter your domain address**

d. Change *email.hsu.edu* to **enter e-mail server address**

e. Delete the paragraph beginning, **This is a.*

f. Save the document as a Word Template file and name it ***[your initials]*WD_Challenge_8-3_Template.**

11. Simulate publishing the template to a blog. Select **Register Later** and save the file as ***[your initials]*WD_Challenge_8-3_Blog.** Close the file and the template.

challenge yourself 2

In this project, a rough draft of a course management advisory committee charter has been sent to you for your comments, touch up, and final approval. You will make changes to the document and return the document via e-mail. You will then create a PDF of the final charter.

1. Start Microsoft Word 2010.
2. Open *Course Management Charter.docx* and save it as
   ***[your initials]*WD_Challenge_8-4_Charter.**
3. Turn on track changes.
4. Change *Advisory Group* to **Advisory Committee** throughout the entire document.
5. Add 6 pt. spacing after each paragraph and after the last item in each list in the document.
6. Make *Ex-officio Members:* bold.
7. Your document should look similar to the one below:

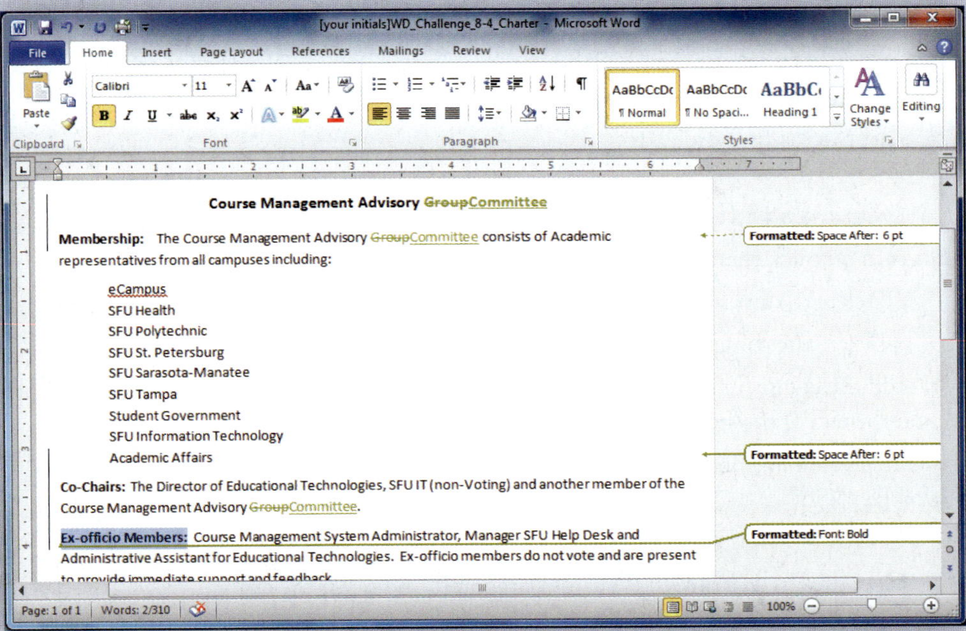

FIGURE WD 8.36

8. Hide the formatting changes in the document and then display them again.
9. Send the document to your instructor as an attachment. If you don't have permission to send the file, practice the steps of sending a document via e-mail, but do not send the document. Close the document when you are done.
10. Now you will take the role as the original sender. Open the file *Course Management Charter Marked Up.docx.* Save the document as
    ***[your initials]*WD_Challenge_8-4_MarkedUp.**
    a. Accept all the changes in the document.
    b. Mark the document as final.
11. Save the document as a PDF file called
    ***[your initials]*WD_Challenge_8-4_MarkedUp.**
12. Close the PDF file. Close the Word document.

on your own

In this project two companies have merged, and the new company, Biscuit Systems, is updating its security policies and guidelines. Boodle Networks suggested the security procedures, and Biscuit Systems' existing policy will be incorporated into one document and then published as a PDF file for the IT security Web page.

1. Start Microsoft Word 2010.
2. Open *BNSG003.docx* and save it in the *Word 97-2003 Document* format as **[your initials]WD_OnYourOwn_8-5_Boodle.**
   a. Turn on track changes.
   b. From the *Word Options* dialog box, change the user name to *Boodle Networks* and the initials to *Boodle.*
   c. At the end of the second bullet under *Picking Good Passwords,* insert the following text before the period: **- hackers use tools with online dictionaries in multiple languages, and names relevant to you or your family can be obtained from publicly available records.**
   d. Save and close the document. This will be your revised document with changes.
3. Open *Biscuit Password Guidelines.docx* and save it as **[your initials]WD_OnYourOwn_8-5_Biscuit.**
   a. Turn on track changes.
   b. Change the user name to *Biscuit Systems* and the initials to *Biscuit.*
   c. Add a bullet below *digit (0–9)* as follows: **- punctuation character (such as ',' '%' or '-')**
   d. Change the sentence in the first bullet under *Picking Good Passwords* to read **at least three of the four groups listed:**
   e. Save the document as a Microsoft Word 2010 document and close. This will be your original document when you combine the two guidelines.
4. Combine *[your initials]WD_OnYourOwn_8-5_Biscuit.docx* with *[your initials]WD_OnYourOwn_8-5_Boodle.doc.*
   a. Choose *[your initials] WD_OnYourOwn_8-5_Biscuit* as the original document.
5. Accept and make changes as follows:
   a. Add a comment to the title as follows: **Jim, please compare the two documents and combine into new guideline for Biscuit Systems.**
   b. Add a comment to the *Introduction* heading as follows: **Keep the introduction from Boodle Networks.**
6. Save document as **[your initials]WD_OnYourOwn_8-5_Combined.**
7. This file will be used for the Fix It project, which follows. You will start with a fresh file in that exercise, but you should compare your results to the start file for Fix It.

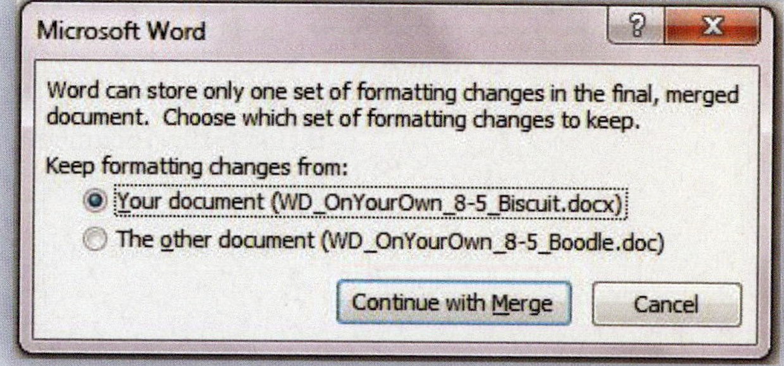

FIGURE WD 8.37

fix it

In this project you will be accepting and rejecting changes made on two separate documents and produce a new document.

1. Start Microsoft Word 2010.
2. Open *Biscuit Password Guideline_Combined* and save it as `[your initials]WD_FixIt_8-6`.
3. Work through the document, accepting and rejecting changes.
   a. Accept Deletion: Choosing Strong
   b. Reject Inserted: (Boodle Networks Security
   c. Accept Inserted: Font format
   d. Accept Inserted: Biscuit Systems Security Policy (BSSP)-003
   e. Accept Inserted: Font format
   f. Reject Inserted:)
   g. Reject Deletion: Introduction
   h. Reject Deletion: Paragraph starting *Passwords*
   i. Reject Inserted: Two
   j. Reject Deleted: two
   k. Reject Inserted: three
   l. Reject Deleted: three
   m. Reject Inserted: four
   n. Accept Inserted: -
   o. Reject Inserted: Paragraph starting *It should NOT*
   p. At this point you can accept all changes.
   q. Turn off track changes.
4. There may be some spelling and grammar errors.
   a. Fix those errors in the document.
   b. Delete *Boodle Networks* where an error is indicated.
5. Save the document.
6. Save the document as a PDF file for the company Web site.
7. Close the document and exit Word.

glossary

a

Artistic effects: Application of different graphic filters to an image. These filters mimic a wide variety of artistic tools, including paint strokes, pencil strokes, watercolors, mosaics, blurs, and glows.

AutoCorrect: Feature that analyzes each word as it is entered in a document. Each word is compared to a list of common misspellings, symbols, and abbreviations. If a match is found, AutoCorrect automatically replaces the text in the document with the replacement entry.

Automatic date stamp: Insertion of the current date from the computer's system clock into the document.

Automatic hyphenation: Insertion of hyphens to words at the end of a line instead of placing the whole word on the following line.

b

Bibliography: A compiled list of sources referenced in a document.

Blog: A personal online journal available for anyone to visit and read.

Bookmark: An invisible marker that allows you to quickly navigate back to a specific location in a document.

Brightness: Control of how dark or light a picture appears.

Building block: A piece of content that is reusable in any document. Building blocks can be text, such as AutoText, or can include graphics, such as a cover page.

Building Blocks Organizer: Feature that lists the building blocks in alphabetical order by the gallery in which they appear and includes *Bibliographies, Cover Pages, Equations, Footers, Headers, Page Numbers, Table of Contents, Tables, Text Boxes,* and *Watermarks.*

Bullet: A symbol that is displayed before each item in a *bulleted list.*

Bulleted list: List type used to organize information that does not have to be displayed in a particular order.

c

Caption: A brief description of an illustration, chart, equation, or table.

Cell: The intersection of a row and column in a table.

Change Case command: Command that manipulates alphabetical characters, changing how the letters are displayed.

Character effects: Effects applied to text to alter its appearance. Effects include bold, italic, underline, shadow, and strikethrough.

Character spacing: The control of the amount of horizontal space between characters on-screen.

Chart: A graphic that transforms numerical data into a more visual representation.

Citation: A reference to source material in a document. Citations include information such as the author, title, publisher, and the publish date.

Clear Formatting: Command that removes any formatting that has been applied to text, including character formatting, text effects, and styles, and leaves only plain text.

Clip art: Copyright-free illustrations, photographs, audio clips, and video clips that are made available through Word to use in documents.

Clips: Images, photographs, animations, sound, video, and other media files from an external source.

Close command: Command that removes a document from your computer screen but leaves the Word application open.

Color theme: A set of colors that complement each other and are designed to work well in a document.

Column: A vertical arrangement of text on-screen. Text at the bottom of one column continues on to the top of the next column.

Combine: Command that creates a single document from two documents. When you combine two documents, the differences between the two documents are displayed as tracked changes.

Comment: A note you add to a document that is not meant to be a part of the document.

Compare: Takes two documents and creates a single document displaying the differences between the two.

Compare Side by Side: Feature that allows two documents to be displayed and compared on-screen at the same time.

Contextual tabs: Ribbon tabs that contain commands specific to the type of object selected and are only visible when the commands might be useful.

Contrast: Feature that changes the range of color intensity within a picture.

Copy: Command that places a duplicate of the selected text or object on the Office Clipboard without changing the file.

Cover page: First page in a document that contains brief information about the document, including the title and the date.

Crop: Remove part of an image, hiding it from sight.

Cross-reference: A link you add to a document that directs the reader to another part of the document for more or related information.

Cut: Command that removes the selected text or object from the file and places it on the Office clipboard for later use.

d

Digital certificate: Electronic certificate issued by a *certificate authority* to verify that the organization or individual is trustworthy.

Digital signature: Electronic identifier attached to a file confirming that the file came from the organization or individual listed in the digital certificate and that the file has not been altered since the signature was added.

Document properties: Information about a document, such as the location of the document, the size of the file, when the document was created and when it was last modified, the title, and the author.

Draft view: Feature that displays a simple version of the text in a document. Draft view does not display headers and footers, page edges, backgrounds, or drawing objects.

Drop cap: Effect added to a paragraph where the first letter of the first word is a specified number of lines tall. Drop caps can be in line with the paragraph text or placed in the margin next to the paragraph text.

e

Embedded object: Independent object that is pasted into a document. Double-clicking an embedded object will open the object inside the Word document, using the source program, but not the source file.

Endnote: A reference in a document that provides the reader with further information. Endnotes are comprised of two parts: a reference mark and the associated text. Endnotes appear at the end of the document.

Enhanced ScreenTip: A ScreenTip that displays not only the name of the command but also the keyboard shortcut (if there is one) and a short description of what the button does and when it is used.

Exit command: Command that removes a document from your computer screen and closes the Word application.

f

File tab: Ribbon tab located at the far left side that opens Microsoft Office Backstage view.

Find: Command that locates specific instances of text in a document and displays the results in the *Navigation* pane.

Font: A set of characters of a certain design. The font is the shape of the character or number as it appears on-screen. Also called the typeface.

Font theme: A set of fonts that complement each other and are designed to work well together.

Footer: Text that appears at the bottom of every page, just above the bottom margin.

Footnote: A reference in a document that provides the reader with further information. Footnotes are comprised of two parts: a reference mark and the associated text. Footnotes appear at the bottom of a page.

Format Painter: Tool that copies and pastes formatting styles from one object to another.

Formula: Used to perform calculations on ranges of numbers. A formula begins with an equal sign and contains arguments, operators, and functions.

Full Screen Reading view: Displays the document in a simple easy-to-read format. In this view, the Ribbon is no longer visible.

g

Go To: Command that allows you to quickly "jump" to a specific page, section, or line number. You can also navigate to a specific bookmark you inserted or comments made by a reviewer.

Grammar checker: Feature that analyzes your entire document for grammar errors and presents any errors in a dialog box, enabling you to make decisions about how to handle each error or type of error in turn.

Graphics: Photographs, clip art, SmartArt, or line drawings that can be added to documents.

Group: Subsection of a tab on the Ribbon; organizes similar commands together.

Group command: Turns multiple objects into a single object.

h

Hard page break: Command that forces the text to a new page no matter how much content is on the present page.

Header: Text that appears at the top of every page, just below the top margin

Header row: The first row in a table. The header row contains headings for each column in the table.

Highlighting: Changing the background color of the selected area to make it stand out on the page.

Home tab: Ribbon tab that contains the most commonly used commands for Word.

Horizontal line: A decorative element that is used as a visual divider to separate a part of a document without changing the underlying content structure.

Hyperlink: Text or a graphic that can be clicked to open another page or file.

i

Index: A list of topics and associated page numbers that typically appears at the end of a document.

k

Keyboard shortcuts: Keys or combinations of keys that when pressed execute a command.

l

Landscape: Page orientation by which the width of the page is greater than the height.

Line spacing: The white space between lines of text.

Linked object: Dependent object that is pasted into a document. Double-clicking a linked object will open the source file in the original application for editing.

Live Preview: The display of formatting changes in a file before actually committing to the change.

m

Mail merge: The process of creating several documents based on a main document, merge fields, and a recipients list.

Margins: The blank spaces at the top, bottom, left, and right of a page.

Merge cells: Command that combines multiple cells in a table into a single cell.

Merge fields: Placeholders that insert specific data from the recipients list you created in a mail merge.

Metadata: Information describing a file, including keyword tags, the file title, and the author.

Microsoft Office Backstage view: *File* tab that contains the commands for managing and protecting files, including *Save, Open, Close, New,* and *Print.* Backstage replaces the *Office Button* menu from Office 2007 and the *File* menu from previous versions of Office.

Mini toolbar: Toolbar that provides access to common commands for working with text. When you select text and leave the mouse over the text, the Mini toolbar fades in.

Multilevel list: List type that divides the content into several levels of organization.

n

Navigation pane: Task pane used for working with long documents. The first tab in the *Navigation* pane displays all the headings in your document, like an outline. The second tab displays a thumbnail of each page of a document. The third tab allows you to search for text in a document.

New command: Command that creates a new file in an Office application without exiting and reopening the program.

Numbered list: List type used to organize information that must be presented in a certain order.

o

Office Clipboard: Task pane that displays up to 24 copied or cut items for use in in the current document or any Office application.

Orphan: The first line of a paragraph that prints at the bottom of a page.

Outline view: Feature that displays the document grouped by heading levels. Outline view is used to check the structure of a document.

p

Page border: The decorative graphic element along the top, right, bottom, and left edges of the page. Borders can be simple lines or include 3-D effects and shadows.

Paragraph: Any text separated by a hard return. A hard return refers to pressing the [←Enter] key to create a new paragraph.

Paragraph alignment: How text is aligned with regard to the left and right margins of a document.

Password: Combination of letters, numbers, and symbols required to be typed before a document can be opened.

Paste: Command that inserts text or an object from the Office Clipboard into a file.

Paste Special: Command that inserts objects from other Office applications into Word. Objects can be pasted as linked or embedded objects.

PDF (portable document file): Adobe's custom file format that preserves the formatting of the document and is easily readable but not easily editable.

Points: Measurement unit for the height of a font. Abbreviated *pt.*

Portrait orientation: Page layout by which the height of the page is greater than the width (like a portrait hanging on a wall).

Print Layout view: The display of how a document will appear on a printed page.

Property control: An element that is added to a document to save time entering the same information over and over again. Property controls can be used as shortcuts for entering long strings of text that are difficult to type, such as e-mail addresses, phone numbers, and street addresses.

Protected View: Read-only format that protects your computer from becoming infected by a virus or other malware.

Pull quote: Text from your document that is "pulled" out and displayed as a graphic element on the page.

q

Quick Access Toolbar: Toolbar located at the top of the application window above the *File* tab. The Quick Access Toolbar gives quick one-click access to common commands.

Quick Parts: Snippets of text that can be saved and then added to any document.

Quick Style: Formatting element, including character and paragraph formatting, that can be applied to text, tables, drawings, or other objects.

r

Recolor command: Command that removes all colors from a picture and replaces them with shades of one color.

Redo: Command that reverses the *Undo* command and restores the file to its previous state.

Reference mark: The superscript character placed next to the text for a footnote or endnote.

Reference style: A set of rules that is used to display references in a bibliography. These rules include the order of information, punctuation, and character formatting.

Replace: Command that is used with the *Find* command to insert specified text in a file with new text.

Research task pane: Task pane that enables searching for information on the Internet. The *Research* task pane also gives you access to reference tools, such as the Encarta Dictionary and Word's Thesaurus.

Reset Picture: Command to remove all Word formatting applied to a picture, reverting the picture to its state before any formatting was applied.

Reviewing pane: Pane that displays all the changes in a document and shows a summary of the revisions in a document, including the number of insertions, deletions, moves, formatting changes, and comments.

Ribbon: Graphic interface across the top of the application window that organizes common features and commands into tabs.

s

Sans serif fonts: Fonts that do not have an embellishment at the end of each stroke (e.g., Calibri and Arial).

ScreenTip (hyperlinks): A bubble with text that appears when the mouse hovers over a hyperlink. Typically, a ScreenTip provides a description of the hyperlink.

ScreenTip (Ribbon): A small information box that displays the name of the command when the mouse hovers over a button on the Ribbon.

Section: A designated part of a document that can be formatted separately from the rest of the document.

Serif fonts: Fonts that have an embellishment at the end of each stroke (e.g., Cambria and Times New Roman).

Shape: A drawing object that can be quickly added to a document.

Sharpness: Feature that removes any blurriness from a picture, giving it a crisper feel.

Shortcut menu: List of commands that appears after an area of the application window is right-clicked.

Sidebar: A block of information separate from the main document. Sidebars are typically aligned along one side of the page or along the top or bottom of the page. They usually contain information related to the main document but not found in the document.

SmartArt: Visual diagram containing graphic elements with text boxes for entering information.

Softness: Feature that removes hard edges from a picture, giving it a smoother feel.

Sort: Arranges the rows in a table in either ascending (A–Z) or descending (Z–A) order.

Spelling checker: Feature that analyzes your entire document for spelling errors, and presents any errors in a dialog box, enabling you to make decisions about how to handle each error or type of error in turn.

Split cells: Divides a cell in a table into multiple cells.

Status bar: Bar that appears at the bottom of the Word window and displays information about the current document. By default, the status bar displays the page number, number of words in the document, and whether or not there are spelling and grammar errors.

Styles: Complex formatting, including font, color, size and spacing, that can be applied to text.

Styles task pane: Lists all the text styles available in a document.

Symbol: Command to insert into your document a special text character that isn't available on a keyboard.

Synchronous scrolling: Feature that allows two documents to be scrolled simultaneously. When the active document is scrolled, the other document will scroll at the same time.

t

Tab: Subsection of the Ribbon that organizes commands into related groups.

Tab leader: Element that fills in the space between tab stops with solid, dotted, or dashed lines.

Tab stop: The location along the horizontal ruler that indicates how far to indent text when the **Tab** key is pressed.

Table: Content element that helps organize information by rows, which display horizontally, and columns, which display vertically.

Table of Contents: List of the topics in a document and the associated page numbers, so readers can easily locate information.

Table of figures: List of all the illustrations, graphs, charts, equations, and pictures in a document, along with their associated page numbers.

Tags: Keywords describing the file.

Template: A file with predefined settings that can be used as a pattern to create a new file.

Theme: A group of formatting options that is applied to an entire document. Themes include font, color, and effect styles that are applied to specific elements in a document.

Thesaurus: Reference tool that provides a list of synonyms (words with the same meaning) and antonyms (words with the opposite meaning) for a selected word or phrase.

Track Changes: Feature that marks any changes made to a document by reviewers. Such changes include deletions, insertions, or formatting.

u

Undo: Command that reverses the last action performed.

w

Watermark: A graphic or text that appears as part of the page background. Watermarks appear faded so that the text that appears on top of the watermark is legible when the document is viewed or printed.

Web Layout view: View that displays all backgrounds, drawing objects, and graphics as they will appear on-screen if the document is saved as a Web page.

Widow: The last line of a paragraph that prints at the top of a page.

Word count: Feature that provides the current statistics of the document you are working on.

Word wrap: Feature that automatically places text on the next line when the right margin of the document has been reached.

WordArt: Predefined graphic styles that are applied to text. These styles include a combination of color, fills, outlines, and effects.

x

XPS (XML paper specification): Microsoft's file format that preserves the formatting of the document and is easily readable but not easily editable. XPS files can be opened with Microsoft's XPS Viewer, which comes installed with Windows Vista and Windows 7.

z

Zoom slider: Slider bar that controls how large or small the document appears in the Word window. It is located at the right side of the status bar at the bottom of the application window.

index

a

b

c

d

e

f

g

h

i

j

k

l

m

n

t

u

photo credits

Page WD-x, © Tom Grill/Corbis
Page WD-1, © Maureen McCutcheon
Page WD-12, © Ocean/Corbis
Page WD-26, © Juice Images/Alamy
Page WD-65, © Rubberball Productions
Page WD-94, © Jack Hollingsworth/Getty Images
Page WD-116, © Stockbyte/Getty Images
Page WD-117, © Ryan McVay/Getty Images
Page WD-141, © Rubberball Productions/Getty Images
Page WD-176, © Ocean/Corbis
Page WD-202, © Comstock/Getty Images